THE GREAT BRITISH BED and BREAKFAST

KGP Publishing
Penrith, Cumbria

Published by: KGP Publishing, 54 Castlegate, Penrith, Cumbria CA11 7HY, England

ßⴰⴺⴹⴺⴳⴺⴺ

ACKNOWLEDGEMENTS	
Edited by:	Ken Plant
Editorials by:	Jenny Elliott
Map and illustrations by:	Jonathan Robinson
Compiled by:	Diane Bowler
Cover Pictures Front Cover, "Looking Down The Valley" Back Cover, "Breakfast" By kind permission of Richard Hagan	Stephen Darbishire Stephen Darbishire

ßⴰⴺⴹⴺⴳⴺⴺ

THE GREAT BRITISH BED & BREAKFAST
54 Castlegate
Penrith
Cumbria
CA11 7HY
England

CONTENTS

FOREWORD

This year *The Great British Bed & Breakfast* is even better. More and more people are discovering the advantages of staying in a guest house or small hotel. *The Great British Bed & Breakfast* not only helps the visitor find the really good places to stay but it also aims to be a mini travel guide highlighting what you can find in all 4 corners of England, Scotland and Wales.

Up to a tenth of both overseas and domestic visitors to the UK have discovered the values of bed and breakfast accommodation. The less formal atmosphere of a guest house gives plenty of opportunity to relax. Opening up your home to guests generally means you enjoy meeting and looking after people and proprietors are usually well able to advise on local attractions and shopping facilities. Yet unlike self catering, bed and breakfast accommodation offers a complete break.

The quest for quality is the emphasis of *The Great British Bed & Breakfast* and the accommodation in this book has been selected for its high standards in cleanliness, comfort and friendliness that separate the best from the rest. The choice of types of accommodation is extremely varied. You can stay in the heart of the country on a working farm or in a Victorian house in the centre of a town. Many of the buildings have historical interest or are in beautiful surroundings.

The range of services on offer is wide, from swimming pools and bars to the high standards of decoration and comfort. Often en-suite facilities, tea/coffee making facilities, and television are available. Bed and breakfast accommodation is always good value for money. Many offer home cooked evening meals as an extra and some cater for special diets.

To help plan your stay we have made this second edition of *The Great British Bed & Breakfast* even better with more accommodation to choose from this year. Each area of the country is introduced in a section pointing out its attractions, history and interesting features. Just to add some local spirit, a few lines of verse have been included and there are more illustrations. Properties are easy to find as they are located on the map of the area. A brief description of the property pinpoints include the nearest road. Prices, as well as the cost of dinner, if available, are also listed.

Your stay with *The Great British Bed & Breakfast* should be one to remember, so please pass on your comments on the accommodation already listed, or on any you can recommend for the future.

Take a look at what *The Great British Bed & Breakfast* has to offer
We think you will be impressed

LONDON

BIG BEN AND THE HOUSES OF PARLIAMENT.

WESTMINSTER ABBEY.

TOWER BRIDGE.

SAINT PAUL'S CATHEDRAL.

LONDON HOME-TO-HOME

London Home-to-Home specialises in arranging Bed and Breakfast accommodation in London with congenial hosts in good quality private homes in delightful, leafy locations. All offer something that is both unique and exceptional value for money.

LONDON LOCATIONS

London Home-to-Home represents a number of homes in the Central London districts of Kensington, chelsea and Swiss Cottage as well as homes on the convenient west side of London in attractive areas 10-25 minutes from the sights. All of these are just a short walk from an underground station, shops and restaurants.

YOUR ACCOMMODATION

London Home-to-Home hosts, who have all been chosen with great care, take pleasure in welcoming guests to their home. The provide up to 3 comfortable guest rooms of high standards of warmth and cleanliness. Television is provided in most rooms or in a guest sitting area. A hospitality tray is provided. Included in the cost is a generous English breakfast.

Our hosts take a genuine interest in sharing their knowledge of London and helping you get the most out of your stay. Whilst making you most welcome, they will respect your privacy and provide a quiet haven at the end of the day.

RESERVING YOUR ACCOMMODATION

You may reserve your booking with us on the booking form or by telephone or fax. Book early for maximum choice. We can, however, often accommodate last minute reservations. *Please note that the minimum booking period is 2 consecutive nights.*

Overleaf is a selection of the homes we represent. To assist us, we request a few personal details and information about any special requirements you may have. Every care is taken to place guests in the home where they will feel most at ease.

SECURING YOUR RESERVATION

Please forward the completed reservation form and deposit of £5 per person per night, leaving the balance to be paid to your hosts during your stay.

London Home-to-Home accepts the deposit payment in British pounds, by cheque, Eurocheque, Travellers cheque (signed twice) or by credit card (Visa, Mastercard and Eurocard). Please note that our hosts are unable to accept credit cards.

CONFIRMING YOUR RESERVATION

We will send you our official confirmation, giving the name, address and telephone number of your hosts, together with a map and directions to your accommodation.

CANCELLATION

Should it be necessary to cancel your booking, we will refund your payment less an administration fee of £30, providing London Home-to-Home receives at least 4 week's notice. We recommend that you take out full travel insurance.

There need never be a dull moment in England's capital city, London. It offers such a bewildering choice of things to do and places to visit that the difficulty is in deciding how to fit it all in to a short stay.

Among the newest of the city's attractions is Buckingham Palace, the Queen having opened her 300-year-old London home to the public in the last couple of years. Eighteen major rooms are included in the tour from the Throne Room, State Dining Room, the Green, Blue and White Drawing Rooms and the Music Room. London Zoo has been undergoing a £1 million major refurbishment project to update and extend the Children's Zoo and at the Science Museum a new £1.2 million gallery explores the rapid development in 20th century medicine with plenty of hands-on exhibits. The Tower of London has a new Jewel House, three times larger than its predecessor, allowing 20,000 visitors a day to pass through.

London was the first capital city in the world to experience the industrial revolution, and its attractions and river still pay tribute to those days. Many of these attractions such as the National Maritime Museum, the Old Royal Observatory, and London's emerging new city, the London Docklands, are best reached by river boat. The docklands rising in the east alongside the Thames is a mini-Manhattan, with new bold and imaginative buildings filling areas where the world's shipping used to load and unload cargo and redundant warehouses have been converted into fashionable apartments or a shopping village.

Getting around the capital city is easy whether the visitor uses the extensive bus or underground network. There are numerous bus companies offering sightseeing tours and if you want to get onto the streets, walking tours are also given.

London is the place where you can really "shop till you drop" but the difficulty could be knowing where to start. There are the large department stores from Selfridges in Oxford Street, to Harrods in Knightsbridge and Liberty in Regent Street while at the other extreme are the wide selection of specialist shops selling everything from cheese to china.

It is the evening when London comes to life. Theatre in London centres mainly around Shaftesbury Avenue, but there is also the Barbican Centre, home to the Royal Shakespeare Company and the Royal National Theatre on the South Bank. As well as classical music, opera there is an array of restaurants unrivalled by other major cities, a range of night-clubs, wine bars and cinemas.

Home A (Nanette & Stylie) Just off Kensington High Street (Central London)   A315, A3220

A beautifully preserved Victorian town house which is tastefully decorated and incorporates all modern facilities for guests' comfort, whilst retaining the authentic features of the period. TV's, hairdryers and hospitality trays are available in all rooms. Vivacious hosts offer high quality accommodation, serving breakfast in the elegant family dining room. A welcoming atmosphere and friendly service is assured.

Home to Home
Tel/Fax 0181 566 7976

B&B from £40, Rooms: 4 en-suite double Non smoking, Nearest underground: Kensington High Street 12 minutes, Earls Court 10 minutes, Buses to sights, A1 Airbus stops nearby at Earls Court.

Home B (Micee & Robert) Holland Park area (Central London)   Nearest Road A40, A3220

THE LAW COURTS

A large elegant town house in a quiet secluded square in the chic, but lively, area of Holland Park. Close to several very beautiful parks and the famous Portobello Road antique market. Second-hand book shops abound. Leafy, cosmopolitan area, steeped in interest, with numerous smart and trendy restaurants nearby.

Home to Home
Tel/Fax 0181 566 7976

B&B from £30, Rooms: 3 double, 1 twin/family (all en-suite), Nearest underground: Holland Park 5 minutes, Many buses to all sights, A2 Airbus stop nearby at Kensington Hilton.

Home C (Beatriz & George) Just off Kings Road (Central London)   Nearest Road A3220

TOWER BRIDGE

Ground floor accommodation with immense flair in this Victorian mansion flat. Situated just off the fashionable Kings Road which is an excellent shopping area with specialist boutiques, antique and design shops. Breakfast is served in the beautiful dining-room with access to the secluded communal garden. Excellent choice of restaurants nearby to suit all pockets and tastes. Cheyne Walk and River Thames 2 minutes walk away.

Home to Home
Tel/Fax 0181 566 7976

B&B from £26, Rooms: 1 double, 1 twin, Non smoking, Nearest underground: Sloane Square 10 minutes by bus, Buses to Harrods at Knightsbridge and many other places of interest

Home D (Diana & Julius) Kensington area (Cental London)   Nearest Road A4, A315

A quiet haven at the end of a busy day! One large, beautiful double room is offered in this tranquil home. The room is decorated with flair. in keeping with the Victorian period of the home, and provides a queen-size bed, TV and hospitality tray. The private bathroom, complete with antique features is adjacent. Diana, who is a picture restorer, serves breakfast in her charming dining room which overlooks a beautifully tended garden and patio. Restaurants and wine bars nearby. A smart area on the edge of Kensington, conveniently situated for Earls Court and Olympia.

Home to Home
Tel/Fax 0181 566 7976

B&B from £26, Rooms: 1 double with private bathroom, Non smoking Nearest underground: Hammersmith 6 minutes, Buses to places of interest, A1 Airbus stop nearby

Home E (Marilyn & Alan) Just off Finchley Road (Central London)   Nearest Road A41

A modern townhouse situated off the Finchley Road. Accommodation comprises a double/triple room with TV and en-suite bathroom and shower, a double/triple, twin, and dble/single, sharing a guest bathroom. Additional toilet and washbasin available also. Geared for comfort and offering a sitting area with TV, payphone, fax and word processing facilities. Between Hampstead Heath and Regents Park; 200 yds from Swiss Cottage underground (6 mins journey on the Jubilee Line to Baker Street for Madam Tussauds and Bond Street in the heart of Oxford Street shops).

Home to Home
Tel/Fax 0181 566 7976

B&B from £22, Rooms: 4 comfortable guest rooms,
Nearest underground: Swiss Cottage 3 mins,
Bus services to sights, A2 Airbus at Baker Street

Home F (Julianna & Harry) Putney Bridge area   Nearest Road A219, A204

Artist/animator and sculptor hosts offer 1 twin bedded guest room with private bathroom in their beautifully restored Victorian home. House has many intriguing features. Guests are made most welcome by these delightful hosts and their young family. Breakfast is served in the light and airy dining area of the kitchen overlooking the garden and river Thames. Guests are welcome to use the small, charming upstairs conservatory with its panoramic views up and down the river. Attractive riverside pubs and interesting restaurants nearby. Ideal location for Wimbledon tennis.

Home to Home
Tel/Fax 0181 566 7976

B&B from £24, Room: 1 twin with private bathroom,
Nearest underground Putney Bridge 8 minutes,
Riverboats to Westminster, Buses to Central sights

Home G (Dolores & Bert) Parsons Green area   Nearest Road A308, A3217

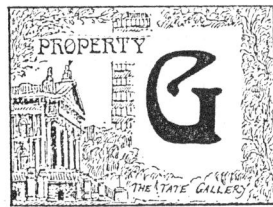

Whether staying for 2 nights or a week you can be sure of a warm welcome with these cheerful and generous hosts. They offer a double room with queen sized bed, TV and hot drinks tray. Shower and wash basin are en--suite. There is also a pretty Laura Ashley single room with wash basin sharing a family bathroom. The atmosphere is friendly and informal. A popular choice! Some of London's trendiest restaurants in the area.

Home to Home
Tel/Fax 0181 566 7976

B&B from £24, Rooms: 1 en-suite double, 1 single,
Nearest underground: Parsons Green 10 minutes,
Buses for Chelsea, Knightsbridge and Central Sights

Home H (Moira & Frank) Parsons Green area   Nearest Road A217, A308

Self contained apartment for 2-4 guests on first floor of a family home. Comprises a twin bedroom with private bathroom, dining/living room with TV and comfortable sofa bed, additional bathroom and fully equipped kitchen. Lounge overlooks a pretty park. Frank & Moira are gracious and welcoming hosts who live on the ground floor in their elegant suite. Ideal for longer stays as guests can be totally self catering. However, hosts are delighted to provide breakfast food if guests prefer not to shop. A popular area for quality interior design/furniture and antiques. Excellent restaurants.

Home to Home
Tel/Fax 0181 566 7976

Self contained apartment from £24 per person,
Nearest underground: Parsons Green 10 minutes,
Buses to various parts of London

Home I (Dianne & Corran) Parsons Green area   Nearest Road A308, A3217

A warm welcome is offered to guests by New Zealand couple in their beautiful town house. Half tester double bed in cosy guest room of great charm with its own TV and hospitality tray. Private bathroom adjacent. Single room also available. Extremely close to the underground and buses as well as excellent restaurants and fashionable shops.

Home to Home
Tel/Fax 0181 566 7976

B&B from £24, Rooms: 1 double with private bathroom, 1 single,
Nearest underground: Parsons Green 2 minutes

Home J (Marjory & Christopher) Hammersmith/Chiswick area   Nearest Road A4, A315

Wonderfully close to the tube, this family home offers a very beautiful and spacious twin/triple guest room with wash basin, TV and hospitality tray. The room overlooks a tranquil garden. Private bathroom is adjacent. Christopher, a linguist, and Marjory, a teacher, are anxious to make their guests' stay as pleasant as possible. Enjoy an evening stroll along a lovely stretch of the river Thames, passing picturesque pubs and lovely gardens Good restaurants and shops nearby.

Home to Home
Tel/Fax 0181 566 7976

B&B from £26, Rooms: 1 twin/triple with private bathroom adjacent,
Nearest underground: Stamford Brook 1 minute, Buses to Trafalgar
Square and Kew Gardens, Non smoking

Home K (Peter & Catriona) Hammersmith/Chiswick area   Nearest Road A4, A315

This lovely couple, an architect and PR consultant, offer 2 double and 1 twin guest rooms in their pretty restored Victorian house built in 1864. A terraced home with a cottagey feel. Situated in the heart of historic Brackenbury Village and near the delightful Ravenscourt Park, their home makes a very comfortable base. Informal atmosphere. Imaginative breakfasts. Many good restaurants and pubs within an easy walk.

Home to Home
Tel/Fax 0181 566 7976

B&B from £19, Rooms: 2 double, 1 twin/single, 2 guests' bathrooms,
Nearest underground: Ravenscourt Park 8 minutes, Goldhawk Road 8
minutes.

Home L (Pat & Ralph) Hammersmith/Chiswick area   Nearest Road A315, A316

These relaxed and adaptable hosts makes guests very comfortable in their home. They offer 3 guest rooms: a spacious family room sleeping 4, as well as a double and a twin, all with wash basins and sharing a guest bathroom. Additional toilet. Lounge with TV available for guests. On summer evening enjoy a walk beside the Thames nearby, or sample the numerous cafes along the High Road! Kew Gardens are a short bus ride away. Children welcome. Non smoking.

Home to Home
Tel/Fax 0181 566 7976

B&B from £15, Rooms: 1 double/family, 1 double, 1 twin
Nearest underground: Turnham Green 8 minutes,
Easy access to Heathrow, Buses to the Central District.

Home M (Peter & Valerie) Chiswick area   Nearest Road A315, B409

Stay in villagey unspoiled Chiswick where writers and actors live. On the Bedford Park Garden Conservation Estate, this 1880's Norman Shaw home is just 3 minutes walk from the tube station, interesting boutiques and eating places. Valerie and Peter offer 3 guest rooms; a double and a twin (which can be triples) with guest bathroom, plus a beautiful double with queen size bed and private bathroom. Sitting room for guests. A fine home beautifully furnished by the retired architect owner.

Home to Home
Tel/Fax 0181 566 7976

B&B from £19, Rooms: 1 double with bathroom, 1 double, twin/triple,
Nearest underground Turnham Green 3 minutes, Easy access to
Heathrow, Buses to Central London.

Home N (Janice & Jeremy) Hammersmith/Chiswick area   Nearest Road A4, M4, A406

Superb accommodation is offered in this home of grace and quality where the hosts delight in providing for guests' every comfort. Beautiful lounge available for guests' sole use. The mock-Tudor home is surrounded by beautiful gardens and is located on a lovely estate with a large park of historic interest close by. Kew Gardens and fascinating pubs along the river's edge within a 30 minute walk. There are 2 guest rooms available: a twin with en-suite bathroom, and a spacious and lovely double room with wash basin and private bathroom close by.

Home to Home
Tel/Fax 0181 566 7976

B&B from £24, Rooms: 1 double, 1 twin (with private facilities),
Nearest underground Acton Town 10 minutes, Ideal for Heathrow

Home O (Anita & David) Ealing area   Nearest Road M4, A406, A40

These friendly hosts offer superb hospitality in their restored Victorian family home. The pretty twin room with washbasin and large, comfortably furnished double or triple room overlook lovely gardens and lawns. A bathroom is reserved for guests. Enjoy the delights of village Ealing, just 5 minutes' walk away, where you find the tube station, a shopping mall and interesting pubs and restaurants!

Home to Home
Tel/Fax 0181 566 7976

B&B from £18, Rooms 1 double/triple, 1 twin (share guest bathroom),
Nearest underground: Ealing Broadway 5 minutes, Direct railway
lines to Paddington, Easy train link to Windsor, Bus to Kew Gardens

Home P (John & Jane) Ealing area   Nearest Road M4, A40, A406

A lovely family home of great character offering 1 twin room with private bathroom adjacent, overlooking landscaped patio and gardens. The home, built in the mid 1880's, has been tastefully furnished. Breakfast is served in the family kitchen/breakfast room which leads onto the garden. Hosts take every care to ensure their guests' comfort. Five minutes walk to a modern shopping mall and several first class restaurants. Open parkland nearby.

Home to Home
Tel/Fax 0181 566 7976

B&B from £24, Room: 1 twin with private bathroom adjacent,
Nearest underground: Ealing Broadway 7 minutes,
Ealing Common 6 minutes

Home Q (Chantal & Benjamin) Ealing area — Nearest Road A40, A406

Three spacious guest rooms are offered in this imposing family residence. Two triples, one overlooking the tranquil garden of Ealing Abbey, share a lovely guest bathroom. Additionally, there is a charming double room with en-suite shower bathroom. Hostess teaches piano and speaks French. A quiet area of beautiful houses within 10 minutes walk of Ealing centre. Excellent selection of restaurants and pubs nearby. Ample room for off-street parking.

Home to Home
Tel/Fax 0181 566 7976

B&B from £16, Rooms: 2 triple sharing bathroom, 1 en-suite double, Nearest underground: Ealing Broadway 10 minutes, Trains to Paddington and buses to Kew and Richmond

Home R (Catherine & Janek) Ealing area — Nearest Road A40, A406

Polish host and his welcoming Scottish wife offer a suite of a double and a single room with guest bathroom on the second floor of their modern town house. Attractive, secluded estate. Guests are happy to return again and again, as the hostess's relaxed welcome encourages them to feel at home. Shops, malls and numerous restaurants and pubs lie 10 minutes walk away, at Ealing Broadway, the attractive local centre. Non smokers.

Home to Home
Tel/Fax 0181 566 7976

B&B from £19, Rooms: 1 double, 1 single, share guest bathroom, Nearest underground: Ealing Broadway 10 minutes, British Rail to Paddington

Home S (Muriel & Neville) Ealing area — Nearest Road M4, A406

This gracious hostess offers 3 single rooms in a home of beauty and charm, decorated with a traditional English quality. A tranquil setting. Muriel, who is a piano teacher and keen gardener, does not accept smokers and is not available in August. At nearby Ealing Common tube station, with its choice of tube lines, is a comprehensive range of shops and restaurants. Easy commuting from Heathrow or Central London.

Home to Home
Tel/Fax 0181 566 7976

B&B from £24, Rooms: 3 single rooms sharing bathroom, Non smoking, Nearest underground Ealing Common 3 minutes

Home T (Rosemary & Ian) Ealing area — Nearest Road M4, A406

Bed and Breakfast with a difference! Australian hosts offer a superb self-contained bed-sitting room in the beautiful, airy loft extension of their home. Overlooking gardens and a pond. Double bedroom, en-suite shower bathroom, kitchenette with microwave, dining/sitting area with TV. Linen provided, also breakfast food. A warm and friendly welcome in a lovely home!

Home to Home
Tel/Fax 0181 566 7976

B&B from £24, Rooms: 1 double with en-suite shower bathroom, Non smoking, Nearest underground: South Ealing 10 minutes, Buses to Kew and Richmond

Home U (Jean & Doug) Ealing area

Nearest Road A40, A406

In the heart of Ealing, 'the Queen of the Suburbs', these congenial hosts offer 1 twin-bedded guestroom with wash basin in their spacious and comfortable ground-floor apartment. Quiet surroundings, overlooking a pretty green. A short stroll to Ealing Broadway Centre for shops, restaurants and tube. Local bus to nearby Kew Gardens, Richmond-upon-Thames, Hampton Court Palace, or Britrail to Windsor.

Home to Home
Tel/Fax 0181 566 7976

B&B from £19, Rooms: 1 twin, sharing bathroom with hosts,
Nearest underground: Ealing Broadway 3 minutes,
Trains and buses nearby

Home V (Margaret & Colin) Ealing area

Nearest Road M4, A40, A406

A good natured and adaptable Australian and her English husband offer a pleasant double room with washbasin and option of private bathroom in their comfortable family home. Non smokers. Easy access to Heathrow.

Home to Home
Tel/Fax 0181 566 7976

B&B from £19, Room: 1 double with washbasin,
Nearest underground: North Ealing 2 minutes

Home W (Wendy & Robert) Ealing area

Nearest Road A40, A406

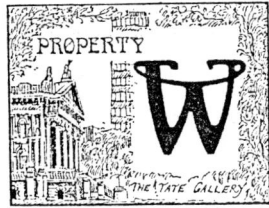

In their immense Victorian home, this lively couple and their young family offer guests superbly decorated double and twin rooms, each with private bathroom. Also available: single, double and very spacious family rooms which share a pretty guest bathroom. TV in all rooms. A quiet location with off street parking. Close to all the amenities at Ealing Broadway Centre.

Home to Home
Tel/Fax 0181 566 7976

B&B from £16, Rooms: double & twin, some with private bathroom
Nearest underground: Ealing Broadway 10 minutes,
Buses to Kew and Richmond. A non smoking home

Home X (Jean & Kevin) Ealing area

Nearest Road A40, A406

This friendly couple offer a comfortable London base which is ideal for a couple or a family of 3 or 4. On the top floor of their home, they provide a suite of a twin bedroom and sitting room with bed-settee and cot bed, plus private bathroom with shower. Jean may offer a substantial continental breakfast during the week and full English breakfast at weekends. Lovely park close by. Very easy access to Heathrow by tube or car. Jean speaks German and Italian.

Home to Home
Tel/Fax 0181 566 7976

B&B from £18, Rooms: 1 twin, plus 1 or 2 beds in guest living area,
Nearest underground: South Ealing 3 minutes,
Trains to Windsor, Buses to Kew and Richmond

Home Y (Marian & Daniel) Ealing area

Nearest Road A406, A40

In their comfortable Edwardian semi-detached home, Marian and Daniel offer a convenient base. The guestrooms comprise a double and a small single sharing a bathroom, plus a double room with small shower bathroom en-suite. Situated on a quiet tree lined street just 5 minutes walk to a parade of shops and 2 tube stations. Easy parking. Ideal accommodation for families.

Home to Home
Tel/Fax 0181 566 7976

**B&B from £19, Rooms: 1 double, 1 single (sharing bathroom),
1 double with en-suite shower bathroom,
Nearest underground: North Ealing 4 minutes, West Acton 7 minutes**

Home Z (Diana & Louis) Ealing area

Nearest Road A40, A406

Relaxed, friendly hosts offer a loft conversion comprising a spacious and airy twin/triple room with private shower bathroom en-suite. TV and hospitality tray. Modern three storey home, conveniently situated for 2 underground lines.

Home to Home
Tel/Fax 0181 566 7976

**B&B from £15, Rooms: 1 twin/triple with en-suite facilities,
Nearest underground: West Acton 7 minutes, North Ealing 7 minutes**

Avon

"Oh! who can ever be tired of Bath?"

(Jane Austen - Northanger Abbey, chapter 10)

AVON

DYRHAM PARK.

Two famous cities put the small county of Avon firmly on the visitors' map - Bristol and Bath. Both cities make an excellent base to explore the surrounding countryside which includes the Quantock, Cotswold and Mendip hills as well as the Wye Valley.

Bath is Britain's best preserved and most complete Georgian city - earning it the title of the country's only World Heritage City. It is also one of the country's oldest cities, famous since Roman times for its warm mineral springs and attracting visitors for over 2,000 years. The hot springs were first discovered by the Celts in 500 BC. It was the Romans who adopted the settlement in AD 44 calling it Aquae Sulis, or the Waters of Sul, a Celtic goddess, who developed them into a sophisticated system of baths. The springs originate in the Eastern Mendip hills, collecting minerals on the way before reaching the surface in Bath.

Bath was prosperous throughout the Middle Ages, but it is most famous for its 18th century life when a handful of architects and arbiters of social taste transformed the city into a fashionable centre. The city became a showpiece of Georgian architecture thanks to the work of John Wood who came to the city in 1727. His building schemes were backed by Ralph Allen, the postal pioneer and the Duke of Chandros. The talented Dandy Richard Beau Nash set the style of the city. Today there is still a rich cultural life in Bath, culminating every year in the Bath International Festival. There are plenty of fine Georgian streets and buildings in Bath. There is the famous circus, designed by John Wood and the Royal Crescent, the work of his son John Wood the Second. Robert Adam designed the Pultney Bridge along with the Upper Assembly Rooms, one of the city's grandest buildings. Bath is also a great place to shop with its indoor markets and narrow lanes lined with shops, cafés and restaurants.

Modern day attractions and excellent shopping facilities combine perfectly with the history of Bristol which grew up around its harbour on the River Avon, flourishing as a port since the 10th century. The city's present day centre was until its excavation in the 13th century an area of marshy ground bordering the western side of the Anglo-Saxon settlement. It was excavated to divert the River Frome and construct an improved harbour for an already expanding port. The city became known throughout the world after John Cabot set sail in 1497 to discover North America and Newfoundland a year before Columbus had landed. By the 18th and 19th centuries the dockside, which had extended outwards to Broadmead, was a bustling quay scene dominated by the masts of tall ships from all over the world. Between 1898 and 1938 this area was gradually covered over to form the gardens and road network of the centre as it now exists. Statues in the centre commemorate two of Bristol's most famous citizens. Edmund Burke, the city's MP from 1774 to 1780 was an exceptional orator and championed the abolition of the slave trade. Edward Colston was one of the city's great benefactors with a great concern for the education of the poor. One of Bristol's main medieval streets is Broad Street, where for 700 years the legal business of the city was carried out from the Guildhall. It was from here that Judge Jeffreys held his "Bloody Assizes" after the battle of Sedgemoor in 1685. Corn Street has been the banking centre of Bristol for over two centuries. The Corn Exchange is generally regarded as the city's finest Georgian, building, built by John Wood the Elder as a meeting place for merchants and ship owners. On the pavement outside are The Nails, four bronze pillars dating from the late 16th century serving as trading tables on which merchants completed their money transactions - hence the famous saying, "to pay on the nail". At the Avon Gorge where the River Avon flows beneath steep limestone cliffs is Bristol's most distinctive landmark, the Clifton Suspension Bridge, 245ft above the water.

14th CENTURY CLEVEDON COURT.

The bridge was designed by the great 19th century engineer Isambard Kingdom Brunel, but not completed until 1864, five years after his death. Avon also has its seaside towns. The quiet resort of Clevedon, just South of Bristol, retains much of its Victorian charm in its houses, hotels and public gardens and it has peaceful seaside and country walks. Weston-super-Mare offers lively entertainment and attractive parks and gardens as well as beautiful countryside surroundings. The town has two piers, a marine lake and miniature railway as well as the Tropicana Pleasure Beach. The winding Burrington Combe winds its way from the foothills of the Mendips to the top which gives fine views across the Bristol Channel. Near the bottom, and market by a plaque, is the Rock of Ages where the Rev A Toplady, sheltering from a storm, received inspiration to write the famous hymn. The Kennet and Avon Canal which stretches 87 miles between Bristol and Reading, is ideal for boating, canoeing, walking, cycling and fishing. Chew Valley Lake is a well loved beauty spot near Bristol. The man-made reservoir is a haven for fishermen, sailors, bird watchers and all who enjoy nature. Another landmark in the area is the Severn Suspension Bridge, with a centre span of 3,240ft, is a vital link on the M4 motorway between Avon and South Wales.

CLIFTON SUSPENSION
BRIDGE, BRISTOL.

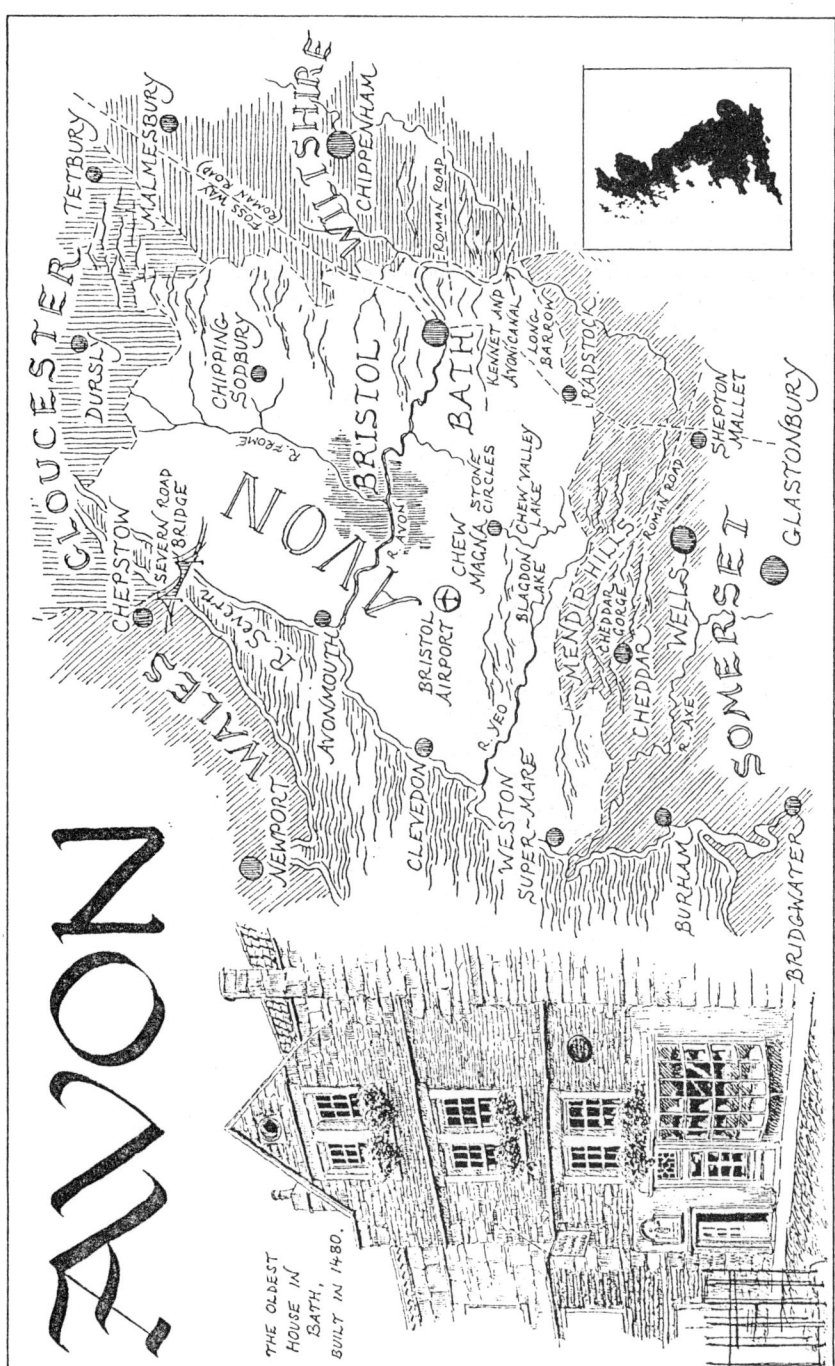

The Old School House, Church Street, Bathford, Bath BA1 7RR   Nearest Road A4, M4

The Old School House is situated in a conservation area and enjoys splendid views of the Avon Valley. Built in 1837 the house has been charmingly decorated and furnished in traditional style. All guest bedrooms are en-suite and offer telephone, colour TV, tea/coffee facilities, hairdryer and trouser press. There is a conservatory for the enjoyment of guests and in winter cheering log fires are lit. Golf and fishing are available nearby and Bath is just 3 miles away.

Sonia and Rodney Stone
Tel: 01225 859593
Fax: 01225 859590

B&B from £30, Dinner from £19.50, Rooms 2 double, 1 family, 2 twin, No smoking, No pets, Open all year, Map Ref: A

The Orchard, 80 High Street, Bathford, Bath, BA1 7TG   Nearest Road A4

Listed Georgian country house home in the hillside village of Bathford and is just 3 miles from Bath. Ideally situated for visiting the surrounding places of great historic interest. The bedrooms, all with TV, are individually designed and furnished to a high standard of comfort and have delightful views across the 1½ acres of walled gardens, hills and countryside.. The elegant drawing room and dining room are filled with fine pieces of period furniture. Ample parking within the grounds.

John & Olga London
Tel: 01225 858765

B&B from £27.50, Rooms: 2 twin all en-suite, 2 double (all with private bathroom), Minimum age 11, No smoking, No pets, Open March to November, Map Ref: A

Wentworth House Hotel, 106 Bloomfield Road, Bath, Avon BA2 2AP   Nearest Road A367

An imposing Victorian residence built in 1887 in Bath stone, standing in mature and secluded gardens with far reaching reaching views. Quietly situated yet within walking distance of the city centre. Bath Abbey and Roman baths. All rooms are tastefully and individually furnished offering colour TV, telephone, and tea/coffee making facilities. There is a elegant lounge and the dining room overlooks the garden and outdoor swimming pool. Licensed bar lounge, Large free car park.

Mrs Avril Kitching
Tel: 01225 339193
Fax: 01225 310460

B&B from £20, Rooms: 11 double, 5 twin, 2 family, 2 single, Minimum age 5, Restricted smoking, Open all year except Christmas and New Year. Map Ref: A

Circus Mansions, 36 Brock Street, Bath, Avon, BA1 2LJ   Nearest Road A4

An elegant Georgian house built in 1769. Circus Mansions has been carefully restored by the resident owners to bring out many of its original features. There is a charming breakfast room which is at garden level The accommodation comprises spacious and comfortably furnished rooms all with private facilities. The price includes English breakfast. Only minutes away from the theatre, restaurants and museums.

Mrs I Lynall
Tel: 01225 336462

B&B from £25, Rooms 3 double, 1 twin (all with private facilities), Restricted smoking, No pets, Open all year except Christmas and New Year, Map Ref: A

Villa Magdala Hotel, Henrietta Road, Bath, Avon BA2 6LX　　　　**5 mins walk to city centre**

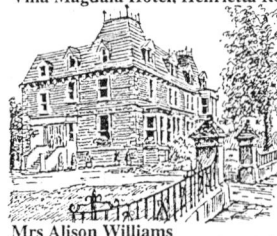

A detached Victorian town house hotel in its own grounds, The Villa Magdala is situated in a quiet residential road only a five minute level walk to the city centre. All bedrooms have private bathroom, telephone, radio/alarms, television, and tea/coffee making facilities, and many overlook the lovely Henrietta Park. The hotel offers ample private parking and is an ideal base for discovering Bath and its many attractions.

Mrs Alison Williams
Tel: 01225 466329　　　　B&B from £25, Rooms: 3 twin, 14 double (all rooms are en-suite),
Fax: 01225 483207　　　　4 posters and triples available, Open all year, Map Ref: A

Grove Lodge Guest House, 11 Lambridge, London Road, Bath BA1 6BJ　　　　**Nearest Road A4 and A46**

Grove Lodge is an elegant Georgian house built in 1788 and set in lovely gardens with views onto the wooded hills surrounding the city. Roy and Rosalie Burridge give you a friendly welcome to their comfortable home which offers 8 excellent large rooms. Each has colour TV and tea/coffee making facilities are available. Continental or 4-course English breakfasts are offered and summer afternoon tea under the apple tree is not to be missed. Bath is an excellent centre for many beautiful and historic locations including the Cotswolds, Stonehenge, Wells and Glastonbury.

Roy & Rosalie Burridge
Tel: 01225 310860　　　　B&B from £17.50, Rooms 3 single, 1 twin, 2 double, 2 family,
Fax: 01225 429630　　　　No smoking, Open all year, Map Ref: A

Cedar Lodge, 13 Lambridge London Road, Bath, Avon BA1 6BJ　　　　**Nearest Road A4**

Cedar Lodge is a listed Grade 2 building of historic interest. It stands in its own grounds with private car park at the rear. The front overlooks the Avon valley and hills surrounding the city. The Kennet and Avon canal and countryside walks are nearby. Frequent bus services pass the door, to and from the city centre. Excellent accommodation in beautifully furnished individually designed rooms. The pine room has a half tester double bed and en suite facilities. the mahogany room with twin beds and the walnut room has 4-poster bed and private bathroom; all rooms have colour TV.

Derek & Maria Beckett　　　　B&B from £18, Rooms 2 double 1 with private bathroom, 1 ensuite,
Tel: 01225 423468　　　　1 twin, No smoking, Open all year except Christmas, Map Ref: A

Wheelbrook Mill, Laverton, Nr Bath, Avon BA3 6QY　　　　**Nearest Road A36**

A warm welcome, log fires on chilly nights and good food awaits you in this picturesque mill nestling in a peaceful valley overlooking the brook, fields and woodland. The pretty, oak beamed bedrooms are centrally heated and furnished with antique pine, Laura Ashley linens and all facilities. Breakfast in the farmhouse kitchen around the refectory table is an informal time where guests can get to know each other. Comfortable sitting room and large garden. An ideal base for touring the West Country.

Shelley & Andrew Weeks　　　　B&B from £22.50, Rooms 1 single, 1 twin, 2 double, Restricted
Tel: 01373 830263　　　　smoking, Pets by arrangement, Open all year, Map Ref: A

The Old Red House, 37 Newbridge Road, Bath, Avon BA1 3HE   Nearest Road A4

We hope you will enjoy your stay at Alfred Taylor's famous "Gingerbread House", which was built 100 years ago and was for many years a high class patisserie and bakers shop. Although the house retains much of its original charm, including stained glass windows, it now enjoys the unmistable atmosphere of a warm and comfortable family home full of pictures and family treasures. Beautifully decorated bedrooms with TV, tea/coffee making facilities, radio alarm clocks and hairdryers. All have en-suite/private facilities. One mile from the heart of the city.

Mrs Chrissie Besley
Tel: 01225 330464

B&B from £20, Rooms: 1 en-suite twin, 1 double with private bathroom, 1 en-suite family, No smoking, Minimum age 4, Pets by arrangement, Open all year, Map Ref: A

Cranleigh, 159 Newbridge Hill, Bath, Avon BA1 3PX   Nearest Road A431

A Victorian house with character and lovely views in a quiet residential area. The spacious en-suite bedrooms are light and airy: one room has a stylish canopied bed, another has a 4-poster. There is a wide choice of delicious breakfasts from scrambled eggs with smoked salmon to pancakes and maple syrup. The atmosphere here is comfortable, relaxed and friendly. There is private parking and a sunny, secluded garden for lazy days. A totally 'non-smoking' house. Minimum 2 nights for summer weekends.

Arthur & Christine Webber
Tel: 01225 310197
Fax: 01225 423143

B&B from £24, Rooms 2 double, 1 family, 2 twin, (all en-suite)
No smoking, Open all year, Map Ref: A

Armstrong House, 41 Crescent Gardens, Upper Bristol Road, Bath BA1 2NB   Nearest Road A4

A beautifully restored city centre Victorian house, offering spacious bedrooms all with private ensuite facilities, tea/coffee, hairdryers, TV and furnished to give maximum comfort. Large English breakfasts are our speciality but special diets can be catered for. A lovely, quiet sitting room for guests is open at all times. Private parking is available, so see Bath the best way - on foot! Only a short level walk to all Bath has to offer. Our interest, good service and best attention is assured.

Nigel and Pat Hunt
Tel: 01225 442211
Fax: 01225 334769

B&B from £25, Dinner not available, Rooms 1 twin, 2 double, 1 family, all have en-suite/private facilities, Minimum age 6, Open all year except Christmas. Map Ref: A

Cheriton House, 9 Upper Oldfield Park, Bath, BA2 3JX   Nearest Rd 10 mins walk to City centre

Dating from the 1880's Cheriton House is located on Bath's southern slopes. Situated in a quiet street with splendid views, yet within easy walking distance of the city. The present owners have carefully restored and redecorated the house and all rooms are attractively furnished. In the dining room a choice of breakfast is offered and in the sitting room there is a plentiful supply of books and brochures to help plan your day. Mike & Jo are pleased to advise guests where to eat, visit; and what to see.

Mike & Jo Babbage
Tel: 01225 429862
Fax: 01225 428403

B&B from £24, Rooms: 6 double, 3 twin
Open all year except Christmas and new year
Map Ref: A

Oakleigh House, 19 Upper Oldfield Park, Bath, BA2 3JX   Nearest Rd 10 mins walk to City Centre

Oakleigh House is situated in a peaceful location 10 minutes from the centre of Bath. Victorian elegance is combined with present day comforts and all bedrooms are en-suite and benefit from tea/coffee making facilities, colour TV, clock radio, hairdryer and tasteful furnishings. There is a car park for guests. A good base for touring Glastonbury, Stonehenge, Bristol, Wells, Salisbury and the Cotswolds.

Jenny King
Tel: 01225 315698
Fax: 01225 448223

B&B from £22.50, Rooms 3 double, 1 twin, all ensuite
Open all year, Map Ref A

Oldfields, 102 Wells Road, Bath, Avon BA2 3AL   Nearest Road A367 (Exeter Road)

This spacious Victorian guest house offers wholefood or traditional English (cholesterol) breakfasts with Mozart in the background, and morning newspapers. Just 10 minutes to the Roman baths and shops to walk off the breakfast! There is off street parking and a garden with views to the hills and crescents. Laura Ashley fabrics and wallpapers lighten the bedrooms which all have TV, tea/coffee trays. Many rooms have private shower/wc. Large lounge with period furniture.

Mr & Mrs A O'Flaherty
Tel: 01225 317984
Fax: 01225 444471

B&B from £20, Rooms: 7 double, 7 twin, 8 rooms have private
shower/wc, Open all year except Christmas. Map Ref: A

Leighton House, 139 Wells Road, Bath, Avon BA2 3AL   Nearest Road A367

Dave and Kathy Slape invite you to enjoy a haven of friendliness at their delightful Victorian home set in award winning gardens, offering views over the city. Ample private parking and only 10 minutes walk from the city centre. The rooms offer every comfort, being tastefully decorated and furnished with en-suite facilities, direct dial telephone, hairdryer, colour TV, radio and beverage making facilities. Superb breakfasts served to suit all tastes. Special breaks available.

David & Kathleen Slape
Tel: 01225 314769

B&B from £28, Rooms: 3 double, 3 twin, 2 family all rooms have en-
suite facilities, Open all year . Map Ref: A

The Hollies, Hatfield Road, Wellsway, Bath, Avon BA2 2BD   Nearest Road A367

Built in 1850 The Hollies is a splendid Grade II listed early Victorian house 1 mile from the city centre. Family run, friendly and personal attention is assured. The 3 pretty guest rooms all have en-suite or private facilities, colour TV and beverage making facilities. A choice of English, Vegetarian or Continental breakfast is served. There is private parking available and a secluded garden with apple trees and shrub roses overlooking the Parish church.

Mrs Nicky Stabbins
Tel: 01225 313366

B&B from £18, Rooms: 2 double, 1 twin, all have en-suite or private
facilities, No smoking, Open all year except Christmas and New Year.
Map ref: A

Gainsborough Hotel, Weston Lane, Bath, Avon BA1 4AB   **Nearest Main Road A4**

A large country house hotel in own attractive grounds near botanical gardens, municipal golf course and park. Both spacious and very comfortable we provide a relaxing and informal atmosphere for our guests stay. The Abbey, Roman baths, and pump rooms are all within easy walking distance via the park. All 16 bedrooms are en-suite with colour TV, tea/coffee making facilities, telephone, hairdryer, etc. The hotel has a friendly bar, satellite TV, 2 sun terraces, large car park and warm welcome.

Mrs R Warwick
Tel: 01225 311380
Fax: 01225 447411

B&B from £28, Dinner from £8.25, Rooms: 16 2 single, 12 twin/double, 2 family (all en-suite), Open all year except Christmas & New Year
Map Ref: A

Arnolds Hill House, Wingfield, Avon BA14 9LB   **Nearest Road A366, A36**

This fine Edwardian country house, set in 5 acres of attractive grounds some 9 miles from Bath, offers personal hospitality in peaceful comfortable surroundings. There are 2 double en-suite bedrooms and 1 twin with private facilities, each with colour TV and tea/coffee making facilities. Guests are free to relax in the sitting room or in the garden around the outdoor swimming pool. Ideally situated for visiting Bath, Longleat House, Stonehenge, Salisbury and Wells.

Marjorie & Derek Dore
Tel: 01225 752025

B&B from £20, Rooms 1 twin with private bathroom, 2 en-suite double, No smoking, Minimum age 16, No pets, Open April - September, Map Ref: A

Box Hedge Farm, Coalpit Heath, Bristol, Avon, BS17 2UW   **Nearest Road Westerleigh Road**

Box Hedge Farm is set in 200 acres of beautiful rural countryside. Local to M4/M5, central for Bristol and Bath. An ideal stopping point for the south west and Wales. We offer a warm family atmosphere with traditional farmhouse cooking. The large spacious bedrooms, one with a four-poster, have colour TV and tea/coffee making facilities.

Mrs Marilyn Collins
Tel: 01454 250786

B&B from £15, Dinner from £7.50, Rooms 1 single, 2 double, 1 family, Restricted smoking, Open all year. Map Ref: B

Please note
'Bed and Breakfast from...'
indicates
the price per person,
based on two people sharing
a room.

Buckinghamshire, Berkshire, Hertfordshire, Bedfordshire

"And ye, that from the stately brow
of Windsor's heights th' expanse below
Of grove, of lawn, of mead survey,
Whose turf, whose shade, whose flowers among
Wanders the hoary Thames along
His silver-winding way:

Ah happy hills! ah pleasing shade!
Ah fields beloved in vain!
Where once my careless childhood stray'd,
A stranger yet to pain!"

(Thomas Gray - Ode on a Distant Prospect of Eton
College)

BEDFORDSHIRE, BERKSHIRE, BUCKINGHAMSHIRE & HERTFORDSHIRE

'JOHN BUNYAN'S CROSS', STEVINGTON, BEDFORDSHIRE.

The counties of Bedfordshire, Berkshire, Buckinghamshire and Hertfordshire have some of the loveliest countryside in England - yet are within an hour's travelling distance from the bustle of central London.

Bedfordshire has a wealth of beautiful countryside, historic sites and fun attractions just waiting to be discovered. Its landscape ranges from the Greensand Ridge in the heart of the county with its wooded slopes abundant with wildlife, to the chalk hills in the South and limestone villages along the banks of the River Great Ouse in the North. Not only is there wonderful landscape, but there are museums, galleries, stately homes, shopping centres, markets, attractive towns and pretty villages. Bedfordshire's famous author and preacher John Bunyan's footsteps can be followed three centuries on. Ampthill is one of Bedfordshire's finest historic towns, lying eight miles South of Bedford. Its picturesque narrow streets are lined mainly with Georgian houses and there are many interesting Tudor bridges. The ancient county town of Bedford dates back to before Saxon times and through it flows the River Great Ouse on its journey to the Wash. Dunstable is on the edge of the highest point in the county, the Dunstable Downs. which offer stunning views and are rich in wildlife.

Royal Berkshire is perhaps one of the most interesting English counties. Stretching from the outskirts of London West to the border with Wiltshire. The River Thames flows through its beautiful countryside, providing many opportunities for boating and walking. The Thames holds a special place in the affections of the British and was immortalised in books like Kenneth Grahame's "The Wind in the Willows" and Jerome K. Jerome's "Three Men in a Boat". From Lechlade in Gloucestershire, the river's 124 miles of non tidal waters pass through five counties on the way to Teddington and the Western outskirts of London. To the West of the county are the market towns of Newbury and Hungerford in the Kennet Valley. Newbury is famous for its racecourse and international spring festival and Hungerford for its serene canal side setting and antiques arcade. The name Royal Windsor conjures up everything that is English and its historic buildings and streets make it an interesting place to visit, with Windsor Castle being the main attraction. Nearby on the banks of the Thames are places like Maidenhead and Eton. At Runnymeade where the Magna Carta was signed there are memorials to John F. Kennedy, The American Bar Association and the Commonwealth Air Forces.

THE CHANTRY CHAPEL ~
THE OLDEST BUILDING IN BUCKINGHAM.

Buckinghamshire is rich in literary and cultural history as well as having beautiful countryside. The Chiltern Hills, running through the South of the county, are known for their incomparable beechwoods - all that remains of a vast forest that once covered the whole of the county. In the North is the new city of Milton Keynes, created around several towns and villages in 1967, now boasting one of the largest indoor shopping centres in Europe. In contrast there are some fine old towns, such as Buckingham and Olney. The Vale of Aylesbury lies in the centre of the county with the county town of Aylesbury at its heart. This rich flat farmland has the occasional high point such as Brill Hill, The Clump at Quainton and Lodge Hill, at Waddesdon. One of the most picturesque parts of the county, the vale is studded with country houses. The county has several of the great homes of the Rothschild family. The River Thames flows along the county's Southern boundary through charming scenery, although mainly residential with pretty villages, parks, heaths and woods. One of the most famous, Burnham Beeches, near Stoke Poges, was a favourite haunt of the poet Thomas Gray.

Hertfordshire has got something for everyone. Peppered among its rolling countryside, picturesque villages and busy market towns, are impressive stately homes and many tourist attractions. As Verulamium, St Albans was once one of the leading cities of the Roman Empire. Today visitors can see the remains and artefacts of this important settlement. Watford is Hertfordshire's largest town with a busy and prosperous centre with modern shopping. Its main role in the middle ages was to act as a market town for neighbouring settlements. Welwyn Garden City was made famous by Ebenezer Howard's Garden City movement. Residential and industrial areas are laid out along curved tree lined boulevards and a neo-Georgian town centre offers excellent shopping. The great Roman road of Watling Street crosses Elstree in the South West with its surrounding parishes of Shenley and Ridge. Nearby Boreham Wood is known primarily for its film studios and modern industrial developments. Hertford is a quiet, charming country town which has many old buildings including the castle. There are numerous antique shops. Both Stevenage and Hemel Hempstead are new towns. Just 30 miles North of London, Stevenage was a small market town until 1946. Hemel Hempstead developed around an existing town and new developments have been skilfully integrated into the town's history which dates back to Roman times.

WINDSOR CASTLE

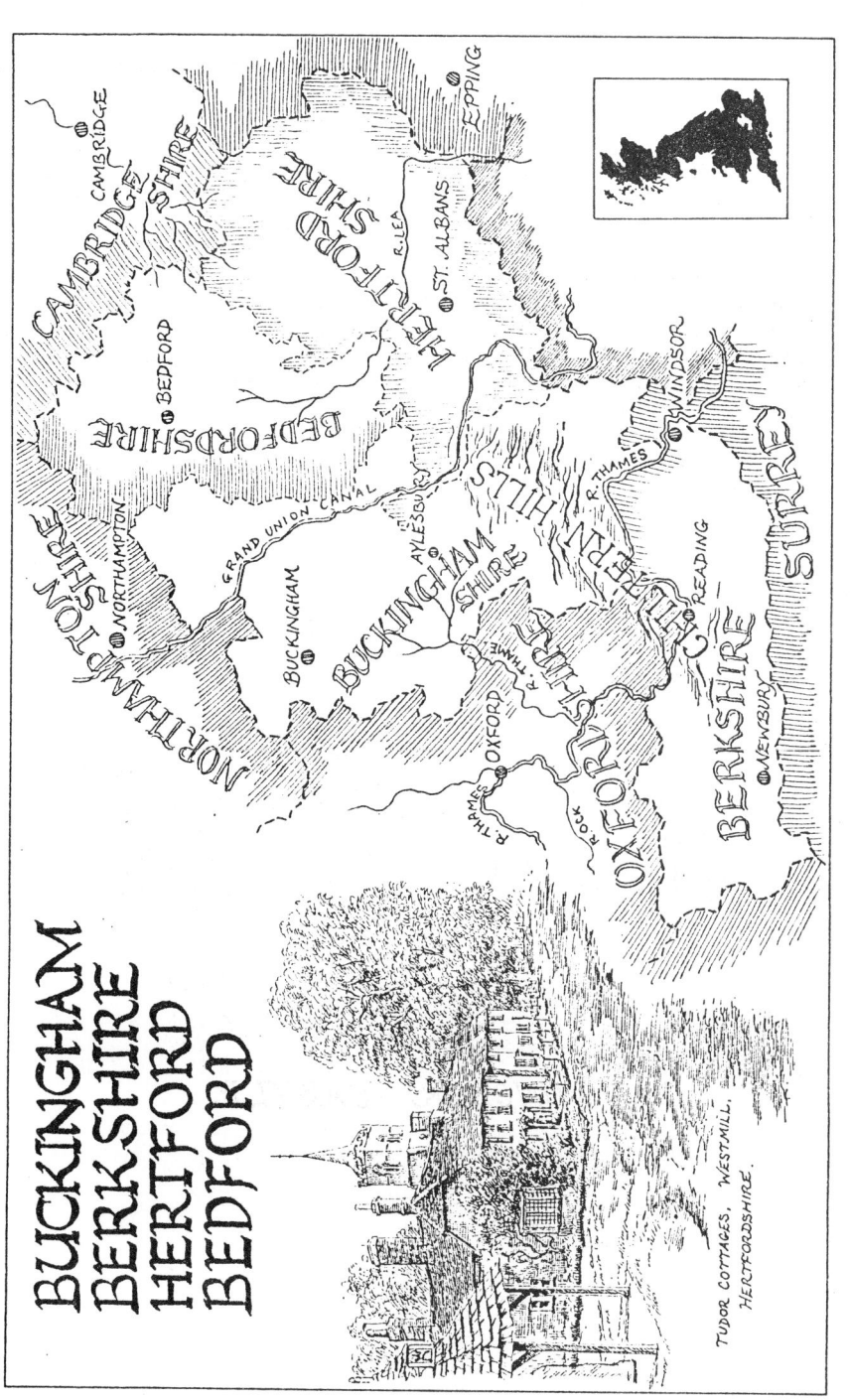

BUCKINGHAM
BERKSHIRE
HERTFORD
BEDFORD

TUDOR COTTAGES, WESTMILL, HERTFORDSHIRE.

CAMBRIDGE

CAMBRIDGESHIRE

HERTFORDSHIRE

EPPING

R. LEA

ST. ALBANS

BEDFORD

BEDFORDSHIRE

WINDSOR

R. THAMES

NORTHAMPTONSHIRE

NORTHAMPTON

GRAND UNION CANAL

AYLESBURY

BUCKINGHAM

BUCKINGHAMSHIRE

CHILTERN HILLS

R. THAME

READING

R. THAMES

OXFORD

OXFORDSHIRE

ROCK

BERKSHIRE

NEWBURY

SURREY

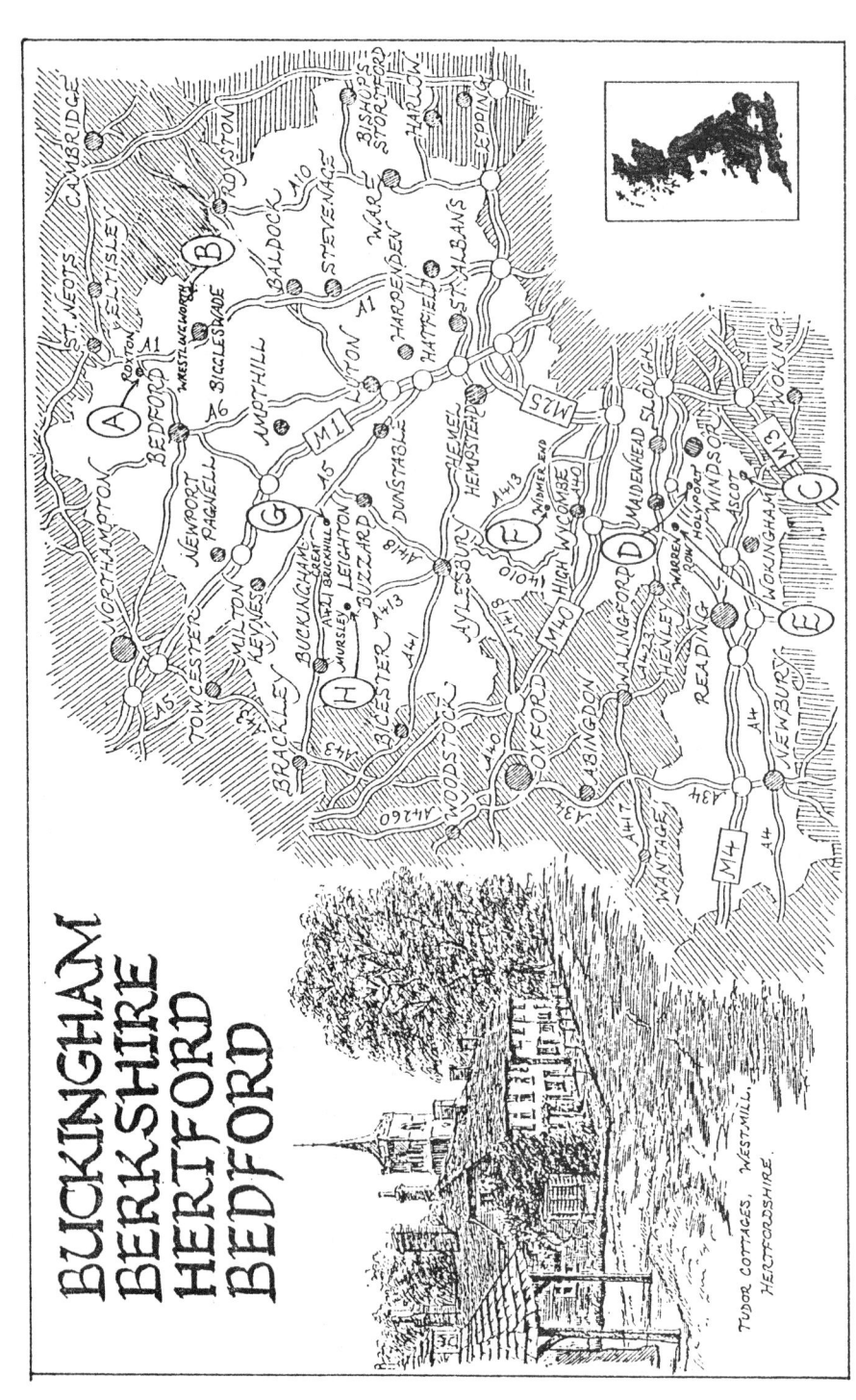

BUCKINGHAM
BERKSHIRE
HERTFORD
BEDFORD

TUDOR COTTAGES, WESTMILL, HERTFORDSHIRE.

Church Farm, 41 High Street, Roxton, Bedford MK44 3EB   Nearest Road A1, A428

A warm welcome is assured at this historic farmhouse situated in a lovely village setting. The house is pleasantly furnished with a mixture of family antiques. The comfortable guest rooms have their own bathroom and staircase, tea/coffee making facilities, and hand basins. There is a lounge for guests with TV and an open fire. Breakfast is served in the 17th century dining room. Highly commended.

Mrs Janet Must
Tel: 01234 870234

B&B from £15, Rooms 1 family, 1 twin, No Smoking,
Open all year, Map Ref: A

Orchard Cottage, 1 High Street, Wrestlingworth, Near Sandy, Beds SG19 2EW   Nearest Rd B1042

Orchard Cottage was at one time the village bakery, and now a comfortable home offering bed and breakfast and a homely atmosphere. Joan and her husband Owen and keen craft workers and their work is evident throughout the house. Much of the furniture was made by Owen and Joan adds the finishing touch with her handmade lace. Nearby is the RSPB headquarters. Cambridge, Wimpole Hall, and Duxford Air Museum are within a short drive. The village offers a post office, village shop, hairdresser, church and a pub where meals are always available.

Mrs Joan Strong
Tel: 01767 631355

B&B from £15, Rooms 2 single, 1 twin, 1 double, No smoking,
Open all year, Map Ref: B

Lyndrick Guest House, The Avenue, North Ascot, Berkshire SL5 7ND   Nearest Road A30, M3, M4

Lyndrick offers good quality accommodation at less than hotel prices and is just 25 minutes from Heathrow. A warm welcome awaits guests and pride is taken in customer service. Full English breakfast is served in a pleasant conservatory and for early departees a continental breakfast can be supplied. London Waterloo is 40 minutes away on British Rail. Wentworth and surrounding golf courses are 10 minutes away. There is easy access to M3, M4 and M25. Bracknell and Windsor are 10 minutes and Reading 25 minutes.

Marjie & Chris Lockrie
Tel: 01344 883520
Fax:01344 891243

B&B from £20, Rooms 1 double, 2 twin, 1 single
(We take Visa and M/C) Open all year, Map ref: C

Moor Farm, Holyport, Nr Maidenhead, Berkshire SL6 2HY   Nearest Road A330, M4

Guests staying at Moor Farm have the exclusive use of a wing of this ancient medieval hall house. The guest bedrooms, all with private facilities, are part of the original house and are attractively furnished with country fabrics, have central heating and comfy beds. They have a Tourist Board rating of 2 crowns and are Highly Commended for quality. Self catering cottages are also available. There are very pleasant village pubs within walking distance which serve good food.

Chris & Gillian Reynolds
Tel: 01628 33761
Fax: 01628 33761

B&B from £19, Rooms 1 double, 1 twin, (all with private facilities),
Restricted smoking, Open all year, Map Ref: D

Woodpecker Cottage, Warren Row Near Wargrave, Berkshire RG10 8QS   Nearest Road A4

A tranquil woodland retreat away from crowds and traffic yet within ½ hour of Heathrow, Windsor, Henley and Oxford. Set in a delightful garden of about 1 acre and surrounded by woods where deer abound. The ground floor accommodation comprises ensuite double room with its own entrance and a twin room with private bathroom. Both have tea/coffee making facilities, and TV. There is a cosy sitting room with log fires in winter. A full English breakfast includes home made bread and jam from fruit grown in the garden. Local pubs and restaurants are within easy reach.

Michael & Joanna Power
Tel: 01628 822772
Fax: 01628 822125

B&B from £18, Rooms 1 twin with private bathroom, 1 en-suite double, No smoking, Minimum age 8, Open all year, MapRef: E

White House, North Road, Widmer End, High Wycombe, Bucks, HP15 6ND   Nearest Road A404

Built as three adjoining brick and flint cottages in the early 1700's, the White House was later extended and provides a restful, self contained, suite to which many of Jane's guests return time and time again. Fully modernised, it contains three rooms - a large restful bedroom, separate bathroom and toilet which remain apart from the rest of the house. The large bedroom locks out onto the large garden and paddocks where ponies and sheep often graze during the year. A traditional or continental breakfast is served.

Mrs Jane Vaughan
Tel: 01494 712221

B&B from £16, Light supper from £2.50, Rooms 1 en-suite twin, or 1 en-suite family (4), Pets welcome, Open all year, Map Ref: F

Three Locks Golf Club, Great Brickhill, Milton Keynes, Bucks MK17 9BH   Nearest Road A5

Three Locks Golf Club - for the golfing enthusiast. All rooms have bath or shower, television, tea/coffee making facilities, and shaving points. There is a bar and lounge for guests and members. Local fishing and wonderful views over open countryside with Milton Keynes and Leighton Buzzard only 3 miles away. The Three Locks Golf Club has a professional and a pro-shop, an excellent practice ground and can offer a golfing challenge to both beginners and experienced golfers. Executive accommodation is available with free golf.

Mrs Patrice Critchley
Tel: 01525 270470

B&B from £29.50, Rooms 1 single, 2 twin, 3 double, 1 family, No smoking, No pets, Open all year, Map Ref: G

Richmond Lodge, Mursley, Milton Keynes, Buckinghamshire MK17 0LE   Nearest Road A421

A country house set in three acres of gardens and orchard with a grass tennis court. Well situated for Woburn and Waddesdon Manor and other National Trust properties. Ideal access for central Milton Keynes and easy train journey to London (35 minutes) Leighton Buzzard to Euston. A warm comfortable house with a friendly welcome. Bedrooms are comfortable and have tea/coffee making facilities, and TV. A non-smoking home. Nearby activities include horse riding, golf and swimming pool.

Christine & Peter Abbey
Tel: 01296 720275
Fax:01296 720275

B&B from £19, Dinner from £12.50 (by arrangement), Rooms 2 twin, 1 double, (1 en-suite), No smoking, Open all year, Map Ref: H

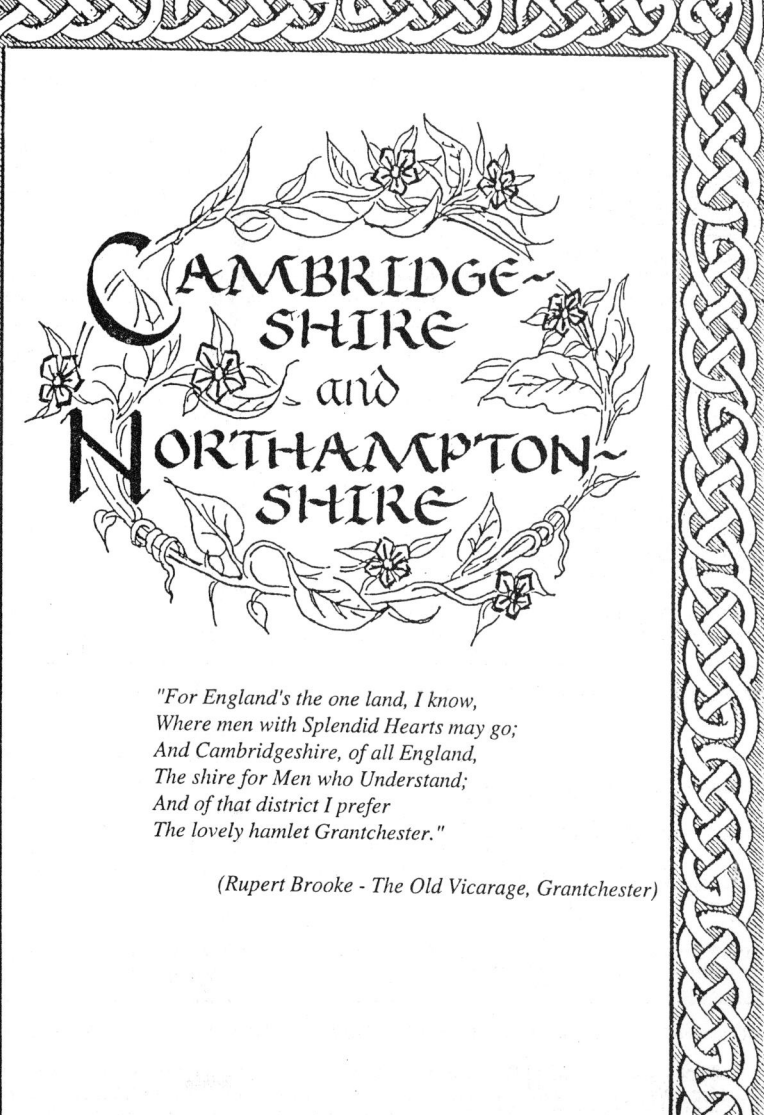

CAMBRIDGESHIRE and NORTHAMPTONSHIRE

"For England's the one land, I know,
Where men with Splendid Hearts may go;
And Cambridgeshire, of all England,
The shire for Men who Understand;
And of that district I prefer
The lovely hamlet Grantchester."

(Rupert Brooke - The Old Vicarage, Grantchester)

CAMBRIDGESHIRE & NORTHAMPTONSHIRE

THE 15TH CENTURY BRIDGE
AND CHAPEL, ST. IVES.

The county of Cambridgeshire has 2 splendid cities rich in cultural heritage - Cambridge and Peterborough.

Cambridge has a great wealth of architectural styles and many interesting features from the courtyards, the bridges and "Backs" along the River Cam. The city has been described as the loveliest in Britain. The establishment of a prospering trading route between eastern and central England led to the real development of the city 900 years ago and Cambridge soon became established as a teaching centre. The university had been founded by the 13th century. The oldest college is Peterhouse, founded in 1284. Others became established over the next 700 years in superb examples of medieval and later styles of architecture. Among the most famous of the colleges are Queen's, Trinity, Magdalene, St John's Clare, Jesus, Emmanuel and King's. King's College Chapel is the city's crowning glory and is best viewed from the "Backs". Today's Cambridge is a bustling city of 100,000 people with good shopping facilities and a wide variety of bookshops. Arts and entertainment are a central part of the city's life, from impromptu classical recitals and plays to full scale musicals, rock concerts and theatre. The city is surrounded by lovely countryside and many attractive villages which contain a wealth of historic buildings.

Peterborough is a perfect blend of past and present. The city has been dominated by its Norman cathedral for more than 750 years. The cathedral's painted ceiling is unique and the West Front is acclaimed as one of the finest in Europe. Peterborough has retained much of its heritage despite being a new city. Careful and tasteful redevelopment, such as the modern shopping complexes of Queensgate and Rivergate, have not resulted in the destruction of the old market town buildings.

Oliver Cromwell (1599-1658, was born, lived and trained troops for the Civil War in Huntingdonshire, centred around the River Great Ouse. The Falcon Inn in Huntingdon's

KING'S COLLEGE CHAPEL, CAMBRIDGE.

Market Square was one of his headquarters. Samuel Pepys (1633-1703) lived close to Huntingdon and was educated at the same school as Cromwell. Queen Catherine of Aragon was sent to Buckden Palace, near Huntingdon, before her death. The poet William Cowper was also a resident of Huntingdon from 1765 to 1767.

The landscape of the Fens is unique in character with vast areas of artificially reclaimed land from its original marsh state. The area was the stronghold of Hereward the Wake, the last Saxon leader to hold out against William the Conqueror.

The market town of Ely is dominated by its architecturally superb cathedral - its octagonal tower is an engineering masterpiece. Wisbech to the North of the county retains its character of a prosperous Georgian market town.

Much of the country between the meandering rivers of the Welland and Nene in Northamptonshire was once held by squires, and many of their farms survive. Here there are forests and water meadows and villages of stone and thatch cluster around elegant church spires. The lovely village of Rockingham is set on a steep hillside overlooking the River Welland. At the summit of the hill is Rockingham Castle, built by William the Conqueror. From here the view extends to five counties

Northampton is one of the largest market towns in England and it is noted for its large number of fine churches. Among the finest is the Holy Sepulchre, a rare round church founded in 1110. The town is probably best known for its shoe industry. During the Civil War, Northampton provided 1,500 pairs of shoes for Cromwell's forces. The scenery in the south of Northamptonshire cannot be described as spectacular but has pleasant, broad landscapes. There are ample opportunities for water sports with its canals, rivers and lakes. This part of the county is steeped in history. A crucial battle in the Wars of the Roses, the Battle of Northampton, fought at Hardingstone Fields in 1460 resulted in the Yorkists capturing Henry VI. The county is also indirectly linked with American independence - George Washington's ancestors lived in the small village of Sulgrave at Sulgrave Manor, build in 1560 by Lawrence Washington. The family coat of arms over the porch is thought to have been the basis for the original Stars and Stripes. Towcester claims to be one of the oldest towns in the county and has been an important road junction ever since the Romans built Watling Street. The Saracen's Head Inn features in Charles Dickens' The Pickwick Papers as one of Mr Pickwick's stopping places.

CAMBRIDGE & NORTHAMPTON

THE WASH

KINGS LYNN

HOLBEACH MARSH

WELLAND

LINCOLNSHIRE

BEDFORD LEVEL

THE FENS

NORFOLK

GREAT OUSE RIVER

HICKWOLD FENS

GREAT FEN

ELY

NEWMARKET

ROMAN ROAD

COGMAGOG HILLS

CAMBRIDGE

R. CAM

ESSEX

DEEPING FEN

MORRIS FEN

R. NENE

PETERBOROUGH

R. NENE (OLD COURSE)

CHATTERIS FEN

WEST FEN

R. OUSE

R. IVEL

GRAFHAM WATER

LEICESTERSHIRE

RUTLANDS

ROCKINGHAM FOREST

MARKET HARBOROUGH

R. NENE

NORTHAMPTONSHIRE

NORTHAMPTON

YARDLEY CHASE

BEDS

BEDFORD

TOWCESTER

R. OUZLE

RUGBY

17TH C. WATERMILL, DUDDINGTON, NEAR NORTHAMPTON.

CAMBRIDGE & NORTHAMPTON

1740. WATERMILL, DUDDINGTON, NEAR NORTHAMPTON.

The Old Bricklayers Arms, Caxton, Cambridge CB3 8PQ

Nearest Road A428

The Old Bricklayers Arms is a Grade II listed building, formerly a pub and now a comfortable family home, with separate accommodation for guests. Bedrooms are all en-suite and are provided with tea/coffee making facilities. Guests may relax in the TV lounge which has inglenook, oak beams and log fires. Dinner and breakfast are served in the traditional dining room. Wimpole Hall and Home Farm, Wood Green Animal Shelter, American Cemetary and Papworth Heart Hospital are a short drive away

Mrs Pauline Benson
Tel: 01954 719228

B&B from 17.50, Dinner from £15, (Reduction for 4 nights or more),
Rooms 1 single, 1 twin, 1 double (all en-suite), Pets by arrangement,
Open all year, Map Ref: A

Springfields, Ely Road, Little Thetford, Ely, Cambridgeshire CB6 3HJ

Nearest Road A10

Springfields is a lovely large home set in an acre of gardens and orchard in which guests are invited to wander, enjoy the tranquillity and smell the roses. The 3 tastefully decorated and furnished bedrooms are in a separate wing. All have tea/coffee making facilities, and TV. A delicious freshly prepared breakfast is served in the pleasant dining room around a large table. Situated just 2 miles from historic Ely with its famous cathedral, museum, and many places to eat. Wicken Fen, and Newmarket Race Course are a short drive away. English Tourist Board listed DeLuxe.

Derek & Dawn Bailey
Tel: 01353 663637
Fax: 01353 663130

B&B from £20, Rooms 2 twin, 1 en-suite double, No smoking,
Minimum age 12, Open January - December, Map Ref: B

Chiswick House, Meldreth, Royston, Hertfordshire, SG8 6LZ

Nearest Road A10

Chiswick House is an original timber-framed building dating from the late 1400's. Over the years it has been altered and extended but it remains fundamentally as it was built 500 years ago. Old beams, polished oak and flowers in every room combined with a warm welcome provide an atmosphere to relax in comfort. The royal crest of King James I is to be found above the fireplace in the drawing room. It is believed that the house was used by King James as a hunting lodge. The Jacobean panelling in the dining room dates from that period.

Mrs Bernice Elbourn
Tel: 01763 260242

B&B £20, Rooms 2 twin, 4 double (all en-suite), No smoking, Open
March - January, Map Ref: C

The Maltings, Aldwincle, Oundle, Northamptonshire NN14 3EP

Nearest Road A605, A14, A1

A lovely 16th century house and former agricultural maltings and granary. The main accommodation is in the granary which has been converted to 2 bedrooms 2 bathrooms and a sitting room. The remainder of the accommodation is in the beamed house which has Inglenook fireplaces. All bedrooms have private bathroom and tea/coffee making facilities. There is a very peaceful atmosphere, a lovely garden with unusual plants which is occasionally open under the National Garden Scheme. Many places of interest, and activities nearby

Margaret & Nigel Faulkner
Tel: 01832 720233
Fax: 01832 720326

B&B from £21.50, Rooms 3 en-suite twin, No smoking,
Minimum age 10, No pets in-doors, Open all year, Map Ref: D

THE ENTRANCE PORCH ~ SULGRAVE MANOR.

CHESHIRE, MERSEYSIDE, GREATER MANCHESTER

"Oh, to be in England now that April's there,
And whoever wakes in England sees, some morning, unaware,
That the lowest boughs and the brushwood sheaf,
While the chaffinch sings on the orchard bough
In England - now!"

(Robert Browning - Home Thoughts, from Abroad)

CHESHIRE AND MERSEYSIDE

HALF-TIMBERED THATCHED COTTAGES NEAR NORTHWICH, CHESHIRE.

Charming countryside, history and the arts meet in Cheshire and Merseyside.

South Cheshire is one of the prettiest areas, famous for its beautiful black and white timbered buildings, waterways and, of course, Cheshire cheese. The Cheshire cheese trail can be followed through the farms, pubs and the countryside.

Chester's history goes back to Roman times and its Medieval influence is still very much in evidence, while in the 19th century the Port of Liverpool was the gateway to the New World. Today the vitality of Merseyside's cultural life is reflected in the range of theatres, art galleries and arts centres. The River Dee runs gently through the Cheshire Plain and past Chester out into the Irish Sea. To protect this fertile land from the Welsh, sea pirates and other marauders, the Romans built their major camp of Deva on what is now called Chester in AD 79. No other British city has such well preserved enclosed ramparts and much of the original Roman wall survives, but many of the town's gates and towers were added in the Middle Ages. A walk around the city walls will take you past the 900 year old cathedral, the Norman castle, the Roman Amphitheatre and the canal in its spectacular rock cutting. The Roodee, once the site of the Roman harbour when the area was submerged by sea, is now Chester Racecourse, right in the centre of the city.

Chester is famous the world over as Britain's finest shopping city outside London. Much of the city's finest architecture now houses shops. Many of them are in two-tier Medieval galleries known as The Rows where shops open onto balustraded walkways reached only by steps from the road. As well as its historic attractions, Chester's lively arts scene draws many

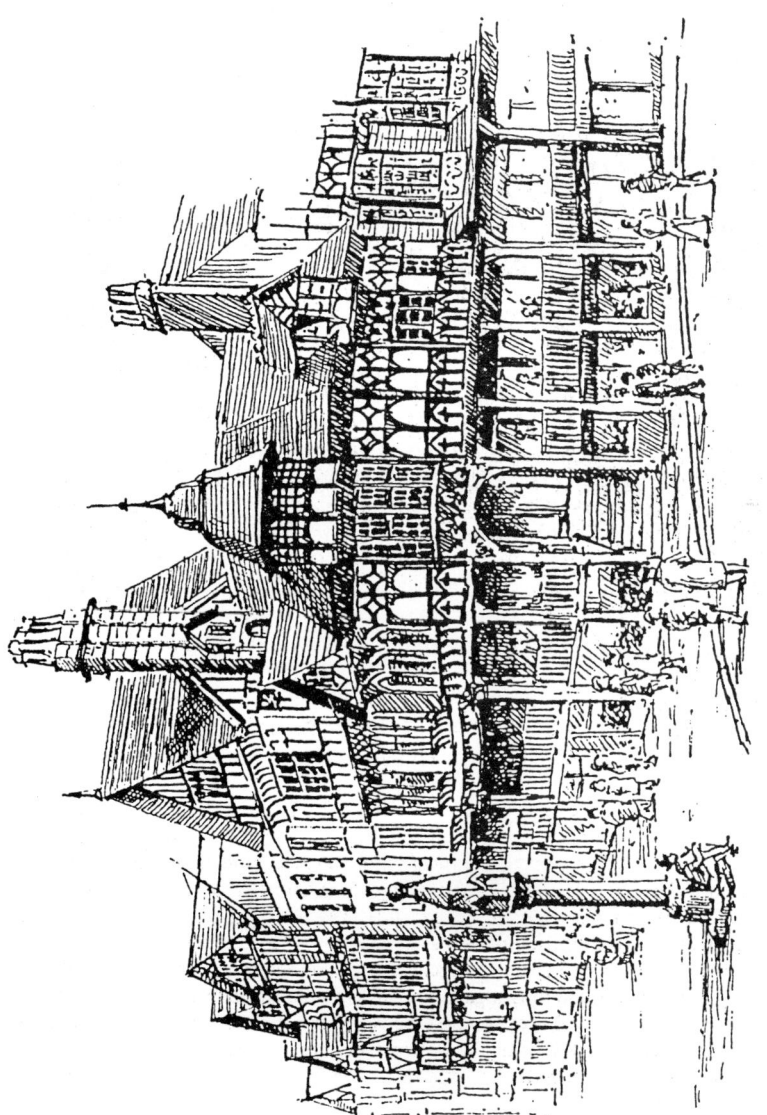

THE ROWS, CHESTER

visitors. The Chester Summer Music Festival has become a celebrated major annual event and the Gateway Theatre runs an innovative programme of traditional and contemporary drama.

To the East of Chester is Tarporley, surrounded by rich farmlands and woodland. North of here is the 4,000 acre Delamere Forest and on a summit to the South is Beeston Castle on the summit of the Peckforton Hills. Knutsford is another attractive town with narrow streets and old black and white houses. Knutsford was the Cranford of Mrs Gaskell's novel of that name. She was married in 1832 in the 18th century parish church and her grave is behind the 17th century Unitarian chapel. Two miles north is Tatton Hall, surrounded by 54 acres of formal gardens and woodland, it is one of the National Trust's most visited properties. Six miles to the South is the giant radio telescope of Jodrell Bank, built for Manchester University in 1957. Nantwich is an old salt mining town on the River Weaver where black and white timbered houses are crowded together in narrow streets. Wallasey on the Wirral Peninsula is connected to the busy shipbuilding and industrial centre of Birkenhead by docks and wharves. Dominating the scene is the Liver Building, the offices of the Royal Liver Friendly Society. Its two main towers are topped by mythical Liver birds from which the city is said to get its name.

During the last century tons of cargo arrived daily from all over the world in the Port of Liverpool. The main trade was from America to supply the cotton merchants and mill owners of the North West during the textile boom. Liverpool's historic waterfront is today one of the country's popular tourist attractions. Converted Victorian warehouses at The Albert Dock are the home of the Merseyside Maritime Museum and next to it, the Tate Gallery houses the most important collection of contemporary art outside London. The Beatles Story, a shrine to the legendary 60's pop group and sons of Liverpool is also within the renovated dockland area. The city also has a wide range of theatres, art galleries and arts centres. Liverpool is known for its boundless artistic talent and for the many playwrights, poets, comedians, musicians and actors who began their careers there. Apart from New York, more films, plays and television series have been made in Liverpool than any other city.

A LIVER BIRD ATOP THE ROYAL LIVER BUILDING.

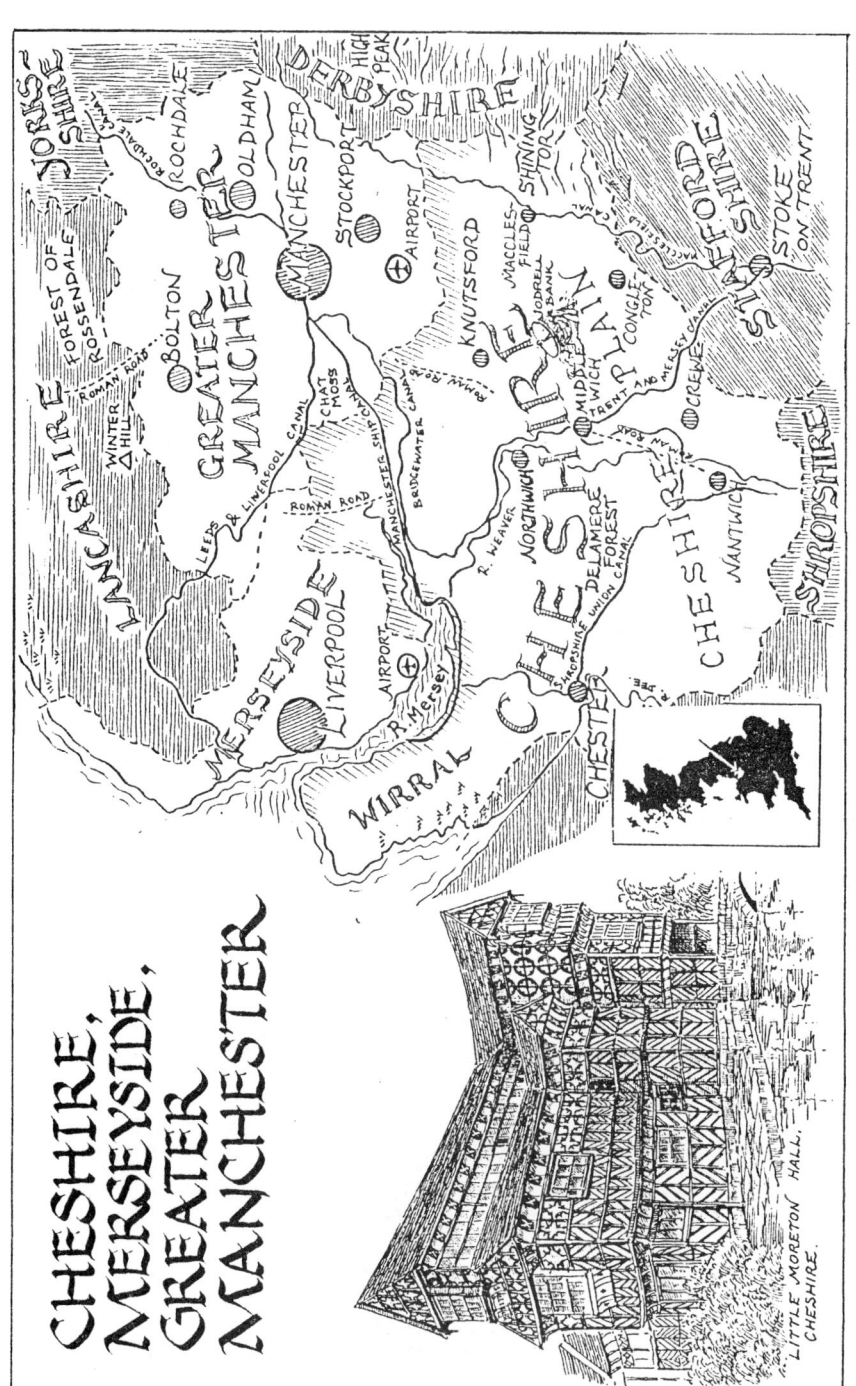

CHESHIRE, MERSEYSIDE, GREATER MANCHESTER

LITTLE MORETON HALL, CHESHIRE.

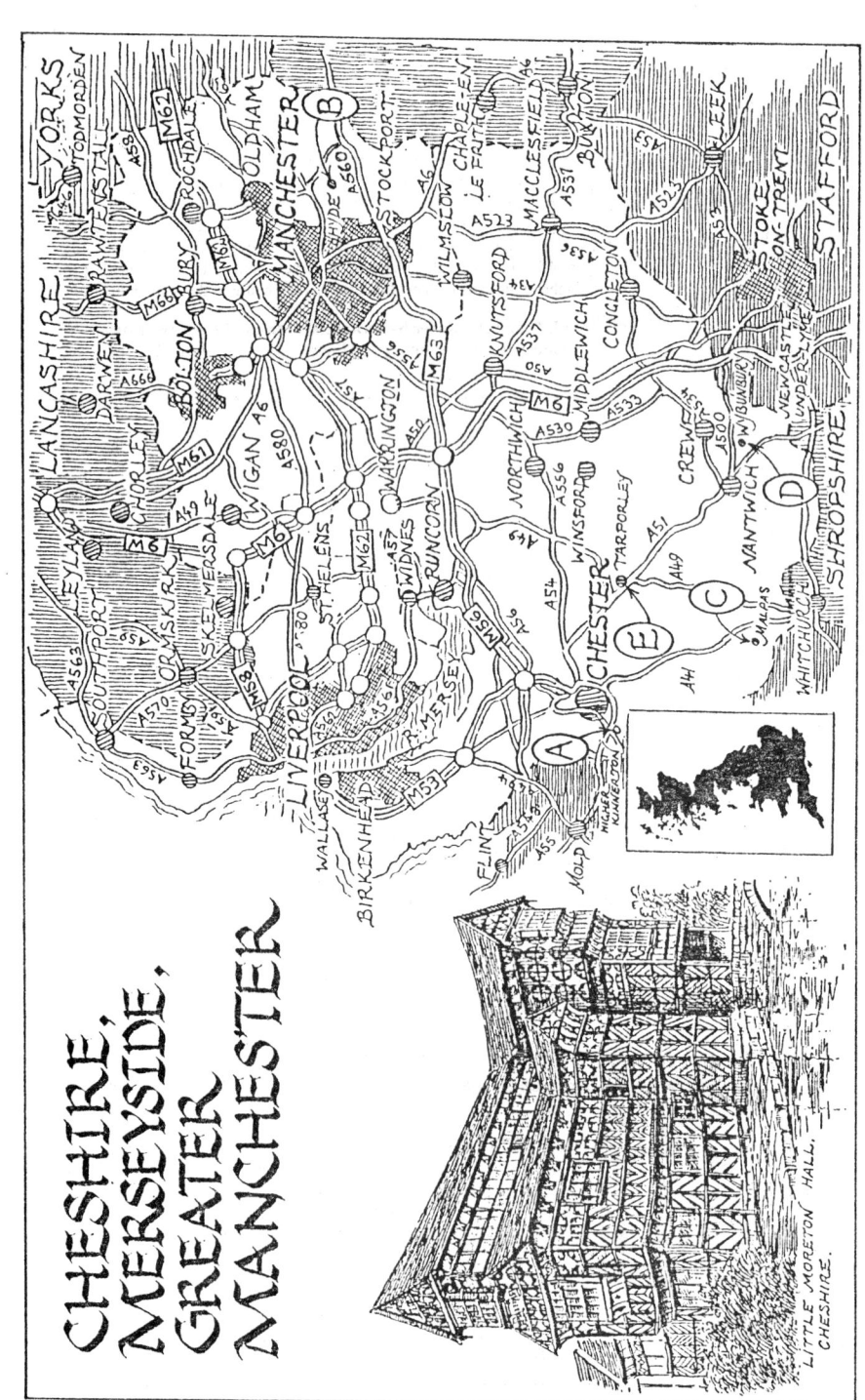

CHESHIRE, MERSEYSIDE, GREATER MANCHESTER

LITTLE MORETON HALL, CHESHIRE.

The Mount, Higher Kinnerton, Chester CH4 9BQ   Nearest Road A55

Attractive Victorian family house on the borders of England and Wales set in own grounds. 3 acre garden; kitchen garden, tennis court and croquet lawn. Within easy reach of Chester, Mold, and North Wales coast. Manchester and Liverpool airports 45 minutes drive. Large comfortable bedrooms with private bathrooms and views over the Cheshire Plain. From Chester take A55 North Wales exit A5104 Broughton. At roundabout left on A5104. Through village of Broughton after about 1 mile left turn Higher Kinnerton (Lesters/Leicesters), only house in the lane on the right.

Mrs Jonathan Major
Tel: 01244 660275

B&B from £19, Dinner by arrangement from £10, Rooms 2 twin, 1 double, Restricted smoking, Minimum age 12, Open all year, Map Ref: A

Needhams Farm, Uplands Road, Werneth Low, Gee Cross Nr Hyde, Cheshire SK14 3AQ   A560

Farmhouse accommodation dating back to the 16th century offering 4 en-suite rooms. Evening meals available each evening. Residential licence. Surrounded by lovely views. Ideal for Manchester Airport and city centre. Courtesy service from airport and Piccadilly station for a small charge. Seven bedrooms in total.

Mrs C Walsh
Tel: 0160 368 4610
Fax: 0160 367 9106

B&B from £18, Dinner from £7, Rooms 4 double, 1 family, 1 twin, 1 single (5 en-suite), Open all year, Map Ref: B

Laurel Farm, Chorlton Lane, Malpas, Cheshire SY14 7ES   Nearest Road A41

South Cheshire has arguably some of the most beautiful countryside in the county. Set in 9 acres of the N Wales/Shropshire borders a lovely 19th century farmhouse sympathetically restored to retain and enhance much character. The emphasis is on peace, tranquility and every comfort in this elegant home. Enjoy a peaceful break or explore many local interests; Chester, walks on 'Sandstone Trail', fine gardens, golf and leisure facilities at Carden Park. A separate 2 bedroom suite (and sitting room) is for guests use at all times; includes a ground floor bedroom with en-suite shower.

Mrs Anthea Few
Tel: 01948 860291
Fax: 01948 860291

B&B from £22, Dinner from £15, Rooms 1 twin/family, 1 twin, 2 double (all en-suite), No smoking, Minimum age 12, Open all year including Christmas, Map Ref: C

Broughton House, Threapwood, Malpas, Cheshire SY14 7AN   Nearest Road A41

Broughton House is a warm and comfortable home within the elegant Georgian stables built for a former 17th century mansion. Traditional breakfasts are served in the conservatory overlooking parkland and the Welsh hills. Peaceful private grounds of 5 acres with hard tennis court. Situated on B5069 England/Wales border. It is convenient for Chester and North Wales.

Valerie & John McGinn
Tel: 01948 770610
Fax: 01948 770610

B&B from £23, Rooms 2 four-poster, 1 twin, (all en-suite and ground floor), No smoking, No pets, Minimum age 10, Open all year, Map Ref: C

Lea Farm, Wrinehill Road, Wybunbury, Nantwich, Cheshire CW5 7NS,   **Nearest Road A500**

Charming farmhouse set in landscaped gardens where peacocks roam on a dairy farm. Ample car parking. In beautiful rolling countryside. Spacious bedrooms. Luxury lounge. Pool, snooker, fishing available. From Nantwich take the A51 turning left at Stapeley Water Gardens. End of road turn right for village of Wybunbury, turn left down Wrinehill Road by church. 1 mile from village.

Mrs Jean Callwood
Tel: 01270 841429

B&B from £14 (children ½ price if sharing with parents),
Dinner from £7.50, Rooms 1 double, 1 family, 1 twin (2 en-suite),
Open all year, Map Ref: D

Roughlow Farm, Chapel Lane, Willington, Tarporley, Cheshire CW6 0PG   **Nearest Road M6, A54**

A delightful 18th century converted farmhouse in quiet situation with wonderful views to Shropshire & Wales. Large garden with cobbled courtyard and tennis court. Elegantly furnished to a high standard with en-suite facilities to 3 twin/double bedrooms. Roughlow Farm is well situated for easy access to Manchester, Chester, Wales, Liverpool, and M6. From M6 (J19) take the A556 towards Chester. A54 Kelsall bypass turn left after passing Morreys Nurseries on right hand side, then left again at the pub in Waste Lane, continue bearing right at the next junction. (150 yds on left).

Mrs P F Sutcliffe
Tel: 01829 751199
Fax: 01829 751199

B&B from £20, Dinner from £15 (minimum 4 persons), Rooms:
3 twin/double, (all en-suite) 1 with own sitting room, Minimum age 6,
No smoking, Open all year except Xmas & New Year. Map Ref: E

CORNWALL

"Cornwall - that strange primordial piece of land
Flung into brilliant light and binding blue
And clinging mists, and all the dangers and delights
Of unpredictable deep seas, that give and take away
with ruthless and beguiling ease."

(ALK)

CORNWALL

ST. MAWES, CORNWALL

Cornwall stretches out into the Atlantic Ocean for nearly 100 miles. This marine county could almost be described as an island for the River Tamar flows along all but 5 miles of its border with Devon. Much of Cornwall's coastline, which is never more than 20 miles away, is designated as of Outstanding Natural Beauty. The Atlantic Ocean crashes onto the North coast's long stretches of beautiful beaches while in contrast the South has numerous fishing villages, sheltered coves and tiny unspoilt bays, as well as sub-tropical gardens and wooded rivers. Cornwall offers opportunities for anglers and water sports enthusiasts. Cornwall is a land of history and tradition. As the Britons were driven west by invading Saxon tribes, Cornwall became, with Wales, a bastion of old Celtic ways. It kept a separate Celtic language until the Middle Ages and the county remained virtually isolated from the rest of the country until modern times.

Legends live on in Cornwall and perhaps the most famous is that of the folk hero King Arthur, who probably did exist and fought the Saxons in the 6th century. Tintagel's precipitous cliff-top castle on the North Cornwall coast was reputedly his birthplace. Tintagel was the stronghold of Gorlois when Uther was head King of Britain. Uther fell in love with Igerne, the wife of Gorlois, and killed her husband to secure his queen - and Arthur was the result of this union. One of the many places claimed to be where Arthur cast his famous sword Excalibur into the water and a ghostly arm caught it is the lake called Dozmary Pool, close to Jamaica Inn on Bodmin Moor.

Bolster is a legendary Cornish giant who lived near St Agnes and liked to have a new wife each year, disposing of the old one. One wife was wiser than he was, making a plot to defeat him and tricking him into bleeding to death in a mine with an entrance to the sea.

Another legend from the far West of Cornwall is the lost land of Lyonesse, a whole country that was drowned by the sea. The waters covered a rich and fertile country with 140 parish churches. The Anglo Saxon Chronicle records two great storms within 100 years which drowned many towns and innumerable people.

Today, St Michael's Mount and the Isles of Scilly are said to be all that remains of the vanished land. St Michael's Mount, with its tiny fishing village and dramatic coastline, can be visited at low tide or by boat.

Twenty eight miles beyond Land's End, the Isles of Scilly have five inhabited islands, including Tresco, with its sub-tropical gardens.. The climate is so mild that the islands are said to have only two seasons - spring and summer.

THE OLD POST OFFICE, TINTAGEL.

Cornwall's history is steeped in its maritime traditions. Working ports such as Newlyn and Megavissey are still important fishing bases, yet retaining a timeless quality with lobster and crab pots lining the quay. It is the tiny fishing villages where time appears to have stood still which attract so many people, many bringing the Cornish heritage of smuggling and contraband to life. At Mousehole colour washed and granite houses surround the small harbour and the popular Polperro maintains its distinctive flavour of a Cornish fishing village. Fowey is a network of narrow streets climbing the hills. The town's fierce seamen, nicknamed the Fowey Gallants, who raided the coast of France during the 100 Years' War, continued their raids even after Edward IV had made peace. Megavissey, one of Cornwall's most celebrated resorts, is another fishing village whose simple beauty has attracted a number of writers and artists. And at Mullion Cove, one of the county's busiest smuggling centres in the 18th and 19th centuries, there is a beautiful cove and a small harbour.

Land's End which tumbles into the sea at the end of the Penwith Peninsula, is the English mainland's furthest point West. Just 5 miles wide, the walker can take in the bracing Atlantic Northern coast and then travel to take in the milder breezes from the Channel shore.

On the South side is the popular resort of Penzance, facing St Michael's Mount, whose climate is so mild that palm trees and other sub-tropical plants thrive. On the North coast is St Ives, whose cluster of coloured stone cottages grew around a small chapel built by St Ia in the 6th century. Once a busy fishing port, it is now internationally known as an artistic centre. The painter Ben Nicholson, potter Bernard Leach and sculptress Dame Barbara Hepworth made the town a workshop of contemporary art.

The most Southerly part of England, the Lizard is made up of rugged cliffs and rocks which stretch down to Lizard Point. Its hazardous waters mean that more sailors have lost their lives here than in any other part of Cornwall. Inland, most of the peninsula is the Goonhilly Downs which burst into flower in May and June.

The towns of Camborne and Redruth run into one, forming the only large industrial area in the west of Cornwall. Camborne was once a centre of tin mining. At the peak of the industry, 600 mines were in operation but the import of cheaper tin forced most to close.

Newquay on the North coast is a popular resort and the centre of a stretch of spectacular coastal scenery and miles of golden beaches. As well as being an important shipping port, Falmouth in its spectacular setting on Falmouth Bay is a leading holiday resort. The area's sub-tropical climate and sparkling blue sea have earned its resemblance to the continental Riviera.

Cornwall's North West has a majestic coast and the bleak and windswept Bodmin Moor. The moor, about 12 miles from North to South and 11 miles from East to West, is crossed by only one major road, from Launceston to Bodmin. The most famous literary pilgrimage in Cornwall is to Jamaica Inn on the lonely road across the moor, immortalised by Daphne du Maurier in her novel of the same name. The place she centred in another novel, Frenchman's Creek, a hidden inlet of the Helford River can also be visited. About ½ a mile West of Helford village, it can be reached by driving down narrow lanes and walking the last mile. Barely a mile from the Devon border, Launceston is a hilly market town retaining its old world character.

CORNWALL

CLOVELLY · BIDEFORD

DEVON

BUDE
BUDE
BAY

HOLSWORTHY

R. TAMAR

TINTAGEL ·
PORT
ISAAC BAY

R. INNY · LAUNCESTON

BROWN
WILLY

R. CAMEL

BODMIN
MOOR

TAVISTOCK
R. TAMAR

PADSTOW

CORNWALL

WATERGATE
BAY

BODMIN

NEWQUAY

R. FOWE

R. LYNHER

SALTASH

ST.
AGNES
HEAD

HENSBARROW
DOWNS

LOOE

WHITE
SAND
BAY

PLYMOUTH

ST.
IVES
BAY

REDRUTH

TRURO

ST. AUSTELL

ST. AUSTELL
BAY

POLPERRO

RAME
HEAD

ST. IVES

WENDRON
MOORS

R. HAYLE

ST.
JUST

PENWITH · PENZANCE

FALMOUTH

LAND'S
END

MARAZION

HELSTON

FALMOUTH
BAY

ST. MICHAELS
MOUNT

THE
LIZARD

LIZARD

The Old Coach House, Tintagel Road, Boscastle, Cornwall PL35 0AS   **Nearest Road A39**

A warm welcome is in store at The Old Coach House which was built some 300 years ago. Sympathetically restored and tastefully furnished all bedrooms have en-suite facilities, TV, tea and coffee makers and there is a peaceful lounge which guests may use. Boscastle is an area of outstanding natural beauy, there is a lovely landlocked harbour, rugged cliffs and babbling streams and is only 2 miles from Tintagel. Breathtaking scenery, unspoilt villages, clean air, swimming, surfing, sandy beaches, birdwatching, fishing, horse riding, walks are all here.

Mrs Sue Miller
Tel: 01840 250398

B&B from £16, Rooms 1 single, 1 twin, 3 double, 1 family (all en-suite), Restricted smoking, Minimum age 6, Open March - October, Map Ref: A

Treworgie Barton, Crackington Haven, Bude, Cornwall EX23 0NL   **Nearest Road A39**

Fresh flowers in pretty bedrooms, private facilities, personal attention, friendly atmosphere and traditional and imaginative farmhouse cooking. These are the priorities at Treworgie Barton. Beautifully situated, 2 miles from Crackington Haven and the rugged North Cornwall coast, with buzzards wheeling overhead and ancient woodland through which to wander. An ideal place to unwind in peace, tranquility and seclusion.

Mrs Pam Mount
Tel: 01840 230233

B&B from £17, Dinner from £13, Rooms 3 double (one 4 poster), 1 twin, 1 family (all en-suite), Open February - September and November, Map Ref: B

Tregaddra Farmhouse, Nr Cury, Cornwall, TR12 7BB   **Nearest Road A3083**

A well kept garden of winding flower beds, spacious heated outdoor swimming pool, and magnificent views of the coast and countryside, is the setting for this early 18th century farmhouse and 220 acres of arable and beef farm. Guests can relax in the comfortable lounge where on chilly evenings log fires blaze in the original inglenook fireplace. All bedrooms are en-suite (2 with balconies), tea/coffee making facilities and toiletries. Traditional farmhouse fare is served in the spacious dining room and there is also a sun lounge.

Jonathan & June Lugg
Tel: 01326 240235

B&B from £18.50, Dinner from £8, Rooms 1 single, 1 twin, 2 family (all en-suite), No smoking, Open all year, Map Ref: C

Treviades Barton, Constantine, Nr Falmouth, Cornwall TR11 5RG   **Nearest Road A39**

A 16th century Manor farmhouse with entrance through courtyard. The exceptionally attractive gardens include a croquet lawn. Vegetables and soft fruit are grown in the garden for the table. Bedrooms are centrally heated, two have a bathroom en-suite and all have tea/coffee making facilities. Wood fires and a comfortable sitting room complete the country house atmosphere. Treviades Barton is north of the Helford River, a mile east of Constantine. There are fine beaches and splendid coastal paths for walkers. Sailing, riding, windsurfing, fishing, and golf, available locally.

Mike & Judy Ford
Tel: 01326 40524
Fax: 01326 340524

B&B from £18, Dinner from £16.50 including wine, Rooms 2 twin, 1 double (most en-suite), Restricted smoking, Pets by arrangement, Open all year except Christmas, Map Ref: D

Treglisson, Hayle, Cornwall TR27 5JT

Nearest Road A30

Treglisson is a working arable farm situated in a peaceful setting yet only 1 mile from the A30, an ideal holiday base for touring West Cornwall. All rooms are en-suite with tea/coffee making facilities, colour TV, and hairdryer. There is also an indoor heated swimming pool. The area abounds with charming fishing villages, craft centres, galleries, historic mines, breathtaking coastal walks and golden sandy beaches. English Tourist Board 2 crowns highly commended.

Mrs C Runnalls
Tel: 01736 753141

B&B from £17, Rooms 2 double, 2 family, 1 twin, Open Dec - Oct, Closed Christmas and New Year, Map Ref: E

Mellan House, Coverack, Helston, Cornwall TR12 6TH

Nearest Road B3294

Mellan House stands in a large garden and is 5 minutes from a safe sandy beach. Fishing, boating and windsurfing are available and a golf course is 6 miles away at Mullion. Coverack is a beautiful small fishing village in an area of outstanding natural beauty. Bedrooms have sea views and tea/coffee making facilities, and there is a comfortable lounge with colour television available for guests' use.

Mrs Muriel Fairhurst
Tel: 01326 280482

B&B from £18, Rooms 2 double, 1 single, No smoking, Pets by arrangement, Open all year except Christmas, Map Ref: F

Cobblers Cottage, Nantithet, Cury, Helston, Cornwall TR12 7RB

Nearest Road A3083

Situated in an area of outstanding natural beauty this delightful 17th century cottage is set in a large well kept garden with a meandering stream, in a sheltered valley just 2 miles drive from the sea. Carefully modernised inside and still retains old world character with beamed ceilings, interesting alcoves and log fires. All rooms are furnished to a high standard and the lounge has a colour TV. The bedrooms are all en-suite and have tea/coffee making facilities. Ideally situated in the centre of the Lizard Peninsula, well known for its coastal walks and magnificent scenery.

David & Hilary Lugg
Tel: 01326 241342

B&B from £17, Dinner from £8, Rooms 3 double (all en-suite) Restricted smoking, Adults only, Open all year, Map Ref: F

Cliff House, Devonport Hill, Kingsand, Cornwall PL10 1NJ

Nearest Road B3247

Cliff House is a Grade II listed 17th century building fully modernised with the addition of central heating, showers, washbasins and tea making facilities in all the bedrooms. There is a first floor drawing room with log fires in the winter and TV, for guests' use. It has a large balcony through french windows overlooking Plymouth Sound, Cawsand bay and the village. Dinner is by arrangement and light supper can also be catered for. All food is freshly cooked and all wholemeal cookery including vegetarian and special diets.

Mrs Ann Heasman
Tel: 01752 823110

B&B from £16, Dinner from £14 (by arrangement), Rooms 1 twin, 2 double (1 en-suite), No smoking, Open all year, Map Ref: G

Allhays Country House, Talland Bay, Looe, Cornwall PL13 2JB

Nearest Road A387

Set in extensive gardens just a few minutes walk from the sea, Allhays stands on a gently sloping hillside overlooking the beautiful Talland Bay. The emphasis is on comfort and the house is fully centrally heated and also has a log fire blazing in the lounge during colder weather. Most bedrooms have breathtaking views and are en-suite; all have tea/coffee making facilities, TV and telephone. Food is of a high standard and a new menu appears each day. Vegetarian and special diets can be catered for. An interesting selection of reasonably priced wines will complete your meal.

Brian & Linda Spring
Tel: 01503 72434
Fax: 01503 72929

B&B from £28, Dinner £13.50, Restricted smoking, Minimum age 10, Pets welcome, Open all year except Christmas, Map Ref: H

Harescombe Lodge, Watergate, Nr Looe, Cornwall PL13 2NE

Nearest Road A387

Harescombe Lodge overlooking the upper reaches of the West Looe River, originally built in 1760, was once the shooting lodge of the Trelawne Estate the home of the Trelawney family. Now tastefully restored and modernised it offers a high standard of comfort with all the bedrooms individually furnished and each having a private bath or shower and toilet en-suite. Situated in its own gardens with waterfalls and old stone bridges over the swiftly running stream in the secluded and picturesque wooded valley of Watergate.

Mr & Mrs B C Wynn
Tel: 01503 263158

B&B from £16, Rooms 2 double, 1 twin, Minimum age 12, Open all year, Map Ref: H

Coombe Farm, Widegates, Near Looe, Cornwall PL13 1QN

Nearest Road B3253

A delightful 8 bedroomed country house superbly situated in over 10 acres of lawns, meadows, woods, streams and ponds. The house is carefully furnished with many antiques, paintings and interesting objects. In cool weather there are open log fires in the lounge and dining room. The en-suite bedooms all have country views, tea/coffee making facilities, and TV. A full English breakfast is served and in the evening there is a 4 course dinner by candlelight and there is a drinks licence. Guests may also use the heated outdoor swim pool. RAC highly acclaimed, AA 4Q, ETB 2 crowns.

Alex & Sally Low
Tel: 01503 240223

B&B from £18, Dinner from £12, Rooms (all en-suite) 3 twin, 3 double, 3 family, No smoking, Minimum age 5, Open March - November, Map Ref: H

Prospect House, 1 Church Road, Penryn, Cornwall TR10 8DA

Nearest Road A39, B3292

Prospect House is a Grade II listed late Georgian 'Gentleman's Residence', sympathetically restored and decorated and furnished with antiques. Two miles from Falmouth it is ideally situated for access to Cornwall's beauty spots, beaches, gardens, walks, National Trust properties and English Heritage monuments, with nearby facilities for sailing, windsurfing, deep sea fishing, riding, golf, etc. Prospect House can add a pleasing flavour of informal country house style living to a holiday or business visit to Cornwall. Bedrooms all have en-suite facilities.

C Paul & B Sheppard
Tel: 01326 373198
Fax: 01326 373198

B&B from £23.50, Dinner from £16.50, Rooms 2 double, 1 twin, (all en-suite), Minimum age 12, Restricted smoking, Pets by arrangement, Open all year, Map Ref: I

Ednovean Farm Cottage, Ednovean Lane, Perranuthnoe, Nr Penzance, Cornall TR20 9LZ   A394, A30

Ednovean Farm cottage is a 16th century farmhouse situated in a hamlet overlooking the village of Perranuthnoe with extensive views of Mounts Bay including St Michael's Mount, Penzance, Newlyn and Mousehole. Each bedroom has tea/coffee making facilities, and a shower room/bathroom next door. Two sitting rooms with TV for guests to relax in. Perranuthnoe has a fine sandy beach with rock pools and a very good pub which serves excellent food and ales. 3 golf courses and 2 riding centres are close by and Penzance, Helston & St Ives are within a short drive.

Jo & Adrian Marsham
Tel: 01736 710065

B&B from £16, Rooms 1 single, 1 twin, 1 double,
No children, Open all year, Map Ref: J

Ednovean House, Perranuthnoe, Penzance, Cornwall TR20 9LZ   Nearest Road A394, A30

Beautifully situated family run 160 year old Victorian house offering delightful, comfortable rooms, most having en-suite facilities and panoramic sea views. Situated in 1 acre of gardens and overlooking St Michael's Mount and Mount's Bay. It has one of the finest views in Cornwall. Relax in a comfortable lounge, library, or informal bar and enjoy fine food and wines in the candlelit dining room, catering also for vegetarians. Pets welcome, Car park. Ideal for coastal walks and exploring from the Lizard to Lands End. ETB 3 crowns, AA recommended 3Q.

Mr & Mrs A Compton
Tel: 01736 711071

B&B from £17, Dinner from £12.50, Rooms 5 double, 2 twin, 2 single (most en-suite), Pets by arrangement, Open all year except Christmas, Map Ref: J

Acton Vean, Trevean Lane, Rosudgeon, Penzance, Cornwall TR20 9PF   Nearest Road A394

On the edge of beyond, 6 miles from Penzance, Acton Vean is a gracious modern home on the southern coastal slope. In a uniquely privileged position, adjacent to Acton Castle, it has uninterrupted outlook to St Michael's Mount and the Bay, with access to the coastal path. The double bedrooms, with tea/coffee making facilities, elegant sitting room, terrace and garden all provide breathtaking views, with frequent spectacular sunsets. Visitors are warmly welcomed as 'house guests'.

David & Pamela Green
Tel: 01736 762675

B&B £20, Rooms 1 twin, 1 double, Restricted smoking,
Minimum age 12, Open March to December, Map Ref: J

Trenderway Farm, Polperro, Cornwall PL13 2LY   Nearest Road A387

Trenderway Farm is a working mixed farm built in the late 16th century overlooking the 400 acre manor for which it is recorded in the Domesday Book. The farm lies upon gentle western slopes at the head of the Polperro valley. Ideal as a base from which to experience the fascination of Cornwall. All bedrooms have en-suite facilities, TV, and tea and coffee makers. A choice of a full English or a lighter continental breakfast is served in the conservatory/breakfast room. A very comfortable sitting room with open fire is available to guests.

Lynne & Anthony Tuckett
Tel: 01503 72214

B&B from £22, Rooms 1 twin, 4 double (all en-suite), No smoking,
No children, Open all year except Christmas & New Year, Map Ref: K

The Wheal Lodge, 91 Sea Road, Carlyon Bay, St Austell, Cornwall PL25 3SH　　　Nearest Road A38

The Wheal Lodge has a superb position just above the sea in an area of outstanding beauty. The hotel, which adjoins the coastal path and is directly opposite the golf course, is a lovely luxury residence with an old fashioned homely atmosphere. There is an attractive residents' lounge and a spacious dining room with licenced bar. All bedrooms have en-suite facilities and courtesy trays, five bedrooms are on the ground floor. Breakfast is either continental or full English. Delicious Cornish food is served. Ample safe parking within the grounds.

Jeanne & Don Martin
Tel: 01726 815543
Fax: 01726 815543

B&B from £30, Dinner from £12.50, Rooms 1 single, 2 twin, 2 double, 1 family (all en-suite), Restricted smoking, Minimum age 8, Open all year except Christmas, Map Ref: L

Bucklawren Farm, St Martin-by-Looe, Cornwall PL13 1NZ　　　Nearest Road B3253

A warm welcome awaits you at Bucklawren, a 500 acre dairy and arable working farm set deep in the Cornish countryside, yet only 1 mile from the beach and 3 miles from the picturesque fishing village of Looe. The original Bucklawren Manor was mentioned in the Domesday Book, but has now been replaced by the spacious 19th century farmhouse. All rooms have tea/coffee making facilities, TV etc. There is a comfortable lounge and an elegant dining room where guests can enjoy good farmhouse cooking using fresh home grown and local produce.

Mrs Jean Henly
Tel: 01503 240738
Fax: 01503 240481

B&B from £16, Dinner from £9, Rooms 1 double, 3 faily, 1 twin, Restricted smoking, Open March - November, Map Ref: H

Rosebud Cottage, Bossiney, Tintagel, Cornwall PL34 0AX　　　Nearest Road A39

Rosebud Cottage is ½ mile from Tintagel in Bossiney. It is ideally located close by footpaths to Bossiney Cove and Rocky Valley, just 2 of the many coves to be found along the north Cornish coastline which justify the classification as an area of outstanding natural beauty. The cottage dates back 200 years. It overlooks farmland and has its own secluded garden with ample car parking. Tintagel is renowned for its castle ruins and the legend of King Arthur.

Mrs Rosemarie de Boyer
Tel: 01840 770861

B&B from £14, Dinner from £6.50, Rooms 1 double, 1 family, 1 twin, Restricted smoking, Pets welcome, Open all year, Map Ref: M

The Old Borough House, Bossiney, Tintagel, Cornwall PL34 0AY　　　Nearest Road A39

The Old Borough House is a charming 17th century guest house in a prestige position in an area of outstanding natural beauty. All rooms are comfortably furnished and have tea/coffee making facilities and most have en-suite facilities. Guests have access to the sitting room, TV and bedrooms at all times as well as the garden. Breakfast is served at 8.30 am and dinner, a superb 4 course meal, at 7 pm. The coast path from Boscastle to Tintagel is probably the finest in Britain. No matter what time of year it is there are seabirds, and sometimes seals, to be seen.

John & Christina Rayner
Tel: 01840 770475

B&B from £15.50, Dinner from £10, Rooms 1 twin, 3 double, 1 family (many en-suite), Restricted smoking, Minimum age 4, Open all year, Map Ref M

Trebrea Lodge, Trenale, Tintagel, Cornwall, PL34 0HR

Nearest Road A39

Grade II listed Georgian manor house set in 4½ acres of wooded hillside with panoramic sea views. All bedrooms are individually decorated with antique and traditional furniture, have private bathrooms and look over open fields to the Atlantic Ocean. The menu changes daily using finest local ingredients, dinner and breakfast are served in the oak panelled dining room. Log fires, peace and tranquility.

John Charlick & Sean Devlin
Tel: 01840 770410

B&B from £29, Dinner from £15.50, Rooms 1 single, 2 twin, 5 double (all en-suite), Restricted smoking, Minimum age 5, Open all year, Map Ref: M

Trevispean-Vean Farm Guest House, St Erme, Truro, Cornwall TR4 9BL

Nearest Road A3076

Trevispean-Vean combines modern comforts and first class food with all the charms of a 300 year old working farm, which is situated ½ mile from Trispen village and 4 miles from the cathedral city of Truro. Ideally situated for sight seeing. Most rooms are en-suite and all have h & c washbasins. There are 3 lounge areas including spacious TV lounge. A pleasant dining room where a meal prepared with great care may be enjoyed with a good variety of home cooking.

Mr & Mrs E Dymond
Tel: 01872 79514

B&B from £17, Dinner from £7, Rooms 5 double, 4 twin, 3 family Open March - September, Map Ref: N

Laniley House, Trispen, Nr Truro, Cornwall TR4 9AU

Nearest Road A3076

Laniley House is a "Gentleman's Residence" built some 150 years ago for a mine owner. The comfortable bedrooms all have tea/coffee making facilities, and TV. It stands in two acres of private landscaped gardens surrounded by beautiful unspoilt countryside, yet only 3 miles away from the Cathedral city of Truro. The house presents itself in a perfect location for the discerning, ideal for discovering the true old Cornwall and within easy reach of major towns, seaside resorts, beaches and National Trust properties.

Jackie Gartner
Tel: 01872 75201

B&B from £16, Rooms 3 double (1 en-suite), Restricted smoking, Minimum age 16, No pets, Open all year except Christmas, Map Ref: N

Boswednack Manor, Zennor, Cornwall TR26 3DD

Nearest Road B3306

Boswednack Manor is a spacious granite farmhouse overlooking one of the wildest and most magnificent promontories in Cornwall - Gurnard's head. If you wish to learn more about the birds, wild flowers, cliff - castles, cromlechs and stone circles, we offer a number of courses during the year. Also guided wildlife walks on a daily basis. A vegetarian evening meal is available. On course weeks picnic lunches are provided and meals are traditional unless vegetarian is requested. A self catering cottage is also available.

Graham & Liz Gynn
Tel: 01736 794183

B&B from £14, Dinner from £8, Rooms 1 single, 1 twin, 2 double, 1 family (2 double en-suite), No smoking, Open all year except Christmas, Map Ref: O

Cumbria

"the loveliest spot that man hath ever found"

(William Wordsworth)

CUMBRIA

Cumbria is a county for all seasons. Visitors are greeted by lambs and daffodils in the spring and the summer is perfect for enjoying the outdoor activities the county has to offer. Autumn's mellow hues and the snow-clad winter peaks of Lakeland have their own magic. It comes as no surprise that Cumbria, most famous for its lakes and mountains, has been a magnet for millions of visitors and has provided inspiration for countless poets and artists. The mountains from the central Lake District National Park meet the varied landscapes of coast, hills and dales. The beauty of the central Lake District inspired the poet Wordsworth to describe it as *"the loveliest spot that man hath ever found"* and few who have visited it would disagree. But the Lake District is surrounded by fertile farmland on the Solway plain and in the Eden Valley and orchards flourish in sheltered valleys such as the Lyth Valley, West of Kendal, which is a mass of damson blossom each spring. Apart from the variety of year-round activities Cumbria has to offer from walking, climbing, riding, golf, bird-watching and watersports, there is a wide choice of scenery.

The county's only city, Carlisle, still retains a fortress air with its mighty sandstone castle, city walls and sturdy cathedral. It was here that the savage raids of the border reivers left their mark. Now the city's traffic free centre has an impressive variety of quality shops surrounding its historic square.

Half a million acres of some of the most breathtaking landscape in the country lie in the Eden Valley. Alston, England's highest town at 1,000 ft above sea level is surrounded by the wild scenery of the North Pennines and villages which along with the town prospered with lead mining.

The red sandstone town of Penrith is a popular shopping and market town, dominated by the Beacon which dates back to the Border Wars. Further up the Eden Valley is the original county town of Westmorland, Appleby. famous for its horse fair in June. Beyond Brough and Kirkby Stephen in the Howgill Fells the River Eden has its source and the sterner landscape reflects the nearby Dales. To the West of the Lakes is St Bees Head with its priory church, extensive beaches and cliff head bird reserve. Other coastal towns include Georgian Whitehaven, Workington and Maryport with its maritime attractions. To the North the road hugs the shore to Silloth, famous for its fine golf course, stunning sunsets and views across the Solway Firth to Scotland.

For many the Lake District with its spectacular scenery, is the jewel in the crown. In the North, Keswick is surrounded by superb walks with glorious views of Derwentwater and neighbouring Bassenthwaite Lake. Derwentwater is the widest lake at 1¼ miles across. Running 5 miles to the south is the beautiful steep-sided Borrowdale Valley. Off here the hamlet of Watendlath was used by Hugh Walpole as the setting for his novel Judith Paris. In the Western Lakes, lanes meander inland from the coast towards peaks and valleys. Wastwater's screes lift straight from the deep dark water at the base of Scafell, England's highest point at 3,210ft. Steep mountain passes such as Hardknott with a gradient of one in three climb over the mountains to the coast. Mountains ring Ennerdale Water, Loweswater, Crummock Water and Buttermere. Cockermouth is the birthplace of Wordsworth. Every fell in Lakeland can be seen from the top of Helvellyn on a clear day, which at 3,118ft is the 3rd highest peak and the most popular in the Lake District, towering above Ullswater.

DERWENTWATER AND SKIDDAW FROM ASHNESS BRIDGE.

South of Ullswater, over Kirkstone Pass, the highest region open to cars, is Ambleside at the head of Windermere, England's longest lake.

Always crowded with walkers, Ambleside is the setting for the customary rush-bearing each July when children parade through the streets carrying rushes and flowers - a tradition handed down from the Middle Ages when rushes carpeted the floors in churches. Boat trips can be taken from Waterhead, just south of Ambleside, along the full length of the lake. The popular tourist centre of Windermere has many easily reached vantage points with spectacular views. Kendal, the southern gateway to the Lakes grew up around the woollen trade and is known for its many fine old houses and buildings in grey limestone. On the western side of Lake Windermere is Far Sawrey where the children's writer Beatrix Potter lived at Hill Top Farm in the early 1900s. Donald Campbell made many attempts on the world waterspeed record at Coniston and was killed there in 1967 when Bluebird crashed at 310 mph. Grasmere is possibly most famous as the home of the poet William Wordsworth (1770-1850) who moved to Dove Cottage in 1799. Wordsworth's home from 1813 until his death was Rydal Mount, south of the village.

WORDSWORTH HOUSE, COCKERMOUTH.

CUMBRIA

HILL TOP, SAWREY

LAKE DISTRICT NATIONAL PARK

SCOTLAND

CANONBIE
LONGTOWN
NORTHUMBERLAND
HADRIAN'S WALL
BRAMPTON
GREENHEAD
TINDALE
CARLISLE FELLS
Solway Firth
R. WAMPOOL
RIVER CALDEW
RIVER EDEN
WIGTON
ALSTON
MIDDLETON-IN-TEESDALE
ASPATRIA
RIVER ELLEN
INGLEWOOD FOREST
PENNINE WAY
THE PENNINES
DURHAM
MARYPORT
COCKERMOUTH
R. DERWENT
SKIDDAW
PENRITH
R. COAL
R. DERWENT
BASSENTHWAITE
WORKINGTON
KESWICK
CRUMMOCK WATER
DERWENTWATER
ULLSWATER
APPLEBY
WHITEHAVEN
RIVER EHEN
BUTTER MERE
ENNERDALE
HELVELLYN
THIRL-MERE
S'HAP
BROUGH
EGREMONT
COPELAND FOREST
GRASMERE
RYDAL
H. WESWATER
GOSFORTH
WAST WATER
R. IRT
R. DUDDON
SCAFELL PIKE
AMBLESIDE
WINDERMERE
TEBAY
CUMBRIAN MOUNTAINS
HOWGILL FELLS
KENDAL
GRIZEDALE FOREST
O. SEDBURGH
HAWES
ULVERSTON
RIVER KENT
KIRKBY LONSDALE
YORK-SHIRE
BARROW-IN-FURNESS

ULLSWATER

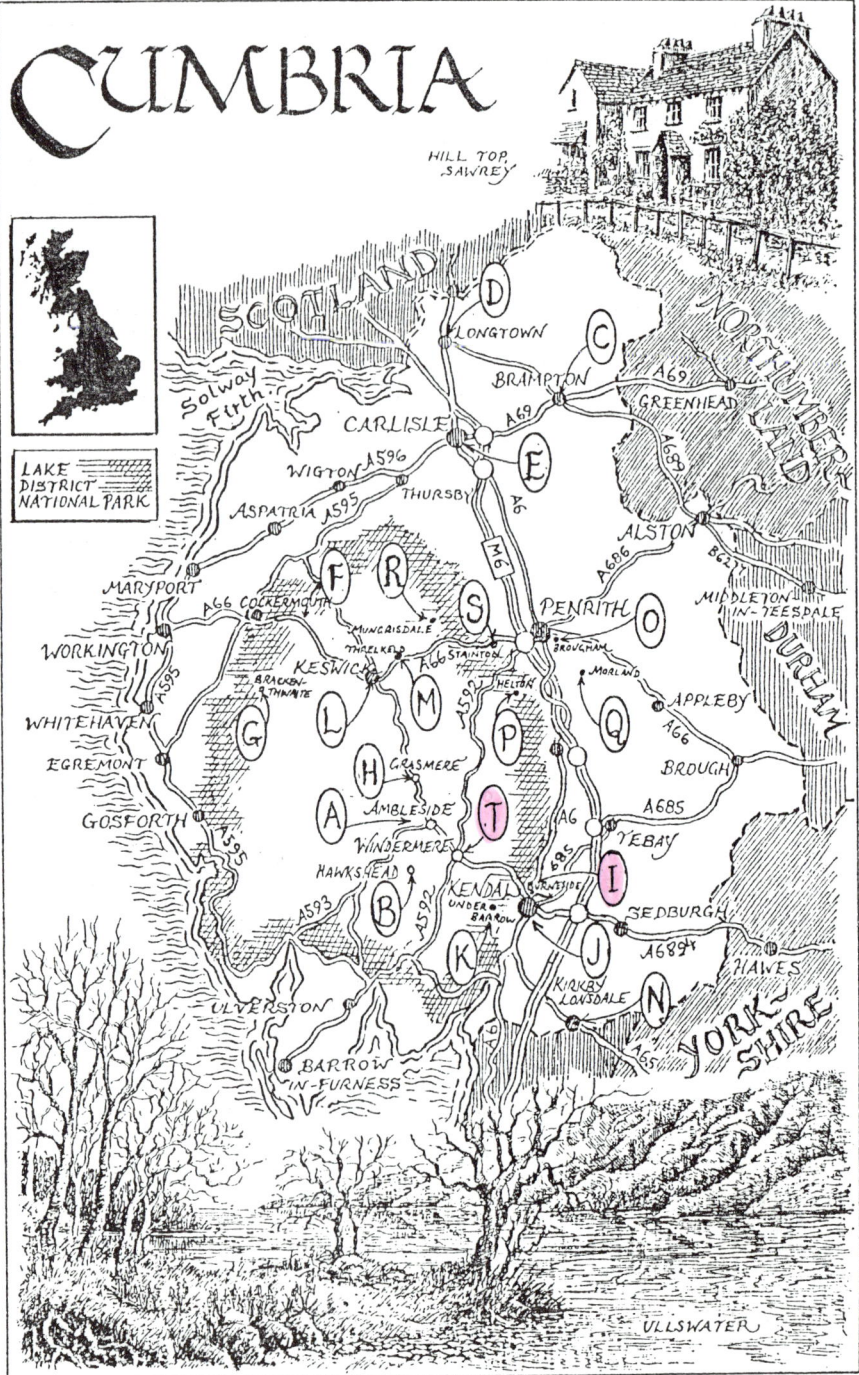

CUMBRIA

HILL TOP
SAWREY

LAKE
DISTRICT
NATIONAL PARK

SCOTLAND

Solway Firth

Longtown

BRAMPTON

CARLISLE

WIGTON A596

ASPATRIA A595

THURSBY

MARYPORT

A66 COCKERMOUTH

MUNGRISDALE

THRELKELD

KESWICK

BRACKEN-
THWAITE

WORKINGTON

WHITEHAVEN

EGREMONT

GOSFORTH

GRASMERE

AMBLESIDE

WINDERMERE

HAWKSHEAD

KENDAL
UNDER-
BARROW

ULVERSTON

BARROW
IN-FURNESS

D

C

GREENHEAD

A69

NORTHUMBERLAND

E

A6

M6

ALSTON

A686

B6277

MIDDLETON
IN-TEESDALE

DURHAM

PENRITH

BROUGHAM

MORLAND

APPLEBY

A66

BROUGH

A685

TEBAY

A685

A6

SEDBURGH

A683

HAWES

KIRKBY
LONSDALE

YORK-
SHIRE

ULLSWATER

F

R

S

O

G

L

M

H

A

B

P

Q

T

I

K

J

N

A69

A66 STAINTON

HELTON

A6

A592

A593

A592

A65

A683

Grey Friar Lodge Country House Hotel, Clappersgate, Ambleside LA22 9NE   Nearest Road A593

The Lodge is a traditional Lakeland stone country house built in 1869 and formerly known as the Brathay Vicarage. Now fully refurbished, whilst retaining a wealth of charm and character, the house offers friendly hospitality in a relaxed yet professional manner. Imaginatively designed menus are a highlight of your stay and all food is carefully prepared daily using the finest fresh produce and herbs from the garden. Special commendation for outstanding accommodation, hospitality, food and service. Winner of the RAC Northern Small Hotel of the Year 1994/95.

Tony Sutton
Tel: 015394 33158

B&B from £20, Dinner from £15.50, Rooms 8 double/twin
Minimum age 12 years, Open February - October, Map Ref: A

Borwick Lodge, Outgate, Hawkshead, Ambleside, Cumbria LA22 0PU   Nearest Road B5286

Borwick Lodge has diploma awards for 'the highest standards of comfort, amenity and hospitality'. It is set in the heart of the English Lake District yet in a delightful and tranquil setting. This is a rather special 17th century country residence of charm and character. Although extensively modernised Borwick Lodge is furnished to a high standard, retaining its olde worlde atmosphere. There is an elegant dining room offering a full English or continental breakfast. All bedrooms are en-suite with colour TV and tea/coffee making facilities. Ground floor and 4-poster rooms available.

Mr & Mrs A Bleasdale
Tel: 015394 36332

B&B from £18, Rooms 4 double, 2 family, Minimum age 8,
No pets, No smoking, Open all year, Map Ref: B

Courtyard Cottages, Warren Bank, Station Road, Brampton, Cumbria CA8 1EX   Nearest Road A69

This is no ordinary B&B, you wont be staying in someone elses home but in a courtyard cottage which provides independence and privacy as well as personal service. Step inside to find luxury furnishings together with colour TV, trouser press, hairdryer, private en-suite shower/bathroom. The ground floor en-suite bedroom has been designed with the disabled and elderly in mind. Awarded category 2 on the national accessibility scheme. Step outside to savour the year round beauty of 3 acres of gardens and surrounding countryside. Several local restaurants cater for all tastes.

Janet & Austen Hempstead
Tel: 016977 41818

B&B from £25, Rooms 2 double, No smoking, No children,
Open early January, Closed December, Map ref: C

Bessiestown Farm, Catlowdy, Longtown, Carlisle CA6 5QP   Nearest Road A7, B6318

One of the nicest farm houses offering many of the delights of a small country hotel combined with the relaxed atmosphere of a comfortable family home. Peaceful and quiet. Delightfully decorated public rooms and warm pretty bedrooms. Delicious traditional home cooking using fresh produce whenever possible. In the interest of all guests smoking is restricted to the bar lounge. The indoor heated swimming pool is open from mid May to mid September. Family accommodation is in comfortable courtyard cottages.

Jack & Margaret Sisson
Tel: 01228 577219
Fax: 01228 577219

B&B from £19, Dinner from £10, Rooms: 2 double, 1 family, 1 twin
Open all year except Christmas and new year, Map Ref: D

Bank End Farm, Roadhead, Carlisle, Cumbria CA6 6NU   Nearest Road B6318

Come and enjoy our self contained suite overlooking garden and river. Your private sitting room has colour TV, tea making and fridge. Enjoy the wild life, flowers and birdsong in our beautiful Lyne Valley; sit in the garden or walk by the river basking in tranquility. Discover the delights of this little known area where the roads are quiet, then return to enjoy delicious meals using fresh and local produce prepared by a distinctive and innovate cook. We provide urban comfort in rural peace. Nearby lie Hadrian's Wall, historic Carlisle and the romantic borderlands of Scotland.

Dorothy & Boy Downer
Tel: 016977 48644
Fax: 016977 48644

B&B from £18, Dinner from £12, Rooms 1 private en-suite twin room in house, 2 self catering cottages, Pets in cottages only, No smoking, Open April - November, Map Ref: E

Link House, Bassenthwaite Lake, Cockermouth, Cumbria CA13 9YD   Nearest Road A66

Link House is a Victorian country house at the head of Bassenthwaite Lake with superb views over forest and fell. All bedrooms have a shower suite, tea/coffee making facilities, and TV. The house is centrally heated and in the evening guests may relax in front of a log fire in the lounge. Meals are freshly prepared; there is always a choice available as is good wine at a modest price. For the energetic there is golf, sailing, riding nearby; others can fish in the lake or walk in any direction. A warm welcome is assured at any time of year.

Brian & May Smith
Tel: 017687 76291

B&B from £20, Dinner from £12, Rooms 2 single, 2 twin, 2 double, 2 family (all en-suite), Restricted smoking, Minimum age 7, Open February - November, Map Ref: F

Pickett Howe, Buttermere Valley Nr Cockermouth, Cumbria CA13 9UY   Nearest Road A66

Peacefully set amidst stunning mountain scenery, this 17th century longhouse offers caring, relaxing hospitality; and an ideal touring/walking base. 1994 Cumbrian finalist in ETB's Best B&B award, it also holds ETB's top quality grading of Deluxe (3 crowns). The cosy bedrooms have Victorian bedsteads, jacuzzi baths, telephone and many extras. Slate floors and oak beams are enhanced by quality furnishings and antiques. Dani's 5-course dinners are a treat for both eyes and palate and the breakfast menu is outstanding - vegetarian choices always available..

David & Dani Edwards
Tel: 01900 85444

B&B £35, Dinner £20, Rooms 1 twin, 3 double (all en-suite) No smoking, Minimum age 10, Pets welcome by arrangement, Open end March - mid November, Map Ref: G

Banerigg Guest House, Lake Road, Grasmere, Cumbria LA22 9PW   Nearest Road A591

Situated in the heart of the Lake District, Banerigg Guest House is a comfortable, a home with wonderful views. It is surrounded by woodland and overlooks the lake. Arrangements can be made for boating and fishing. All bedrooms are comfortable and have tea/coffee making facilities. A pleasant lounge, with log fire, for guests to relax in. Drying facilities are available.

Angela & Martin Clark
Tel: 015394 35204

B&B from £22, Rooms 1 single, 1 twin, 2 double, 3 family (many of which are en-suite), No smoking, Children welcome, Open March - November and New Year. Map Ref: H

Silverholme, Graythwaite, Hawkshead, Cumbria LA12 8AZ   Nearest Road A590

Built in 1840, Silverholme is a fine example of a small Georgian mansion. Set in its own grounds in an elevated position overlooking Lake Windermere the house is approached down an azalea and rhododendron lined drive. Retaining most of its original features the large, beautifully proportioned rooms have been traditionally furnished, all helping to create a special atmosphere for relaxations. All rooms have superb views over the lake. Bedrooms are all en-suite and tea/coffee making facilities. There is a guests' lounge with TV and a log fire in which to relax,.

Diane Rackham
Tel: 05395 31332

B&B from £19.50, Dinner from £9.50, Rooms 1 twin, 2 double, 1 family (all en-suite), No smoking, Open all year, Map Ref: B

High Grassings, Sunny Brow, Outgate, Hawkshead, Cumbria LA22 0PU   Nearest Road B5286

Here is one of the most tranquil settings near the heart of the Lakes. The house nestles against a Woodland Trust coppice and has seven acres of wildlife grounds. Views are over Curlew fields and woods to mountain range. Walk by bridle path to a pub or drive four minutes into quaint Hawkshead for your evening meal. Enjoy log fires in the beamed lounge and take breakfast in our spacious conservatory. If you would like to escape from life's bustle and crowds rest at High Grassings for a while.

Edward & Anne Miller
Tel: 015394 36484

B&B from £19.50, Rooms 2 twin, 2 double, 1 family, Restricted smoking, Minimum age 4, Open all year, Map Ref: B

Garnett House Farm, Burneside, Kendal, Cumbria LA9 5SF   Nearest Road A591

Garnett House Farm is an AA listed RAC acclaimed 15th century farmhouse on a large dairy and sheep farm, situated between Kendal and Windermere. The guests' lounge has 16th century oak panelling, old beams and very thick walls. All bedrooms have colour TV for watching your favourite programme, tea making facilities and most are en-suite. Good parking and close to village and public transport. Lovely views and many country walks from the farm. Food is good and plentiful with choice for breakfast and dinners served most evenings.

Mrs Sylvia Beaty
Tel: 01539 724542

B&B from £14, Dinner from £7, Rooms 5 double and family, No pets, Open all year except Christmas, Map Ref: I

Burrow Hall Country Guest House, Plantation Bridge, Kendal LA8 9JR   Nearest Road A591

Built in 1648 Burrow Hall has been sympathetically extended to provide modern comforts including a TV lounge, yet the principal lounge has a log fire and the original oak beams. Paul and Honor Brind are congenial hosts who enjoy having guests in their home. The set main course for dinner is complimented by a mouth watering range of starters and puddings and a small wine list. Breakfast is also impressive, offering a good selection of dishes.

Paul & Honor Brind
Tel: 01539 821711

B&B from £22.50, Dinner £12.50, Rooms 1 double, 2 twin, No pets, No children, Open all year, Map Ref: J

Low Jock Scar, Selside, Kendal, Cumbria LA8 9LE   **Nearest Road A6**

A small well appointed country guest house built in Lakeland stone and located in a wonderfully secluded riverside setting surrounded by 6 acres of garden and woodland. An idyllic spot offering easy access to the Lake District and the Yorkshire Dales and is en route for Scotland. Perfect for a few days away from it all with some excellent walking nearby. Kendal is a historic market town and is 6 miles away, Windermere 10 miles and Ullswater 20 miles. A very warm and welcoming atmosphere. All rooms have tea/coffee making facilities, and there is a guests lounge with TV.

Alison and Philip Midwinter
Tel: 01539 823259

B&B from £20, Dinner £14, Rooms 2 twin, 3 double (most en-suite), No smoking, Pets allowed on request, Open March - November, Map Ref: J

Tranthwaite Hall, Underbarrow, Near Kendal, Cumbria LA8 8HG   **Nearest Road M6, A6**

Tranthwaite Hall, which dates back to the 11th century, is a 225 acre working dairy and sheep farm in an idyllic and peaceful setting up an unspoilt country lane where deer and other wild- life can be seen. This is a magnificent "olde worlde" farmhouse with huge oak beam doors and a rare antique iron fire range in the guest lounge. All bedrooms have tea/coffee making facilities, central heating and electric blankets. Home make jam and marmalade with breakfast. Golf, pony trekking, and good country pubs are all nearby. AA selected and Cumbrian Tourist Board commended.

Mrs D M Swindlehurst
Tel: 015395 68285

B&B from £16, Rooms 2 double, 1 twin, 1 family room (en-suite available), No smoking, Open all year, Map Ref: K

Greystones, Ambleside Road, Keswick-on-Derwentwater, CA12 4DP   **Nearest Road A66**

Greystones is a small comfortable family run hotel situated in a quiet area of Keswick. It is only a short distance from the town centre, the lake and the fells. Eileen and David aim to create a friendly atmosphere to ensure a happy and relaxed holiday. Many guests return to sample Eileen's cooking which is imaginative, excellent quality, made with fresh produce, and attractively presented. There is also an excellent wine list.

David & Eileen Davenport
Tel: 01768 73108

B&B from £20.50, Dinner from £12.50, Rooms 5 double, 2 twin, 1 single, No smoking in bedrooms, No pets, Minimum age 8, Open February - November. Map Ref: L

Scales Farm Country Guest House, Scales,Threlkeld, Keswick CA12 4SY   **Nearest Road A66**

Alan and Sheila welcome you to stay at Scales Farm, a 17th century farmhouse which has been beautifully renovated and converted. The farm is set on the lower slopes of Blencathra, just 10 minutes by car from Keswick and has wonderful open views to the south. All bedrooms are en-suite (2 ground floor) and have tea/coffee making facilities, fridge and TV. The guests' beamed sitting room has a woodburning stove and a full choice breakfast is served in the attractively decorated dining room. Ample parking space and pretty gardens. ETB 3 crowns highly commended.

Alan & Sheila Appleton
Tel: 017687 79660

B&B from £20, Rooms 1 twin, 3 double, 1 family/double (all en-suite) Restricted smoking, Dogs welcome, Open all year except Christmas, Map Ref: M

Hipping Hall, Cowan Bridge, Kirkby Lonsdale, Cumbria LA6 2JJ Nearest Road A65

Hipping Hall is the remnant of a hamlet stemming from the 15th century. Today the Hall is a handsome country house set in 4 acres of walled gardens and perfectly placed for touring both the Lakes and the Dales and easy to find, just 10 minutes from the M6 (junction 36). Dinner is a 5 course affair served with accompanying wines and a 3 course supper on Sundays. All food is freshly prepared byJocelyn from home and local produce. A truly enjoyable experience.

Josely Ruffle & Ian Bryant B&B from £39, Dinner from £20, Rooms: 5 double, 2 twin,
Tel: 015242 71187 Minimum age 12, Open mid February - mid November,
Fax: 015242 72452 Map Ref: N

Hornby Hall, Brougham, Penrith, Cumbria CA10 2AR Nearest Road A66

Hornby Hall is a Grade II listed building built about 1550. It is situated on a working farm in tranquil countryside 1 mile off the A66 and 3 miles south east of Penrith. Dry fly fishing is available on a 2 mile stretch of the River Eamont. There are 2 double bedrooms with en-suite bathrooms, 3 twin rooms sharing a bathroom and a shower room and 2 single rooms. Nearby places of interest to visit include Carlisle Castle and Tullie House Museum. Penrith is a red sandstone market town with historic interest and only a few miles from the Lake District.

Ros Sanders B&B from £18, Dinner from £13.50, Rooms: 2 double, 2 single
Tel: 01768 891114/01831 482108 Open all year, Map Ref: O

Holywell Country Guest House, Helton, Penrith, Cumbria CA10 2QA Nearest Road A6

Holywell House is a splendid spacious Victorian property situated in an elevated position enjoying superb views of the unspoilt Lowther Valley from all rooms. Peacefully located between Ullswater and Haweswater but convenient for the wealth of lake and leisure facilities available for you to enjoy. Bedrooms are individually furnished to a high standard with full central heating, en-suite and private facilities. Comfortable sitting room and dining room with open fires. Hearty breakfast in a relaxed atmosphere. Mature garden and parking. Brochure available.

Anne & Rob Hunt B&B from £20, Rooms 2 double, 1 twin, Minimum age 10,
Tel: 01931 712231 No smoking, Open February to November, Map Ref: P

Hill Top Guest House, Morland, Penrith, Cumbria CA10 3AX Nearest Road A6, A66, M6

A family run Georgian house that has been completely refurbished to provide comfortable and relaxing accommodation in a friendly atmosphere. Situated in the heart of Morland and the Eden Valley it enjoys lovely views of the Pennines. All rooms are en-suite and have colour TV, hairdryer, tea/coffee making facilities, etc. Resident's lounge has an open log fire for cosy evenings. ETB classification 2 crowns commended.

Michael & Marilyn Tuppen B&B from £19, Dinner from £10, Rooms 2 double, 1 twin,
Tel: 01931 714561 Minimum age 5, Open all year, Map Ref: Q

Near Howe Farm Hotel, Mungrisdale, Penrith CA11 0SH   Nearest Road A66

A Cumbrian family home which is situated amidst 300 acres of moorland.. 5 of the 7 bedrooms have private facilities and all have tea/coffee making facilities. Meals are served in the comfortable dining room and great care is taken to produce good home cooking with every meal freshly prepared. Comfortable residents lounge with colour TV, games room, smaller lounge with well stocked bar and for the cooler evenings an open log fire. The surrounding area can provoide many activities and past-times including golf, fishing, pony trekking, boating and walking. Commended 3 crowns.

Mrs Christing Weightman
Tel: 017687 79678
Fax: 017687 79678

B&B from £16, Dinner from £9, Rooms 3 double, 3 family, 1 twin
Open March to November, Map Ref: R

The Old Vicarage, Mungrisdale, Penrith, Cumbria CA11 0XR   Nearest Road A66

The Old Vicarage is a spacious Victorian house of extreme charm and character with central heating and log fires. It is situated in large gardens in the unspoilt Lakeland village of Mungrisdale which nestles at the foot of Souther Fell and Bowscale Fell. The village has a pub, an internationally recommended restaurant and Post Office. Fishing, golf, pony trekking, swimming, theatre and craft workshops are all close at hand. There are walks to suit everyone, from gentle strolls and energetic climbs and an abundance of wild flowers, birds and animals.

Gordon & Pauline Bambrough
Tel: 017687 79274

B&B from £17, Rooms 1 double, 1 family, 1 twin, 1 single,
No pets, No smoking, Open all year, Map Ref: R

Gill House, Stainton, Penrith, Cumbria CA11 0ES   Nearest Road A66

Lovely house in its own grounds, situated in pretty village which has 2 places for good bar meals. The house is centrally heated. Television lounge and tea/coffee making facilities. Bedrooms have wash basins, 1 twin en-suite and 2 double bedrooms, one with shower. Three miles to Lake Ullswater and 2 miles to the M6 (exit 40).

Mrs Julia Thompson
Tel: 01768 890785

B&B from £15, Rooms 2 double, 1 twin, No pets,
Open March to October, Map Ref: S

Orrest Head House, Kendal Road, Windermere, Cumbria LA23 1JG   Nearest Road A591

Orrest Head House, Windermere, is a charming country house dating back to the 16th century. All bedrooms are en-suite and have colour TV, and tea/coffee making facilities. It is set in 3 acres of garden and woodland and has distant views to mountains and lake. Close to the station and village with a very homely atmosphere.

Mrs Brenda Butterworth
Tel: 015394 44315

B&B from £18.50, Rooms 3 double, 2 twin (all en-suite),
Rooms 3 double, 2 twin, Minimum age 6, No smoking,
Open all year except Christmas day, Map Ref: T

Rosemount, Lake Road, Windermere, Cumbria LA23 2EQ
Nearest Road A591

Rosemount is a family run guest house catering exclusively for the non-smoker offering warm hospitality and value for money and is ideally situated midway between the charming villages of Windermere and Bowness-on-Windermere. Eight tastefully furnished and comfortable bedrooms all with private facilities. Scrumptious, sizzling breakfasts (or refreshing fruit alternative) come highly recommended by their many regular guests. Ample car parking.

Alan & Dorothy Fielding
Tel: 015394 43739

B&B from £17.50, Rooms 5 double, 1 family, 1 twin, Minimum age 5, No smoking, Open January - November, Map Ref: T

St John's Lodge, Lake Road, Windermere, Cumbria LA23 2EQ
Nearest Road A5704

St John's Lodge takes pride in personal recommendations received and the owner/managers, Doreen and Ray Gregory, are most anxious to meet your personal requirements. The hotel's residents' lounge is available at any time and a warm welcome awaits you at the friendly residents' bar where you can relax with your pre dinner drink. A 4 course dinner is served each evening at 7 pm. St John's Lodge is situated midway between the villages of Windermere and Bowness, just a 10 minutes walk from the lake pier.

Doreen & Ray Gregory
Tel: 015394 43078

B&B from £17.50, Dinner from £10, Rooms 9 double, 3 family, 1 twin, 1 single, Minimum age 3, Open from February - November Map Ref: T

Kirkwood Guest House, Prince's Road, Windermere, Cumbria LA23 2DD
Nearest Road A591

Kirkwood is a large Victorian stone house situated on a quiet corner between Windermere and Bowness ideally situated for exploring the Lake District. All rooms are en-suite with colour TV, tea/coffee making facilities and radios. Some rooms have 4 poster beds, ideal for honeymoons, anniversary, or just a special treat. There is a comfortable lounge in which to relax and for breakfast an extensive menu is offered including vegetarian and special diets (with prior notice). Help with planning walks and drives or choosing a mini bus tour is all part of the personal service.

Carol & Neil Cox
Tel: 015394 43907

B&B from £18.50, Rooms 3 twin, 3 double, 4 family (all en suite), Restricted smoking, Children welcome, Pets by arrangement, Open all year, Map Ref: T

Quarry Garth Country House Hotel, Windermere, Cumbria LA23 1LF
Nearest Road A591

This gracious and mellow Edwardian country house is set in eight acres of peaceful Lakeland gardens and woodland near Lake Windermere. The individually designed bedrooms are all en-suite with television, telephone and beverage tray. Huw and Lynne are friendly and caring hosts who combine high standards with kindness and good humour. ETB 4 crown highly commended and 2 AA rosettes awards for unmissable dinners taken in the oak panelled restaurant with log fires. An ideal base from which to see the celebrated Lake District.

Huw & Lynne Phillips
Tel: 015394 88282
Fax: 015394 46584

B&B from £35, Dinner from £19.50, Rooms 2 twin, 7 double, 1 family (all en-suite), Restricted smoking, Pets by arrangement, Open all year, Map Ref: T

Please mention

THe
GREAT
BRITISH
BED
and
BREAKFAST

when
booking your
accommodation

Derbyshire and Staffordshire

"It has everything that England has . . . It is England in little, lost in the midst of England, unsung by searchers after the extreme; perhaps occasionally somewhat sore at this neglect, but how proud in the instinctive cognizance of its representative features and traits!"

(Arnold Bennett - The Old Wives' Tale, chapter 1

DERBYSHIRE & STAFFORDSHIRE

DOVEDALE

Rich upland scenery and industrial heritage offer a wide variation for the visitor to Derbyshire and Staffordshire. A focus of the area is the Peak District National Park, England's most Southerly highland country with Britain's first national park more than 40 years ago at its heart. Most of the Peak District's 555 square miles are in Derbyshire, but include parts of surrounding counties, one of them being Staffordshire. Rich and varied countryside from moorland, grassy hills and dales to craggy rocks rises to 2,088ft at Kinder Scout. It is not surprising that the area offers plenty of activities, whether on foot, horseback or by bicycle. The area has over 4,000 miles of public paths and other areas where walkers have free access for most of the year there is also climbing, caving, sailing and gliding.

A large part of the Peak District occupies the North Eastern corner of Staffordshire. At Three Shires Head the River Dane tumbles down to the meeting place of Cheshire, Derbyshire and Staffordshire, continuing on its journey West along the Staffordshire-Cheshire border.

Buxton is in the heart of the national park and although one of the highest towns in England at 1,007ft, is sheltered by the surrounding hills. The spa town owes its fame to the 5th Duke of Devonshire who, at the end of the 18th century, built the town's beautiful Crescent as a rival to fashionable Bath. Just as they did in Roman times, the town's springs, charged with nitrogen and carbon gas, emerge at a constant temperature of 28°c.

LICHFIELD CATHEDRAL.

Not far from Buxton, at Edale is the start of the 250 mile Pennine Way, which runs along the Pennine chain to the Scottish border. Some of England's most beautiful river valley country intersperses these high rides in mid Derbyshire, along the courses of the rivers Wye, Derwent and Dove. The Wye flows from Bakewell where the surrounding wooded hills stretch up to high moorland. The town is perhaps most famous for its Bakewell Tarts. Known locally as Bakewell pudding, the recipe began when the cook from the Rutland Arms spread egg mixture on top of the jam in a strawberry tart instead of using it in the pastry.

At the centre of South Derbyshire is the city of Derby with its wide range of parks, theatre, shopping, sporting facilities and varied attractions. Derby's recent history was founded on silk and the railways. Some of the city's finest houses date from the 18th century. England's first silk mill was established in Derby by Thomas Cotchet and John Lombe, and it produced silk that was famous throughout Europe.

A century later following the rapid expansion of industry came the building of the Midland Railway's locomotive and coach works. In 1908 Sir Henry Rolls along with the Hon C S Rolls established Rolls Royce. Sir Henry's monument can be seen in one of the city's 20 parks, the Arboretum.

The area around Stoke-on-Trent in Staffordshire is dominated by industry. The novelist Arnold Bennett (1867-1931) focused the cluster of the "Five Towns" in most of his famous novels. Today the towns of the Potteries have plenty to offer the visitor with many of the pottery shops and factories open to the public. The area was a natural place for the making of pottery with its ample supplies of clay, as well as water and coal. Fragments of pottery dating back to Neolithic times and Roman and Saxon wares have also been discovered. The area's broad belt of rich pasture land is also home to the brewing industries at Burton-on-Trent where several museums and exhibitions tell the story of brewing.

The area has its share of pleasant old towns. The county town of Stafford on the River Saw was listed as a borough in the Domesday Book in 1086. Both Leek and Uttoxeter are market towns. Uttoxeter is known for its National Hunt steeplechase course where 19 meetings are held each year. Stone and Tutbury are picturesque towns. The River Trent and the Trent and Mersey Canal run parallel South of Stone while Tutbury is set on the banks of the River Dove.

Between Stafford, Cannock and Rugeley is Cannock Chase, 3,000 acres of wild heath and woodlands - the last remnants of the once extensive oak forest and hunting ground which covered much of the county in Norman times. This is riding and walking country with many trails and picnic areas. A large herd of fallow deer are descendants of those which escaped the arrows of the Plantagenets.

Lichfield is dominated by its cathedral's three sandstone spires, known as "The Ladies of the Vale". Dr Samuel Johnson was born in Breadmarket Street, Lichfield in 1709.

DERBYSHIRE AND STAFFORDSHIRE

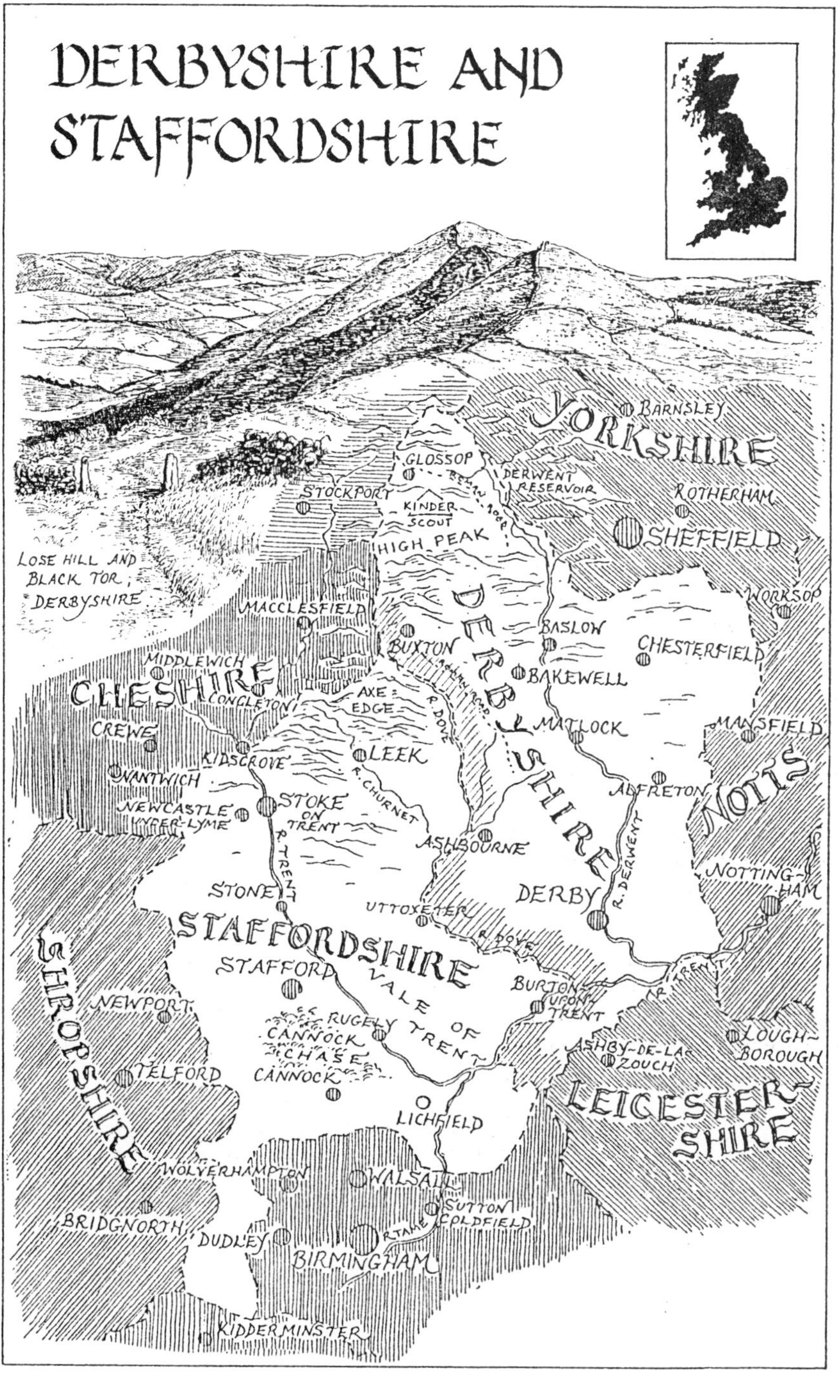

BARNSLEY

YORKSHIRE

GLOSSOP

DERWENT RESERVOIR

STOCKPORT

ROTHERHAM

KINDER SCOUT

SHEFFIELD

HIGH PEAK

LOSE HILL AND BLACK TOR, DERBYSHIRE

WORKSOP

MACCLESFIELD

BUXTON

BASLOW

CHESTERFIELD

MIDDLEWICH

DERBYSHIRE

BAKEWELL

AXE EDGE

R. DOVE

MATLOCK

MANSFIELD

CHESHIRE

CONGLETON

CREWE

LEEK

NOTTS

KIDSGROVE

R. CHURNET

ALFRETON

NANTWICH

NEWCASTLE UNDER LYME

STOKE ON TRENT

ASHBOURNE

NOTTING-HAM

R. TRENT

R. DERWENT

STONE

DERBY

UTTOXETER

R. DOVE

STAFFORDSHIRE

VALE OF

STAFFORD

BURTON UPON TRENT

TRENT

NEWPORT

RUGELEY

CANNOCK CHASE

ASHBY-DE-LA-ZOUCH

LOUGH-BOROUGH

SHROPSHIRE

TELFORD

CANNOCK

LICHFIELD

LEICESTER-SHIRE

WOLVERHAMPTON

WALSALL

BRIDGNORTH

DUDLEY

R. TAME

SUTTON COLDFIELD

BIRMINGHAM

KIDDERMINSTER

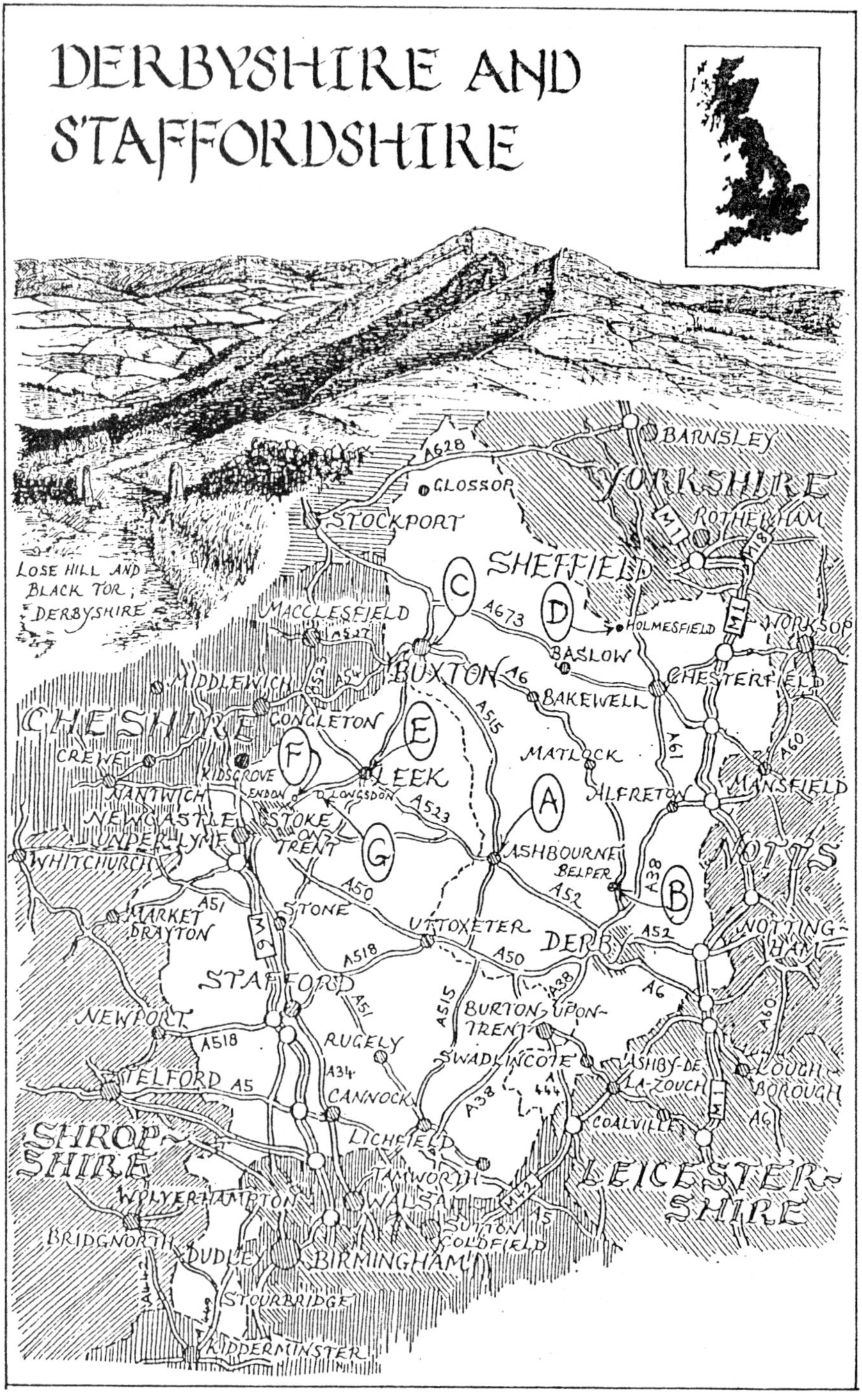

DERBYSHIRE AND STAFFORDSHIRE

LOSE HILL AND
BLACK TOR;
DERBYSHIRE

BARNSLEY

A628

GLOSSOP

STOCKPORT

YORKSHIRE

ROTHERHAM

M1

SHEFFIELD

C

A673

D

HOLMESFIELD

WORKSOP

MACCLESFIELD
A537

MIDDLEWICH

BUXTON

A6

BASLOW

CHESTERFIELD

M1

CHESHIRE

CONGLETON

E

A515

BAKEWELL

A6

CREWE

KIDSGROVE

F

LEEK

MATLOCK

A61

A60

MANSFIELD

NANTWICH

ENDON

LONGSDON

A523

ALFRETON

NEWCASTLE
UNDER LYME

STOKE ON
TRENT

A

A38

WHITCHURCH

G

ASHBOURNE
BELPER
A52

B

NOTTS

MARKET
DRAYTON

A51

A50

STONE

A52

NOTTING-
HAM

3 6

UTTOXETER

DERBY

A6

A60

NEWPORT

STAFFORD

A518

A51

RUGELY

A5

A518

A50

A515

A38

ASHBY-DE-
LA-ZOUCH

LOUGH-
BOROUGH

A61

TELFORD A5

A34

CANNOCK

BURTON-UPON-
TRENT

SWADLINCOTE

M

A38

COALVILLE

SHROP-
SHIRE

LICHFIELD

LEICESTER-
SHIRE

BRIDGNORTH

WOLVERHAMPTON

TAMWORTH

WALSALL

M6

SUTTON
COLDFIELD

DUDLEY

BIRMINGHAM

STOURBRIDGE

KIDDERMINSTER

Stanshope Hall, Stanshope, Nr Ashbourne, Derbyshire DE6 2AD **Nearest Road A515**

Stanshope Hall, part of which dates from the 16th century, stands on the brow of a hill between the Manifold and the Dove Rivers in the tranquil farming hamlet of Stanshope. The hall faces south across rolling landscape. Lovingly restored and retaining many of its original features. All bedrooms are en-suite and have tea/coffee making facilities. There is a guests' drawing room with piano and record player and local information is available. Centrally heated throughout. Dinner available using garden and local produce and there is a residents licence. Extensive breakfast menu.

Naomi Chambers & NickLourie
Tel: 01335 310278
Fax: 01335 310470

B&B from £20, Dinner from £16.50, Rooms 1 twin with private facilities, 2 en-suite double/family, Restricted smoking, Open all year except Christmas, Map Ref: A

Dannah Farm Country Guest House, Shottle, Belper, Derbys DE56 2DR **Nearest Road A517**

Dannah is a beautiful 18th century Georgian farmhouse with its own tranquil atmosphere and character. Close to the Peak District and the many and varied attractions that Derbyshire has to offer, all within easy reach. The house has been lovingly restored and all rooms have private facilities, colour TV, radio and hot drinks trays. There are 2 sittings rooms exclusively for guests use and large safe gardens. Winners of the 1992 National Award and 1993 Food Services Award. ADAS/Sunday Telegraph.

Joan & Martin Slack
Tel: 01773 550273
Fax: 01773 550590

B&B from £27, Dinner from £14, Rooms 3 double, 2 twin, 1 family, 1 single, No smoking, Open all year except Christmas, Map Ref: B

Biggin Hall, Biggin-by-Hartington, Buxton, Derbyshire SK17 0DH **Nearest Road A515**

Beautifully restored, this stone built house dating from the 17th century, set 1,000 feet up in the Peak District National Park, is delightful in every way. Antiques, a log fire, a 4 poster bed give this home a wealth of charm. The food is outstanding with the owners priding themselves on the use of only the freshest and best produce available. The home baked bread is excellent! Perfect in every way. Easy access to the Spa town of Buxton, Chatsworth House, Haddon Hall, etc. Beautiful uncrowded footpaths from the grounds.

Mr & Mrs J M Moffett
Tel: 01298 84451

B&B from £22.50, Dinner from £14.50, Rooms and Apartments, Minimum age 12, Open all year, Map Ref: C

Springwood House, Cowley Lane, Holmesfield, Nr Sheffield, Derbys S18 5SD **Nearest Road M1, A57**

Springwood House is situated in the Cordwell Valley amidst glorious countryside on the edge of the Peak District yet within a few miles of Sheffield and Chesterfield. The rooms are spacious, well furnished and have private facilities, hot drinks tray and TV. The house stands in 1½ acres of garden with beautiful views all around A warm friendly welcome awaits each guest on arrival.

Mr A Turner
Tel: 01742 890253
Fax: 01742 891365

B&B from £17.50, Dinner by arrangement, Rooms 1 double, 1 twin, with private facilities, Restricted smoking, Open all year except Christmas and new year. Map Ref: D

Pethills Bank Cottage, Pethills Lane, Bottom House Nr Leek, Staffs ST13 7PF   **Nearest Road A523**

Pethills Bank Cottage is located on the southern slopes of the Peak National Park. Formerly a Derbyshire stone farmhouse of the 18th century, the property has been extensively modernised and extended to provide an attractive and comfortable retreat in a peaceful and relaxing atmosphere. The cottage style accommodation is contained on 2 levels with low beams and stone walls. Bedrooms are to a high standard and have TV, radio/alarm, and tea/coffee making facilities, etc. A full English or continental breakfast is served and a 3 course dinner available by prior arrangement.

Yvonne & Richard Martin
Tel: 01538 304277/304555
Fax: 01538 304575

B&B from £20, Dinner from £15 (by prior arrangement),
Rooms 3 double (all en-suite),No smoking, Minimum age 5,
Open March - December (not Christmas), Map Ref: E

The Hollies, Clay Lake, Endon, Stoke-on-Trent, Staffs ST9 9DD   **Nearest Road B5051, A53**

A warm welcome awaits you in this delightful Victorian house which has been sympathetically developed to its present comfortable standard. Situated in a quiet country setting in Endon and within easy reach of The Potteries, Staffordshire Moorlands and Alton Towers. Bedrooms are spacious, comfortable and have central heating, wash basins, shaver points, colour TV and tea/coffee making facilities. The lounge and dining room overlook a secluded garden. There is a choice of breakfast and home made preserves. Private parking.

Mrs Anne Hodgson
Tel: 01782 503252

B&B from £16, Rooms 3 en-suite double/family, 2 double/family,
No smoking, Open all year, Map Ref: F

The Old Vicarage, Leek Road, Endon, Stoke-on-Trent, Staffordshire ST9 9BH   **Nearest Road A53**

A traditional Victorian/Edwardian former vicarage, in a quiet setting, with good sized rooms. The comfortable bedrooms have TV, tea/coffee making facilities, and hairdryer. Guests have their own sitting room which overlooks the front garden. Breakfast is served at a large single table and there is a varied menu. Nearby is the Plough Inn which serves good luncheons and evening meals. Places of interest to visit include The Potteries, Peak Park and Staffordshire Moorlands.

Mrs I Grey
Tel: 01782 503686

B&B from £15, Rooms 2 twin, 1 double/family, No smoking,
Open all year, Map Ref: F

Micklea Farm, Micklea Lane, Longsdon, Stoke on Trent, Staffs ST9 9QA   **Nearest Road A53**

A lovely 18th century cottage set in pleasant gardens complete with a swing for children. Micklea farm is ideally situated for visits to Alton Towers, the Peak District and the Potteries. The food is excellent, much of which is home grown garden produce. There is a cosy sitting room with an open fire and the house is traditionally furnished and decorated. Whether relaxing or sightseeing this is an ideal base and a warm welcome is guaranteed.

Mrs Barbara White
Tel: 01538 385006
Fax: 01538 382882

B&B from £15, Dinner from £10, Rooms 2 single, 2 twin/double,
No smoking,No pets, Open all year except Christmas, Map Ref: G

DEVON

"Tom Pearse, Tom Pearse, lend me your grey mare,
All along, down along, out along lee,
For I wants for to go to Widdicombe Fair,
Wi Bill Brewer, Jan Stewer, Peter Gurney,
Peter Davy, Dan'l Whiddon, Harry Hawk,
Old Uncle Tom Cobley and all . . . "

(Sabine Baring-Gould)

DEVON

THE PICTURESQUE FISHING VILLAGE OF CLOVELLY.

Devon provides the cream of coast and country. Inland the countryside is ideal for a relaxed holiday, with opportunities to explore on foot, horseback or by bike. Around the coast is a wealth of lovely resorts with some of the best beaches in the country.

Dartmoor stretches over much of inland Devon offering a feeling of remoteness surrounding the granite uplands, the relics of volcanic upheaval 400 million years ago. Yet to the North, the coast has sandy beaches, bracing winds and stark cliffs while sub-tropical flowers and palm trees grow along the South coast.

From Welcombe on the west facing coast near the Cornish border to Trentishoe on the North coast is Devon's most dramatic stretch of coastal scenery. Cliffs, which in some parts drop sheer into the sea are interspersed only by Woolacombe Sands and long sand flats stretching South from Saunton.

There are several popular seaside resorts in the region. Ilfracombe is the largest seaside resort in North Devon and is built around its old harbour. There are many good shingle beaches, two of them reached by tunnels through the rocks. Coastal walks take advantage of the hilly landscape.

Lundy Island, 12 miles North West of Hartland Point, can be reached by a two hour steamer journey from Ilfracombe. Now owned by the National Trust, the island is named after the old Norse word for puffin - and puffins still nest on the narrow cliff ledges along with other birds.

At Appledore the Rivers Taw and Torridge meet before entering the sea about two miles away - an ideal site which made Appledore a famous shipbuilding town. Clovelly is one of Britain's show places. Cars cannot drive through the narrow, cobbled main street, which drops 400ft in a series of steps to an inn by the harbour. The cottages lining the street are decked with flowers for most of the year.

Westward Ho! was named after Charles Kingsley's famous novel published in 1855. It has good beaches, a golf course and the famous two mile long Pebble Ridge. It was the Victorian novelist who described north Devon's climate as combining the soft warmth of South Devon with the bracing freshness of the Welsh mountains.

BERRY POMEROY CASTLE.

The most important centres of commerce and industry are Barnstaple and Bideford. Both are near the estuary where the Rivers Taw and Torridge meet and they were prosperous ports before the estuary silted up. Barnstaple is one of the oldest towns in Britain, an established borough minting its own coins as early as the 10th century. The long bridge over the River Taw with its 16 arches dates from the 13th century.

Bideford's narrow streets climb the steep hill on the West bank of the River Torridge. The town's most famous landmark is the bridge over the river - its 24 arches span 677 ft and incorporate part of the original 15th century stone bridge

Dartmoor is the largest tract of open country left in Southern England and most of it lies in the Dartmoor National Park which covers 365 square miles between Okehampton and Ivybridge, Tavistock and Christow. The market town of Okehampton, the "capital of the Northern moor" is set on the River Okement. South of the town are the highest tors or peaks of Dartmoor - High Willhays at 2,039ft and Yes Tor, 2028 ft. Another important market town is Tavistock, traditionally regarded as the Western capital of the moor which grew up around its Benedictine abbey, founded in the 10th century. Widdecombe in the Moor is a picturesque village in a high fold of Dartmoor. Widdecombe Fair, made famous by the Uncle Tom Cobleigh song, is held in September. To the West is Hameldown Beacon which has on its west side a well preserved group of Bronze Age barrows. Princetown, the moor's largest town and the bleakest standing at 1,400ft above sea level, was named after the Prince of Wales (later George IV) who gave land from the Duchy of Cornwall to build a prison to house the captives of the Napoleonic Wars.

The rich agricultural region of South Hams stretches from Totnes to Prawle Point and from Dartmouth to Plymouth. Plymouth is the largest city in the west country and has one of the grandest sites of any city in Britain, lying between the mouths of the Tamar and Plym. During the Second World War virtually the whole of the city centre was obliterated. In 1620 the Pilgrim Fathers sailed from Plymouth to America in the Mayflower and in 1772 James Cook departed on his three year round the world voyage. Totnes was settled and fortified by the Saxons and in the middle ages grew rich on the cloth trade. Dartmouth is another town of historical and architectural importance. An important harbour site since Roman times, many historic naval expeditions have set sail from here.

From Brixham to Dawlish the Devon coast has colourful, luxuriant vegetation, golden sands and vivid blue sea. Visitors can enjoy a variety of activities from golf to boating and fishing and other seaside amenities. Brixham is in two parts - the old village climbing a hill and the fishing village half a mile below with early 19th century houses clustered around the harbour. Dawlish became a resort in the late 18th century, its elegant Regency character captured in The Strand, a street built in the early 1800s. The town was favoured by Jane Austen and Dickens made it the birthplace of Nicholas Nickleby.

Teignmouth is one of Devon's oldest resorts with a long history of fishing and ship building. Torquay's superb setting has helped make it the largest and most famous seaside resort in the county. East Devon is a region of contrasts. The Westernmost chalk headland along the Channel coast is at Beer Head and not far away are the vivid red cliffs of Budleigh Salterton. Axminster, a small town on the River Axe, is famous for its carpets and likewise Honiton is famous for its lace, produced since Elizabethan times.

The seaside resort of Sidmouth is full of Regency and Victorian buildings. The Duke and Duchess of Kent stayed here at Woolbrook Cottage in 1819 with their infant daughter, later to be Queen Victoria.

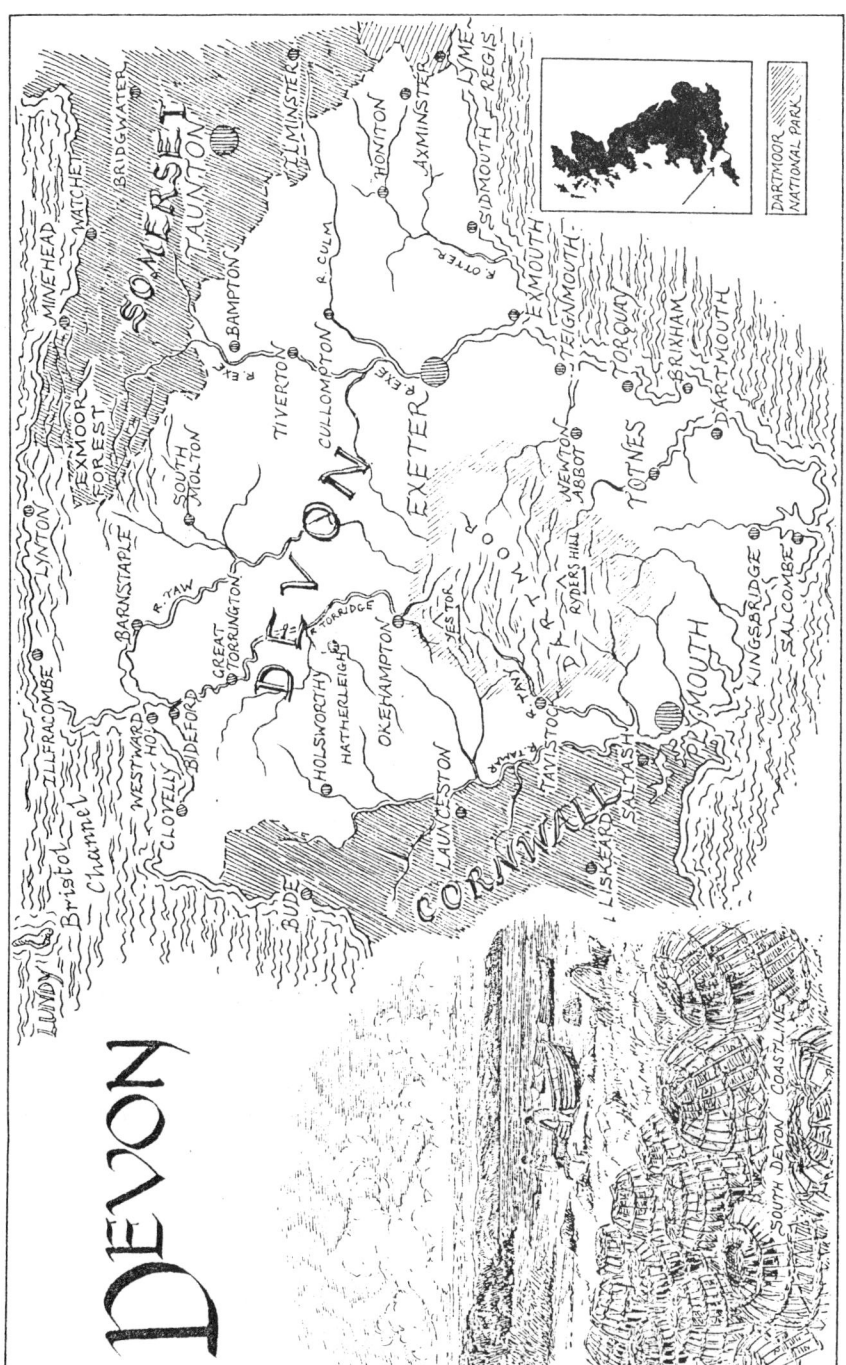

DEVON

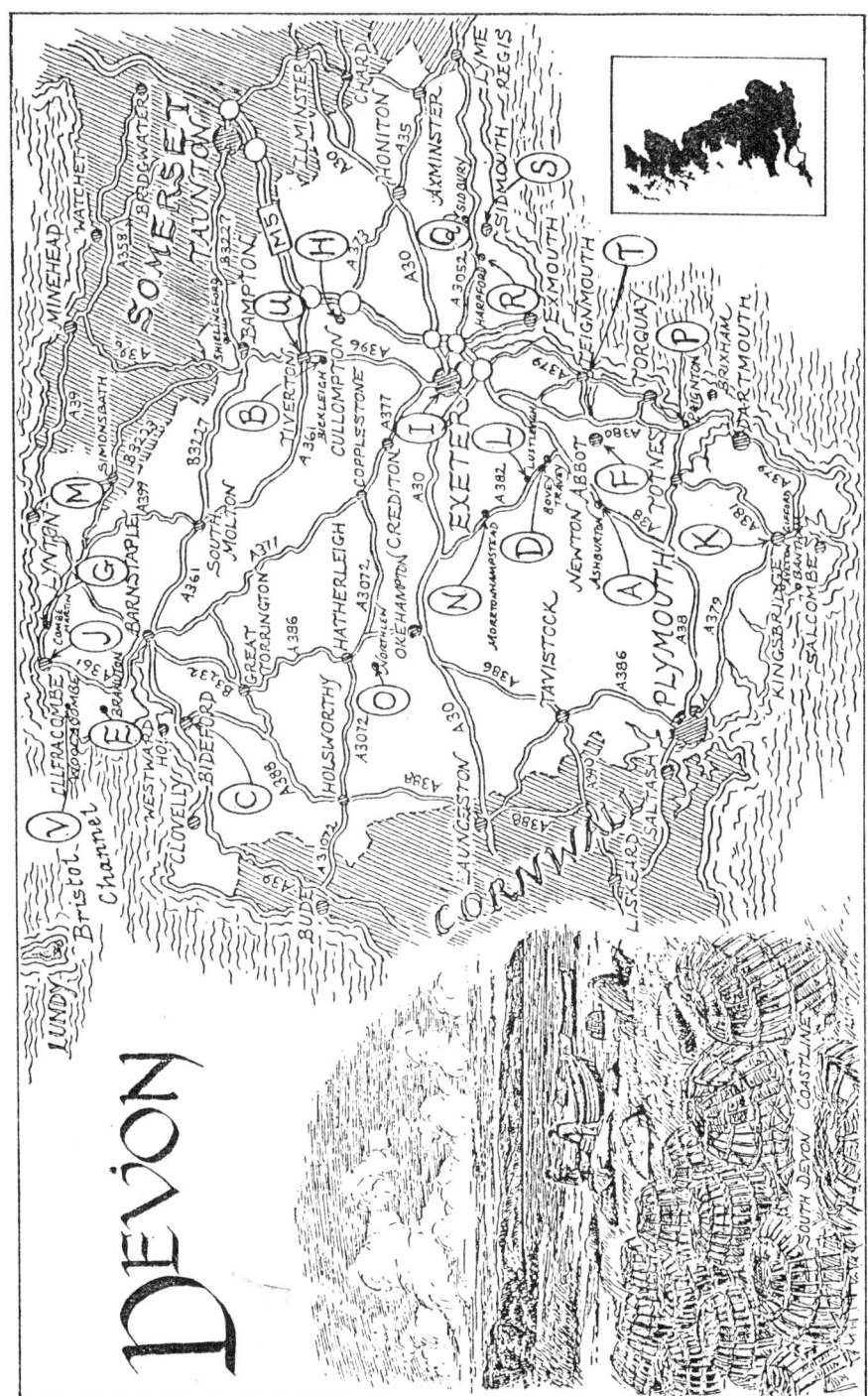

Wellpritton Farm, Holne, Ashburton, Devon TQ13 7RX   Nearest Road A38

A warm welcome, personal attention, mouthwatering farm produced food, and Devonshire cream every day awaits you at Wellpritton a beautiful farmhouse on the edge of Dartmoor, where there are goats, donkeys, rabbits and chickens. Set in the heart of the countryside and yet only 3 miles from the A38 and ½ hour from Exeter, Plymouth and Torbay. Riding, fishing, walking sailing and golf are all nearby. The farmhouse is modernised to a high standard, most rooms are en-suite and all rooms have tea/coffee makers. There is a games room also an outdoor swimming pool.

Mrs Sue Townsend
Tel: 01364 631273

**B&B from £17, Dinner from £9, Rooms 2 twin, 2 double
(most en-suite) Restricted smoking, Open all year, Map Ref: A**

Bickleigh Cottage Hotel, Bickleigh, Devon EX16 8RJ   Nearest Road A396

Situated on the bank of the River Exe near Bickleigh Bridge, a landmark famous for its scenic beauty, Bickleigh Cottage Country Hotel has been privately owned by the Cochrane family since 1933. The original cottage was built circa 1640 with additions in the 1970's. All bedrooms are en-suite and have tea/coffee making facilities. The location of Bickleigh makes it a perfect centre for touring Devon. Exeter with its cathedral and maritime mueseum, Tiverton castle, Knightshayes Court and Killerton House are all nearby.

R S H & P M Cochrane
Tel: 01884 855230

**B&B from £23.50, Dinner from £11.40, Rooms 2 single, 3 twin,
4 double, (all en-suite), Restricted smoking, Minimum age 14,
Open April to October, Map Ref: B**

Lower Winsford, Abbotsham Road, Bideford, Devon EX39 3QP   Nearest Road A39

Everyone is made very welcome at Lower Winsford to share our family home, tastefully furnished have a relaxing atmosphere, surrounded by lovely countryside. Caring attention at all times. Within easy reach are Exmoor and Dartmoor as is the beach at Westward Ho. Many coast walks.

Mrs Margaret Ogle
Tel: 01237 475083
Fax: 01237 425802

**B&B from £16, Rooms 1 double en-suite, 1 twin with private
bathroom, No smoking, Open Easter - September, Map Ref: C**

Corbyns Brimley, Higher Brimley, Nr Bovey Tracey, Devon TQ13 9JT   Nearest Road A382

Corbyns Brimley is a 16th century Grade II listed longhouse in Dartmoor National Park in the hamlet of Higher Brimley with extensive rural views facing almost due south. The house has been attractively furnished in a style in keeping with its age and the bedrooms have tea/coffee making facilities and one has private bathroom. Snack suppers are available on request. Several nearby pubs and restaurants offer good food.

Hazel & Chris White
Tel: 01626 833332

**B&B from £20, Rooms 2 twin (1 en-suite), No smoking,
Minimum age 12, Open all year except Christmas and New Year,
Map Ref: D**

Denham Farm & Country House, North Buckland, Braunton, Devon EX33 1HY   Nearest Road A361

This traditional farmhouse, dating back to the 1700's, is set in the centre of a totally unspoilt hamlet and offers log fires, soft lighting, and relaxing atmosphere. All rooms are en-suite with colour TV, hair dryer, clock/radio, and tea/coffee making facilities. Denham Farm is renowned locally for good home cooking. Close by are many attractions including market towns, Exmoor National Park, golf, horse riding, bird sanctuary and a nature reserve.

Mrs Jean Barnes
Tel: 01271 890297
Fax: 01271 890297

B&B from £20, Dinner from £12, Rooms 6 double, 2 family, 2 twin, Restricted smoking, Open all year except Christmas, Map Ref: E

Oakfield, Chudleigh, Devon TQ13 0DD   Nearest Road A38

Oakfield is a elegant country house standing in 20 acres of formal gardens, orchards and paddocks, offering perfect peace and tranquility. This family home has been tastefully restored providing all modern facilities whilst retaining its original period charm. Guests have use of drawing room, library, billiards room and heated swimming pool. Bedrooms are ensuite, have TV and tea/coffee making facilities. The kitchen garden provides produce for the dining table. Situated 1 mile from the ancient wool town of Chudleigh. An ideal centre for touring Dartmoor and the coast.

Peter & Patricia Johnson-King
Tel: 01626 852194
Fax: 01626 852194

B&B from £30, Dinner from £20, Rooms 1 twin, 2 double, (all en-suite)
No smoking, Minimum age 12, Open Easter - end October, Map Ref: F

Brinscott Farmhouse, Berry Down, Nr Combe Martin, Devon EX34 0PA   Nearest Road A3123

Tucked into the hills above Combe Martin, situated between Ilfracombe and Exmoor, Brinscott Farmhouse is a 16th century Grade II Devon longhouse. Guests' lounge has a beamed ceiling, Inglenook fireplace with feature bread ovens and creamer. Colour TV, videos, games, books and music are all available. Modern bathrooms, some en-suite. All bedrooms have tea/coffee making facilities, and central heating. Within easy access of golden beaches, golf, riding, shooting, surfing and plenty of beautiful walks, etc

Jackie & John Kingsley
Tel: 01271 883146

B&B from £15, Dinner from £8, Rooms 1 double, 2 family/double, 2 twin, Open March - December, Map Ref: G

Rullands, Rull Lane, Cullompton, Devon EX15 1NQ   Nearest Road M5 (junction 28)

A comfortable 15th century house set amidst beautiful, peaceful, rolling countryside and yet only a few minutes from the M5 and historic Tiverton and the market town of Cullompton. Within easy reach of all country pursuits - golf, shooting, fishing, riding, etc. Hard tennis court in grounds. There is an elegant dining room where delicious home cooked meals are served and en extensive wine list is available. All bedrooms are en-suite, have colour TV and courtesy trays.

Georgina Charteris
Tel: 01884 33356
Fax: 01884 35890

B&B from £25, Dinner from £13.50, Rooms 3 double, 1 twin, 2 single, Restricted smoking, Open all year, Map Ref: H

Raffles, 11 Blackall Road, Exeter, Devon EX4 4HD   Nearest Road Exeter Central

Raffles is a spacious Victorian house furnished in keeping with that period. All rooms are provided with private bathroom, central heating, TV, and tea/coffee making facilities. A traditional English breakfast is served between 7.30 and 9.30 am, an alternative lighter breakfast is also available. A 3 course evening meal can be provided on request and there is a residential table licence. Only 5 minutes walk from the centre of this historic city with all its amenities including the beautiful Norman Cathedral, 14th century Guildhall, shops, gardens, etc.

Sue & Richard Hyde
Tel: 01392 702200

B&B from £19, Dinner from £12, Rooms 2 single, 1 twin, 2 double, 2 family (all en-suite), Pets by arrangement, Open all year, Map Ref: I

Higher Bagmores Farm, Woodbury, Exeter, Devon EX5 1LA   Nearest Road A376, B3179

Higher Bagmores Farm is a working beef, sheep and cereal farm set in delightful countryside. Within a few miles are the towns of Exeter, the Cathedral city; and Exmouth, with a good sandy beach and sports centre. Budleigh Salterton, Dartmoor, Torbay, Plymouth and Lyme Regis are also within an easy drive. The house has full central heating and all bedrooms have tea/coffee making facilities.

Mr & Mrs B Glanvill
Tel: 01395 232261

B&B from £13.50, Rooms 1 double, 1 family, 1 single, Open all year, Map Ref: I

Varley House, Chambercombe Park, Ilfracombe, Devon, EX34 9QW   Nearest Road A361

A warm welcome and friendly atmosphere are assured at Varley House which is situated opposite Hillsborough overlooking the harbour which, like the High Street, is a short stroll away. All bedrooms are en-suite and situated on the ground and first floors. All have sea or country views, central heating, together with comforts such as tea/coffee facilities, radio alarm, hairdryer & CTV. Breakfast is a choice of either traditional or an array of lighter fare and special diets can be catered for. Guests are able to relax in the comfortable lounge and the licensed bar. There is a carpark.

Roy & Barbara Gable
Tel: 01271 863927
Fax: 01271 863927

B&B from £21, Dinner from £9.50, Rooms 1 single, 1 twin, 5 double, 2 family (all en-suite), Restricted smoking, Minimum age 5, Pets by arrangement, Open Easter - end October. Map Ref: J

Helliers Farm, Ashford, Aveton Gifford, Kingsbridge, Devon TQ7 4ND   Nearest Road A379

Helliers Farm is a small working sheep farm situated on a hillside. Dating from 1749 Helliers is set in the heart of Devon's unspoilt countryside, one mile from the village of Aveton Gifford and 4 miles from Kingsbridge. Recently modernised the farmhouse offers spacious accommodation - traditional dining room, comfortable lounge with TV, and a games room. Adjoining the paved courtyard, spring water feeds a water garden and down the hill there is an extensive fish pool. The charming bedrooms all have tea/coffee making facilities, and one of the double rooms is en-suite.

Mrs C Lancaster
Tel: 01548 550689
Fax: 01548 550689

B&B from £16, Rooms 2 double/twin, 1 family (1 en-suite), No smoking, Open all year except Christmas, Map Ref: K

Court Barton Farmhouse, Aveton Gifford, Kingsbridge, Devon TQ7 4LE   **Nearest Road A379**

Court Barton is a 16th century Grade II listed manor house. The farm dates from before Domesday times and is now a small mixed farm. There is a cosy lounge with colour TV and lots of holiday reading. Many of the pleasant bedrooms are en-suite. Central heating throughout with log fires in colder weather. English breakfast, or special diets can be catered for by arrangement. Walking, bird watching, sailing, swimming, golf, tennis and horse riding all close by.

Jill Balkwill
Tel: 01548 550312

B&B from £16, Rooms 2 double, 2 family, 2 twin, 1 single
(most are en-suite), Open all year except Christmas, Map Ref: K

The Sloop Inn, Bantham, Nr Kingsbridge, Devon TQ7 3AT   **Nearest Road A379**

This 400 year old inn by the sea has a history of smuggling. One of its owners was a notorious wrecker, luring ships (by means of lights) onto rocks in order to plunder them. All bedrooms are en-suite, have central heating, TV, and tea/coffee making facilities. There is an extensive menu of fresh fish, shellfish, and local steaks plus a wide selection of homemade sweets. To accompany this there is a good quality wine list and a fine range of draught and bottled beers and ciders. Just 500 yds away is one of the best surfing beaches on the south coast. Also excellent for sand castles!

Mr Neil Girling
Tel: 01548 560489
Fax: 01548 560489

B&B from £25, Dinner from 5.50, Rooms 3 double, 2 family
(all en-suite), Pets by arrangement, Open all year except Christmas
and New Year, Luxury self-catering also available, Map Ref: K

Old Walls, Combe, Nr Salcombe, Kingsbridge, Devon TQ7 3DN   **Nearest Road A381**

Old Walls is a beautiful 17th century traditional cob and thatch cottage set in mature private garden with stream. The hamlet of Combe nestles in a steep sided valley which leads to the beach at South Sands, from there the ferry takes passengers to Salcombe in about 10 minutes (avoiding the hassle of parking). The cottage is set into a hillside and is overlooked by the National Trust Tor Woods. Bread is baked fresh every morning, muesli and preserves are home made and dinner is available by arrangement. Bedrooms are en-suite and have tea trays, and TV.

Barry & Michelle Sames
Tel: 01548 844440

B&B from £16, Dinner from £9.50, Rooms 1 twin, 2 double
(all en-suite), Restricted smoking, Open all year except Christmas,
Map Ref: K

The Thatched Cottage, 9 Crossley Moor Road, Kingsteignton, Newton Abbot, TQ12 3LE   **(A380)**

The Thatched Cottage Restaurant a Grade II listed 16th century thatched longhouse of great character together with a resident friendly ghost! This is a licenced restaurant offering an extensive, and mouth watering menu combined with comfortable bed and breakfast accommodation. Many of the, well appointed, nicely decorated and furnished, bedrooms are en-suite and all have TV and tea/coffee making facilities. A well positioned property for exploring the coast and Dartmoor.

Klaus & Janice Wiemeyer
Tel: 01626 65650

B&B from £16, Dinner from £6.50, Rooms 1 single, 2 double,
1 family, (many en-suite), Restricted smoking, Open all year,
Map Ref: F

Kemerton, Lustleigh, Devon, TQ13 9TG   **Nearest Road A382**

Kemerton is a peaceful and comfortable Edwardian house on the edge of the delightful village of Lustleigh at the foothills of the Dartmoor National Park. It has secluded gardens and glorious views. There are wonderful walks on the doorstep and the coast and open moor are a short drive away. It is the ideal place for a few days break if you want to "get away from it all". Relax and be well looked after.

Mr Tim Daniel
Tel: 016477 340

B&B from £16.50, Dinner from £13.50, Rooms 1 single, 1 twin, 2 double (some en-suite), Restricted smoking, Open all year, Map Ref: L

Southcliffe, Lee Road, Lynton, Devon EX35 6BS   **Nearest Road A39**

This attractive Victorian house, is comfortable, warm, friendly and relaxing. All bedrooms have private bathroom, tea/coffee making facilities, colour TV, and hairdryer. Two rooms have balconies. Food is appetising and the hotel is licensed so you may enjoy wine with your meal and perhaps relax with a drink in the guests' lounge after dinner. Packed lunches can also be provided on request. Lynton is an unspoilt holiday resort which, with its twin town Lynmouth, sits on Devon's north coast. This is a very beautiful part of England's countryside.

June & Adrian Kamp
Tel: 01598 53328
Fax: 01598 53328

B&B from £20, Dinner from £11, Rooms 1 single, 2 twin, 5 double (all with private bathroom), No smoking, Minimum age 8, Pets welcome by arrangement, Open March - October, Map Ref: M

Cross Tree House, Moretonhampstead, Devon TQ13 8NL   **Nearest Road B3212**

Cross Tree House is situated at the edge of the village adjoining National Trust land and next to the famous granite Almshouses dating back to 1637 and below the 15th century St Andrew's church. The listed house, which gets its name from the old dancing tree and ancient stone cross at its entrance, has a fine Georgian staircase and wings which date back to Tudor times. The bedrooms are spacious and furnished in style. All have en-suite or private bath and tea/coffee making facilities. Lounge with colour TV shared with owners.

Mr & Mrs S R Landor
Tel: 01647 440726

B&B from £18, Dinner from £14, Rooms 2 twin with en-suite facilities, 1 double with private facilities, Pets welcome by arrangement, Open March - December, Map Ref: N

Great Sloncombe Farm, Moretonhampstead, Devon TQ13 8QF   **Nearest Road A382**

Great Sloncombe is a 13th century listed granite and cob built Dartmoor farmhouse which has been sympathetically restored and traditionally furnished. The farm with its 170 acres is set in a peaceful valley with beautiful meadows and woodland that provide habitat for a variety of wildlife. Guests are welcome to watch the farming activities. All bedrooms are en-suite with every facility provided for an enjoyable country break. Breakfast and dinner are served in the small, cosy dining room and many of the ingredients used are home produce.

Trudie, Robert, Helen
Merchant
Tel: 01647 440595

B&B from £18, Dinner from £9, Rooms 2 double, 1 twin, Minimum age 8, No smoking, Open all year. Map Ref: N

Penpark, Bickington, Newton Abbot, Devon TQ12 6LH   **Nearest Road A38**

Penpark is a beautiful and elegant country house designed by the famous arthitect Clough Williams Ellis. It has magnificent hill top views, 5 acres of secluded gardens and woodland, a hard tennis court and is situated within Dartmoor National Park. Guests have a large and luxurious room with balcony overlooking the peaceful woodland gardens. There are twin beds which can be zipped together making a kingsize double, washbasin, colour TV, tea/coffee making facilities, , sofa and chairs. There is a single room next door and a private bathroom.

Mrs Madeleine Gregson
Tel: 01626 821314
Fax: 01626 821101

B&B from £20, Dinner from £10 (by arrangement), Rooms 1 single. 1 twin/double with private bathroom, No smoking, Open all year, Map Ref: F

Lower Elsford Cottage, Bovey Tracey, Newton Abbot, Devon TQ13 9NY   **Nearest Road A382**

Lower Elsford Cottage is very pretty, 17th century stone cottage, full of character with spectacular views. Set high above the Wrey Valley in a peaceful setting giving views of the wooded valley across to Dartmoor and the village of Lustleigh. The charming bedrooms are well appointed one being en-suite. A full English breakfast is provided. Ideally situated for touring, walking and fishing in the nearby reservoirs.

Pauline & Eden Griffiths
Tel: 016477 408

B&B from £17, Rooms 1 single, 1 en-suite double, No smoking, Minimum age 8, Pets by arrangement, Open all year, Map Ref: F

Sampsons Farm, Preston, Newton Abbot, Devon TQ12 3PP   **Nearest Roads A38, A380, B3193**

Thatched 14th century longhouse with oak beams, panelling and inglenook fireplaces. Sampsons is a Grade II listed building, low beams, creaky floors and hidden away in the hamlet of Preston with lovely walks along River Teign. Always a warm welcome and a cheerful atmosphere. All rooms have tea/coffee making facilities, and colour TV. The restaurant has an excellent reputation with only the finest produce being used. There is a licensed bar and cellar containing wines from around the world. Sampsons is well placed to explore Devon and Cornwall.

Nigel & Hazel Bell
Tel: 01626 54913
Fax: 01626 54913

B&B from £15, Dinner from £6.95, Rooms 3 double, 2 family Open all year, Map Ref: F

Howards Gorhuish, Northlew, Devon EX20 3BT   **Nearest Road A30**

Howards Gorhuish is a pretty pink 16th century Devon longhouse with beams and inglenook fireplaces - log fires are lit on cooler days. Enjoying spectacular views of Dartmoor it is surrounded by gardens, orchards and flower filled meadows where geese, ducks and chickens range. Northlew is situated in the rural and picturesque heart of Devon - ideally situated between Dartmoor and Exmoor and mid-way between the north and south coast beaches. The RHS garden at Rosemoor and many National Trust properties are within an easy drive. A car is essential.

Paul & Heather Richards
Tel: 01837 53301

B&B from £18, Dinner from £10, Rooms 1 single, 1 twin, 2 en-suite double, No smoking, Minimum age 10, Pets by arrangement, Open all year except Christmas and new year, Map Ref: O

Elberry Farm, Broadsands, Paignton, Devon TQ4 6HJ   Nearest Road A3022

Elberry Farm is a working farm with beef, poultry and arable production. The farmhouse is between 2 beaches both within a 2 minute walk. Broadsands being a safe bathing beach has been awarded the European Blue Flag 1994. As an alternative there is a 9 hole pitch and putt golf course opposite; and a short drive away there is the zoo, town centre and the National Park. The comfortable bedrooms all have tea/coffee making facilities. Guests are welcome to relax in the lounge; and stroll around the secluded garden. Baby sitting service available by arrangement.

Mrs Mandy Tooze
Tel: 01803 842939

B&B from £13, Dinner from £5.50, Rooms 1 twin, 3 double/family, Restricted smoking, Pets by arrangement, Open January - November, Map Ref: P

Jubilee Cottage, 75 Chapel Street, Sidbury, Devon EX10 0RQ   Nearest Road A375

Jubilee Cottage with its thatched roof, thick Devon cob walls and delightful gardens with open view of the Sid Valley and Buckley Hill dates back to the 16th century. Bedrooms all have central heating, drink making facilities, radio, hairdryer, etc. There is a separate guests' bathroom as well as a separate guests' shower room. The guests' lounge has inglenook fireplace, colour TV, an assortment of games, and tourist information. The dining room with inglenook fireplace offers traditional English and international cuisine.

Marianne & Bob Coles
Tel: 01395 597295

B&B from £16, Dinner from £10, Rooms 2 twin, 2 double, No smoking, Minimum age 9, Open all year, Map Ref: Q

Otter House, Harpford, Nr Sidmouth, Devon EX10 0NH   Nearest Road A3052

Otter House is a 16th Century Grade II listed house with stunning views across the Otter Valley, on the edge of Harpford. Harpford is a very picturesque hamlet 3 miles from Sidmouth and the sea, just off the A3052 and about 10 miles from the Cathedral city of Exeter. There are wonderful walks from the hamlet through the peaceful east Devon countryside and nearby Sidmouth is an unspoiled seaside town with 'olde worlde' charm. There are 2 comfortable bedrooms which share a private bathroom and both have tea/coffee making facilities.

Mrs Joanna Vollers
Tel: 01395 568330

B&B from £17.50, Rooms 1 twin, 1 double, No smoking, Open all year, Map Ref: R

Cheriton Guest House, Vicarage Road, Sidmouth, Devon EX10 8UQ   Nearest Road A3052

Cheriton Guest House is a large town house which backs on to the River Sid, with the 'Byes' parkland beyond. There are private parking spaces at the rear. The half mile walk to the seafront, via the town centre, is all on level ground. Cheriton is notorious for its fine cooking and varied menus. There is a comfortable lounge with colour TV. Beautiful secluded rear garden for the exclusive use of guests. All bedrooms have central heating, colour TV and tea/coffee making facilities and most rooms are en-suite.

Diana & John Lee
Tel: 01395 513810

B&B from £18 pp, Dinner from £7, Rooms 3 single, 5 double/twin, 2 family, (most en-suite), Restricted smoking, Pets welcome by arrangement, Open all year, Map Ref: S

Fonthill, Torquay Road, Shaldon, Teignmouth, Devon TQ14 0AX   **Nearest Road B3199**

Fonthill is peacefully situated 2 minutes from the delightful village of Shaldon where there are 5 village pubs and several excellent restaurants. Spacious and beautiful grounds with views of the sea, river and Dartmoor. There is also a hard tennis court. The coastal path to Torquay is a few minutes away as is an 18 hole golf course and Shaldon Wildlife Trust. Dartmoor National Park is within easy reach, also Exeter and Plymouth and several fine National Trust properties.

Mrs Jennifer Graeme
Tel: 01626 872344
Fax: 01626 872344

B&B from £22, Rooms 3 twin with private or en-suite bathroom, No smoking, No pets, Open all year, Map Ref: T

Hornhill, Exeter Hill, Tiverton, Devon EX16 4PL   **Nearest Road A361, M5**

Originally an 18th century coaching inn situated at the top of a hill with panoramic views overlooking the Exe Valley. Set amidst 75 acres of farmland and surrounded by mature gardens. Here you will find comfort, warmth, excellent food and a happy relaxed atmosphere. The bedrooms have private bathrooms, tea/coffee making facilities, TV and one has a Victorian 4-poster bed. The ground floor double room has an en-suite shower room and is suitable for the partially disabled. A perfect base for touring. ETB 2 Crowns Highly Commended, AA 5Q Premier Selected.

Barbara Pugsley
Tel: 01884 253352

B&B from £17.50, Dinner from £12 by arrangement, Rooms 2 double, 1 twin (with private bathrooms), Minimum age 12, No smoking, Open all year, Map Ref: U

Great Bradley Farm, Withleigh, Tiverton, Devon EX16 8JL   **Nearest Road B3137**

Great Bradley is a dairy farm of 155 acres. The 16th century farmhouse, once owned by Lord de Bradleigh in medieval times, still retains its original oak screens and cruck beams. The centrally heated bedrooms are comfortable and attractive with tea/coffee facilities, and private bathrooms. The guests' lounge with TV and books overlooks the garden and beautiful view towards Dartmoor. Delicious tempting dinners; traditional or light breakfast. An excellent touring base for the charming villages, historic cities and Nat Parks of Devon and Somerset. Highly Commended WCTB.

Mrs Sylvia Hann
Tel 01884 256946

B&B from £35, Dinner from £10 by arrangement, Rooms, 1 twin, 1 double (private bathroom), NO SMOKING, Minimum age 10, Open March to October, Map Ref: U

Sandunes Guest House, Beach Road, Woolacombe, Devon EX34 7BT   **Nearest Road A361**

Sandunes is a small guest house situated within 5 minutes walk of Woolacombe Sands and village, with outstanding views of the sea and National Trust land. Woolacombe itself is an ideal base for touring the area, with a superb sandy beach, for those wish to relax, but within easy reach of Ilfracombe, Lynton and Lynmouth, Barnstaple, Clovelly and Exmoor. All bedrooms are en-suite and have tea/coffee making facilities, some have sea views. Comfortable guests' lounge and sun patio.

Jean & Charles Boorman
Tel: 01271 870661

B&B from £16, Dinner £9.50, Rooms 1 single, 1 twin, 5 double, (all en-suite), No smoking, No children, No Pets Open March to October, Map Ref: V

Sunnycliffe Hotel, Chapel Hill, Mortehoe, Woolacombe, Devon EX34 7EB **Nearest Road A361**

Small award winning quality hotel set above picturesque Devon Cove on heritage coast. All bedrooms have sea views, colour TV, tea/coffee making facilities, and are en-suite. Delicious traditional English food by highly qualified proprietor chef. Plenty of walks through hidden valleys, coastal paths where countryside greets the sea in breathtaking scenic beauty. Regret no children or pets. Brochure available.

Mr & Mrs V B Bassett
Tel: 01271 870597

B&B from £25, Dinner from£15, Rooms 6 double, 2 twin,
Minimum age 12, Restricted smoking, Open February - November,
Map Ref: V

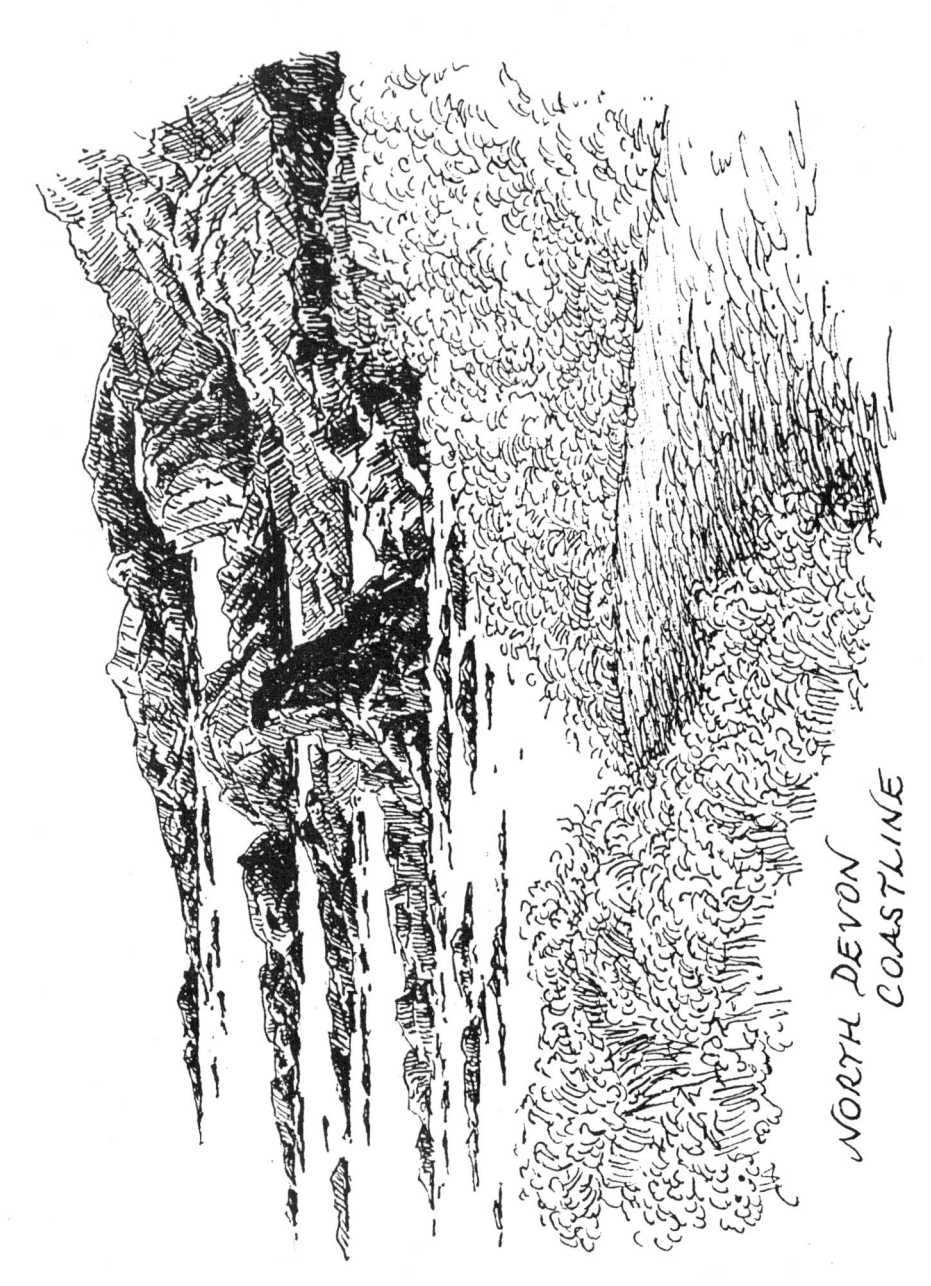

NORTH DEVON COASTLINE

DORSET

"In zummer when the sheades do creep
Below the Zunday steeple, round
The mossy stwones, that love cut deep
Wi neames that tongues noo mwore do sound
the Leane do lose the stalken team,
An' dry-rimm'd waggon-wheels be still,
An' hills do roll their down-shot stream
Below the resten wheel at mill.
O holy day, when tweil do cease,
Sweet day o'rest an' greace an' peace."

(William Barnes - A Dorset Sunday)

DORSET

THOMAS HARDY'S COTTAGE, BOCKHAMPTON.

So beautiful is the county of Dorset that it has been almost entirely designated as an Area of Outstanding Natural Beauty. It has a wealth of rolling chalk hills and fertile green valleys. Its villages of thatch and golden sandstone contrast with the large lively resorts.

Dorset has remained a rural county mainly because it has not been carved up by major roads. Even the seaside resorts have kept their character along with the villages and country towns.

Dorset has never been better captured than in the writings of Thomas Hardy - the country of Tess of the d'Urbervilles, Jude the Obscure, Far From the Madding Crowd and Wessex Tales. Thomas Hardy country is the heathland of mid Dorset where the novelist lived all his life. Hardy was born in Higher Bockhampton, near Dorchester and the neighbouring village of Stinsford is the original Mellstock of his novel Under the Greenwood Tree. Mid Dorset's wild stretch of bracken and briars, Winfrith Heath is the Egdon Heath described in Hardy's Return of the Native. The church at Bere Regis has become a place of pilgrimage for admirers of Hardy's novel, Tess of the d'Urbervilles. Its heroine Tess was buried there and a 15th century window bears the crest of the old Dorset family of Turberville on whom Hardy based his novel.

In the heart of mid Dorset is Dorchester, a bustling county town and shopping centre. The lines of its main road were laid by the Romans and there is plenty of other evidence of Roman life in the town.

GOLD HILL, SHAFTSBURY.

At Milton Abbas thatched cottages line the street of this 18th century model village while Wool, a mellow village on the River Frome, has one of the most beautiful 17th century bridges in the county. Along the coast are unspoilt chalk cliffs and the notable beauty spot of Lulworth Cove. Here the cliffs suddenly end and Portland and Purbeck stone almost encircle a lake of water. The climb and walk westwards leads to Man O'War Bay and the huge limestone arch, Durdle Door, jutting out into the sea.

Rolling chalk hills stretch to the sea in West Dorset. from South of Sherborne to Lyme Regis. Sherborne is an ideal place from which to explore the area. Close by are the remains of ancient tracks and earthworks cut from the chalk, including the Cerne Abbas Giant, cut out of the turf about 1,500 years ago. Sherborne abounds in old inns and 16th and 17th century houses built in the same golden stone as the town's imposing abbey which has one of the most graceful fan-vaulted roofs in England. Sherborne Old Castle, where Sir Walter Raleigh lived for 5 years, is now a ruin while Sherborne New Castle is rich in art treasures.

Lyme Regis, once a medieval port, became a seaside resort in the 18th century, earning its royal title when Edward I used its harbour during the war against the French. The resort was a favourite of the novelist Jane Austen, who set part of Persuasion in the town. Lyme Regis and neighbouring Charmouth are a paradise for fossil collectors. The constantly crumbling cliffs are formed of shale and beds of limestone and in them are sea animals with shells that lived 100 to 320 million years ago.

Portland, the two mile wide mass of rock which stretches into the sea was called by Thomas Hardy "the Gibraltar of Wessex". The peninsula is scarred with quarries - the Portland stone has been used for buildings ever since Sir Christopher Wren used it for St Paul's Cathedrral in London. Portland's highest point at 496ft gives good views to the West along Chesil Beach. The long blue-clay reef lying the ten miles from Abbotsbury to Portland is covered with a wall of shingle. This natural sea wall encloses a long body of water known as the Fleet.

The undulating country of North East Dorset reflects rural tranquillity. Shaftesbury, built on the edge of a 700ft plateau, has fine views over the Blackmoor Vale and figures under its old name, Shaston, in Hardy's novels. Grey-green sandstone houses line the steep, cobbled gold Hill. There are numerous other little farming villages.

East Dorset is an area of contrasts from rich agricultural land to wild heathland and bleak and high hills.

Poole, Dorset's largest town has a harbour with an 18th century atmosphere. Swanage is a busy holiday resort. Once a Saxon port, it is referred to in the Domesday Book as Swanic.

The handsome Georgian town of Blandford Forum was burnt to the ground in 1731 and its buildings in Market Street, East Street and Salisbury Street are well designed in red or rust brick and stone.

The prosperity of the little market town of Wimborne Minster was based on wool but now comes from market gardening.

DORSET

Bere Marsh House, Shillingstone, Blandford, Dorset DT11 0QY   Nearest Road A357

Dorset cob built family home over 200 years old with inglenooks, bread ovens and old fireplaces. Set in its own 2 acres with tennis court and a summer house overlooking a rock garden. The large conservatory breakfast room is adorned by a mature grape vine and there is also a dining room with mahogany tables. Felicity runs a small licensed restaurant and creates wonderful freshly made dishes. This is the place to go and enjoy a superb gourmet dinner with courses like chateaubriand or breast of duck with bagarde sauce followed by baklova or banoffi pie.

James & Felicity Roe
Tel: 01258 861133

B&B from £17, Dinner from £12, Rooms 1 twin, 1 double with tea/coffee making facilities, Minimum age 6, Pets by arrangement, Open February - December, Map Ref: A

Sandhurst Hotel, 16 Southern Road, Southbourne, Bournemouth, Dorset BH6 3SR   Nearest Road A35

A small private hotel in a tree lined road, 2 minutes walk from the cliff lift and sandy beach of Southbourne a quiet suburb of Bournemouth with its many theatres, cinemas, shops and restaurants. A warm friendly atmosphere with high standards. Large comfortable bedrooms all have colour TV, with one being on the ground floor. Guest lounge and ample car parking. Colin is an accomplished artist and his pictures can be seen and purchased. Jean prepares a good value traditional evening meal which is optional. Lovely displays of flower tubs and hanging baskets complete this well kept hotel.

Colin & Jean Du Faur
Tel: 01202 423748

B&B from £16, Dinner from £6.50, Rooms: 1 single, 2 twin, 3 double, 2 family (most en-suite), All with tea/coffee making facilities, Restricted smoking, Open March to November, Map Ref: B

Silver Trees, 57 Wimborne Road, Bournemouth, Dorset BH3 7AL   Nearest Road A347

A charming Victorian house standing in wooded grounds with sweeping lawns, colourful flowers and shrubs. There is car parking available for 10 cars. All bedrooms are en-suite and have tea/coffee making facilities, as well as colour TV. Nearby activities include the beach and the town centre is only 1 mile away. Silver Trees is graded AA 4Q and RAC Acclaimed.

Jo & Bill Smith
Tel: 01202 556040
Fax: 01202 556040

B&B from £19, Rooms: 2 double, 2 twin, 1 family (all en-suite), Minimum age 5, Open all year, Map Ref: B

Britmead House, West Bay Road, Bridport, Dorset DT6 4EG   Nearest Road A35

Britmead is a small licensed hotel with a reputation for friendliness, hospitality and high standards and is pleasantly located just a short walk from the harbour of West Bay. Most of the 7 spacious rooms are en-suite and have colour TV, radio clock alarm, hairdryer, tea/coffee making facilities, and a mini bar. The lounge and dining room overlook the garden beyond which is open countryside. There is a car park. Food is renowned for its excellence using local fresh produce when possible. Swimming, golf, seafishing and walks are all nearby. ETB 3 Crown Commended.

Ann & Dan Walker
Tel: 01308 422941

B&B from £19, Dinner £12, Rooms 4 double, 3 twin (most en-suite) Open all year, Map Ref: C

Lamperts, Sydling St Nicholas, Near Cerne Abbas, Dorset DT2 9NU   **Nearest Road A37**

16th century thatched listed farmhouse with stream running in front. Situated in a peaceful village in the beautiful Sydling Valley. Bedrooms are prettily decorated with dormer windows. Breakfast is served in the dining room which has an Inglenook fireplace, bread oven and beams. Guests have their own sitting room with TV, central heating and tea/coffee makers. West Dorset is an ideal touring centre with beaches. The countryside is excellent for walking with footpaths over chalk hills and through hidden valleys. Guidebooks and maps available to borrow.

Nicky Willis - 01300 341659
Rita Bown - 01300 341790

B&B from £17, Dinner from £10, Rooms 2 double, 2 twin, 1 family (many en-suite), Open all year including Christmas, Map Ref: D

The Creek, Ringstead, Dorchester, Dorset DT2 8NG   **Nearest Road A353**

Ringstead is situated on the Heritage Coastal path approximately 7 miles from both Weymouth and Dorchester. It is within easy reach of many important National Trust properties and is ideally situated for artists, bird watchers, walkers and watersport enthusiasts. The house has a large garden overlooking the seashore and surrounded by farmland. There is full central heating and showers in all bedrooms and a spacious sitting room and comfortable dining room. Gourmet evening meals available by arrangement. A heated swimming pool during summer months.

Mrs Fisher
Tel: 01305 852251

B&B from £17.50, Dinner from £9, Rooms 2 double, Minimum age 8, No smoking, No pets, Open all year, Map Ref: E

Lower Lewell Farmhouse, West Stafford, Dorchester, Dorset DT2 8AP   **Nearest Road A35, A352**

A 17th century farmhouse authentically improved and situated among a patchwork of fields in rolling Dorset countryside. Reputed to be Talbothays Dairy from Thomas Hardy's "Tess of the D'Urbervilles". Built in Portland stone under a red tiled roof with a Victorian brick and slate extension, this is a homely farmhouse with beams, log fires and plenty of space. Hearty breakfasts from the farmhouse kitchen are served at separate tables in the dining room with Inglenook fireplace. There is a good local pub offering snacks and restaurant meals.

Mrs Marian Tomblin
Tel: 01305 267169

B&B from £15, Rooms 1 twin, 1 double, 1 family all with tea/coffee making facilities, TV lounge, Open all year, Map Ref: E

Vartrees House, Moreton, Dorchester, Dorset DT2 8BE   **Nearest Road B3390, A35**

A peaceful, secluded, character country house built by a friend of Thomas Hardy, set in 3 acres of picturesque woodland gardens which attract wildlife. Accommodation enjoyed by guests is spacious and comfortable. Tea/coffee making facilities in all rooms. Situated near the pretty village of Moreton with its renowned church and burial place of Lawrence of Arabia. Excellent local pubs nearby.

Mrs D M Haggett
Tel: 01305 852704

B&B from £30, Rooms 2 double, 1 twin, Minimum age 10, Pets by arrangement, Open all year, Map Ref: E

Churchview Guest House, Winterbourne Abbas, Dorchester, Dorset DT2 9LS   **Nearest Road A35**

This 17th century licenced guest house noted for warm, friendly hospitality, traditional breakfasts and delicious evening meals, makes an ideal base for touring beautiful West Dorset. Our character bedrooms are comfortable and well appointed. Meals are taken in our beautiful period dining room, with relaxation provided by two lounges, one non-smoking, and well stocked bar. Your hosts, Jane and Michael Deller, will be pleased to give every assistance with local information on attractions, walks and touring to ensure you of a memorable stay at Churchview.

Michael & Jane Deller   **B&B from £18, Dinner from £10, Many bedrooms are en-suite,**
Tel: 01305 889296   **Restricted smoking, Open all year except Christmas, Map Ref: E**

Apple Tree Cottage, Fifehead Magdalen, Gillingham, Dorset SP8 5RT   **Nearest Road A30**

This is a quietly situated modern stone built house situated in an attractive Dorset hamlet. Well maintained and decorated in pastel shades with comfortable traditional furnishings. Convenient for visiting Bath, Stourhead, Longleat, Sherborne, etc. The south facing double room as open countryside views and the larger twin share a modern bathroom with shower. Moira enjoys cooking and is happy to discuss breakfast and dinner menus and will be pleased to serve favourite dishes with prior notice. There is parking and a small garden. A friendly service is assured.

Mrs Moira Wootton   **B&B from £17.50, Dinner by arrangement from £12, Rooms: 1 twin,**
Tel: 01258 820689   **1 double, All rooms have tea/coffee making facilities, Dogs by**
    arrangement, Open all year, Map Ref: F

The Beehive, Church Lane, Osmington, Dorset DT3 6EL   **Nearest Road A353**

The quaint village of Osmington with its enchanting array of pretty stone and thatched cottages like, "The Beehive" is probably one of Dorset's best kept secrets. This is an area of great natural beauty with scenic coastal and inland walks. Mary is a most convivial host having lead an interesting life working in Africa for some years. Light suppers of imaginative soups with local cheese, bread and fruit. In winter Dorset dinners are offered using local recipes of tipsy rabbit or long piddle lamb followed by Tyneham pears or buttered oranges, served around the cosy kitchen table.

Mary Kempe   **B&B from £15, Light suppers from £4.50, Dinner from £9.00, Rooms 1**
Tel: 01305 834095   **twin, 2 double (1 en-suite), all with tea/coffee makers, No smoking,**
    Min. age 6, Pets by arrangement, Open Feb - Dec. Map Ref: G

Almshouse Farm, Hermitage, Sherborne, Dorset DT9 6HA   **Nearest Road A352**

This charming, listed, old farmhouse was a monastery during the 16th century and was restored in 1849. A family run working dairy farm surrounded by 160 acres overlooking the Blackmore Vale. Accommodation is in 3 comfortable rooms with private or en-suite facilities and have tea/coffee makers. Dining room with Inglenook fireplace and separate tables, lounge with TV for guests use. Large garden and spacious lawns. Plenty of local information provided for this area. Situated 6 miles from Sherborne with its Abbey and castles and 15 miles from Dorchester.

Mrs Jenny Mayo   **B&B from £16, Rooms 1 double, 1 twin, 1 double/twin (private/en-**
Tel: 01963 210296   **suite), No pets, Open all year, Map Ref: H**

Stourcastle Lodge, Gough's Close, Sturminster Newton, Dorset DT10 1BU   **Nearest Road B3092**

Built in 1732 this residence offers very high standards and quality throughout. The bedrooms have impressive Victorian bedsteads, stencilled borders, antique furniture and modern well equipped bathrooms some with whirlpool baths. Peacefully situated down a lane yet moments from the town centre or fields and riverside walks. Oak beams, log fires and view of the lovely garden from every room. Jill is a gold medallist chef so with dishes like baked poussin with creamy curry sauce followed by boozy bread and butter pudding this is an excellent place to both stay and eat.

Ken & Jill Hookham-Bassett
Tel: 01258 472320
Fax: 01258 473381

B&B from £20, Dinner from £15, Rooms 2 twin, 2 double, 1 family (all en-suite) all have tea/coffee making facilities, Restricted smoking Open all year, Map Ref: I

Lovells court, Marnhull, Sturminster Newton, Dorset DT10 1JJ   **Nearest Road A303, A30**

Lovells Court is a rambling country house of character furnished with antique pine and offering spacious en-suite accommodation. It is situated in the peaceful village of Marnhull, commanding fine views across the Blackmore Vale. There are many villages and towns of interest nearby offering good food. This makes an excellent base for discovering Dorset and Somerset. Nearby places of interest include the market town of Sturminster Newton, Abbeys of Sherborne and Milton Abbas, Salisbury and Wells Cathedrals, National Trust properties, Bath,. etc.

Mrs Mary Ann Newson-Smith
Tel: 01258 820652
Fax: 01258 820487

B&B from £20, Rooms 2 double, 1 twin, No smoking, No pets, Open all year including Christmas, Map Ref: I

Bucknowle House, Bucknowle, Wareham, Dorset BH20 5PQ   **Nearest Road A351**

Bucknowle is a large Victorian house, midway between Corfe Castle and Church Knowle on the Isle of Purbeck, with extensive views across the Corfe Valley. The three bedrooms have recently been decorated and all have en-suite facilities. Breakfast is served in the spacious dining room which has views across the garden to the Valley and Corfe Common. Ideally situated for exploring the magnificent Dorset coastline as well as the many interesting historical sites and monuments in the area. Golf, swimming, sailing, fishing, riding and walking all to hand.

Mr & Mrs R N Harvey
Tel: 01929 480352
Fax: 01929 481275

B&B from £20, Rooms 2 double, 1 twin (all en-suite), Open all year, Map Ref: J

The Old Granary, The Quay, Wareham, Dorset BH20 4LP   **Nearest Road A351**

This 250 year old former grain store nestles beside the River Frome and the Quay in this interesting old town. On the restaurant menu fresh grilled sea bass followed by raspberry mousse are popular choices. The bedrooms are beamed on the two upper floors and have bathrooms. Scenic water colours by a local artist cover the walls. The restaurant, with swagged curtains and riverside terrace full of flower baskets and tubs makes, a delightful setting to enjoy drinks and cream teas with food served all day. Staff are friendly and efficient. Mooring, boat hire and trips arranged locally.

Mr & Mrs D Sturton
Tel: 01929 552010
Fax: 01929 552482

B&B from £19.50, Dinner from £13.95, Rooms 2 double, 2 twin (many are en-suite) all have tea/coffee making facilities, No smoking, Open all year. Map Ref: J

Essex

"This is the land that the sea mists muffle,
This is the land where the marsh-creeks fill,
Green-lit dawns that the black wings ruffle,
Smoke-red tides where the sunsets spill.

This is the land where the farmsteads muster,
Field on field till the sky sweeps down,
Where the earth lies bare to the bold winds' bluster
And the trees sing shrill on the hills' low crown.

(. . .)

This is the land where the old lanes ramble,
Cloudy with dust in the heat of June,
Where September's hedgerows are brave with bramble
And the grasses sing to the streams' thin tune.

This is the land where London's river
Breaks from its channel to seek the sea,
Where the flat fields fade and the first waves quiver,
And the wide skies light and the winds fly free."

(N Longhurst - Essex)

ESSEX

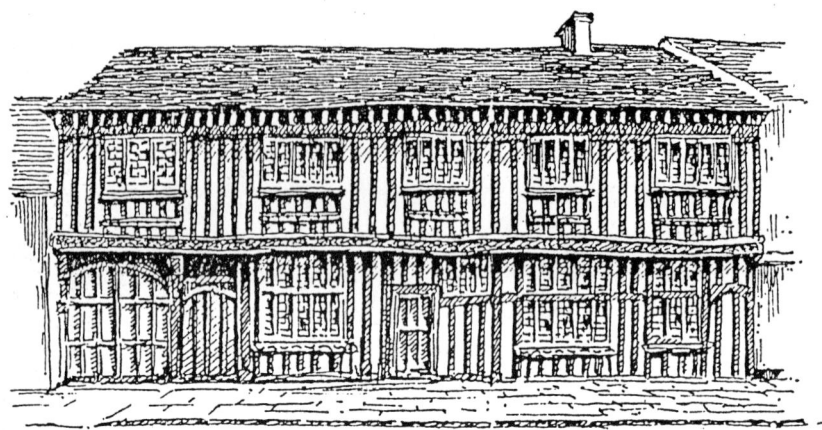

PAYCOCKE'S HOUSE, COGGESHALL.

Essex is a county of many parts. The South of the county between London and Chelmsford can be divided into three. On the fringe of Greater London is Epping Forest, covering almost 6,000 acres, the remnant of a 60,000 acre hunting ground of Saxon, Norman and Tudor kings. Epping, now a busy little market town, dates from the 13th century and was once an important coaching centre and some of the old coaching inns still survive along the attractive main street. Epping's long High Street follows the line of one of the 'purlieu banks' that marked the edge of Epping Forest, which extends for 270 acres north of the town. In contrast to the rough heaths and trees of the forest is the built-up area along the Thames from Purfleet to Shoeburyness, including Southend with its pier and illuminations - London's own Blackpool. Sweeping north from Shoeburyness to the Blackwater estuary, and peculiar to the area, is the coastal belt of marsh reclaimed from the sea by the Dutch in the 17th century. Behind the sea wall the miles of mudflats, saltings and remote islands are a haven for wildlife.

Esssex's county town, Chelmsford, has lost much of its rural charm to housing and industrial development but some early buildings survive, such as the Church of St Mary the Virgin, which became a cathedral in 1914. Only two miles west of the city centre is Writtle, which has one of the loveliest greens in the county. Maldon is one of the county's least spoilt old towns. Lying on the rivers Chelmer and Blackwater, it is important yachting centre and home of the Thames sailing barges which can be seen by the Hythe quay. It stands on a hill where Brythnoth's Anglo-Danish troops were defeated by the Viking invaders in AD 991. All Saints' Church has the only triangular tower in England. Granted a Royal Charter in 1171, the town has many other interesting old buildings.

Essex has numerous seaside resorts. Southend-on-Sea has seven miles of beach-lined promenades, fringed with pretty parks, elegant esplanades and lively amusements. It has the longest pleasure pier in the world with unique pier trains. The resort was winner of the Tidy Britain Group Seaside award for cleanliness of beach and water at East Beach, Shoeburyness and Three Shells Beach. Clacton-on-Sea's South facing seven mile long sandy beach forms the sunshine holiday coast of Essex. The strikingly clean town has tree lined streets and

SAFFRON WALDEN

colourful gardens. Nearby Holland-on-Sea has good sandy beaches which are usually quieter than Clacton. Frinton-on-Sea is for the more energetic. It has a first class golf course plus excellent cricket, tennis and squash facilities. Burnham-on-Crouch is the largest town in the area known as the Dengie Hundred, a peninsula stretching into the North Sea, bounded by the River Blackwater in the north and the River Crouch in the south. Dating back to prehistoric times it has maintained its strong maritime flavour which still earns it the title of the "Pearl of the East Coast".

The focus of North East Essex is Colchester, one of the greatest Roman fortress cities in England after London. The town is a marvellous mix of the old and new with centuries old streets blending in with modern shopping centres. Colchester's famed history is everywhere from parts of the original Roman wall to the Norman castle keep, the largest in Britain. Over the centuries Colchester has been a great centre for weaving and Britain's oyster trade.

Both Braintree and Coggeshall were wool centres. Braintree now depends on the manufacture of silk and other textiles. Coggeshall is on the route of the old Roman Stane Street and among its many fine old houses is Paycocke's, a well known wool merchant's house of 1500.

The ancient town of Saffron Walden has revolved around its market for many generations. The medieval market rows are well preserved and there are many timber-framed buildings, many decorated by the traditional pargetting. The Saffron Crocus can be seen flowering outside the town's museum in the autumn.. The town made its wealth from saffron and wool.

To the South are the Rodings, a group of farming villages along the valley of the River Roding, rich in half timbered houses, moated manor farms and ancient churches. The Victorian novelist Anthony Trollope loved 'the Roothings' as Essex people call them, and hunted there each winter.

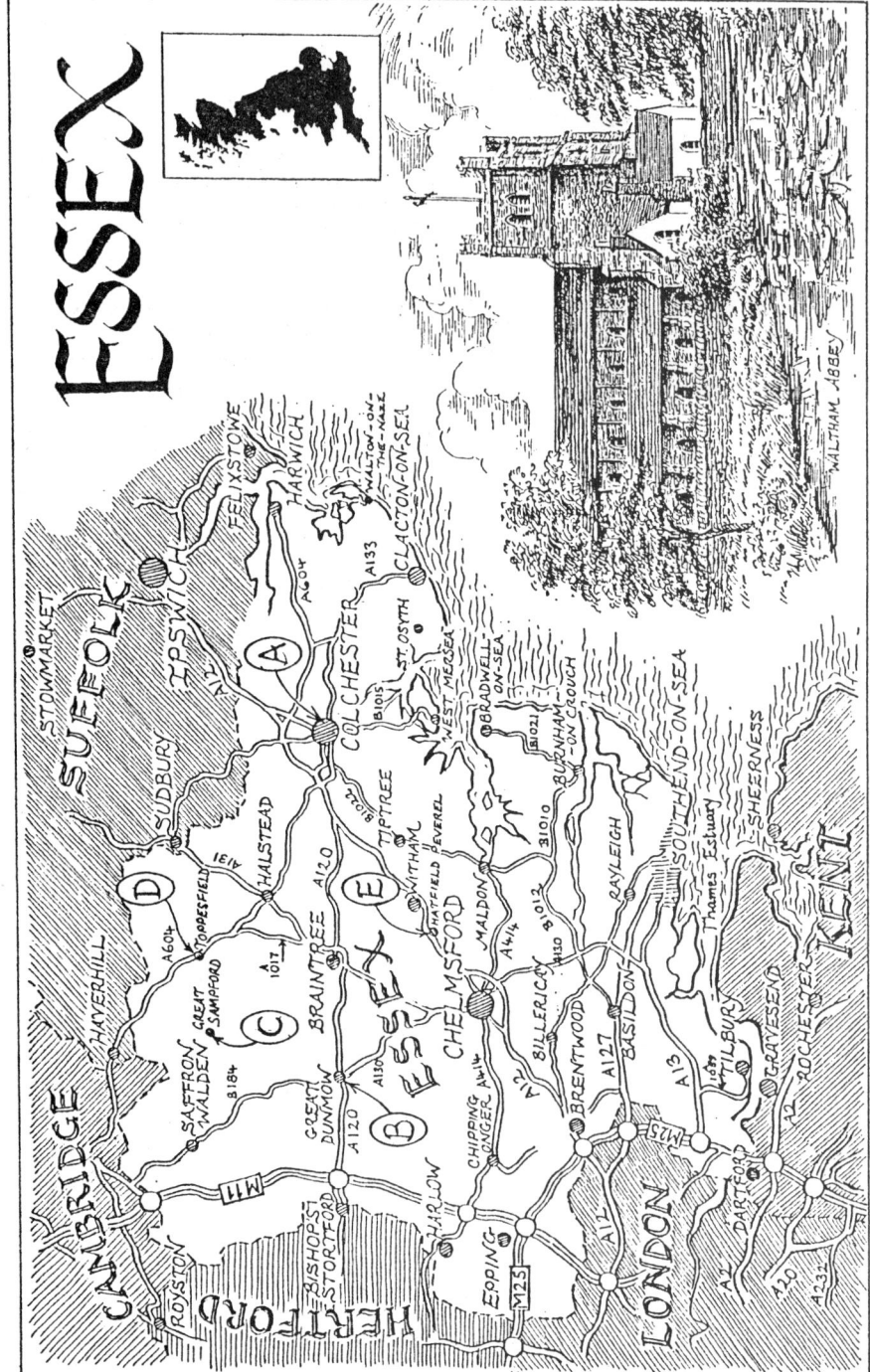

The Bauble, Higham, Colchester, Essex CO7 6LA **Nearest Road A12**

The Bauble is a period property carefully modernised and lying on the edge of the picturesque hamlet of Higham in the heart of Constable country and Dedham Vale. Guests are invited to relax in 1½ acres of lovely gardens, play tennis or swim in the heated pool. The accommodation is attractive and comfortable with antiques throughout. Bedrooms have, colour TV, radio, tea/coffee trays, and all rooms have private or en-suite facilities. In winter the guests' sitting room enjoys a log fire.

Mr & Mrs N Watkins
Tel: 01206-37254
Fax: 01206 37263

B&B from £120 Rooms 1 single, 2 twin, (all have private or en-suite facilities), Minimum age 12, Open all year, Map Ref: A

Greys, Margaret Roding, Nr Great Dunmow, Essex CM6 1QR **Nearest Road A1060**

'Greys' was formerly two cottages and now has three double rooms for guests, one with twin beds. Pleasantly situated on the family farm - arable and sheep. The house is beamed throughout, with dining and sitting rooms, and large garden. Ideal for short breaks, exploring and relaxing. Discover the Essex countryside, its history, pretty villages, old towns, creeks and estuaries. Please check the map - we are eight miles from Gt Dunmow; just off the A1060 - Bishops Stortford to Chelmsford Road (by telephone kiosk in the village), Half mile along, second house on left.

Mrs Joyce Matthews
Tel: 01245 231509

B&B from £16, Rooms 1 twin, 2 double, No smoking, Minimum age 10, Open all year except Christmas, Map Ref: B

The Stow, Great Sampford, Essex CB10 2RG **Nearest Road B1053, A184**

The Stow is a 16th century farmhouse with an attractive garden leading onto open fields for walks and is situated in the delightful village of Great Sampford between Thaxted and Saffron Walden. It provides an excellent base from which to tour East Anglia. Historic Audley End is nearby and Cambridge and Newmarket half an hour away. Bedrooms have either private or en-suite bathroom with tea/coffee making facilities. There is a charming sitting room with colour TV for the use of guests and a warm welcome is assured by Arthur and Susan Collins.

Arthur & Susan Collins
Tel: 01799 586354

B&B from £22.50, Supper from £10, Rooms 2 twin, 1 single
Open all year, Map Ref: C

Olliver's Farm, Toppesfield, Halstead Essex CO9 4LS **Nearest Road A604**

A very interesting 16th century farmhouse with historic American connections, in quiet idyllic situation. Comfortable bedrooms all with tea/coffee making facilities and one is en-suite. The garden is **'a must'** for garden lovers and is open under the National Gardens Scheme 3 times a year. Although dinner is not available at present at Ollivers there are excellent restaurants and pubs within 5 miles. Ideally placed for visiting Cambridge, Newmarket, and Colchester Britain's oldest recorded town.

Mr & Mrs J Blackie
Tel: 0787 237642
Fax: 0787 237642

B&B from £18, Rooms 1 single, 1 twin, 1 family,
No smoking, Minimum age 10, Pets welcome on request,
Open all year except Christmas, Map Ref: D

The Wick, Hatfield, Peverel, Essex CM3 2EZ   **Nearest Road A12**

The Wick is a Grade II listed 16th century farmhouse in a pleasant rural setting with a large garden, duck ponds and stream. The drawing room is nicely furnished as is the pretty dining room. Bedrooms are pleasantly decorated and have tea/coffee making facilities. Delicious home cooked evening meals are available on request. Well situated for London, Suffolk and East Coast ports.

Mrs Linda Tritton
Tel: 01245 380705

B&B from £17.50, Dinner from £10, Rooms 1 twin, 1 single, Minimum age 10, Open all year, Map Ref: E

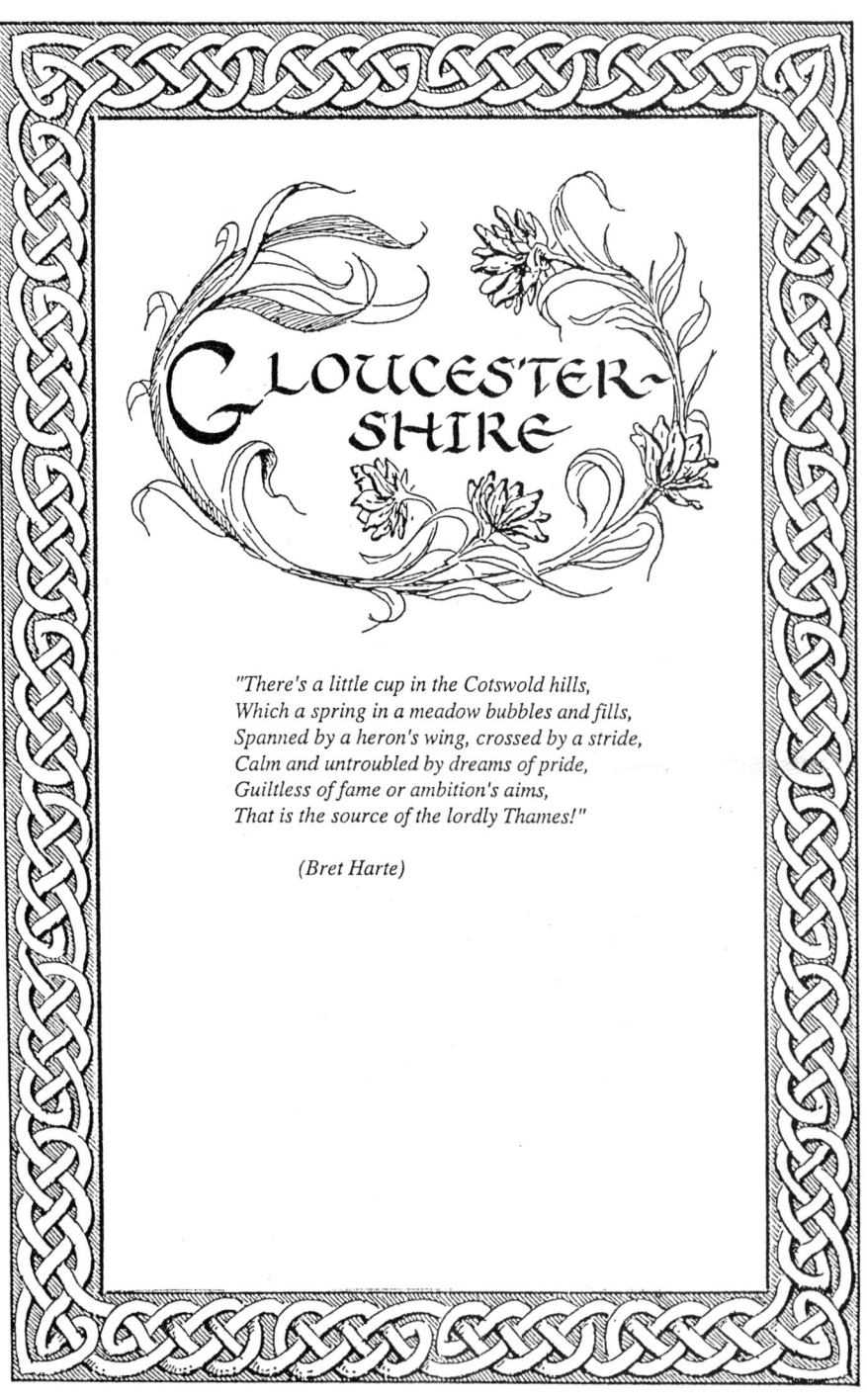

GLOUCESTERSHIRE

"There's a little cup in the Cotswold hills,
Which a spring in a meadow bubbles and fills,
Spanned by a heron's wing, crossed by a stride,
Calm and untroubled by dreams of pride,
Guiltless of fame or ambition's aims,
That is the source of the lordly Thames!"

(Bret Harte)

GLOUCESTERSHIRE

ARLINGTON ROW, BIBURY.

Mention the county of Gloucestershire and the immediate image is one of mellow Cotswold villages surrounded by true English countryside. As well as many picturesque towns and villages, a focus of the county is the Regency spa town of Cheltenham, along with nearby Gloucester, with its magnificent cathedral. The Forest of Dean stretches for 20 miles between the rivers Severn and Wye in the West of the county. More than 27,000 acres of the ancient forest are crown land. Traditional industries helped shape the character of Gloucestershire. Between the 15th and 17th centuries the prosperity brought by the wool industry to the Cotswolds led to the building of many lovely churches and manor houses. Evidence of this bygone industry is at Chipping Campden in the Woolstaplers Hall, built in 1340 for merchants to buy the staples of Cotswold fleece, and now a museum.

Stow-on-the-Wold was once a bustling centre of the wool industry, its importance growing in the Middle Ages because it stood at the junction of several main roads. As well as the wealth of the wool trade and its heritage of superb buildings, the area is also characterised by its soft, natural limestone used in its buildings and abundant dry stone walls.

There are world famous larger villages such as Bourton-on-the-Water, Broadway, Chipping Campden and Bibury, but plenty of smaller "undiscovered" villages like Stanton, Snowshill and Bisley offer true local character. With a number of long distance footpaths, the area is a

TINTERN ABBEY.

walker's paradise. These include the Cotswold Way, Offa's Dyke Path, the Oxfordshire Way and the Wye Valley Walk. The countryside is dissected by swift flowing streams such as the Windrush, the Coln and the Evenlode, which are rich in trout and crayfish. The River Windrush is a feature of the beautiful village of Bourton-on-the-Water, flowing through the main street, under bridges and past lawns.

The Cotswolds are just as famous for their inns and antiques. Real is best and can be enjoyed in front of a blazing log fire in a Cotswolds village inn. The region has probably more genuine antique shops than anywhere in England.

The source of the Thames is three miles South West of the Roman town of Cirencester , an excellent centre for walking or touring. In the 2nd century the town called Corinium by the Romans was the largest outside London. Three Roman roads - Akeman Street, the Foss Way and one of the two Ermine Streets radiate from Cirencester, whose many Roman finds can be seen in the Corinium Museum.

Cheltenham is a centre of music, art and sport. The Cheltenham Music Festival was started in 1944 with the intention of fostering contemporary music in Britain. It is one of the most famous spa towns in England. The only alkaline springs in England run underground and are available at the Pittville Pump Room, the town's most beautiful building.

Also with Roman origins is Gloucester, for centuries the guardian to the routes to Wales which converged at the lowest crossing point of the River Severn. It history dates back 2,000 years and it eventually became a "Colonia" - a settlement that was to last 400 years. Today it is a bustling marketing and manufacturing centre. The city's industrial heritage can be seen at Gloucester Docks, a collection of Victorian warehouses, restored with shops, restaurants and cafe bars. It has superb shopping facilities, pubs which are 500 years old and plenty of night life. To the West of the River Severn is the beautiful Wye Valley, dominated by the splendour of Symonds Yat and the ruined Tintern Abbey, and the Forest of Dean.

The Forest of Dean has an estimated 20 million trees, mainly oak and beech but with birch, ash, conifers and massive holly trees. Decreed a Royal hunting ground in 1016, the forest offers facilities for quiet recreation such as walking and other outdoor activities. Traditional industries include charcoal making and mining. Foresters, the people who live and work in the forest, have traditional privileges granted to them centuries ago. Miners have the right to dig coal free and the quarrymen can cut stone. Half the forest is fenced and the other half is grazed by Foresters' sheep. A natural phenomenon is the Severn Bore, when the river meets the incoming tide and forms a great wave.

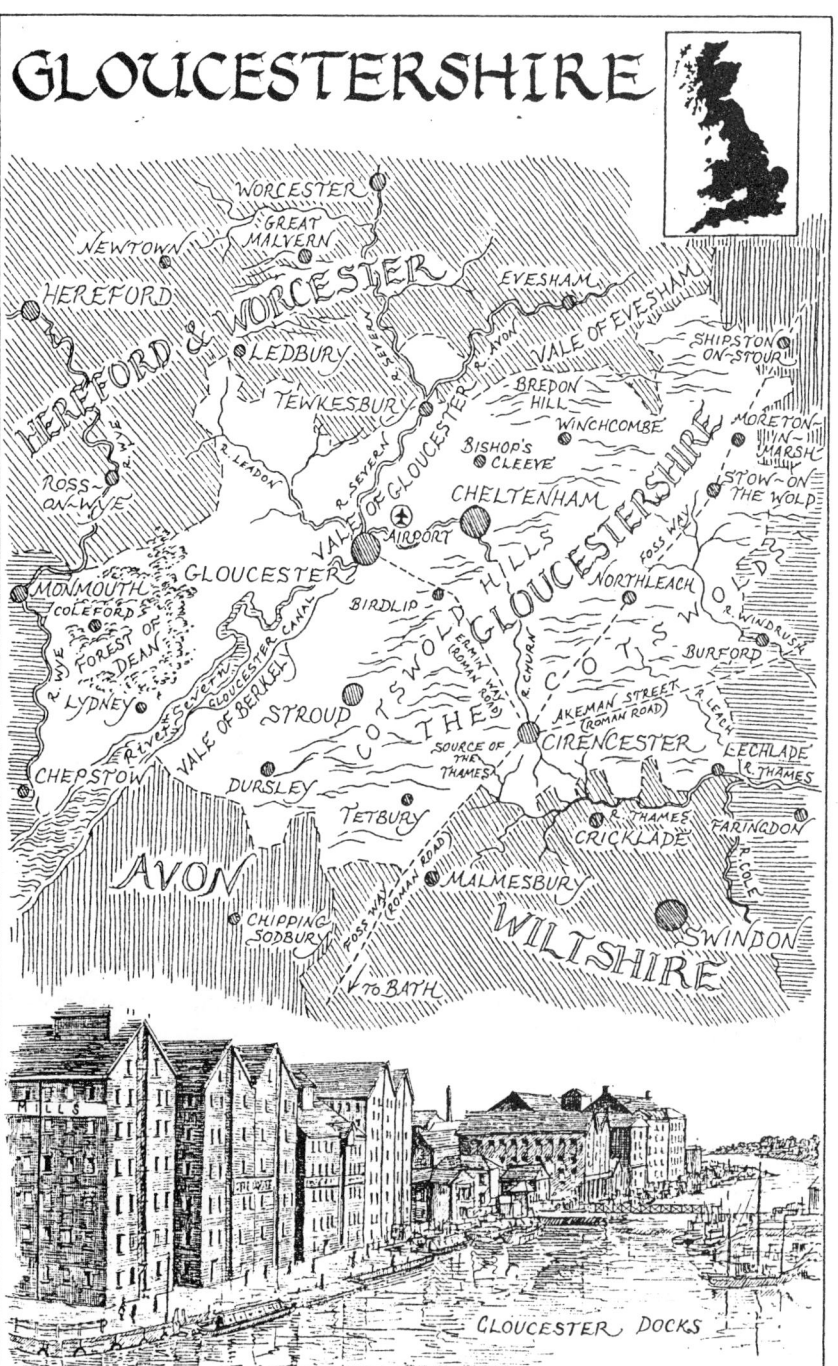

GLOUCESTERSHIRE

NEWTOWN
HEREFORD
ROSS-ON-WYE
MONMOUTH
COLEFORD
FOREST OF DEAN
LYDNEY
CHEPSTOW

WORCESTER
GREAT MALVERN
HEREFORD & WORCESTER
LEDBURY
TEWKESBURY
R. LEADON
R. SEVERN
VALE OF GLOUCESTER
GLOUCESTER
AIRPORT
BIRDLIP
SEVERN & GLOUCESTER CANAL
RIVER SEVERN
VALE OF BERKELEY
STROUD
DURSLEY
TETBURY

EVESHAM
R. AVON
VALE OF EVESHAM
BREDON HILL
WINCHCOMBE
BISHOP'S CLEEVE
CHELTENHAM
COTSWOLD HILLS
ERMIN WAY (ROMAN ROAD)
R. CHURN
SOURCE OF THE THAMES
AKEMAN STREET (ROMAN ROAD)
CIRENCESTER
R. THAMES
CRICKLADE

SHIPSTON-ON-STOUR
MORETON-IN-MARSH
STOW-ON-THE-WOLD
GLOUCESTERSHIRE
THE COTSWOLD
FOSS WAY
NORTHLEACH
R. WINDRUSH
BURFORD
R. LEACH
LECHLADE
R. THAMES
FARINGDON
R. COLE

AVON
CHIPPING SODBURY
FOSS WAY (ROMAN ROAD)
MALMESBURY
WILTSHIRE
SWINDON
↓ TO BATH

CLOUCESTER DOCKS

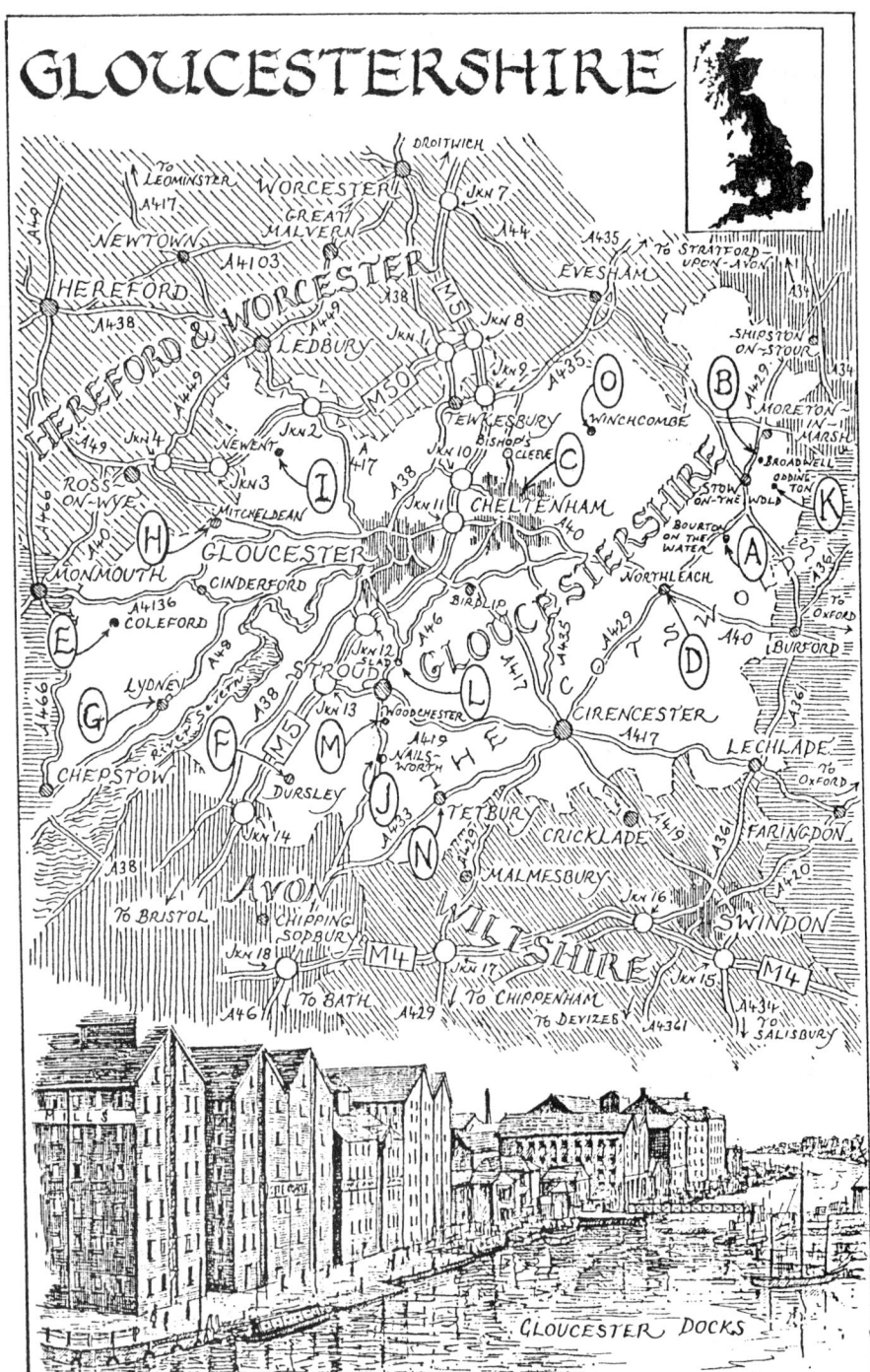

GLOUCESTERSHIRE

GLOUCESTER DOCKS

Clapton Manor, Clapton on the Hill, Near Bourton on the Water, Glos GL54 2LG   Nearest Road A429

Clapton Manor is a 17th century Cotswold stone house located at the top of the village with spectacular views across the Windrush Valley. The layout of the house lends itself to either complete privacy or more integration with the family as preferred. The interior with its beams and huge inglenook fireplaces is both informal and comfortable. Karin loves cooking and makes her own jams and marmalades. James is a garden designer and historian and is delighted to advise on gardens to visit in the area. Children of all ages are most welcome.

James & Karin Bolton
Tel: 01451 810202

B&B from £15, Dinner from £10, Rooms 1 twin, 1 double,
No smoking, Pets allowed by arrangement, Open all year,
Map Ref: A

Upper Farm, Clapton on the Hill, Bourton on the Water, Glos GL54 2LG   **Nrst Road A429**

A working family farm of 140 acres in a peaceful undiscovered Cotswold village 2 miles from the famous Bourton-on-the-Water. The listed 17th century stone farmhouse has been tastefully restored and offers a warm and friendly welcome with exceptional accommodation and hearty farmhouse fayre. The heated bedrooms are of individual character some are en-suite with TV and one is ground floor. From its hill position Upper Farm enjoys panoramic views of the surrounding countryside and being centrally located makes it an ideal base for touring, walking or merely relaxing.

Helen Adams
Tel: 01451 820453

B&B from £15, Rooms 3 double, 1 family, 1 twin, (many en-suite),
No smoking, Minimum age 8, Open March - November, Map Ref: A

College House, Chapel Street, Broadwell, Glos, GL56 0TW   **Nearest Road A429**

College House is a 17th century house located in a quiet and enchanting Cotswold village. It has delightful accommodation with luxurious bedrooms and bathrooms two of which are en-suite. Exposed beams, shutters, flagstone floors and mullioned windows abound. Sitting room with large stone fireplace for exclusive guest use. Breakfast and, if desired, 3 course dinners are served in the beamed dining room. The popular villages of Bourton on the Water and Chipping Camden are close by and Cheltenham, Oxford and Stratford are easily accessible.

Sybil Gisby
Tel: 01451 832351

B&B from £19.50, Dinner from £14.50, Minimum age 16, No pets,
Open all year except Christmas, Map Ref: B

Cleeve Hill Hotel, Cheltenham, Gloucestershire GL52 3PR   **Nearest Road B4632**

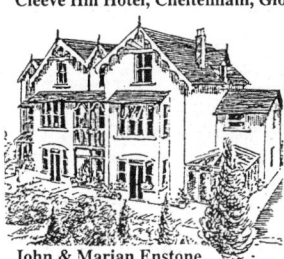

Cleeve Hill Hotel is personally run by the proprietors. All bedrooms are en-suite and have telephone, TV with movie channel, tea/coffee making facilities, and radio alarm clocks. All enjoy superb views of either the Malvern Hills or Cleeve Common and the golf course. The excellent breakfasts are renowned for being extremely generous and will provide the perfect start to the day. The comfortable lounge provides a pleasant place to relax and enjoy a quiet drink from the licensed bar. AA premier selected 5Q, RAC high acclaimed, ETB highly commended.

John & Marian Enstone
Tel: 01242 672052

B&B from £30, Rooms 5 double, 2 twin, 1 family, 2 single
(all en-suite), No smoking, No pets, Minimum age 8,
Open all year, Map Ref: C

Market House, The Square, Northleach, Cheltenham, Glos GL54 3EJ   **Nearest Road A40, A429**

A 400 year old Cotswold stone house of 'olde worlde' charm characterised by exposed beams and inglenook fireplace. Located in the centre of an unspoilt town in the heart of the Cotswolds. Offering three cosy bedrooms (one en-suite). Tea/coffee making facilities. Travel information available. Full central heating makes for a very comfortable stay.

Theresa & Mike Eastman
Tel: 01451 860557

B&B from £16, Rooms 2 double, 1 twin, No smoking, No pets, Minimum age 12, Open all year, Map Ref: D

Tudor Farmhouse Hotel, Clearwell Near Coleford, Gloucestershire GL16 8JS   **Nearest Road A466**

Set in a gentle valley between the Forest of Dean and the Wye Valley, this peaceful and welcoming old farmhouse has stood since the 13th century and features oak beams and original wall panelling throughout. The bedrooms are tastefully furnished in traditional style, some have 4 poster beds and all have colour TV, tea/coffee making facilities, central heating and en-suite bath or shower and wc. In the lounge there is an inglenook fireplace. The dining room has open stonework, oak beams and is the ideal way to enjoy the imaginative freshly prepared cuisine.

Deborah & Richard Fletcher
Tel: 01594 833046
Fax: 01594 837093

B&B from £24.50, Dinner from £15, Rooms 6 double, 1 family, 2 twin, (all en-suite), Open all year, Map Ref: E

Drakestone House, Stinchcombe, Dursley, Gloucestershire GL11 6AS   **Nearest Road B4060**

A delightful Cotswold country house where guests receive a warm welcome. Drakestone is elegantly furnished with family antiques and treasures from Hugh and Crystal's life abroad. Set in beautiful Edwardian gardens on the edge of beech woods the house overlooks the Vale of Berkeley and distant Welsh hills. Ideally situated for visiting Berkeley Castle, Slimbridge Wildfowl Trust, Westonbirt Arboretum, Bath and the Cotswolds.

Hugh & Crystal
   St John Mildmay
Tel: 01453 542140

B&B £23, Dinner by arrangement £15, Rooms 2 twin, 1 double, No smoking, Pets allowed in stable, Open April - October, Map Ref: F

Upper Viney Farmhouse, Viney Hill, Lydney, Gloucestershire GL15 4LT   **Nearest Road A48**

This lovely stone built grade II listed farmhouse has feature oak spiral staircase, beams and Inglenook fireplaces; also an early 18th century child's coal mining boot which is to be found under the stairs. Situated just off the A48 between the Royal Forest of Dean and the River Severn and is acclaimed for home cooking and warm hospitality. An ideal base from which to explore the Forest of Dean, Wye Valley, Wales and The Marches. Gloucester, Cheltenham, Chepstow and Bath are all within easy reach. Special weekends, 3 days breaks with guided walks available.

Malcolm & Mary Litten
Tel: 01594 516672

B&B from £17, Dinner from £12, Rooms 1 twin, 1 double, 1 family, all en-suite or with private facilities, all have tea/coffee making facilities, Restricted smoking, Open all year, Map Ref: G

Gunn Mill House, Lower Spout Lane, Mitcheldean, Glos GL17 0EA   **Nearest Road A40, A48**

Nestling in Flaxley Valley in the Forest of Dean, Gunn Mill House stands in 5 acres of gardens and paddocks, bounded by its mill stream which flows to a 17th century mill. The Andersons have refurbished their Georgian home to a high standard, filling it with collectables from their travels around the world. By day enjoy the beauty of the Royal Forest, between restful nights in this peaceful spot. Large outdoor swimming pool, a couple of bikes may be borrowed. So also can the family dog! A roaring log fire and great hospitality add to the dinner party atmosphere.

David & Caroline Anderson
Tel: 01594 827577
Fax: 01594 827577

B&B £19.50, Dinner on request £16.50, Liquor Licence,
Rooms 1 twin/family, 2 double (all en-suite), No smoking, Children &
Pets welcome by arrangement, Open all year, Map Ref: H

Orchard House, Aston Ingham Road, Kilcot, Near Newent, Glos GL18 1NP   Nearest Road M50, B4222

Orchard House is a delightful Tudor style country house completely surrounded by 5 acres of peaceful gardens. A beautifully appointed home with a relaxed and friendly atmosphere, every modern comfort and delicious food. A very high standard of accommodation, including a Regency style dining room, luxurious double and en-suite bedrooms, original oak beams, TV lounge and winter log fires, a conservatory, fountain courtyard and croquet lawn.

Mrs Anne Thompson
Tel: 01989 720417

B&B from £19.50, Dinner from £14.50, Minimum age 12, No pets,
No smoking, Open all year, Map Ref: I

The Laurels, Inchbrook, Nailsworth, Gloucestershire GL5 5HA   **Nearest Road A46**

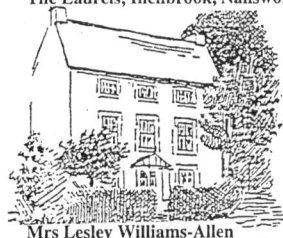

The Laurels is a lovely, rambling old house with a warm atmosphere which has been completely renovated. Relax and unwind in front of an open fire in the panelled study,or play snooker or board games in the beamed lounge. Take dinner or a bar meal in the licensed dining room where excellent home cooked meals are served. Wander in the garden, listen to and watch the large variety of birds, badgers and foxes who regularly visit the feeding station by the stream. All bedrooms are en-suite and there is a heated swimming pool for guests' use.

Mrs Lesley Williams-Allen
Tel: 01453 834021
Fax: 01453 834004

B&B from £16, Dinner from £10.50, Snacks from £1.50,
Rooms 2 double, 1 family, 1 twin, No smoking,
Open all year including Christmas. Map Ref: J

The Vicarage, Nailsworth, Gloucestershire GL6 0BS   **Nearest Road A46 - Avening Road**

Nailsworth Vicarage was built in 1894, it has spacious and well proportioned rooms with lovely views, it stands in 2 acres of mature gardens which look over the hills and woodland. The town centre is 2 minutes walk with a nationally renowned delicatessen and several restaurants providing for different tastes and budgets. Nailsworth is ideally situated for visits to Bath, Bristol, Cirencester and Cheltenham and an excellent base for many local walks including the Cotswold Way. The house is warm and cosy with open fires and central heating throughout.

Mrs P Strong
Tel: 01453 832181

B&B from £18, Rooms 2 single, 1 twin, No smoking, Pets welcome,
Open all year except Christmas, Map Ref: J

Orchard Cottage, Back Lane, Upper Oddington, Moreton-in-Marsh, GL56 0XL   Nearest Road A436

This attractive stone cottage, with its log fires to enjoy in winter and pretty garden for summer, provides the warmest of welcomes. The whole emphasis is on quality and personal attention. Jane Beynon has an extensive knowledge of the Cotswolds and helps you plan your itinerary, then provides you with a sumptuous evening meal on your return. Both bedrooms have their own bath/shower and toilet and also tea/coffee making facilities.

Jane Beynon
Tel: 01451 830785

B&B from £17.50, Dinner from £14, Rooms 1 double 1 twin (with private facilities), Tea/coffee makers, No smoking, Minimum age 5, Pets by arrangement, Open February - November, Map Ref: K

Down Court, Slad, near Stroud, Gloucestershire GL6 7QE   Nearest Road B4070

Down Court stands in an acre of cottage garden and is situated at the head of the beautiful Slad Valley. When first built, around 1620, Down court consisted of 5 cottages used to house the farm workers for Down Farm. The house was used in the BBC production of "Cider with Rosie". The comfortable bedrooms offer splendid views, tea/coffee making facilities, and radio. There is a large drawing room with colour TV, music and table games. Afternoon tea is available from 4.30 pm and full English breakfast is served at times convenient to guests.

Mrs Anne Mills
Tel: 01452 812427

B&B from £16.50, Dinner from £12.50, Rooms 1 double with private facilities, 2 en-suite twin, Minimum age 12, Open all year, Map Ref: L

Southfield Mill House, Woodchester, Stroud, Gloucester GL5 5PA   Nearest Road A46

Southfield House is an historical Cotswold mill house dating from 1560 and situated in its own gardens. The accommodation comprises 2 twin rooms (one with bathroom ensuite and one with private bathroom); also an en-suite single room. A short walk away is the local village which has 3 pubs which serve good food. Woodchester is ideally situated for golf, walking, etc and very central for visiting a number of historic monuments and houses. Yours hosts are widely travelled and very welcoming.

Mrs S Richardson
Tel: 01453 873437
Fax: 01453 872049

B&B from £20, Rooms 1 single, 2 twin (all en-suite), Restricted smoking, No children, Pets by arrangement, Open all year except Christmas, Map Ref: M

Tavern House, Willesley, Near Tetbury, Gloucestershire GL8 8QU   Nearest Road A433

Delightfully situated 17th century grade II listed former staging post, this elegant Cotswold stone country house has been sympathetically restored to its former glory. Overlooking Silk Wood and only 1 mile from the famous Westonbirt Arboretum. All rooms have private bath and shower en-suite, telephone, TV, hairdryer, etc. A charming secluded walled garden offers peace and tranquility with an interesting and varied contrast of colour from the many flowers and plants. Convenient for visiting Bath, Gloucester, Cheltenham, and Stow. A warm welcome is assured.

Janet & Tim Tremellen
Tel: 01666 880444
Fax: 01666 880254

B&B from £27.50, Rooms 1 twin, 3 double, Restricted smoking, Minimum age 10, Open all year, Map Ref: N

Gower House, 16 North Street, Winchcombe, Glos., GL54 5LH   **Nearest Road B4632**

Gower House, a 17th century town house, is situated close to the centre of Winchcombe, a small picturesque country town on the 'Cotswold Way', and is an ideal base for exploring the Cotswolds. Ramblers, cyclists and motorists are all equally welcome and there is ample parking to the rear. The three comfortable bedrooms all have radio, tea/coffee making facilities, washbasins, full central heating and are served by 2 bathrooms each with shower and bath. In addition a TV lounge and a large secluded garden are available for guests' use.

Sally & Mick Simmonds   **B&B from £16, Rooms 2 twin, 1 double, Restricted smoking,**
Tel: 01242 602616   **Open all year except Christmas, Map Ref: O**

THE
14TH CENTURY
HIGH STREET, CHIPPING CAMDEN.

Hampshire

"Each rural sight, each sound, each smell, combine;
The tinkling sheep-bell, or the breath of kine;
The new-mown hay that scents the swelling breeze,
Or cottage chimney smoking through the trees."

(Gilbert White)

HAMPSHIRE

JANE AUSTEN'S HOUSE AT CHAWTON.

Hampshire's vital role in England's defence from sea invasion spans many centuries. In the many busy ports such as Portsmouth, Southampton and Gosport, this maritime past is depicted in museums and heritage sites. Inland, high, rolling downs dip to small villages, complete with Norman churches and thatched cottages. The county is dissected by great trout rivers, the Test and the Itchen. Hampshire's great history is echoed in the 450 ancient monuments from Neolithic long barrows, to cathedrals and country mansions. While many old dock and port areas have been restored to modern and cosmopolitan shopping and marina areas, the relics of the county's maritime heritage are still evident. In Portsmouth, historic ships, castles, forts and museums combine with the city's resort of Southsea to create an excellent holiday centre from which to explore the area. For much of England's history Portsmouth has been the traditional home of the Royal Navy and was the strongest fortress in medieval England. At its heart is Nelson's flagship, HMS Victory, and nearby the remains of the Mary Rose, Henry VIII's favourite warship, are being conserved. Portsmouth is the birthplace of Charles Dickens and his home has been furnished in early 19th century style.

Years of traditional seaside holidays have developed the city's own resort of Southsea - the largest in Hampshire - into the grandstand of the Solent, with 4 miles of seafront offering leisure activities. The New Forest occupies the south Western Corner of Hampshire on its border with Dorset. For centuries it was the haunt of English kings. Nova Foresta, as it was named by William the Conqueror, is still subject to the special laws which he created to protect his sport of the forest's red deer. Over 900 years later visitors can explore the mosaic of ancient forest and heathland that is a unique survivor of England's royal hunting forests.

On the western edge of the New Forest is the seaside town of Christchurch, on the confluence of the Rivers Stour and Avon. Dating from Saxon times, Christchurch was originally known

THATCHED COTTAGES, NETHER WALLOP.

as Twynham - the place between the waters - and today it still retains its Saxon street layout. The annual regatta is held in mid-August with rowing on the River Stour, displays on the quay and culminating in a spectacular fireworks display.

To the East of the town and at the entrance to Christchurch Harbour is Mudeford, a popular holiday area with sandy beaches and good watersports facilities. Basingstoke is a thriving commercial centre set in unspoilt rural North Hampshire. A large part of the borough has been designated as part of the North Wessex Downs Area of Outstanding Natural Beauty. Less than an hour away from both London and the South coast makes it a popular tourist area. To the North of Basingstoke, is Watership Down, immortalised in Richard Adams' novel of the same name.

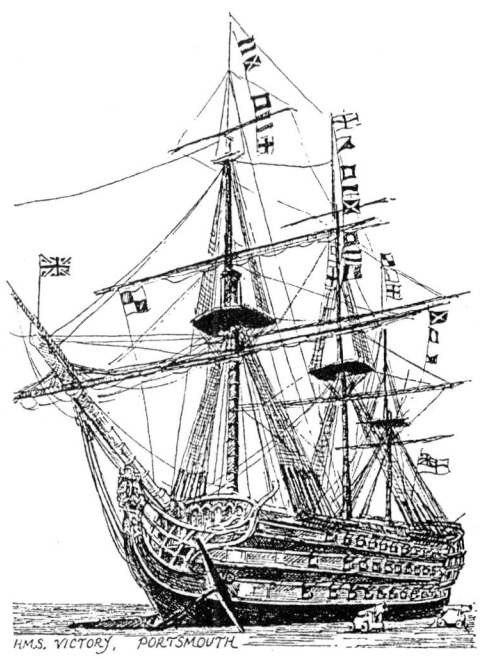

H.M.S. VICTORY, PORTSMOUTH

Winchester, founded by the Romans, was King Alfred's capital and it first acquired a church in 648, and its cathedral was built nine centuries ago by William the Conqueror. The famous Arthurian Round Table, weighing well over a ton, is housed in the Great Hall, the only remaining part of Winchester's castle where the first English Parliament met. Winchester College was founded as far back as 1382.

East Hampshire has been featured in the work of literary figures such as Flora Thompson, W H Hudson, William Cobbett and Edward Thomas. Jane Austen once lived in the historic village of Chawton where she wrote such classics as Emma and Pride and Prejudice. Gilbert White, the pioneer 18th century naturalist, was born in Selborne and it was here that he recorded his observations of birds, plants and animals in The Natural History of Selborne.

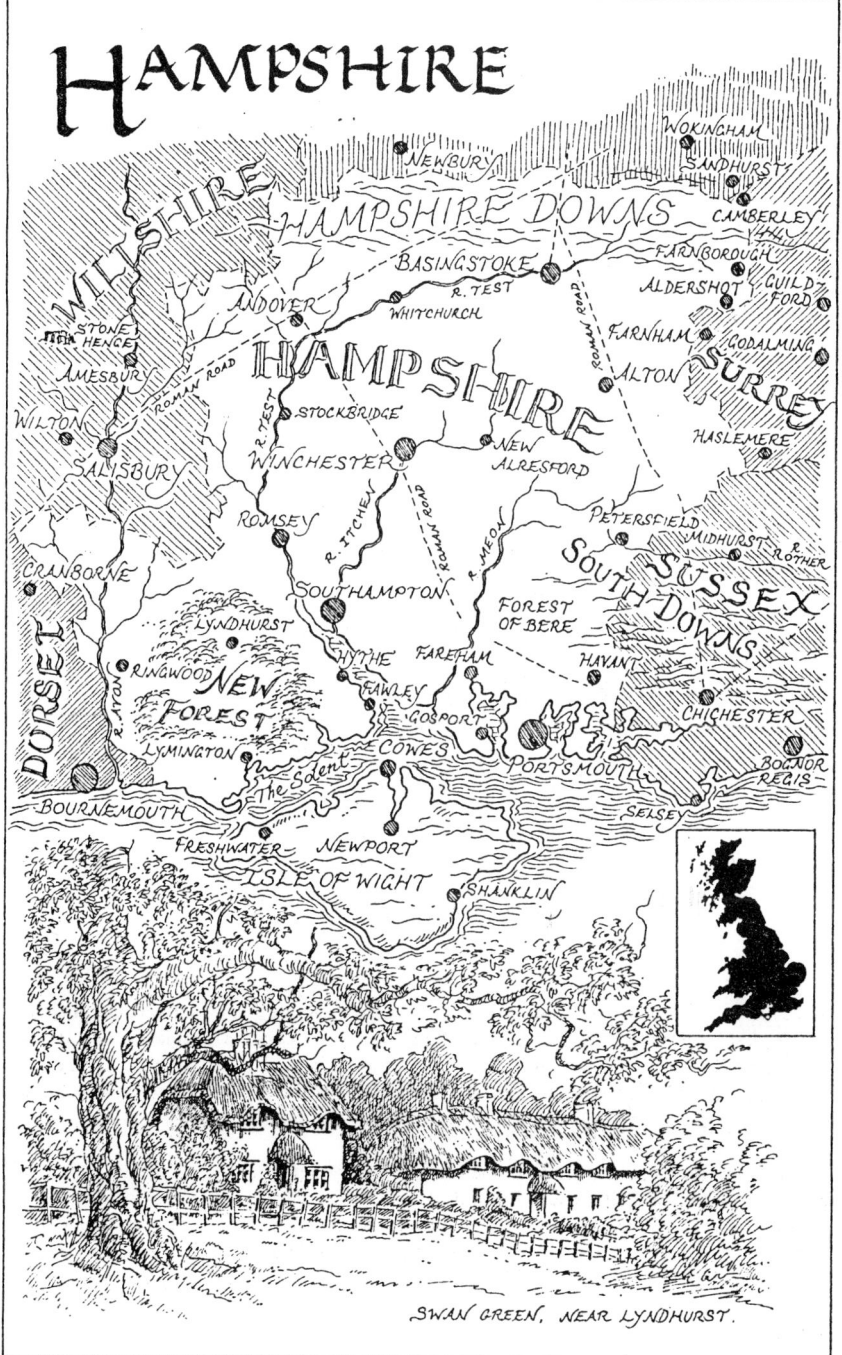

HAMPSHIRE

WILTSHIRE

WOKINGHAM
SANDHURST
NEWBURY
HAMPSHIRE DOWNS
CAMBERLEY
FARNBOROUGH
BASINGSTOKE
ANDOVER
R. TEST
ALDERSHOT
GUILD-
FORD
WHITCHURCH
STONE
HENGE
HAMPSHIRE
FARNHAM
GODALMING
AMESBURY
ALTON
SURREY
ROMAN ROAD
WILTON
R. TEST
STOCKBRIDGE
WINCHESTER
HASLEMERE
NEW
ALRESFORD
SALISBURY
ROMSEY
R. ITCHEN
PETERSFIELD
MIDHURST
R. ROTHER
CRANBORNE
R. MEON
SOUTH DOWNS
SUSSEX
ROMAN ROAD
SOUTHAMPTON
FOREST
OF BERE
DORSET
LYNDHURST
HYTHE
FAREHAM
HAVANT
R. AVON
RINGWOOD
NEW
FOREST
FAWLEY
CHICHESTER
LYMINGTON
GOSPORT
BOURNEMOUTH
The Solen
COWES
PORTSMOUTH
BOGNOR
REGIS
SELSEY
FRESHWATER
NEWPORT
ISLE OF WIGHT
SHANKLIN

SWAN GREEN, NEAR LYNDHURST.

HAMPSHIRE

WILTSHIRE

WOKINGHAM

NEWBURY

SANDHURST

CAMBERLEY

D

A339

A343

A34

BASINGSTOKE
B3400

HARTLEY
WINTNEY

M3

FARNBOROUGH

ALDERSHOT

GUILD-
FORD

ANDOVER

WHITCHURCH

A30

FARNHAM

A31

STONE-
HENGE

A303

A34

A303

A339

ALTON

GODALMING

SURREY

AMESBURY

A338

HAMPSHIRE

A31

STOCKBRIDGE

A272

NEW
ALRESFORD

HASLE-
MERE

WILTON

A30

A30

WINCHESTER

A

BRAMDEAN

A3

MIDHURST

SALISBURY

A3057

MORESTEAD

RAMSDEAN

PETERSFIELD

PETWORTH

A36

ROMSEY

A33

L

A272

BURITON

A272

CRANBORNE

EASTLEIGH

A32

H

SUSSEX

FORDINGBRIDGE

J

SOUTHAMPTON

K

DENMEAD

G

A286

DORSET

C

RINGWOOD

A337

LYNDHURST

326

M27

FAREHAM

HAVANT

A27

CHICHESTER

BROCKENHURST

HYTHE

BOGNOR
REGIS

BURLEY

B3054

FAWLEY

A27

BEAULIEU

GOSPORT

B

LYMINGTON

A337

COWES

PORTSMOUTH

E

SELSEY

BOURNEMOUTH

F

The Solent

A3054

RYDE

FRESHWATER

NEWPORT

SANDOWN

ISLE OF WIGHT

SHANKLIN

I

VENTNOR

SWAN GREEN, NEAR LYNDHURST.

Woodcote Manor, Bramdean, Alresford, Hampshire SO24 0LL   Nearest Road A272

A long private drive leads to this impressive manor house set in 1000 acres of farmland. Mentioned in the Domesday Book parts date from Medieval times with later additions in the 15th and 16th centuries. Throughout there are high ceilings, huge windows, solid oak doors, polished floors and oak panelled walls. The entrance hall has a chequered marble floor and ancient refectory table. There is a grass tennis court and wonderful garden. The twin room has a private bathroom and the large family unit is en-suite. Breakfast is served in the library.

Caroline McLaughlan
Tel: 01962 771793

B&B from £20, Rooms: 1 twin, 1 family all with en-suite facilities and tea/coffee making facilities, No smoking, Open March to November, Map Ref: A

Tothill House, Black Lane, Off Forest Road, Burley, Christchurch BH23 8DZ   Nearest Road A35

Tothill House is in an idyllic woodland setting on the southern fringe of the New Forest adjoining Poors Common, an area designated for outstanding natural beauty and noted for its flora and fauna. All bedrooms are en-suite, have colour TV, and tea/coffee making facilities. A wide variety of local sporting and recreational activities available with fine sailing waters on the Solent, bathing beaches and an excellent selection of golf courses. Private fishing lakes nearby.

Mrs Wendy Witt
Tel: 01425 674414
Fax: 01425 672235

B&B from £25, Rooms 2 double, 1 twin (all en-suite) Minimum age 15, No pets, No smoking, Open all year except Christmas & new year . Map ref: B

Weir Cottage, Bickton, Fordingbridge, Hampshire, SP6 2HA   Nearest Road A338

This historic 18th century cottage is set in a picturesque hamlet overlooking the famous Hampshire Avon as it flows beneath Bickton Mill. Converted from a grain and sack store it is now a fine family home. Guests can relax in the 'Garden Room' which leads to an English cottage garden. Breakfast is in the splendid first floor raftered drawing room overlooking the river. There is a profusion of wildlife including many swans. Your hosts enjoy sharing their home and you can dine 'en famille' on fresh garden produce often with home caught trout and pheasant.

Geoffrey & Philippa Duckworth
Tel: 01425 655813

B&B from £19, Dinner by arrangement from £12, Rooms 1 twin, 1 en-suite double and have tea/coffee making facilities, No smoking, Minimum age 8, Open all year, Map Ref: C

Shearings, Rockbourne, Fordingbridge, Hampshire SP6 3NA   Nearest Road A354

Located beside a stream in a delightful village this picturesque 16th century listed thatched cottage is the epitome of 'olde worlde' charm. Oak beams, inglenooks, fresh flowers and birdsong in abundance. The cosy sitting room has a wealth of useful information. Beautiful well kept gardens with a croquet lawn, shrubs, sunny patios; with breakfast outside under the grape vine in summer. Colin & Rosemary invite guests to dine with them in a house party atmosphere for candlelit dinners of freshly prepared, very tasty, home cooked dishes. Private parties can be catered for.

Brigadier & Mrs A C D Watts
Tel: 01725 518256
Fax: 01725 518255

B&B from £23, Dinner from £13, Rooms 1 single, 1 twin, 1 double (all en-suite) all with tea/coffee making facilities, Restricted smoking, Minimum age 12, No petsOpen February - December, Map Ref: C

Cotterstone, Mount Pleasant, Hartley Wintney, Hampshire RG27 8PW   Nearest Road A30

Cotterstone is a large turn of the century Edwardian home set within a walled garden in a quiet tree lined road leading to Hartley Wintney's famous cricket green. The village has several antique shops, pubs and restaurants and is the home of Westgreen House a National Trust property. Hampshire is a delightful area and has many villages, country houses and walks but retains its charm although less than an hour from London and within easy reach of the M3. The light pretty double room has a bathroom and tea/coffee makers. Small single child's room is also available.

Mrs Frances Chidley
Tel: 01252 842783

B&B from £17.50, Rooms 1 single, 1 double (with private facilities)
No smoking, Open all year, Map Ref: D

Cockle Warren Cottage Hotel, 36 Seafront, Hayling Island, Hampshire PO11 9HL   Nearest Road A27

Cockle Warren is a delightful Cottage Hotel set back in its own grounds on the seafront. David and Diane have won many national and regional awards from the AA and RAC for their accommodation, hospitality and food. Enjoy the candlelit dinners, log fires and garden with its heated swimming pool. Hayling Island is renowed for its clean air and mild climate. It is equally situated between the Roman city of Chichester and the historic city of Portsmouth with its HMS Victory and The Mary Rose.

Diane & David Skelton
Tel: 01705 464961

B&B from £26, Dinner £24.50, Rooms 5 double, 5 single
Minimum age 12, Pets by arrangement, Open all year, Map Ref: E

St Mary's Lodge, Captains Row, Lymington, Hampshire SO41 9RR   Nearest Road M27

An elegant Georgian interior designed house situated in the old area of Lymington close to the town quay. Quaint with fishing boats and visiting yachts. Boutiques, shops, pubs and first class restaurants minutes away. Well known Saturday antiques market. Two marinas and ferry to the Isle of Wight. Wonderful walks in the New Forest and Beaulieu. Convivial hosts providing a memorable stay.

Mrs P A Thomson
Tel: 01590 678576

B&B from £25, Rooms 2 double, 1 twin, 2 single, Minimum age 8,
No smoking, Pets by arrangement, Open all year, Map Ref: F

Albany House, Highfield, Lymington, Hampshire SO41 9GB   Nearest Road A337

Built in 1820, this elegant Regency residence has large, well proportioned rooms with quality furnishings and sumptuous bathrooms. Situated in a quiet position overlooking a green yet only moments from Lymington's thriving shopping centre with interesting boutiques, narrow cobbled streets and ancient Saturday market. A ferry to the Isle of Wight operates during summer months. A comfortable lounge with books and log fire. An excellent dinner is served in the elegant dining room. Bedrooms have tea/coffee making facilities, TV and are en-suite.

Mrs Wendy Gallagher
Tel: 01590 671900

B&B from £24, Dinner from £10.50, Rooms 1 twin, 1 double, 1 family
(all en-suite), Pets by arrangement, Open all year except Christmas.
Map Ref: F

Pillmead House, North Lane, Buriton, Petersfield, Hampshire GU31 5RS   Nearest Road A3

This Victorian family house built of local malmstone overlooking a valley its garden descending steeply with herbaceous borders and roses. Breakfast is served in the dining room with views of the Queen Elizabeth Country Park and Butser Hill. The village of Buriton is on the South Downs Way a popular walking route in a once thriving hop growing area - it boasts a pond, Norman church and 2 pubs serving excellent food. Pillmead House is centrally placed for visiting Portsmouth, "The Flag Ship of Maritime Britain" Chichester with cathedral and theatre and Winchester.

Mrs Sarah Moss
Tel: 01730 266795
Fax: 01730 264042

B&B from £18.50, Rooms 1 double, 1 twin, and have tea/coffee making facilities and TV, There is no smoking, Pets by arrangement, Open all year, Map Ref: G

Twentyways Farm, Ramsdean, Petersfield, Hampshire GU32 1RX   Nearest Road Ramsdean Road

Twentyways Farm is a converted 17th century barn nestling in 20 acres of paddocks and gardens tucked beneath the brow of ancient Butser Hill in the picturesque Meon Valley. Maureen and David Farmer offer you a warm welcome in either of the 2 comfortable bedrooms with en-suite facilities and TV. Tea or coffee can be taken in the spacious galleried drawing room or relaxing in the flint walled courtyard around the pool with Italian fountain playing and an abundance of gaily coloured flowers. Breakfast, taken in the oak dining room, has to be experienced to be believed.

Maureen & David Farmer
Tel: 01730 823606

B&B from £20, Rooms 2 en-suite twin, No smoking, No children, Open all year, Map Ref: H

Fortitude Cottage, 51 Broad Street, Old Portsmouth, Hampshire PO1 2JD   Southern end of A3

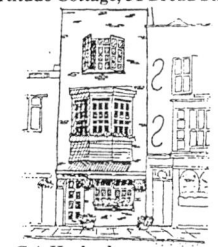

A charming unusual town house overlooking the quayside in the heart of Old Portsmouth. Built on the site of a 16th century cottage destroyed during the 2nd war and named after an 18th century warship. The immaculately maintained bedrooms and bathrooms are decorated in delicate pastel shades and needlepoint pictures and flowers abound. Breakfast is served on pine tables in a beamed room with views over the water. Carol has won 'Britain in Bloom' awards for her window boxes and hanging baskets; and 'Heartbeat' for healthy food choices.

Mrs C A Harbeck
Tel: 01705 823748

B&B from £20, Rooms: 1 twin (en-suite), and 1 double, both with tea/coffee making facilities, No smoking, No children, Open all year, Map Ref: I

The Nest, 10 Middle Lane off School Lane, Ringwood, Hants BH24 1LE   Nearest Road A31, B3347

A lovely Victorian family house. Situated in a quiet residential lane within 5 minutes walk of Ringwood town centre, an ancient market town with many restaurants and inns. Ample parking. Beautifully decorated, very clean and well maintained. Breakfast times are flexible and served in the delightful sunny conservatory overlooking the gardens. Pretty colour co-ordinated 'Laura Ashley' style bedrooms with pine furnishings. Local activities include fishing, golf, riding and forest walks. An excellent base to explore the New Forest. AA selected. Highly recommended.

Mrs Yvonne Nixon
Tel: 01425 476724

B&B from £16, Rooms 2 double, 1 twin, 1 single,No smoking, Pets by arrangement, Open all year, Map Ref: J

Forest Gate, Hambledon Road, Denmead, Waterlooville, Hampshire PO7 6EX   Nearest Road B2150

This is a fine Grade II listed Georgian residence, built around 1790, and is situated on the outskirts of the village overlooking farmland. Set in approximately 2 acres of garden with lawns, rose beds, pond and tennis court. The elegant drawing and dining rooms have mahogany floors with French doors opening onto a paved garden terrace. The comfortable bedrooms are en-suite and have tea/coffee making facilities. Nestling in the South Downs Denmead is on the Wayfarers Way, a scenic 70 mile walk from Emsworth to Newbury. Dinner is available by arrangment.

B&B from £16, Dinner from £10.50, Rooms 2 twin (en-suite),

Torfrida & David Cox
Tel: 01705 255901

No smoking, Minimum age 10, Open all year except Christmas and New Year. Map Ref: K

Morestead Grove, Morestead, Winchester, Hampshire SO21 1LZ   Nearest Road M3

Dating from 1836 this large imposing Georgian family residence was formerly a rectory. Set in 2 acres of lawned gardens and tucked away behind a 12th century church. Morestead is a quiet hamlet amidst Hampshire's rolling countryside yet close to historic Winchester. The very spacious double room with private bathroom, tea/coffee making facilities, amd TV can also accommodate a family. Dinner is available by prior arrangement and home produced eggs, honey and vegetables are always available.

Katherine Sellon
Tel: 01962 777238

B&B from £18, Dinner from £12, Rooms 1 en-suite double,
No smoking, Open all year, Map Ref: L

Hereford and Worcester

"Dappled very close with shade,
Summer-snow of apple-blossoms, running up from glade to glade"

(Elizabeth Barrett Browning)

HEREFORD & WORCESTER

LOWER BROCKHAMPTON MANOR

The English plains meet the Welsh mountains in the county of Hereford and Worcester.

In the West of the county rugged countryside bears testimony to an angry past and border warfare. While in the east, the Rivers Severn and Avon water flat, fertile land. This fertile land means it is a county of food and drink - from beef to cider and fruit and vegetables. With few exceptions, the towns are market towns, trading in the rich produce of the surrounding orchards and fields.

Hereford and Worcester is steeped in history and its two principal cities reflect this. Worcester is famed as a Royalist city: Charles I passed through on his way West and Charles fought his last battle South of Worcester and then fled, hiding from Cromwell's troops in the famous Royal Oak. Worcester Cathedral is in a beautiful situation on the River Severn and away from the town centre. Its modern day claims are cricket and porcelain. The county cricket ground is an archetypal feature of an English summer and there is an all year round programme of racing at Worcester Racecourse.

It was thanks to the richness of the surrounding agricultural land that Hereford grew up on the banks of the River Wye. Hereford Cathedral, built on a site overlooking the river and associated with the church since the 7th century, is famous as the home of the Mappa Mundi, a unique map of the world drawn at the end of the 13th century.

In South Herefordshire the River Wye dissects some of the finest farming country in Britain - yet the area is also secluded, wild in places and an area of outstanding natural beauty. A horse shoe gorge has been carved through sandstone by the river at Symonds Yat forming spectacular cliffs 500 ft above the water.

THE MALVERN HILLS.

Ross-on-Wye, South Herefordshire's largest town, stands on a stone outcrop overlooking the river and its 17th century market hall still hosts two markets a week. The area is popular for a variety of outdoor activities from angling and watersports to climbing and rambling. Offa's Dyke Footpath, the long distance trail, runs for 177 miles along the entire length of the border between England and Scotland. It passes the unique town of Hay-on-Wye which has the world's largest second hand and antiquarian book centre. To the North of Hereford, Leominster is a beautiful old wool town on the River Lugg, with a number of black and white half-timbered houses as well as a church dating back to the 12th century. Ledbury, to the east of Hereford, also has a number of half timbered houses. It makes a good centre from which to explore the Malvern Hills to the North. The Malverns are a feature of the landscape, running ten miles from North to South and rising to 1,395 ft at the Worcestershire Beacon. The hills have a number of walks and trails and it is said that 14 counties can be seen from the ridge on a fine day. Much of the building of Great Malvern was carried out by the Victorians who came to take the waters. The area also has a strong connection with the composer Sir Edward Elgar, who lived in the area for much of his life and is buried at Little Malvern. Malvern is the site of the Three Counties Showground which hosts the Three Counties Agricultural Show in June and the Spring Gardening Show in May.

THE RIVER WYE NEAR SYMONDS YAT.

The area around Evesham and Pershore has the greatest concentration of market gardening and fruit orchards and in the spring motorists can follow the lanes for the Blossom trail. Towards Droitwich and Ombersley the land is more rolling and Bromsgrove is set in undulating farm land. Redditch grew up in the Industrial Revolution becoming, among other things, the needle capital of the world - at one time 90 per cent of the world's needles were made here. Today it is a prime example of a new town, over half is made up of countryside, parks and woodlands.

The Ancient Forest of Wyre covers 6,000 acres and is one of Britain's most important broadleaved woodlands.

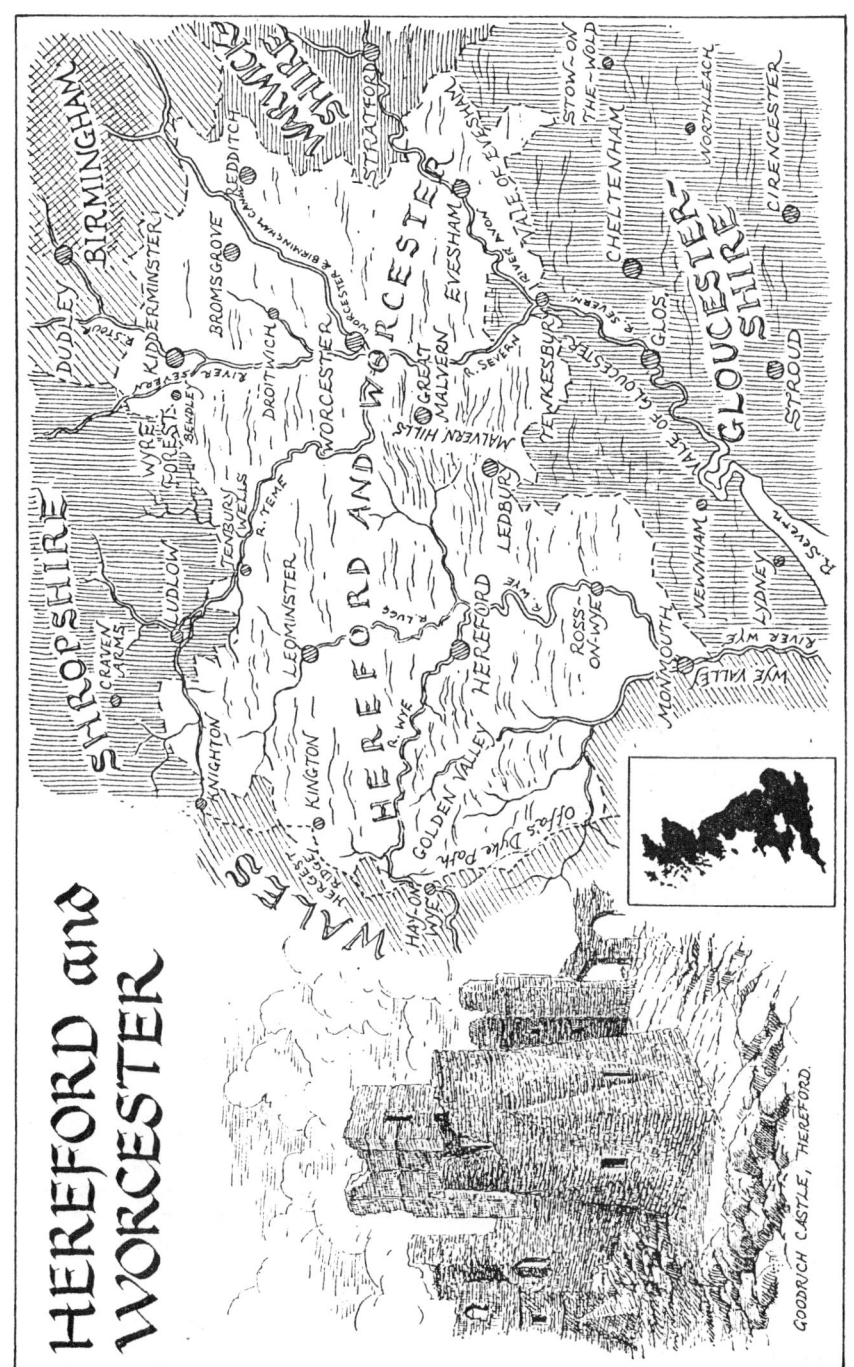

HEREFORD and WORCESTER

WARWICKSHIRE

SHROPSHIRE

GLOUCESTERSHIRE

HEREFORD AND WORCESTER

WALES

BIRMINGHAM
DUDLEY
R. STOUR
KIDDERMINSTER
REDDITCH
BROMSGROVE
WYRE FOREST
BEWDLEY
DROITWICH
RIVER SEVERN
WORCESTER CANAL & BIRMINGHAM
STRATFORD
GREAT MALVERN
EVESHAM
VALE OF EVESHAM
RIVER AVON
STOW-ON-THE-WOLD
NORTHLEACH
CIRENCESTER
CHELTENHAM
R. SEVERN
TEWKESBURY
GLOS.
VALE OF GLOUCESTER
STROUD
R. SEVERN
MALVERN HILLS
LEDBURY
HEREFORD
R. WYE
ROSS-ON-WYE
NEWNHAM
LYDNEY
RIVER WYE
WYE VALLEY
MONMOUTH
GOLDEN VALLEY
R. WYE
KINGTON
LEOMINSTER
R. LUGG
TENBURY WELLS
R. TEME
LUDLOW
CRAVEN ARMS
KNIGHTON
HEREFORD BEACON
HAY-ON-WYE
Offa's Dyke Path

GOODRICH CASTLE, HEREFORD

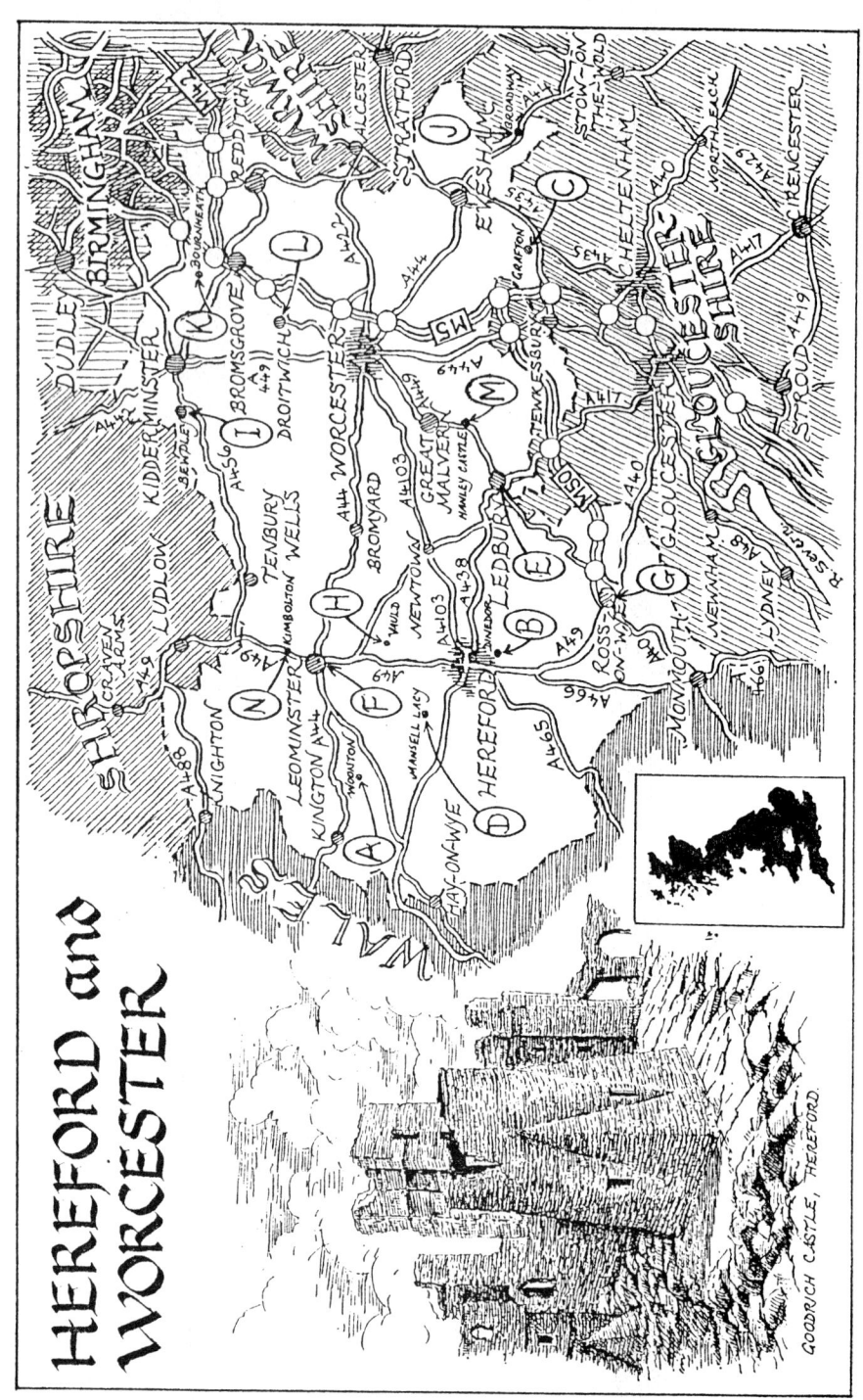

HEREFORD and WORCESTER

WALES

SHROPSHIRE

WARWICKSHIRE

GLOUCESTERSHIRE

BIRMINGHAM

DUDLEY

WORCESTER

HEREFORD

LUDLOW

KIDDERMINSTER

BROMSGROVE

DROITWICH

REDDITCH

ALCESTER

STRATFORD

EVESHAM

STOW-ON-THE-WOLD

CHELTENHAM

CIRENCESTER

STROUD

GLOUCESTER

NEWNHAM

LYDNEY

MONMOUTH

ROSS-ON-WYE

LEDBURY

GREAT MALVERN

TEWKESBURY

HANLEY CASTLE

BROMYARD

TENBURY WELLS

LEOMINSTER

KINGTON

KNIGHTON

HAY-ON-WYE

NEWTOWN

MANSELL LACY

WOONTON

WIGMORE

MULD

KIMBOLTON

BENTLEY

BOURNHEATH

CRAVEN ARMS

BROADWAY

NORTHLEACH

A

B

C

D

E

F

G

H

I

J

K

L

M

N

GOODRICH CASTLE, HEREFORD.

Rose Cottage, Woonton, Almeley, Herefordshire, HR3 6QW   Nearest Road A480

A romantic 16th century cottage set in 2 acres of period gardens and grounds. Peaceful location with fine views towards the black mountains. There are 3 delightful double bedrooms all with drinks tray, hairdryer, clock/radio and central heating. One has 4 poster and en-suite facilities. The oak panelled hall leads to the cosy oak beamed breakfast room and sitting room with log fires in winter. Furnished with antiques and interesting collection of china and samplers. Hearty breakfasts and vegetarian available. Come and meet our pet sheep! 2 Crowns.

Mrs Jackie Kingdon
Tel: 01544 340436

B&B from £16, Rooms are 3 double 1 of which is en-suite, all have tea/coffee making facilities, Restricted smoking, Pets by arrangement, Open all year. Map Ref: A

Dinedor Court, Dinedor, Herefordshire HR2 6LE   Nearest Road A49

Beside the River Wye, surrounded by rolling farmland and cider orchards, Dinedor Court is a rambling 16th century farmhouse. We have the peace and quiet of the countryside but are only 3 miles from the cathedral city of Hereford. Spacious bedrooms, oak panelled dining hall, guests' sitting room, log fires in season. All bedrooms have tea/coffee making facilities.

Mrs Rosemary Price
Tel: 01432 870481

B&B from £15, Rooms 1 double, 1 twin, Minimum age 10, No smoking in bedrooms, Open March - November. Map Ref: B

Grafton Villa Farm, Grafton, Herefordshire HR2 8ED   Nearest Road A49

An early 18th century farmhouse beautifully appointed, furnished with antiques and complimented by beautiful fabrics and decor. Centrally heated throughout. All rooms are comfortable and have tea/coffee making facilities, and TV. Guests can relax in a log fired lounge or enjoy delicious meals in a separate sun filled dining room overlooking the garden and patio. Breakfast is a choice of cereals, fresh grapefruit or prune and apricot compote, followed by an English breakfast, or a choice from the extensive menu.

Mrs Jennie Layton
Tel: 01432 268689

B&B from £16, Rooms 1 twin, 1 double, 1 family (all have en-suite or private facilities), Pets are allowed by prior arrangement, Open all year except Christmas, Map Ref: C

Appletree Cottage, Mansell Lacy, Hereford, Herefordshire, HR4 7HH   Nearest Road A480

Appletree Cottage was originally one cottage and then a cider house and eventually 2 converted farm cottages. One cottage was built in 1450 and the more modern one around the late 16th century. The house is fully centrally heated. There is an open plan sitting room with wood burning stove and dining room. English country breakfasts are served and evening meals and packed lunches are available by prior arrangement. We are surrounded by many places of historical interest.

Mrs Monica Barker
Tel: 0198122 688

B&B from £15, Dinner by prior arrangement, Rooms: 1 single/double, 2 twin (1 en-suite), All rooms have tea/coffee making facilities, No smoking, Open all year, Map Ref: D

Wall Hills Country Guest House, Hereford Road, Ledbury, HR8 2PR   **Nearest Road A438, M50**

This elegant Georgian mansion house stands on the hill slopes overlooking Ledbury. The views over the surrounding Herefordshire countryside are superb and the house itself is of some historical interest, having a 15th century Cruck barn as part of the property. The food is excellent using only the best quality fresh ingredients. Children of all ages are most welcome and parents will enjoy the relaxing atmosphere of the spacious house. This peaceful country location provides an excellent centre from which to explore the many attractions that the region has to offer.

David & Jennifer Slaughter
Tel: 01531 632833

B&B from £22.50, Dinner from £16.50, Rooms 1 double, 1 family, 1 twin, Restricted smoking, Open all year except Christmas and New Year, Map Ref: E

New House Farm, Much Marcle, Ledbury, Herefordshire HR8 2PH   **Nearest Road A449, M50**

Anne and Tom Jordan offer you a warm welcome to their delightful, fully modernised farmhouse enjoying panoramic views over Herefordshire, Worcestershire and Gloucestershire. Comfortable bedrooms with wash basins and tea/coffee making facilities. Guests bathroom, sitting room with log fire and an outdoor swimming pool.

Mrs Anne Jordan
Tel: 01531 660604

B&B from £15, Dinner from £10, Rooms 1 double, 1 twin, Minimum age 6, Open all year except Christmas, Map Ref: E

Highfield, Newtown, Ivington Road, Leominster, Herefordshire HR6 8QD   **Nearest Road A44**

Highfield stands in a large garden with unspoilt views of open farmland and distant mountains and enjoys a pleasant rural situation just 1½ miles from the old market town of Leominster. The house was built around the turn of the century and accommodation is elegant, comfortable and friendly being well proportioned and attractively decorated. Meals are carefully prepared from good fresh ingredients and delightfully served in the charming dining room. All gastronomic needs and desires are catered for and a modest wine list is available. Groups and house parties welcome.

Catherine and Marguerite
Fothergill
Tel: 01568 61 3216

B&B from £18.50, Dinner from £10 by arrangement, Rooms 1 double, 2 twin ensuite/private facilities, Open all year, Map Ref: F

Lower Bache, Kimbolton, Near Leominster, Herefordshire HR6 0ER   **Nearest Road A4112**

Just 4 miles from the historic town of Leominster lies Lower Bache a sympathetically restored 17th century farmhouse nestling in 14 acres of a tiny tranquil unspoilt Herefordshire valley. The self contained suites, each with bath/shower room and private sitting room, are delightfully furnished in period country style. The dining room, converted from the cider making annexe and featuring the original cider mill, is the setting for meals from the renowned cuisine of Rose & Leslie Wiles. ETB Highly commended Lower Bache is a fitting retreat for lovers of comfort and fine food.

Rose & Leslie Wiles
Tel: 01568 87 750304

B&B from £24.50, Dinner from £11.50, Rooms 2 double, 1 twin (all en-suite), Restricted smoking, Minimum age 8, Open all year except Christmas, Map Ref: N

The Hills Farm, Leysters, Leominster, Herefordshire HR6 0HP   **Nearest Road A4112**

A 15th century farmhouse in the heart of rural north Herefordshire with fine views over the surrounding countryside. The dining room, which was once a dairy, has separate tables and adjoins a pretty sitting room with wood burning stove. A 3 course dinner is served at 7 pm and a vegetarian menu is available. The 4 luxury bedrooms are all heated, have colour TV, clock radios and tea/coffee making facilities. Leysters is ideally situated for touring and exploring Herefordshire, Worcestershire, Shropshire and the Welsh borders.

Peter & Jane Conolly
Tel: 01568 750205

B&B from £20, Dinner from £15, Rooms 1 twin en-suite, 3 double (1 with private bathroom, 2 en-suite), No smoking, Minimum age 12, Pets allowed on request, Open February - November, Map Ref: F

Sunnymount Hotel, Ryefield Road, Ross-on-Wye, Herefordshire HR9 5LU   **Nearest Road A40**

All rooms are well appointed, bright and cheerful and full central heating, en-suite facilities and tea/coffee trays. There is a choice for breakfast and' in the evening a set 4 course dinner with home and locally grown vegetables. A vegetarian menu is available. The hotel is well placed for touring Upper and Lower Wye Valley, The Brecon Beacons, Forest of Dean and the Malverns. The region has many recreational facilities and tourist attractions including golf, bird watching, Symonds Yat and the Falconry Centre.

Geoff & Peggy Williams
Tel: 019895 63880

B&B from £23, Dinner £15, Rooms 1 single, 2 twin, 3 double (all en-suite), Restricted smoking, Open all year except Christmas, Map Ref: G

Vauld Farm, Vauld, Herefordshire, HR1 3HA   **Nearest Road A49**

This ancient farmhouse, built in 1510, has black timbered walls, which have become lopsided with age. Step through the door and you enter into a great room with stone slabbed floor, half timbered walls, log fire and beams overhead. The granary suite has a private sitting room, bedroom, bathroom and gallery with double bed. The ground floor oak room has a 4 poster bed. Further accommodation is in the converted 17th century barn. This is in an area of picturesque villages, medieval churches and stately gardens.

Mrs Jean Bengry
Tel: 01568 797 898

B&B from £15, Dinner from £15 (4 courses), Rooms: 1 twin, 3 double, 1 family, (2 double en-suite), tea/coffee making facilities in all rooms, Restricted smoking, Minimum age 12, Open all year, Map Ref: H

Lightmarsh Farm, Crundalls Lane, Bewdley, Worcs., DY12 1NE   **Nearest Road B4190**

Lightmarsh Farm is a small pasture farm which lies a little over 1 mile north of the picturesque and historic settlement of Bewdley. The 18th century farmhouse enjoys an elevated position with fine views southwards towards Worcester. Inside there is a cosy lounge with inglenook fireplace where a log fire burns on chilly evenings and the bedrooms which enjoy pleasant views, have tea/coffee making facilities. At the front of the house is a small garden where many species of birds are often to be observed. ETB highly commended.

Mrs P A Grainger
Tel: 01299 404027

B&B from £16.50, Rooms 1 double, 1 twin, (both with private facilities), Minimum age 10, Restricted smoking, Open all year except Christmas, Map Ref: I

Cowley House, Church Street, Broadway, Worcestershire WR12 7AE   Nearest Road A44

Cowley House was originally a Cotswold stone barn and farmhouse, dating from the 17th century, recently restored and refurbished with period antiques, retaining the character and atmosphere of the original, combined with modern facilities. Standing in its own grounds of $^2/_3$rds of an acre in a secluded central position just off the village green, but only 2 minutes walk from Broadway's numerous shops and restaurants, the beamed rooms are tastefully furnished with central heating, TV, radio alarms and en-suite facilities including 4-poster en-suite.

Mrs Mary Kemp
Tel: 01386 853262

B&B from £20, Rooms 1 single, 1 twin, 3 double, 1 family (all en-suite), No smoking, Minimum age 3, Open all year, Map Ref: J

Manor Farm, Broadway, Worcestershire WR12 7NL   Nearest Road B4632

Once this house was known as Charity Farm because 'dole' was dispensed to wayfarers. Now known as Manor Farm this is an attractive period farm house opposite the Church in the quiet village of Wormington. Being about 4 miles from Broadway it is ideally situated for touring the Cotswolds. There are leaded casements in the sitting room, a stone Inglenook in the hall, Welsh slate on the floor and old beams everywhere. Access to 400 acres of farm with horses and cattle. There is a trout stream and fishing can be arranged on request.

Mrs Pauline Russell
Tel: 01386 584302

B&B from £15, Rooms 1 twin, 2 double all with en-suite/private facilities and have tea/coffee trays, Restricted smoking, Minimum age 5, Pets by arrangement, Open all year, Map Ref: J

Windrush House, Station Road, Broadway, Worcester WR12 7DE   Nearest Road Station Road

Broadway is a beautiful Cotswold village and sometimes called, "The Showcase Village of England". It is an ideal touring centre for visiting Worcester, Stratford-upon-Avon, Cheltenham, Warwick and Cirencester. Windrush is an Edwardian guest house which is situated 300 yards from the centre of the village. Evening meals are available by prior arrangement. A tarrif of 10 % discount after 2 days. All rooms have en-suite showers, TV, hairdryer and teasmade. This is a non-smoking establishment.

Alex & Ruth Travers
Tel: 01386 853577

B&B from £18, Dinner from £12 (by arrangement), Rooms 1 twin, 3 double (all with private facilities), No smoking, Pets by arrangement, Open early February - end November, Map Ref: J

Hill Farm, Rocky Lane, Bournheath, Bromsgrove, Worcs., B61 9HU   Nearest Road M42

Hill Farm has overlooked the peaceful countryside of Bournheath for 250 years. This Georgian listed building, with its medieval cruck barn, makes the ideal base for touring the heart of England. Four generations of the Rutter family have lived and worked on the farm and, during the summer months, guests can enjoy the delights of 'pick your own' fruits. There is a spacious lounge/dining room with colour TV overlooking south facing gardens. Birmingham Convention Centre, National Exhibition Centre and Birmingham Airport are 20 minutes drive away along the M42.

Mrs Lily Rutter
Tel: 01527 872403

B&B from £17.50, Dinner from £11.50 on request, Rooms 1 double, 2 twin, 2 single, Minimum age 3, Open all year, Map Ref: K

Caulin Court, Ladywood, Near Droitwich, Worcestershire WR9 0AL   **Nearest Road A449, A389**

Caulin Court is a beautiful country residence set in 20 acres. It has a tennis court and swimming pool which residents are welcome to use. There is a stable yard behind the house and all pets are welcome to use the spacious stables. All rooms are centrally heated with private bathroom, colour TV, and tea/coffee making facilities. Caulin Court is 10 minutes drive from both Droitwich and Worcester. It has easy access to junction 6 of the M5 which leads to M42/M40/M6 Birmingham, B'ham Airport, NEC, Stratford and Cotswolds. A warm welcome assured.

B&B from £20, Dinner by arrangement from £10,

Mrs S Harfield
Tel: 01905 756382

Rooms 1 single, 1 twin, 1 double (all en-suite), Restricted smoking, Pets allowed in stables only, Open all year, Map Ref: L

Old Parsonage Farm, Hanley Castle, Worcester WR8 0BU   **Nearest Road M5, M50**

Old Parsonage Farm is a fine mellow brick 18th century country residence. The location is superb enjoying beautiful views of the Malvern Hills and surrounding countryside. The house is beautifully decorated with attention to detail thanks to Ann Addison's natural flair for interior design. Besides this she is an accomplished cook producing imaginative dishes of a high standard. To complement this, husband Tony, is a wine expert. There are over 100 wines in stock. All in all a very impressive house.

B&B from £20.50, Dinner £14.75, Rooms 2 double/twin, 1 family,

Mrs Ann Addison
Tel: 01684 310124

Restricted smoking, Minimum age 12, Open January to December, Map Ref: M

WORCESTER CATHEDRAL.

KENT

"As I went down by Dymchurch Wall,
I heard the South sing o'er the land;
I saw the yellow sunlight fall
On knolls where Norman churches stand."

(John Davidson - In Romney Marsh)

KENT

SANDWICH; THE MEDIEVAL BARBICAN.

Kent is a county for all seasons with its orchards and gardens but is also a county steeped in history. Its great passenger port, Dover, is the Gateway to Britain, whose harbours are thronged with cross-Channel ferries, cargo boats and yachts, all overlooked by the grey walls of Dover Castle. Known since the height of the Cinque Ports - powerful, prosperous ports whose men and ships guarded their king and country - as the Key to England, Dover is one of the most strategic strongholds in Europe. Inland there are also dramatic castles. The 13th century splendour of Leeds Castle has been enlarged and enriched over the century by Kings of England. Both Leeds and Lullingstone were loved by Henry VIII and Anne Boleyn, whose childhood home was Hever Castle.

Kent has hundreds of well preserved historical buildings and many eminent people have been associated with the county, leaving houses as reminders of their lives and times. One of the county's most famous landmarks is Canterbury Cathedral. Canterbury is the cradle of Christianity in Saxon England, standing on a site that had been occupied for 350 years when the Romans arrived in AD 43. The long grey cathedral is the mother church of Anglicans throughout the world. It dates from Norman times and for 350 years after the murder of Thomas Becket in the cathedral in 1170 it was the destination of countless pilgrims.

Maidstone, the county town of Kent, is a thriving commercial and business centre with excellent shopping and leisure facilities - but there are many reminders of the town's historical past from the old gatehouse to the Archbishop's Palace.

Sevenoaks is still a typical market town, despite its closeness to London. In the town centre there are many old buildings including the Market House and the Red House, the home of Jane Austen's uncle whom she often visited.

CANTERBURY CATHEDRAL, MAIN TOWER.

Royal Tunbridge Wells was a fashionable spa in the 17th to 19th centuries and in Georgian times the aristocracy flocked here to indulge in high society life.

Kent's holiday coast in the North thrives on its good sands, safe bathing and record for long hours of sunshine and low rainfall. The towns mix the grace and charm of Regency houses with Victorian Gothic, yet there is plenty of modern entertainment. Off the coast are 2 islands. Thanet is an island in name only although in Roman and Saxon times it was separated from the mainland by the Rivers Stour and Wantsum. Sheppey (Isle of Sheep) is cut off from the mainland by the narrow Swale Channel and crossed only by the Kingsferry Bridge. Margate and neighbouring Ramsgate are popular resorts and both have miles of safe sands and plenty of entertainment, although Ramsgate is more of a sea-going and olde worlde town. Broadstairs is another popular seaside town and there are reminders of the Flemish weavers in Sandwich, an ancient Cinque Port now two miles from the sea.

DOVER CASTLE.

KENT

TUDOR BUILDINGS, SANDWICH.

LONDON
ESSEX
SOUTHEND-ON-SEA
GRAVESEND
ROCHESTER
RIVER MEDWAY
NAVAL
CHATHAM
GILLINGHAM
SHEERNESS
ISLE OF
SHEPPEY
THE SWALE
MARGATE
BROADSTAIRS
RAMSGATE
PEGWELL BAY
SANDWICH BAY
SANDWICH
DEAL
MARGARET'S BAY
EAST WEAR BAY
HERNE BAY
ISLE
OF THANET
WHITSTABLE
ROMAN ROAD
FAVERSHAM
CANTERBURY
STOUR
DOVER
FOLKESTONE
STONE STREET (ROMAN ROAD)
ASHFORD
PILGRIMS' WAY
NORTH DOWNS
MAIDSTONE
R. MEDWAY
SEVENOAKS
PILGRIMS' WAY
R. BEULT
TONBRIDGE
ROYAL
TUNBRIDGE
WELLS
VALE OF KENT
BIDDENDEN
CRANBROOK
R. ROTHER
TENTERDEN
THE WEALD
ROMNEY
ROMNEY MARSH
WALLAND
MARSH
RYE
RYE BAY
DUNGENESS
R. ROTHER
UCKFIELD
HEATHFIELD
SUSSEX
BEXHILL
HASTINGS

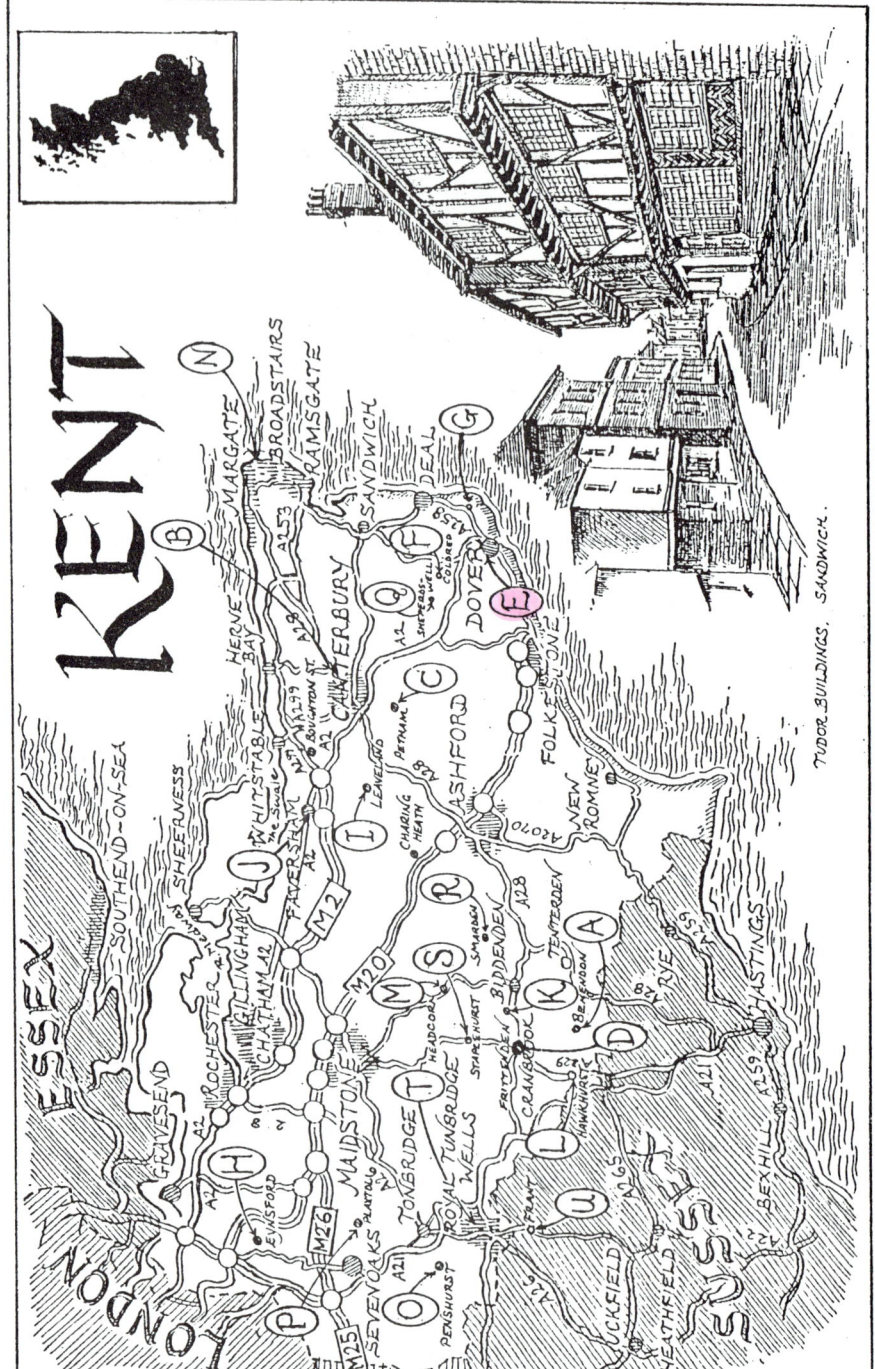

KENT

TUDOR BUILDINGS, SANDWICH.

Crit Hall, Cranbrook Road, Benenden, Kent TN17 4EU   **Nearest Road A262, A229**

Crit Hall, an elegant classic Georgian house with extensive views over the Weald of Kent. It is equipped to accommodate the most discerning of guests and is now recognised to be one of the most acclaimed private houses in the south of England offering bed & breakfast and (optional) imaginative dinners. Guests have their own drawing room and convervatory. Bedrooms are either en-suite or have a private bathroom and are exceptionally well and fully appointed. Crit Hall is licenced and ideally situated for visiting the gardens and historic houses of Kent and Sussex.

Sue & John Bruder
Tel: 01580 240609
Fax: 01580 241743

B&B from £24, Dinner from £16.50, Rooms 2 twin, 1 double,
No smoking, Minimum age 12,
Open mid January - mid December, Map Ref: A

Zan Stel Lodge, 140 Old Dover Road, Canterbury, Kent, CT1 3NX   **Nearest Road M2/A2**

A warm and friendly welcome is assured at Zan Stel Lodge which is situated adjacent to the Kent County Cricket Ground and only 10 minutes walk to the city centre. The spacious, comfortable, bedrooms all have colour TV and tea/coffee making facilities. Two of the double bedrooms are en-suite. A full English breakfast is provided and vegetarians can be catered for on request. An attractive patio area for guests to sit in when warm and sunny, leading to an attractive garden. Private carpark and garage available.

Zandra & Ron Stedman
Tel: 01227 453654

B&B from £34, Rooms 1 twin, 3 double (en-suite available),
No smoking, Minimum age 9, Open all year, Map Ref: B

Upper Ansdore, Duckpit Lane, Petham, Canterbury, Kent CT4 5QB   **Nearest Road B2068/A2**

Upper Ansdore Farmhouse dates from the 14th century with later additions. Situated in a sylvan setting with far reaching views across the valley overlooking a Kent trust nature reserve. All bedrooms have en-suite facilities and tea/coffee trays. A full English breakfast is provided with free range eggs. This is an excellent location for walking, cycling, and exploring the surrounding areas.

Roger & Susan Linch
Tel: 01227 700672

B&B from £18, Rooms 1 twin, 3 double, 1 family (all en-suite),
No smoking, Open all year except Christmas, Map Ref: C

Thanington Hotel, 140 Wincheap, Canterbury, Kent CT1 3RY   **Nearest Road A28**

Thanington House was built in approximately 1800 and is listed Grade II of architectural interest. The hotel now offers 'up market' bed and breakfast accommodation for the discerning traveller, whether it be for business or pleasure. All bedrooms are en-suite and boast toiletries, telephone, TV, trouser press, hairdryer, hot beverage making facilities and a personal wall safe. In the evening you can enjoy a quiet drink in the bar and during the day the walled garden is quite delightful. Heated indoor swimming pool and snooker room. 10 minutes walk to city centre.

Jill & David Jenkins
Tel: 01227 453227

B&B from £27.50, Rooms 5 double, 2 family, 3 twin,
Open all year, Map Ref: B

Hancocks Farmhouse, Tilsden Lane, Cranbook, Kent, TN17 3PH   Nearest Road A229

Hancock's Farmhouse is a well preserved timber framed listed building situated just outside the attractive Wealden town of Cranbook with its famous windmill and fine parish church. Surrounded by farmland, the house is comfortably furnished with antiques. Guests have the use of the spacious drawing room which has a large inglenook fireplace with log fires for cooler evenings. Good home cooking. There is a lovely garden for guests to enjoy. Cranbrook is an ideal centre for visiting picturesque villages and places of interest. Close to Sissinghurst Gardens.

Bridget & Robin Oaten
Tel: 01580 714645

B&B from £22.50, Dinner from £15, Rooms 2 double, 1 twin,
Minimum age 12, No smoking, Open all year, Map Ref: D

Castle House, 10 Castle Hill Road, Dover, Kent CT16 1QW   Nearest Road A2/M2 and A20/M20

Close to the town centre at the foot of Dover Castle, this small guest house dates from 1830 and provides comfortable accommodation, good food and a warm welcome from Rodney and Elizabeth. All rooms have private facilities and colour television. There is a small lounge for guests and a payphone. Ideally situated for the ferries and hoverport and 10 minutes from the channel tunnel.

Rodney & Elizabeth Dimech
Tel: 01304 201656
Fax: 01304 210197

B&B from £15, Rooms 4 double, 1 twin, 1 single,
No smoking, Open all year, Map Ref: E

Coldred Court Farm, Church Road, Coldred, Nr Dover, Kent CT15 5AQ   Nearest Road A2

Coldred Court Farm is a charming red brick 16th century farmhouse with a warm and welcoming atmosphere. Situated on an historic site in attractive countryside between Dover and Canterbury. Beautifully decorated with patchwork quilts, embroidered curtains, dried and fresh flowers. Bedrooms have tea/coffee making facilities and are all en-suite. Good position for visiting Dover and Canterbury and several historic monuments, etc.

Mrs Truda Kelly
Tel: 01304 830816
Fax: 01304 830816

B&B from £19, Dinner from £10, Rooms 2 double, 1 twin (all en-suite),
Restricted smoking, Open all year except Christmas and New Year,
Map Ref: F

Wallett's Court, West Cliffe, St Margaret's, Dover, Kent CT15 6EW   Nearest Road A258, A2

Wallett's Court is an old manor house set in lovely open countryside within easy reach of spectacular cliff scenery, the channel ports, championship golf courses and the cathedral city of Canterbury. The house has great character with beamed ceilings, red brick walls, inglenook fireplaces, and leaded lights. The en-suite bedrooms have tea/coffee making facilities, TV and telephone. All are furnished with flair and one room has a 4 poster bed. There is a guests' lounge. The renowned restaurant is open to non residents all week and offers a special 5 course menu on Saturdays.

Chris & Lea Oakley
Tel: 01304 852424
Fax: 01304 853430

B&B from £25, Dinner from £20.25, Rooms 2 twin, 8 double,
(all en-suite), Restricted smoking, Open all year, Map Ref: G

Home Farm, Riverside, Eynsford, Kent DA4 0AE   **Nearest Road M25, M20, A225**

We welcome you to our arable farm in the heart of the Darent Valley, an area of outstanding natural beauty. Home Farm is an 18th century listed house near the centre of the picturesque village of Eynsford. The accommodation is spacious and comfortable and all bedrooms are en-suite. We offer a full English breakfast and for the evening there is a choice of restaurants and pubs in the village. An ideal base for those visiting London or Brands Hatch and the many National Trust properties within easy reach.

Mrs Sarah Alexander
Tel: 01322 866193

B&B from £18, Rooms 2 double, 1 twin, (all en-suite)
No smoking,Open March - November, Map Ref: A

Leaveland Court, Leaveland, Faversham, Kent ME13 0NP   **Nearest Road A251, M2**

15th century Leaveland Court is an enchanting timber framed farmhouse with adjoining granary and stables. In a quiet rural setting the house nestles between 13th century Leaveland church and woodlands retaining its true character being at the heart of a 300 acre working downland farm. Offering high standard of accommodation and cuisine, a warm welcome is always assured. All bedrooms are en-suite and have tea/coffee making facilities. Guests are invited to use the heated outdoor swimming pool set in secluded and attractive gardens.

Mrs Corrine Scutt
Tel: 01233 740596

B&B from £20, Dinner from £10.50, Rooms 1 double, 2 twin
(all en-suite), No smoking, Open all year, Map Ref: I

Frith Farm House, Otterden, Faversham, Kent ME13 0DD   **Nearest Road A20, A2**

Frith Farm is situated on the North Downs in an area of outstanding natural beauty. The house, an elegant Georgian building, is reached by a sweeping drive and surrounded by well looked after lawns and gardens. The interior is decorated with flair and great individuality using fine fabrics and antiques. A delightful and relaxing place to stay. One bedroom has a 4 poster and all have en-suite shower, tea/coffee making facilities, and TV. Horse riding, golf, Pilgrims and North Downs Way are all nearby. A warm welcome is assured.

Markham & Susan Chesterfield
Tel: 01795 890701
Fax: 01795 890009

B&B from £23.50, Dinner £17.50, Rooms 1 twin, 2 double (all en-suite), No smoking, Minimum age 10, Open all year, Map Ref: J

Maplehurst Mill, Mill Lane, Frittenden, Kent, TN17 2DT   **Nearest Road A229**

Maplehurst Mill is a beautiful watermill lying in tranquil countryside with many gardens, castles, country houses and medieval towns just a short distance away, yet surprisingly only an hours journey from London. The mill's 11 acres, surrounded by water, are full of wildlife and guests are free to explore them. The mill has 3 pretty en-suite bedrooms and a large comfortable drawing room all with views over the water. Breakfast and dinner are served in the connecting medieval miller's house. There is a heated swimming pool for guests use.

Mrs Heather Parker
Tel: 01580 852203

B&B from £27, Dinner from £17, Rooms 1 double, 2 twin (all en-suite),
Minimum age 12, No smoking, Open all year, Map Ref: K

Conghurst Farm, Conghurst Lane, Hawkhurst, Kent TN18 4RW

Nearest Road A268

Conghurst is a Georgian farmhouse situated on the Kent and Sussex border in beautiful unspoilt countryside. It is totally peaceful and undisturbed, surrounded by farmland, yet within easy reach of the many historic houses and gardens this area has to offer. The bedrooms are well furnished with either private or en-suite facilities and tea and coffee trays. There is an elegant drawing room and a separate guests' television room. Excellent evening meals are available, by prior arrangement, using fresh local produce as much as possible.

Mrs Rosemary Piper
Tel: 01580 753331
Fax: 01580 754579

B&B from £20, Dinner from £12 (by arrangement),
Rooms 2 twin, 1 double (all private/en-suite) No smoking,
Minimum age 12, Open February - November, Map Ref: L

Vine Farm, Waterman Quarter, Headcorn, Kent TN27 9JJ

Nearest Road A274, M20

Vine Farm is a working sheep farm centered around a 16th century listed farmhouse, in a peaceful position along its own private track and surrounded by ponds and garden - Jane Harman is a keen gardener. The house is attractively furnished with antiques; there is a guests' sitting room and 3 charming bedrooms all with en-suite/private bathrooms and tea/coffee making facilities. Vine Farm is 2 miles south of Headcorn (BR 1 hour London) and being in the centre of Kent is an excellent base for visiting the county's many historic sites and gardens (Sissinghurst 4 miles).

Mrs Jane Harman
Tel: 01622 890 203
Fax: 01622 891 819

B&B from £19.50, Dinner from £15, Rooms 2 double, 1 twin,
(all en-suite or private facilities), Minimum age 12, No pets,
No smoking, Open all year except Christmas, Map Ref: M

The Greswolde Hotel, 20 Surrey Road, Cliftonville, Margate, Kent CT9 2LA

Nearest Road A28

This elegant Victorian terraced house, retaining much of its original character and charm, is situated close to the sea at Walpole Bay. The house is filled with Victorian memorabilia and is cosy and welcoming. The lounge/reading room has winged armchairs with the original Victorian fireplace and is a pleasant place to relax. Breakfast is taken in the attractively decorated dining room The spacious bedrooms offer a good degree of comfort with en-suite, CTV and tea/coffee making facilities. This hotel is popular with business travellers and tourists from many countries.

Mrs Ann Earl
Tel: 01843 223956

B&B from £18, Rooms 3 double, 3 twin (all en-suite),
Restricted smoking, Pets by arrangement, Open all year, Map Ref: N

Swale Cottage, Old Swaylands Lane, Off Poundsbridge Lane, Penshurst, Kent TN11 8AH

A26

Swale Cottage was part of a 13th century yeoman farm. Surrounded by a country cottage garden, this Grade II listed barn and hayloft conversion is as pretty as any in Kent. Behind leaded light windows is a frilly 4 poster, a draped brass knobbed bedstead and twin beds, all with TV and tea trays. A delicious breakfast is served at a communal antique table. A few yards from where *Peter Pan's friend Wendy lived.* AA 5Q's, Awarded Best New Guesthouse in the South of England, ETB listed Highly Commended. A26 off B2176, ½ mile south east of Penshurst Place.

Mrs Cynthia Dakin
Tel: 01892 870738

B&B from £25, Rooms 1 twin (with private facilities), 2 double (en-suite), No smoking, Minimum age 10, Open all year, Map Ref: O

Jordans, Sheet Hill, Plaxtol, Sevenoaks, Kent TN15 0PU   **Nearest Road A227**

An exquisite picture postcard Tudor house, dating from the 15th century, and which has been awarded the "Historic Building of Kent" and has a plaque to this effect. The atmosphere is enhanced by its leaded windows, inglenooks and oak beams. The delightful double bedrooms have there own TV. Mrs Lindsay is a keen gardener and her garden is a gem; she is also an artist and her work is displayed throughout the house. Quietly situated in a picturesque village, an ideal base for visiting many historic places including Hever Castle, Chartwell, Leeds Castle, Igntham Mote, etc.

Mrs Jo Lindsay   **B&B from £24, Rooms 1 single, 2 double, Minimum age 11,**
Tel: 01732 810379   **No smoking, Open mid February - mid December, Map Ref: P**

Sunshine Cottage, The Green, Shepherdswell, Kent CT15 7LQ   **Nearest Road A2**

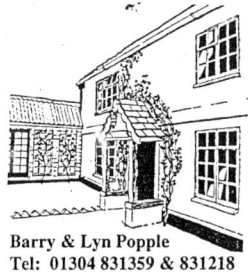

A Grade II listed cottage overlooking Shepherdswell village green between Canterbury and Dover, 25 mins from Channel Tunnel. The 1635 cottage has been carefully restored with a wealth of beams, inglenook in the sitting room and wood burning stove in the lounge. Breakfast, evening meal, and supper are served in the dining room where there is a display of antique china. The bedrooms are cosily furnished have tea/coffee makers, some have antique brass bedsteads and some with private facilities. Guests are welcome in the garden & courtyard and there is a guests' lounge with TV.

Barry & Lyn Popple   **B&B from £18.50, Dinner from £13, Supper from £6, Rooms 1 twin,**
Tel: 01304 831359 & 831218   **5 double (2 en-suite), No smoking, Open all year. Map Ref: Q**

Munk's Farm, Smarden, Kent TN27 8PN   **Nearest Road A274**

There will be a warm welcome at Munk's Farm set in one acre of garden with a large swimming pool and 2 natural ponds surrounded by fields. It is a Grade II listed building built in the 18th century. It is heavily oak beamed with inglenooks. The bedrooms are tastefully furnished with private bathroom, colour television, and hairdryer. Guests have breakfast in the attractive dining hall (formerly the farmhouse kitchen) and may use the drawing room (formerly the stables), the garden and swimming pool (when open). This is a perfect base for touring Kent.

Ian & Josephine Scott   **B&B from £20, Dinner from £16, Rooms 2 twin (en-suite),**
Tel: 01233 770265   **No smoking, Minimum age 12, Open all year, Map Ref: R**

Little Pagehurst, Pagehurst Road, Staplehurst, Tonbridge, Kent TN12 0JA   **A20, M20, A229**

Little Pagehurst is a 500 years old Grade II listed house set in peaceful countryside, which looks as though it had been planted in its beautiful 4 acre garden. The house faces south and has warm, gracious rooms, exposed beams, inglenook fireplaces and comfortable antique furniture. All bedrooms have hand basin, tea/coffee making facilities, their own bathroom and lovely views of the garden with its roses, lawns, shrubs and borders. There is a heated outdoor swimming pool, tennis court and croquet, while Leeds and Sissinghurst castles are both within easy reach.

Mrs Anna Emanuel   **B&B from £24, Rooms 1 twin, 2 double, Restricted smoking,**
Tel: 01580 891486   **Minimum age 12, Open March - December, Map Ref: S**

Ash Tree Cottage, 7 Eden Road, Tunbridge Wells, Kent TN1 1TS   **Nearest Road A26/A264**

A very attractive bungalow in a very quiet area of Tunbridge Wells close to High Street and Pantiles. Beautifully decorated throughout with fine furniture and a homely and friendly atmosphere. The comfortable en-suite bedrooms have tea/coffee making facilities and TV. Excellent centre for travelling around Kent and East Sussex.

Richard & Sue Rogers
Tel: 01892 541317

B&B from £20, Rooms 2 en-suite twin, No smoking, Minimum age 9, Open February - end November, Map Ref: T

Blundeston, Eden Road, Tunbridge Wells, Kent TN1 1TS   **Nearest Road A26, A264**

Blundeston is a beautifully decorated home situated in central Tunbridge Wells within easy walking distance of the Pantiles, shops and mainline station to London. Mrs Day is an interior designer and her flair is apparent throughout. The comfortable double bedroom has its own en-suite facilities, courtesy tray and television. This is a very convenient base from which to visit many country homes, castles and gardens.

Timothy & Gillian Day
Tel: 01892 513030
Fax: 01892 517682

B&B from £22, Rooms 1 en-suite double, No smoking, Minimum age 9, Open all year, Map Ref: T

The Old Parsonage, Church Lane, Frant, Tunbridge Wells, Kent, TN3 9DX   **Nearest Road A267**

The Old Parsonage is a magnificent Georgian house in a quiet, pretty village providing superior accommodation; luxurious en-suite bedrooms including 2 4-posters, antique furnished reception rooms and a spacious sunny conservatory, where guests may relax in armchair comfort with afternoon tea, overlooking the ballustraded terrace and secluded walled garden. For evening meals the village pub restaurants are 2 mins walk away. Short drive to many historic houses and gardens. This is first class accom with friendly, helpful hosts. AA Premier selected. ETB Deluxe.

Mrs Mary Dakin
Tel: 01892 750773
Fax: 01892 750773

B&B from £25, Rooms 1 twin, 2 double (all en-suite), Restricted smoking, Pets by arrangement, Open all year, Map Ref: U

---

10 Modest Corner, Nr Tunbridge Wells, Kent TN4 0LS   **Nearest Road A26**

Quiet cul-de-sac with views. Three twin-bedded rooms, with tea/coffee making facilities, and TV. Two bathrooms each with excellent shower. Good walking and sight seeing centre and only one hour from London. Dutch and German. A unique and welcoming atmosphere.

Mrs Anneke Leemhuis
Tel: 01892 522450

B&B from £18, Dinner from £7.50 (by arrangement), Rooms - 3 twin, Restricted smoking, Pets by arrangement, Open all year, Map Ref: T

LANCASHIRE

"But oh the wild hills that look up to the skies,
Where the green bracken wave to the wind as it flies!
Sing, hey for the moorland!"

(Edwin Waugh)

LANCASHIRE

LANCASTER CASTLE

Natural beauty, industrial heritage and seaside resorts are just some of the reasons for visiting Lancashire. East Lancashire is wild moorland rising to 1,836 feet, interspersed with wooded dales and river valleys. The coastal "lung" has been the north's most popular resort area since the mid 18th century.

Lancashire's industrial centres are in an arc North of Manchester, in the South of the country and include the important cotton spinning towns of Bolton, Blackburn, Rochdale and Oldham. The towns are wedged between ridges running from North to South, including the Forest of Rossendale and Pendle Hill, rising to 1,831 ft 4 miles to the east of Clitheroe.

The Weaver's Shuttle long distance walk around Pendle, land of the famous Pendle Witches, takes ramblers around the splendour of Lancashire's hill country with views of the mills and towns. Bolton was the birthplace of Samuel Crompton (1753-1827), inventor of the spinning mule which revolutionised the textile industry and Blackburn's history of cotton weaving goes back to the 14th century when it became the home of the Flemish weavers. Cotton weaving was the main industry of Burnley and Chorley. One of Chorley's sons was Henry Tate the sugar magnate and founder of the Tate Gallery in London, who was born in the town in 1819. As well as being the birthplace of the war time singer Gracie Fields, Rochdale was also the birthplace of the Co-operative Movement. The depression of the early 19th century prompted a group of men to set up their own co-operative shop in 1844, dividing the surplus for the benefit of all. Wigan's rows of back to back houses were described by George Orwell in The Road to Wigan Pier. One of the oldest boroughs in Lancashire, the town's leading tourist attraction, Wigan Pier, takes a step back in time to the year 1900.

Lancashire boasts some of Britain's most famous seaside resorts, visited by millions of people each year . Blackpool, Britain's premier seaside resort, attracts over 17 million visits a year. Blackpool Pleasure Beach is Europe's greatest amusement park with more big thrills and attractions than any other park in the world.

THE MAIN
GATEWAY, LANCASTER CASTLE.

While much of the resort's original charm remains, these days hi-tech fund fair rides blend with gentle diversions such as tea dances in the Tower Ballroom. One of the country's most famous traditions is the Blackpool Illuminations - every Autumn the display is more spectacular than the previous year. Neighbouring Lytham St Annes is famous for its golf courses and offers a gentler pace of life. The area is renowned for its delightful parks, gardens and floral displays and its miles of sandy beaches - sand yachting is a favourite pastime.

LEIGHTON HALL , CARNFORTH.

This stretch of coast is the only place in the UK where traditional trams are still used. To the North of Blackpool the tram goes to Thornton Cleveleys, with sandy beaches and creeks to explore. Further North it reaches the famous seaside town of Fleetwood, once one of Britain's largest fishing ports. Today fishing is still important but there is plenty of other nautical activity from yachting to power boats and wind surfing.. Further North is one of Britain's most beautiful coastal stretches, Morecambe Bay. Two ancient villages - Morecambe and Heysham - have combined to form one lively resort famous for its annual music festival. There are spectacular views to the North over the Lake District hills and to the West across Morecambe Bay. At low tide it is possible to walk across Morecambe Bay from Hest Bank to Grange-over-Sands.

Lancaster, an important university city these days, has a seafaring history still in evidence today with its Georgian Quay and Maritime Museum. The home of wealthy cotton, rum and sugar merchants, the city's history goes back much further. Its skyline is dominated by Lancaster Castle which tells 800 years of history and whose royal lineage goes back to Henry IV's father. It is probably best known for its imprisonment of the Lancashire Witches.

Preston, lying at the crossroads of the region's motorway network, makes an ideal touring centre. To the West is beautiful moorland country. From the M6 motorway at Forton Services the road goes through ancient hunting forest to Abbeystead. From here a road goes by Marshaw to Dunsop Bridge through the Trough of Bowland, the wild pass along with the 20 Lancashire witches were taken from Pendle.

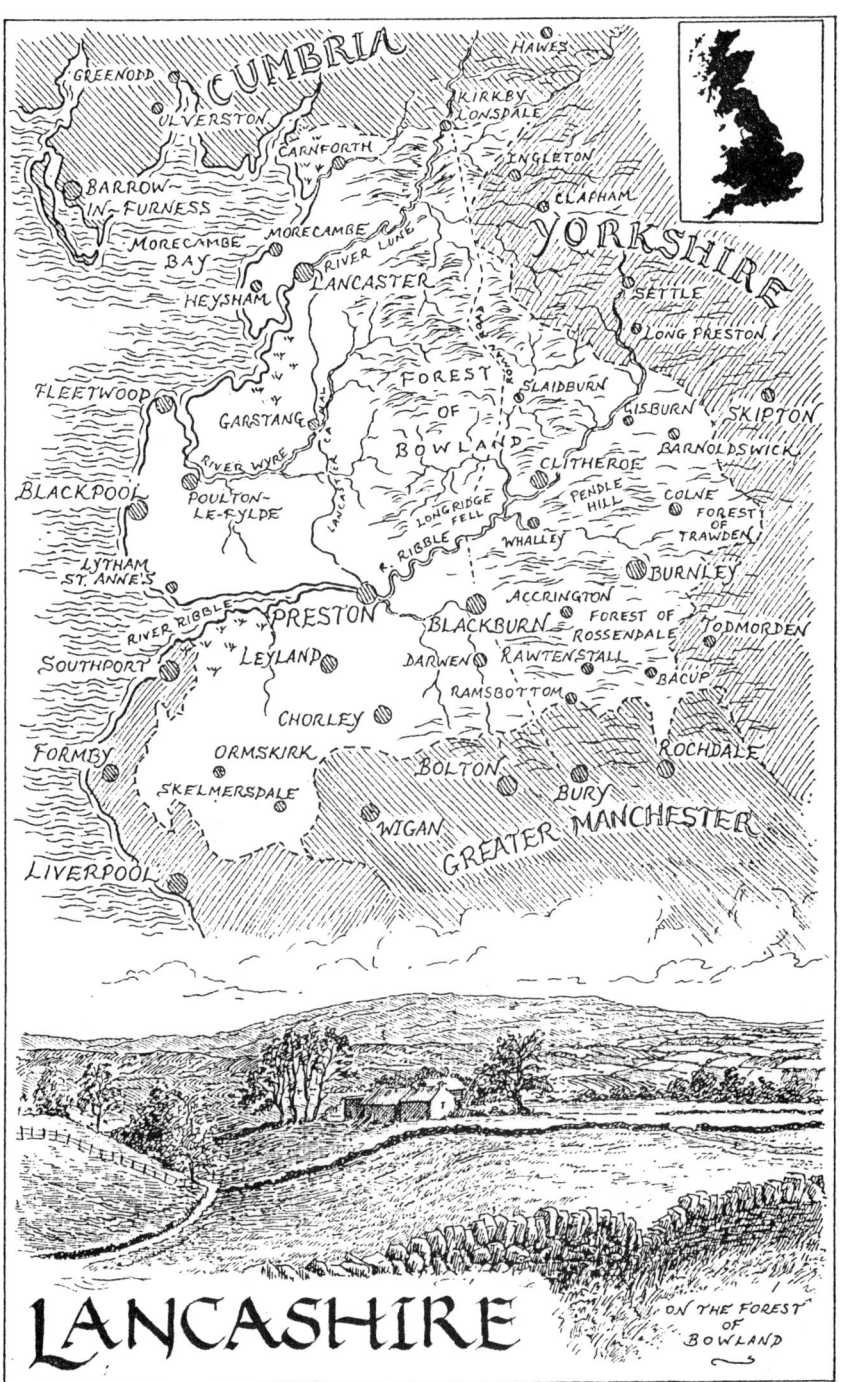

GREENODD
CUMBRIA
HAWES
ULVERSTON
KIRKBY
LONSDALE
CARNFORTH
INGLETON
BARROW-IN-FURNESS
CLAPHAM
MORECAMBE
MORECAMBE BAY
RIVER LUNE
YORKSHIRE
HEYSHAM
LANCASTER
SETTLE
LONG PRESTON
FLEETWOOD
FOREST OF BOWLAND
SLAIDBURN
GARSTANG
GISBURN
SKIPTON
RIVER WYRE
BARNOLDSWICK
BLACKPOOL
POULTON-LE-FYLDE
CLITHEROE
PENDLE HILL
COLNE
FOREST OF TRAWDEN
LONGRIDGE FELL
RIBBLE
WHALLEY
LYTHAM ST. ANNE'S
BURNLEY
RIVER RIBBLE
PRESTON
BLACKBURN
ACCRINGTON
FOREST OF ROSSENDALE
TODMORDEN
SOUTHPORT
LEYLAND
DARWEN
RAWTENSTALL
BACUP
RAMSBOTTOM
FORMBY
CHORLEY
ORMSKIRK
BOLTON
BURY
ROCHDALE
SKELMERSDALE
WIGAN
GREATER MANCHESTER
LIVERPOOL

LANCASHIRE

ON THE FOREST OF BOWLAND

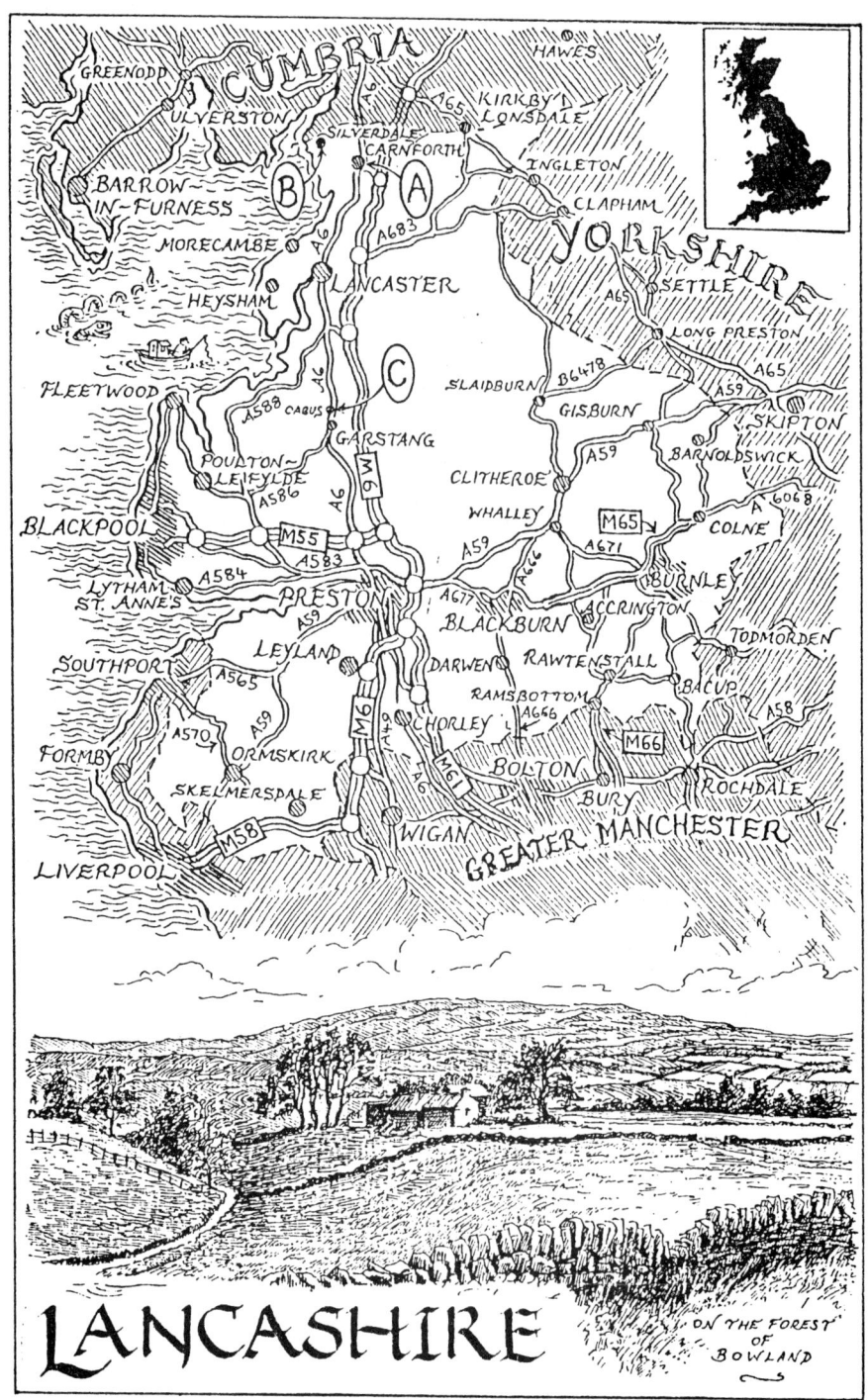

LANCASHIRE

ON THE FOREST OF BOWLAND

New Capernwray Farm, Capernwray, Carnforth, Lancashire LA6 1AD   Nearest Road M6 (exit 35)

A most convenient stop en-route London-Scotland. Three miles from exit 35 (M6). Set in beautiful countryside between the Lake District and Yorkshire Dales. High quality accommodation in award winning 17th century former farmhouse. Renowned for warm hospitality, comfort and excellent candlelit dinners. Delightful, fully equipped bedrooms with private/en-suite facilities. By arrangement personal pick up from Manchester airport or Lancaster station and personally conducted tours in Landrover Discovery ETB 3 Crowns Highly Commended, AA 5Q's.

Peter & Sally Townend
Tel: 01524 734284
Fax: 01524 734284

B&B from £26, Rooms 2 double, 2 twin, Minimum age 10, Restricted smoking, Open all year. Map Ref: A

The Limes Village Guest House, 23 Stankelt Road, Silverdale, Nr Carnforth, Lancs LA5 0TF   A6, M6

The Limes, a charming Victorian house set in beautiful landscaped gardens, has been tastefully refurbished. The spacious bedrooms, decorated with flair, have private bathrooms, TV, easy chairs, and tea and coffee tray. The owners serve delicious food, with an incredibly wide breakfast choice and an optional five course candlelit dinner. Silverdale, an area of outstanding natural beauty, with a wealth of coastal and wooded footpaths, is in close proximity to the Lake District, and Yorkshire Dales and an ideal stopover between England and Scotland.

Noel & Andree Livesey
Tel: 01524 701454
Fax: 01524 701454

B&B from £16.65, Dinner £11.50, Rooms 1 twin, 1 double, 1 family, (all with private bathrooms), No smoking, No pets, Open all year, Map Ref: B

Clay Lane Head Farm, A6 Road, Cabus, Garstang, Lancs PR3 1WL   Nearest Road A6

Clay Lane Head Farm is conveniently situated for breaking a long journey between the South of England and the Lake District or Scotland, being within easy reach of the M6 motorway. A warm and friendly welcome is offered to weary travellers. The old farmhouse has oak beams and open firest plus full central heating and 2 of the rooms have en-suite facilities. All rooms have tea and coffee making equipment. The farm makes a good base for exploring the Fylde coast, Lancashire Fells and the Lune & Ribble Valleys. Only a 1 hour drive to the Lake District. Fishing and golf nearby.

Joan & Clifford Higginson
Tel: 01995 603132

B&B from £17, Rooms 1 twin, 1 double, 1 family, Restricted smoking, Open 1 March - 23 December, Map Ref: C

THE 'TROUGH OF BOWLAND'.

Leicestershire and Nottinghamshire

"This royal throne of kings, this sceptred isle,
This earth of majesty, this seat of Mars,
This other Eden, demi-paradise,
This fortress built by Nature for herself
Against infection and the hand of war,
This happy breed of men, this little world,
This precious stone set in the silver sea
(. . .)
This blessed plot, this earth, this realm, this England."

(William Shakespeare - Richard II, III)

LEICESTERSHIRE & NOTTINGHAMSHIRE

NEWARK CASTLE.

There's plenty of opportunities to delve into the past in Leicestershire and Nottinghamshire. Throughout history the area has been at the heart of events which are still evident in the number of museums, castles, historic houses and heritage centres.

The English Civil War began here in 1642 when Charles I raised his standard beside Nottingham Castle, beginning years of bitter conflict. Mary Queen of Scots spent long years in captivity before her execution at Fotheringhay, Northamptonshire in 1587. Over a hundred years earlier, Richard III lost his crown and his life to the future Henry VII at the Battle of Bosworth field in 1485. The Battlefield Trail can be followed at Bosworth today, where visitors can relive the sights and sounds of the famous battle.

The story of the Pilgrim fathers began in the villages of Babworth and Scrooby in north Nottinghamshire. At Worksop the library and museum houses a special exhibition.

Home of the Dukes of Rutland since Henry VIII's time is Leicestershire's Belvoir Castle - a must for art lovers, housing works by Poussin, Rubens, Holbein and Reynolds. During the summer months it plays host to numerous special events, including medieval jousting tournaments.

Leicester's Castle Park turns back the clock. The city's historic core has a host of museums, wonderful architecture, peaceful gardens and waterside walks. The history of Leicester can be traced from the Jewry Wall, the grand entrance to the town's public baths in Roman times, to the Saxon church of St Nicholas.

Fascinating narrow streets wind back to St Martin's Square with its Victorian lights and specialist shops, through one of the largest permanent open air markets to the modern department stores of the Shires Centre and the theatres.

A warm and friendly welcome awaits in Leicestershire's market towns. Ashby-de-la-Zouch has a five-aisled church and a ruined castle. The former Saxon settlement of Lutterworth has ancient inns and Melton Mowbray is famed for its pork pies and Stilton cheese.

CLUMBER PARK.

The city of Nottingham is known throughout the world for Nottingham Lace. The city's Lace Hall gives a fascinating insight into the history of lace and display panels in the Lace Centre, one of the city's oldest buildings, tell the story of lace from medieval times. The city has many museums, including the Brewhouse Yard Museum, five 17th century cottages at the foot of Nottingham Castle, which houses displays on the city's social history.

The market town of Southwell has two claims to fame: It is home of the popular Bramley apple and it also has a fine Minster, dating back to 1108.

Nearby Newark was the scene of a lengthy seige during the Civil War and today visitors can enjoy the riverside walk beneath the massive castle walls, browsing for antiques or taking in the air museum or local history collections.

Leicestershire's charming countryside is just waiting to be explored. From the warm-toned villages of the East to the grey stone buildings of the West and the craggy outcrops of Charnwood to the tranquil expanse of Rutland Water, there is plenty of opportunity to relax.

At Rutland Water there is a 27 mile cycle track around the shoreline and there are numerous waterside paths which encircle one of the largest man-made lakes in western Europe.

Red and fallow deer roam in Bradgate Park among the 850 acres of natural parkland with its rocky hills, woods, heath and bracken. From the summit of Beacon Hill Country Park there are superb views and there are nature reserves at Watermead and Melton Country Parks.

Nottinghamshire provides a variety of ever-changing landscapes. Rolling arable farmland and ancient oak woodlands blend harmoniously with grand ducal estates and picturesque villages.

Clumber Park is a notable example of 18th century landscape design. It is famed for its Dukes Drive, a double avenue of lime trees over two miles long. The 3,800 acre National Trusts site has nature walks, a lake and a beautiful chapel built for the 7th Duke of Newcastle.

There are more woodland walks at Rufford Country Park, with its 25-acre lake and formal gardens. Close by is the most famous parkland of all, the Sherwood Forest Country Park at Edwinstowe. In the days of the Norman kings when Sherwood was a royal hunting forest, it covered 100,000 acres, although it is much smaller today. It is preserved much as it it would have been in Robin Hood's time with its thousand ancient oak trees. Waymarked paths lead to the Mighty Major Oak and an interpretative exhibition "Robin Hode and Mery Scherwode". The legends really come to life in the Robin Hood Festival, a week long feast of medieval entertainment held every summer, with jousting, story-telling and hunt the outlaw games.

LEICESTERSHIRE & NOTTINGHAMSHIRE

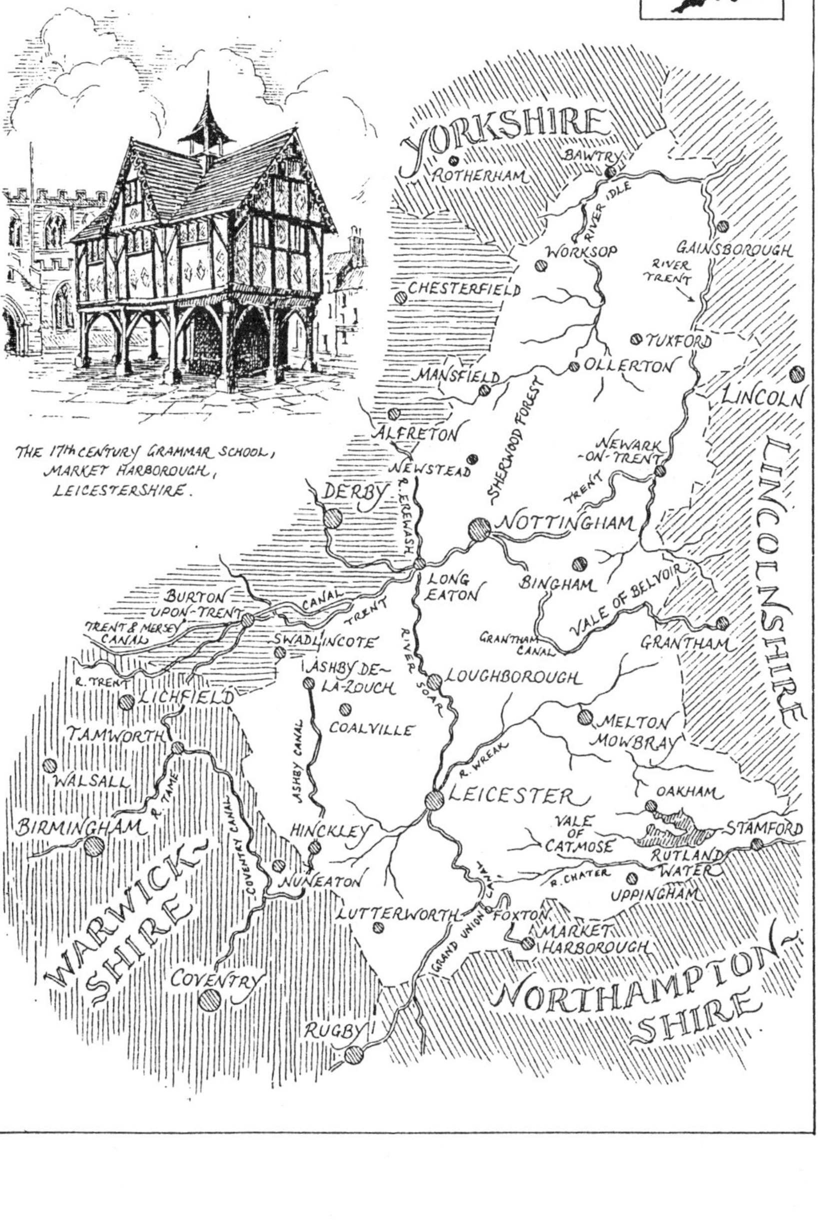

THE 17th CENTURY GRAMMAR SCHOOL,
MARKET HARBOROUGH,
LEICESTERSHIRE.

YORKSHIRE
ROTHERHAM
BAWTRY
RIVER IDLE
WORKSOP
GAINSBOROUGH
RIVER TRENT
CHESTERFIELD
TUXFORD
MANSFIELD
OLLERTON
LINCOLN
SHERWOOD FOREST
ALFRETON
NEWARK-ON-TRENT
NEWSTEAD
R. EREWASH
DERBY
TRENT
NOTTINGHAM
LINCOLNSHIRE
LONG EATON
BINGHAM
VALE OF BELVOIR
BURTON-UPON-TRENT
CANAL
TRENT
TRENT & MERSEY CANAL
SWADLINCOTE
GRANTHAM CANAL
GRANTHAM
R. TRENT
ASHBY-DE-LA-ZOUCH
RIVER SOAR
LOUGHBOROUGH
LICHFIELD
COALVILLE
MELTON MOWBRAY
TAMWORTH
R. WREAK
WALSALL
ASHBY CANAL
LEICESTER
OAKHAM
STAMFORD
BIRMINGHAM
HINCKLEY
VALE OF CAT-MOSE
RUTLAND WATER
WARWICKSHIRE
COVENTRY CANAL
NUNEATON
R. AVON
R. CHATER
UPPINGHAM
LUTTERWORTH
FOXTON
GRAND UNION CANAL
MARKET HARBOROUGH
COVENTRY
NORTHAMPTONSHIRE
RUGBY

LEICESTERSHIRE & NOTTINGHAMSHIRE

THE 17TH CENTURY GRAMMAR SCHOOL,
MARKET HARBOROUGH,
LEICESTERSHIRE.

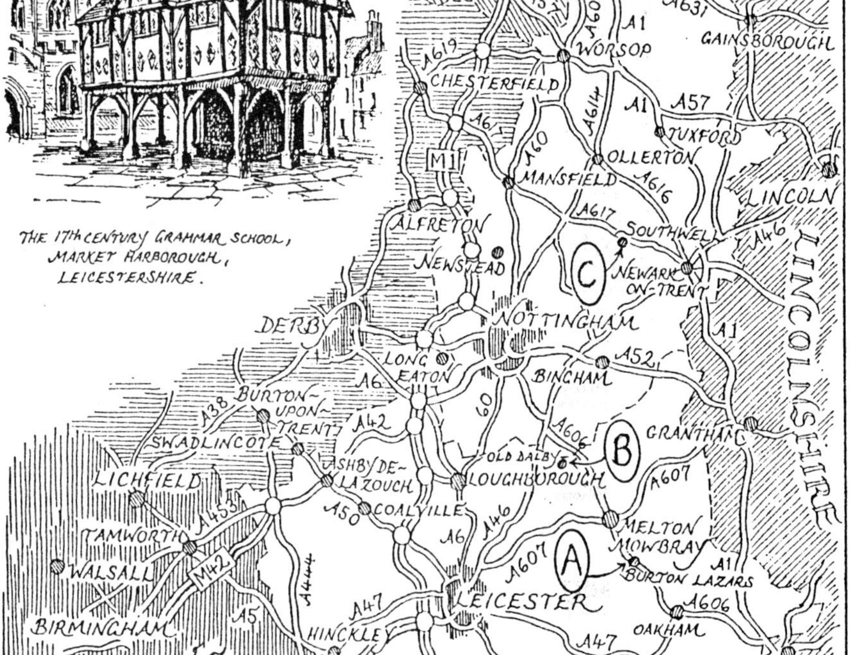

Hillside House, 27 Melton Road, Burton Lazars, Melton Mowbray, Leics LE14 2UR   A606

Charming converted comfortable old farm buildings with superb views over rolling countryside. Accommodation comprises 3 double rooms, one is en-suite, with a separate bathroom and shower-room. All rooms have colour TV and tea/coffee making facilities. Pleasant garden. Situated within easy reach of Belvoir Castle, Stamford and Rutland Water - or just enjoy the villages and countryside.

Mrs Sue Goodwin
Tel: 01664 66312

B&B from £15, Rooms 2 twin (1 en-suite), 1 double, Minimum age 10 Open all year except Christmas, Map Ref: A

Home Farm, Church Lane, Old Dalby, Leicestershire, LE14 3LB   Nearest Road A606, A46

A charming host and hostess with a warm welcome. This is a lovely old farmhouse with good facilities and a very relaxed atmosphere. A peaceful haven from the madding crowd! Bedrooms are comfortable and all are en-suite and have tea/coffee making facilities. Excellent evening meals at acclaimed Crown Inn across village green.

Sean & Val Anderson
Tel: 01664 822622

B&B from £17.50, Rooms 2 single, 3 twin (all en-suite), No smoking, Euro, Visa & Mastercard accepted, Open all year, Map Ref: B

The Old Forge, Burgage Lane, Southwell, Nottinghamshire NG25 OER   Nearest Road A612

Quietly but centrally situated in this charming little town known for its beautiful and historic Minster. Once an old working forge, now a comfortable house with character. Attractive decorations throughout and mainly antique furniture. A secluded patio to relax on complete with fish pond and waterfall. Restaurant and pubs within an easy walk. Rooms are en-suite, have telephone, tea/coffee making facilities, TV, and 2 are on the ground floor. Continental or English breakfast is served in conservatory/dining room. Private parking. ETB 3 Crowns Highly Commended.

Mrs Hilary Marston
Tel: 01636 812809/816302
Mobile: 0850 237908

B&B from £20, Rooms 3 twin, 3 double (all private/en-suite), No smoking, Pets by arrangement, Open all year, Map Ref: C

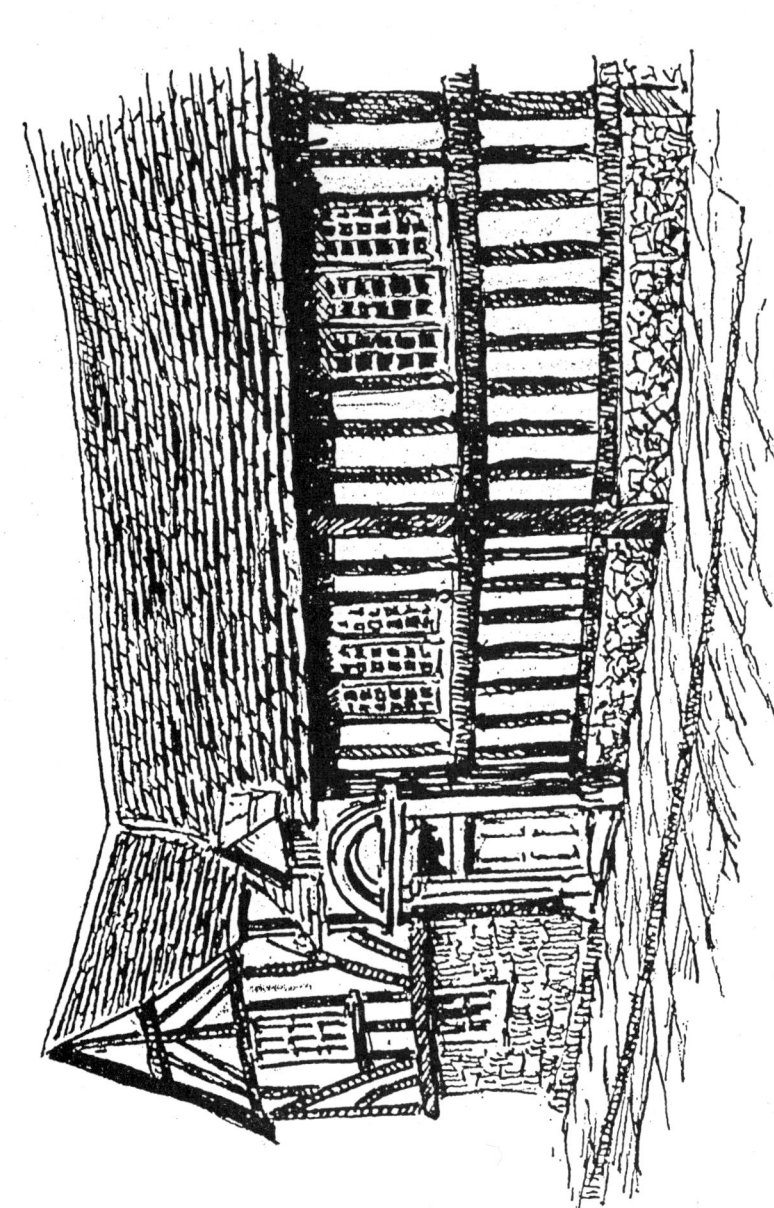

THE 15TH CENTURY GUILDHALL, LEICESTER.

LINCOLNSHIRE

"Calm and deep peace on this high Wold"

(Alfred Lord Tennyson)

LINCOLNSHIRE

ON THE LINCOLNSHIRE WOLDS.

If you think of the county of Lincolnshire as being flat and dull, take a look for yourself. The gentle rolling landscape of the peaceful Wolds, ancient woods, winding roads and pretty villages along with the mysterious beauty of the Fens will all come as a surprise. The Wolds are a 40 mile stretch of chalk upland containing rolling hills and deep valleys, rising to 552ft near Normanby le Wold. The area is one of England's most prosperous for growing wheat and peas. There are 3,000 miles of public rights of way and another 1,000 miles of Green Lanes so there is plenty of opportunity to explore Lincolnshire's unspoilt countryside. There are plenty of quiet roads with places of interest to discover. From Woodhall Spa, set amid splendid pine woods, there are numerous picturesque walks. From the top of nearby Tattershall Castle's brick tower, both Lincoln Cathedral and the Boston "Stump", the octagonal church tower of St Botolph's Church, can be seen on a clear day. The bulb-growing region of the Lincolnshire Fens is a riot of colour in the spring time when daffodils and tulips come into flower around Holbeach and Spalding. Here the highlight of the year is the Spalding Flower Parade in early May, with its floats covered in brilliant coloured flower heads. One of the country's premier show gardens, Springfields, has over a million spring bulbs and Summer bedding plants. Lincolnshire's coast stretches from Gibraltar Point to the mouth of the River Humber. Here the North Sea often retreats so far it almost disappears. Cleethorpes is at the mouth of the river and neighbouring Grimsby, until the mid 1970s was one of the world's greatest fishing ports.

12TH CENTURY
JEWS HOUSE, LINCOLN.

Skegness has always been described as "bracing" because of its East winds. It is not surprising that windmills are a feature of the Lincolnshire landscape - the 5 sailed tower mill at Alford was built in 1837. As well as beautiful countryside, Lincolnshire has many places of historic interest. The poet Alfred Lord Tennyson was born in the village of Somersby where his father was rector. The gardens of Gunby Hall were Tennyson's "haunts of ancient peace" and exhibitions commemorating his work can be seen at Stockwith Mill and in Lincoln's Usher Gallery. Lincolnshire's busy market towns offer a wealth of attractions for visitors. Horncastle was a walled settlement in Roman times and is now noted for its many antique shops. Stamford with its honey-coloured stone buildings was England's first conservation area.

THE GATEWAY, LINCOLN CASTLE.

LINCOLNSHIRE

ST. BOTOLPH'S CHURCH, THE BOSTON STUMP.

LINCOLNSHIRE

ST. BOTOLPH'S CHURCH,
THE BOSTON STUMP.

The Lanchester Guest House, 84 Harrowby Road, Grantham, Lincs NG31 9DS   **A1, A52**

This well established Edwardian guest house is run professionally to high standards and has retained its warm and friendly atmosphere. Located in a pleasant tree lined road close to the town centre. Accommodation is in 3 comfortable bedrooms, 1 with en-suite facilities, all with modern amenities, TV and tea/coffee making facilities. A TV lounge and separate dining room are also available. A good choice of restaurants nearby, ask for recommendations on your arrival. ETB 2 crowns, RAC acclaimed.

Mrs J M Standish
Tel: 01476 74169

B&B from £15, Dinner by arrangement, Rooms 1 double, 2 twin, Restricted smoking, Open all year. Map Ref: A

Sycamore Farm, Bassingthorpe, Grantham, Lincoln NG33 4ED   **Nearest Road A1**

Sycamore Farm is a working family farm with a spacious Victorian farmhouse set in the peaceful surroundings of south Lincolnshire. Relax in the guest lounge with colour television, board games, and piano. Three pretty bedrooms offer a choice of either washbasin or en-suite facilities. All have unspoilt views across open countryside. Tea/coffee making facilities. Hair dryer available on request.

Mrs Sue Robinson
Tel: 0147658 274

B&B from £16, Dinner by arrangement, Rooms 2 double (1 can be family), 1 twin, Minimum age 6, No smoking, No pets, Open all year except Christmas & New Year, Map Ref: A

Pipwell Manor, Saracens Head, Holbeach, Spalding, Lincs PE12 8AL   **Nearest Road A17**

This Georgian manor house was built around 1740 and is a Grade II listed building. It has been tastefully restored and redecorated in the appropriate style and retains many of its original features. All 4 bedrooms are attractive and well furnished and have tea/coffee making facilities. Parking is available and guests are welcomed with home made cakes and tea. Pipwell Manor stands amid gardens and paddocks in a small village just off the A17 in the Lincolnshire Fens. A lovely place to stay.

Lesley Honor
Tel: 01406 423119

B&B from £17, Rooms 2 double, 1 twin, 1 single, No smoking, No pets, Open all year except Christmas & New Year, Map Ref: B

Greenfield Farm, Mill Lane/Cow Lane, Minting, Near Horncastle, Lincs LN9 5RX   **A158**

Judy and Hugh welcome you to stay at their lovely farmhouse set in a quiet location yet centrally placed for all the major Lincolnshire attractions. Relax by the large pond or enjoy the forest walks that border the farm. Guests have their own sitting room with colour television and wood burning stove, pretty en-suite shower rooms with heated towel rails, and tea/coffee making facilities. ETB 2 crowns, AA recommended QQQ, All private facilities.

Judy & Hugh Bankes Price
Tel: 01507 578457

B&B from £17, Rooms 2 double, 1 twin, No smoking, Pets by arrangement, Open all year except Christmas & New Years, Map Ref: C

Please mention

THE GREAT BRITISH BED and BREAKFAST

when booking your accommodation

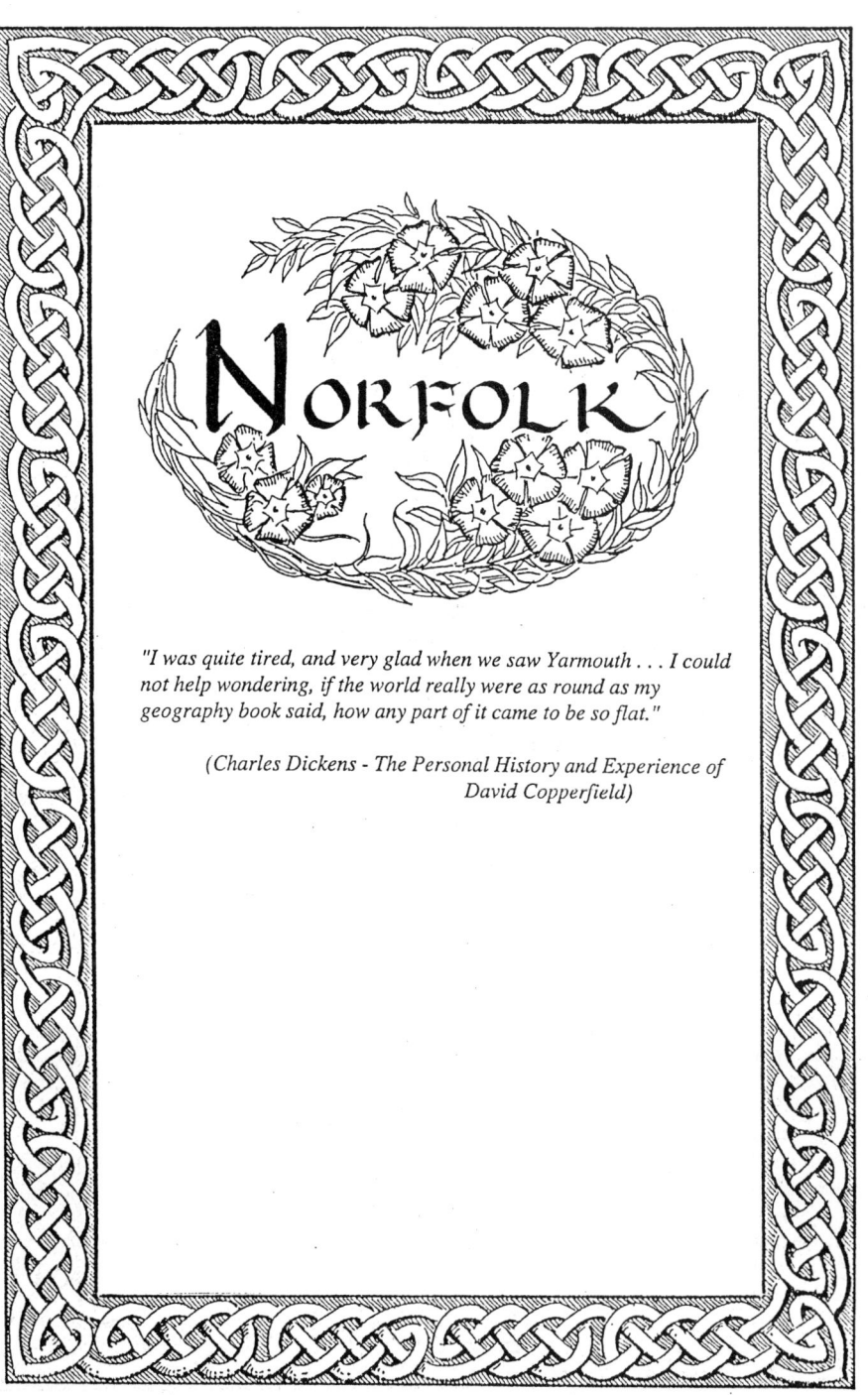

NORFOLK

"I was quite tired, and very glad when we saw Yarmouth . . . I could
not help wondering, if the world really were as round as my
geography book said, how any part of it came to be so flat."

(Charles Dickens - The Personal History and Experience of
David Copperfield)

NORFOLK

THE GARDENS AT BLICKLING HALL, NORFOLK.

Norfolk is probably best known for the Broads and the seaside resorts of Great Yarmouth, Cromer and Hunstanton - but the county has much more to offer. Peaceful and unspoilt, Norfolk is easy to reach with good road and rail links to the rest of the country. Once there is it easy to relax, whether walking, using the excellent sporting facilities or turning back the clock by visiting some of the many historical buildings. Norfolk is known for its numerous medieval churches and in particular for its vast Norman cathedral in Norwich. There are many historic houses open to the public which, along with the ruined castles and religious foundations, testify to the county's important place in history.

Nature lovers will find reserves to visit, most of which offer the novice some guidance. Bird watchers will already be aware of the North coast's importance, particulary during the spring and autumn migrations. Norfolk with its gentle terrain is ideal walking and cycling country. For the energetic there is the Around Norfolk Walk which joins the Peddars Way from Thetford to the Coastal Path, running from Holme to Cromer, and then along the Weavers Way to Great Yarmouth.

For visitors interested in more formal sporting pursuits there are a number of golf courses, sports centres, swimming pools and other sports facilities. The kingdom of East Anglia was originally made up of the North Folk (Norfolk) and the South Folk (Suffolk). Its boundaries were practically impregnable with the sea to the North and East and the Fens to the West.

The landscape of the Fens with its patchwork of fields has its own dramatic beauty. The original marshland was drained by Dutch engineers in the 17th century and the remains of the wind pumps used are still visible - without them the water contained within the high banks of the rivers and dykes would still cover this fertile, black farmland

THE OLD CHAIN FERRY, HORNING, ON THE NORFOLK BROADS.

The coastline stretches from the flat tidal marshes of the Wash, past Hunstanton with its red and white cliffs, and along the salt marshes and lonely beaches and dunes passing a number of picturesque villages. The cliffs re-emerge at Weybourne Hope and climb steadily past the resorts of Sheringham and Cromer to Trimingham and Mundesley. Here the coast curves Southwards and dunes replace the cliffs, which between Sea Palling and Winterton are all that prevent the sea from flooding into the Broads at Horsey Mere. South of Winterton are the holiday areas of Hemsby, Scratby, Caister, Great Yarmouth and Hopton.

Within the triangle from Norwich, Lowestoft and Sea Palling lie more than 30 Broads, networks of rivers and lakes, formed by flooded medieval peat digging, which today form 125 miles of lock free waterways. For long stretches the waterways are below the level of the surrounding flat countryside. The real character of the Broads is best appreciated from a boat and many boatyards offer craft to hire for the day. For the fisherman the waters are a delight, offering roach, bream, rudd, perch and tench.

Breckland contains some of the oldest settlement sites in Norfolk. It is a mixture of farmland, pine belts, conifer plantations and wild heaths, the latter providing an important refuge for some unusual plants and animals. The 50,000 acres of Thetford Forest Park have plenty of picnic sites, many of which are the beginnings for circular walks.

One of the earliest industrial sites can be seen at Grimes Graves, a 30 ft deep pit where flint was excavated over 4,000 years ago.

Norwich is Norfolk's county town and has one of England's best preserved historic centres with its medieval street pattern contained by the remains of the old city walls. Once the second largest city in England, the large number of substantial medieval buildings reflect the city's wealth based on the wool and cloth trade of the time. The city has exceptionally good shopping and also hosts a regular arts festival, with events held in various venues around the centre. Great Yarmouth is an unusual combination of a large bustling seaside resort and an historic port. The seafront has its traditional visitor attractions while the river quay has been home of the herring and merchant fleet for centuries, but is now more familiar to oil rig supply vessels and cargo ships. Cromer, known as "the Gem of the Norfolk Coast", became a seaside resort in Victorian times with the coming of the railway and has remained popular ever since King's Lynn was one of England's foremost ports as early as the 11th century. It has a colourful maritime past with a wealth of historic buildings and a thriving shopping and commercial centre. Unusually, the town has 2 market places and 2 medieval guildhalls, one of which is now the town hall with a magnificent chequered frontage. Thetford is an ancient town and 1,000 years ago was the capital of East Anglia. Its continuing importance during the middle ages left a legacy of historic sites.

NORFOLK

THE BEACH AT CROMER.

LINCOLNSHIRE

SKEGNESS

The Wash

HOLKHAM BAY

NORFOLK COASTAL PATH

SALT MARSHES

BLACKENEY POINT

SHERINGHAM

HUNSTANTON

WELLS-NEXT-THE-SEA

CLEY-NEXT-THE-SEA

CROMER

HEACHAM

HOLT

FAKENHAM

NORTH WALSHAM

LONG SUTTON

GREAT OUSE

KING'S LYNN

AYLSHAM

R. WENSUM

SMALLBURGH

WISBECH

EAST DEREHAM

NORFOLK BROADS

HEMSBY

R. NAR

NORWICH

R. BURE

THURNE

CAISTER-ON-SEA

DOWNHAM MARKET

SWAFFAM

R. YARE

BURE

GREAT YARMOUTH

R. WISSEY

WATTON

WYMONDHAM

R. CHET

THETFORD FOREST

ATTLEBOROUGH

LOWESTOFT

LITTLEPORT

BUNGAY

BECCLES

ELY

THETFORD

DISS

R. WAVENEY

R. LITTLE OUSE

SOUTHWOLD

CAMBRIDGESHIRE

SUFFOLK

NEWMARKET

SAXMUNDHAM

BURY ST. EDMUNDS

STOWMARKET

ALDEBURGH

PEDLAR'S WAY

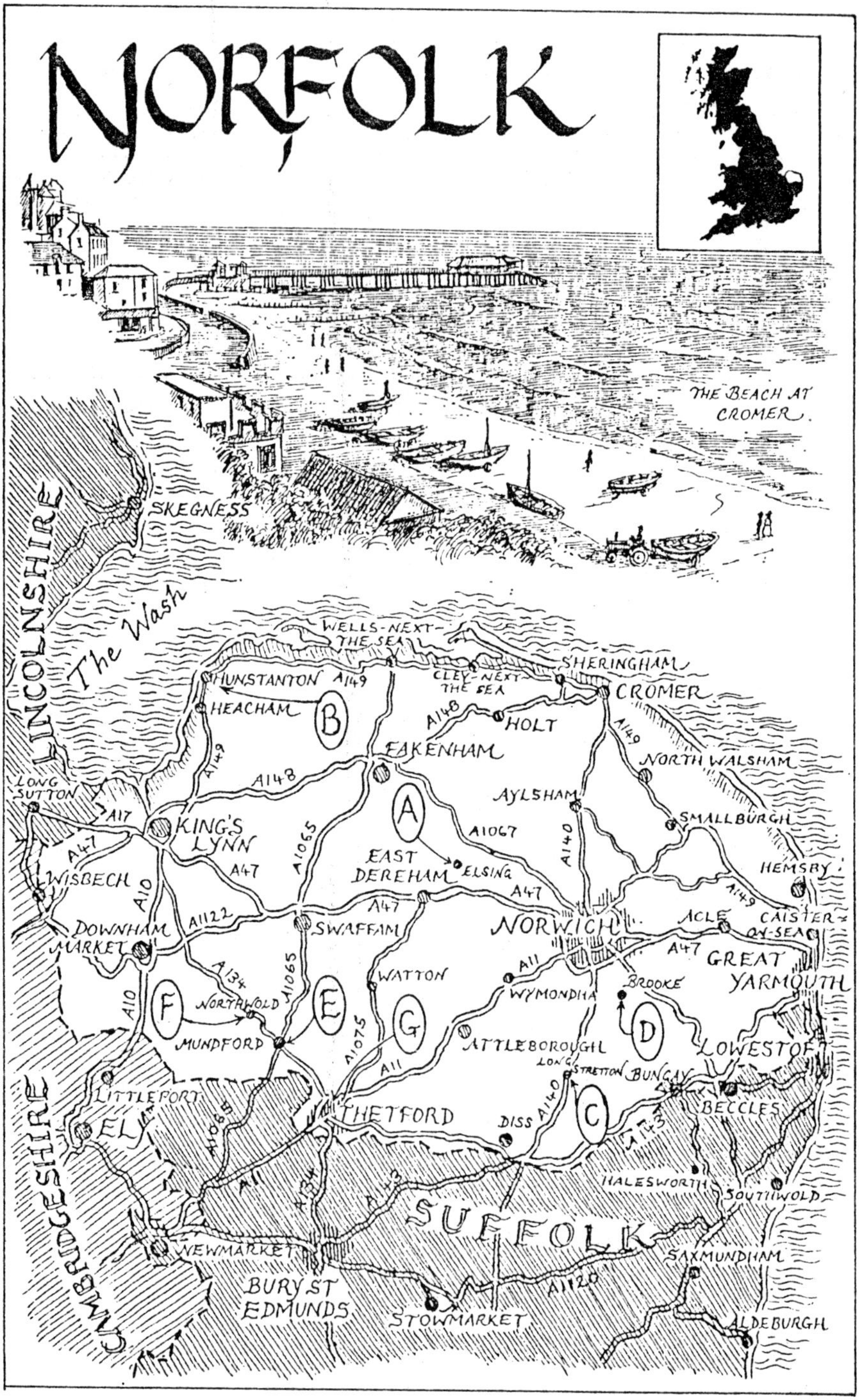
NORFOLK
THE BEACH AT CROMER
SKEGNESS
LINCOLNSHIRE
The Wash
WELLS-NEXT-THE SEA
SHERINGHAM
CLEY-NEXT THE SEA
CROMER
HUNSTANTON
A149
HEACHAM
B
A148
HOLT
A149
EAKENHAM
NORTH WALSHAM
A148
LONG SUTTON
A17
KING'S LYNN
A1065
A
AYLSHAM
SMALLBURGH
A47
A1067
A140
EAST DEREHAM
ELSING
HEMSBY
WISBECH
A47
A47
A149
A10
A1122
A47
NORWICH
ACLE
CAISTER-ON-SEA
DOWNHAM MARKET
SWAFFAM
A47
GREAT YARMOUTH
A134
A1065
WATTON
A11
BROOKE
A10
F
NORTHWOLD
E
G
WYMONDHAM
D
MUNDFORD
A1075
ATTLEBOROUGH
LOWESTOFT
A11
LONG STRETTON
BUNGAY
LITTLEPORT
THETFORD
DISS
A140
C
A143
BECCLES
ELY
A1088
CAMBRIDGESHIRE
A11
A134
A143
HALESWORTH
SOUTHWOLD
SUFFOLK
NEWMARKET
SAXMUNDHAM
BURY ST EDMUNDS
A1120
STOWMARKET
ALDEBURGH

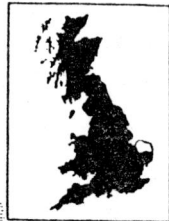

Bartles Lodge, Church Street, Elsing, Dereham, NR20 3EA   **Nearest Road A47, A1065**

Bartles Lodge is a period farmhouse and stables which has been beautifully renovated and converted. The house is set within 5 acres of peaceful meadowland and has its own well stocked private fishing lake. All bedrooms are en-suite and have tea/coffee making facilities, and TV. Bazrtles Lodge is idylically situated opposit the superb 14th century church in the delightful village of Elsing. There is a traditional country inn only 50 metres away.

David & Annie Bartlett
Tel: 01362 637177

B&B from £22, Rooms 3 double, 1 family, 3 twin,
Minimum age 10, Open all year, Map Ref: A

Pinewood House, 26 Northgate, Hunstanton, Norfolk, PE36 6AP   **Nearest Road A149**

A family run Victorian hotel offering comfort, relaxation, good food and an excellent base from which t tour the beautiful north west Norfolk countryside between King's Lynn and Blakeney. Pinewood is within 100 yards of glorious sandy beaches which provide miles of wonderful walks. All bedrooms are well furnished some being en-suite and have sea views. All have central heating, colour TV, tea/coffee making facilities. There is a small inviting restaurant, a pleasant bar and a lounge with log fire.

Mrs Susan Porter
Tel: 01485 533068

B&B from £18.50, Dinner from £12.95,
Rooms 4 double, 3 family, 1 twin, (many en-suite),
Open Feburary - Mid December, Map Ref: B

Greenacres Farm, Woodgreen, Long Stratton, Norfolk NR15 2RR   **Nearest Road A140**

This peaceful retreat is in an idyllic rural situation and yet only 1½ miles from Long Stratton. There are a variety of shops, public houses, restaurants, and a sport centre. Golf, riding, fishing, swimming facilities are all nearby. The comfortable, en-suite bedrooms are provided with tea/coffee making facilities, and TV. Guests are welcome to use the all weather tennis court (proper tennis shoes must be worn). There is also a games room equipped with snooker table, darts, table tennis and carpet bowls; or guests may relax in the comfortable lounge. Also self catering

Mrs Joanna Douglas
Tel: 01508 30261

B&B from £18, Dinner from £8, Rooms 1 twin, 1 double
(both en-suite), Self catering accommodation also available,
Restricted smoking, Open all year, Map Ref: C

Waterfield Cottage, High Green, Brooke, Norwich NR15 1JE   **Nearest Road B1332**

Waterfield Cottage, is an attractive 400 year old thatched cottage, set in an acre of delightful gardens and surrounded by a moat. It is situtated on the edge of a conservation village amongst fields and woodlands. The accommodation is very comfortable, bedrooms have tea/coffee making facilities, and TV. A delightful lounge is available for guests to relax in. The fine cathedral city of Norwich is only 15 minutes away by car, and the Norfolk Broads and coasts of Norfolk and Suffolk are within easy reach.

Mrs Rosemary Price
Tel: 01508 550312

B&B from £18, Dinner from £10, Rooms 1 double, 1 twin,
1 bed/sitting room en-suite, Restricted smoking, Minimum age 5,
Open March - November, Map Ref: D

Old Bottle House, Granwich, Mundford, Thetford, Norfolk IP26 5JL

Nearest Road A134

A warm welcome is assured at The Old Bottle house. This is a 275 year old former coaching inn, which has a lovely garden and rural views set in a wonderful position on the edge of Thetford Forest. The spacious colour co-ordinated bedrooms have tea/coffee making facilities, and colour television. Delicious meals are served in the dining room which has an inglenook fireplace. There is a pleasant lounge where guests may relax after a busy day.

Mrs Marion Ford
Tel: 01842 878012

B&B from £16.50, Dinner from £10, Rooms 2 twin, 1 double/family, No smoking, Minimum age 5, Open all year, Map Ref: E

The Grange, Northwold, Thetford, Norfolk, IP26 5NF

Nearest Road A134

This beautiful 18th century Regency house has easy access to Cambridge, Norwich, King's Lynn and Bury St Edmunds. It is also well situated for the North Norfolk coast, Sandringham and many National Trust properties. The comfortable bedrooms are all on the first floor and have central heating, tea/coffee making facilities. TV and clock radio. There are a drawing room and dining room with log fires both with views over the lawns with peacocks and ducks strolling around. Guests are welcome to use the heated swimming pool.

Sue & Malcolm Whittley
Tel: 01366 728240

B&B from £17, Dinner £12.50, Rooms 1 twin, 2 double (both en-suite), 2 singles, Pets by arrangement, Open all year except Christmas & new year, Map Ref: F

White Hall, Carbrooke, Nr Watton, Thetford, Norfolk IP25 6SG

Nearest Road B1108

White Hall is an elegant listed Georgian house standing in delightful grounds of 3 acres with large natural pond, surrounded by fields and providing a haven of peace and tranquillity. Spacious accommodation, full central heating, log fires on chilly evening, early morning tea and evening drinks ensure your stay is enjoyable and relaxing. Situated on the edge of Carbrooke village and in the centre of the interesting and attractive area of Breckland, we are ideally situated for the many attractions in both Norfolk and north Suffolk. Good choice of local eating places. ETB 2 Crowns Highly Commended.

Mrs S Carr
Tel: 01953 885950

B&B from £17, Rooms 1 double en-suite, 1 twin and 1 double, Restricted smoking, Open all year, Map Ref: G

Northumbria

"Oh where is the boatman,
I'd give any money,
And you for your trouble
Rewarded shall be,
To ferry me over the Tyne
To me Hinney, and scull her across
That rough river to me"

(Northumbrian folk song)

NORTHUMBRIA

HADRIAN'S WALL.

The former ancient kingdom on Northumbria now encompasses 4 counties - Northumberland, Tyne and Wear, Durham and Cleveland - and each has its own unique identity. Excellent motorways and trunk roads link the region with the rest of Britain. In just 3 hours British Rail's InterCity 225 service will bring the visitor from the centre of London to Newcastle upon Tyne. Once in the area, quiet roads lead through unspoilt countryside and Areas of Outstanding Natural Beauty. The area has wild National Parks and a spectacular coastline with high cliffs, castles and golden beaches. Northumbria's miles of unspoilt beaches are guarded by a string of fortresses built hundreds of years ago that bear witness to the area's violent past. England's most Northerly town, Berwick-upon-Tweed boasts a compelling history. The town changed hands 14 times as the English and Scots fought to control the border and the town was first fortified in the 13th century..

Lindisfarne Castle to the South on Holy Island was given to the National Trust in 1944. It was originally built as a fortress in the mid 1500s and it was converted into a residence in 1903 by architect Sir Edwin Lutyens. Holy Island is set apart from the mainland and is accessible at low tides by a causeway. The village of Bamburgh is dominated by its castle, which dates from the 12th century when it was the capital of the region ruled by the Saxon Kings. The nearby town of Seahouses is the embarkation point for the Farne Islands, a collection of 28 islands, some only visible at low tide. Inner Farne became a retreat for St Aidan and St Cuthbert and chapel remains can still be seen there. Today the islands are a sanctuary for oyster catchers, puffins, kittiwakes and other seabirds as well as a grey seal colony. The eerie ruin of Dunstanburgh Castle can be seen from the tiny fishing village of Craster, famous for its oak smoked kippers. At Warkworth a magnificent ruined castle stands high above the River Coquet. There are popular resorts at Tynemouth and Whitley Bay, which both have stretches of golden sands and leisure facilities. There is a superb promenade at South Shields, the country of the novelist Catherine Cookson. The ancient market town of Alnwick grew up around its castle, erected in the 10th century as a defence against the Scots.

BAMBURGH CASTLE.

It is not surprising that the area is peppered with battle sites. Otterburn was the site of one of the most desperate border battles immortalised in the Ballad of Chevy Chase in 1388. In 1513 the battle of Flodden was the last to be fought in Northumberland between James IV of Scotland and the Earl of Surrey. The Scottish king was killed. History goes back even further the Roman times with Hadrian's Wall. Large sections of the wall built nearly 2,000 years ago remain with the surrounding moors and valleys forming a stunning backdrop.

The Cheviot Hills form the backbone of Northumberland and make up the 400 square mile Northumberland National Park, popular with ornithologists, ramblers and archaeologists. South of the River Tyne, one of the area's main rivers, is the rural district of Weardale, once governed by the wealthy and all powerful Prince Bishops, who assumed the role when William the Conqueror declared Durham a palatinate. The River Tees rises at Cross Fell and courses down to Middleton-in-Teesdale. Teesdale's scenery has been recognised by its inclusion in the North Pennines Area of Outstanding Natural Beauty. High Force, in upper Teesdale, drops 70ft over the Great Whin Sill. Barnard Castle is the gateway to Teesdale and has associations with the present royal family. Darlington is known as the birthplace of the railway and George Stephenson's steam engine Locomotion 1 can be seen at the Railway Museum in North Road.

DURHAM CATHEDRAL

NORTHUMBRIA

GALASHIELDS

KELSO
R. TWEED
NEWTOWN
SAINT BOSWELLS

JEDBURGH

KIRK
YETHOLM

HAWICK

SCOTLAND

CARTER
BAR

BYRNESS

KIELDER

KIELDER
WATER

FOREST

OTTER
BURN

PENNINE WAY

BERWICK-
UPON-TWEED

COLDSTREAM

HOLY ISLAND
(LINDISFARNE)

FARNE ISLANDS

BAMBURGH

WOOLER

SEAHOUSES

THE
CHEVIOT

ROMAN ROAD (DEVIL'S CAUSEWAY)

ALNWICK
R. ALN

ALNMOUTH

WARKWORTH

R. COQUET

AMBLE

DRURIDGE
BAY

ROTHBURY

MORPETH

ASHINGTON

R. WANSBECK

NEWBIGGIN

PONTELAND

R. BLYTH

BLYTH

R. PONT

CRAMLINGTON

GILSLAND

HADRIAN'S

WALL

NEWCASTLE
UPON TYNE

WHITLEY BAY

CORBRIDGE

BRAMPTON

HAYDON
BRIDGE

R. TYNE

HEXHAM

TYNEMOUTH

SOUTH SHIELDS

TYNE & WEAR

GATESHEAD

BLANCHLAND

WASHINGTON

SUNDERLAND

ALSTON

CONSETT

CHESTER-
LE-STREET

CUMBRIA

STANHOPE

DURHAM

WEARDALE

COUNTY DURHAM

PETERLEE

R. WEAR

HARTLEPOOL

APPLEBY

MIDDLETON
IN
TEESDALE

BISHOP
AUCKLAND

TEESDALE

BARNARD
CASTLE

STOCKTON-
ON-TEES

REDCAR

CLEVELAND

BROUGH

BOWES

DARLINGTON

R. TEES

MIDDLESBROUGH

TEBAY

YORKSHIRE

WHITBY

NORTHUMBERLAND
NATIONAL
PARK

ALNWICK CASTLE, NORTHUMBERLAND.

NORTHUMBRIA

ALNWICK CASTLE, NORTHUMBERLAND

The Coach House at Crookham, Colnhill-on-Tweed, Northumberland TD12 4TD   Nearest Road A697

Highly commended by the best guides, The Coach House offers warm spacious bedrooms surrounding a sunlit courtyard. The large lounge with peach leather furniture and fine pictures overlooks a west facing terrace. A flock of Soay sheep graze beneath the damson trees. Food is fresh and varied reflecting modern ideas on healthy eating with some Mediterranean influence. Local fish, game and meat are used, organically reared where possible. Special diets catered for. Excellent facilities for disabled guests. Lovingly renovated to a high standard.

Mrs Lynne Anderson
Tel: 01890 820293

B&B from £19, Dinner from £14.50, Rooms 2 single, 5 twin, 2 double, (all en-suite), Restricted smoking, Dogs welcome, Open March - October, Map Ref: A

Clive House, Appletree Lane, Corbridge, Northumberland NE45 5DN   Nearest Road A68, A69

Originally built in 1840 as part of Corbridge village school, Clive House has been tastefully converted to provide 3 lovely bedrooms, one of which has a four-poster and its own sitting area. All are en-suite with tea/coffee making facilities, colour TV, hairdryer and telephone. At the centre of Hadrian's Wall country, historic Corbridge is an ideal base for exploring Northumberland and a convenient break between York and Edinburgh.

Mrs Ann Hodgson
Tel: 01434 632617

B&B from £18, Rooms: 2 double, 1 twin (all en-suite), No smoking, Minimum age 12, Open all year, Map Ref: B

Grove House, Hamsterley Forest, Nr Bishop Auckland, Co Durham, Northumbria DL13 3NL   A68

Grove House is set in an idyllic situation in the middle of Hamsterley Forest amongst 5,000 acres of mixed woodland, moors and becks. The house which was once an aristocrat's shooting box is shown in the grandeur of the downstairs rooms. All bedrooms are en-suite, have tea/coffee making facilities, comfortably furnished and with central heating throughout, creating a relaxed atmosphere. Helene prepares and cooks all the food with fresh ingredients and game from the forest, such as pheasant and venison, is ofen on the menu

Mrs Helene Close
Tel: 01388 488203

B&B from £20.50, Dinner from £12, Rooms 1 double, 2 twin No smoking, Minimum age 8, Open all year, Map Ref: C

The Coach House, Whorlton, Nr Barnard Castle, Co Durham, DL12 8XQ   A66, A67

A warm welcome awaits you at this converted stable in the tiny picturesque village of Whorlton on the banks of the River Tees, 3 miles east of Barnard Castle. This is an ideal situation for those visiting the Land of the Prince Bishops as well as the Yorkshire Dales as well as lovely Teesdale. The two bedrooms are comfortable and nicely decorated and furnished. A private sitting room with tea/coffee making facilities, and colour television is available for guests to use. Breakfast is a choice of a full English or vegetarian alternative.

Helen & Keith Calder
Tel: 01833 627237

B&B from £17.50, Dinner from £13, Rooms 1 twin, 1 double, No smoking, No children, No dogs, Open April - December, Map Ref: D

Partridge Close Stud, Lanchester, Co Durham, Northumbria DH7 0SZ   Nearest Road A68, A1

An exquisite house set in an unspoilt valley. Partridge Close is a stud farm for thoroughbred horses. Cooking is of a very high standard. A comfortable drawing room is open for guests and a log fire is lit on cool evenings. The charming bedrooms all have private bathroom together with tea/coffee making facilities. Durham city, Lanchester and Barnard Castle are all within a short drive.

Mr & Mrs Alexander
Tel: 01207 520896
Fax: 01207 520066

B&B from £21, Dinner from £11.50, Rooms 1 single, 1 twin, 1 double, 1 family (all with private facilities), Minimum age 8, Pets by arrangement, Open all year, Map Ref: E

Holmhead Farm, Hadrian's Wall, Greenhead-in-Northumbria, Via Carlisle CA6 7HY   A69, B6318

Holmhead is 150 year old traditional farmhouse which is now the home of Pauline and Brian Staff who take great pleasure in welcoming guests to this delightful old house which stands on the line of Hadrian's Wall and is built with Roman stones. The food is excellent and Holmhead prides itself on the 'longest breakfast menu in the world' and a BTA excellence award. Guests dine together for evening meals at a large oak candlelit table. 3 crowns commended, AA listed 4Q. Also S/C apartment, sleeps 4, 4 keys commended.

Brian & Pauline Staff
Tel: 016977 47402
Fax: 016977 47402

B&B from £21.50, Dinner from £16, Rooms 1 double, 1 family, 2 twin (all with shower and toilet), No smoking, Open all year except Christmas, Map Ref: F

East Peterel Field Farm, Hexham, Northumberland NE46 2JT   Nearest Road A68, A69

East Peterel Field Farm is a charming home only 2 miles away from Hexham and yet hidden away in stunning countryside. It is primarily a stud farm with a large stable block housing thoroughbred horses. The bedrooms, 2 of which are en-suite, have tea/coffee making facilities, and TV. There is a lovely snug, where guests may relax, with log fire in the winter. Mrs Carr is a Cordon Bleu cook and will be happy to prepare dinner. This is an excellent base to explore the area. Hadrians Wall, Beamish, Wallington, Kielder Water are among nearby attractions.

David & Susan Carr
Tel: 01434 607209

B&B from £20, Dinner from £13.50, Rooms 2 double, 1 twin, 1 single, Open January - December, Map Ref: G

West Close House, Hextol Terrace, Hexham, Northumberland NE46 2AD   Nearest Road B6305

This charming, immaculate 1920's villa is set in lovely gardens with a revolving summer-house. The quiet, leafy cul-de-sac with private parking is only a ten minute stroll from the centre of historic Hexham with its Abbey, theatre, restaurants and attractive shops with the tranquil Northumbrian countryside surrounding the town on all sides. Whether on holiday, on business or visiting friends or family, every comfort, excellent food and a welcoming and relaxing atmosphere awaits in this delightful home. ETB. 2 crown. Highly Commended.

Patricia Graham-Tomlinson
Tel: 01434 603307

B&B from £17.50, Rooms 2 single, 1 en-suite double, 1 family, No smoking, Open all year, Map Ref: G

Rye Hill Farm, Slaley, Hexham, Northumbria NE47 0AH　　　　**Nearest Road A68, A69, B6306**

Rye Hill Farm offers you the freedom to enjoy the pleasures of Northumberland throughout the year whilst living comfortably in the pleasant family atmosphere of a cosy farmhouse adapted especially to receive holidaymakers. Bedrooms are all en-suite and centrally heated. A full English breakfast is served and an optional 3 course evening meal is served in the dining room which has an open log fire and a table licence. Telephone and tourist information in the reception lounge. Guests are invited to use the upstairs games room.

Mrs E A Courage
Tel: 01434 673259

B&B from £18, Dinner from £10, Rooms 2 double, 2 family 2 twin, Pets welcome by arrangement, Open all year, Map Ref: G

Shieldhall, Wallington, Morpeth, Northumbria NE61 4AQ　　　　**Nearest Road A696**

Shieldhall has been charmingly and elegantly restored from the original 18th century house, nestling in the rolling landscape and overlooking the National Trust estate of Wallington. The main buildings form a well ordered courtyard onto which each of the guests' suites have their own entrances. The suites are self contained with independent heating, and tea/coffee making facilities. The oak dining room has Inglenook fireplace and antiques. The lounge and library both have french doors which open into the garden with croquet lawn.

Stephen & Celia Gay
Tel: 01830 40387
Fax: 01830 40387

B&B from £17, Dinner from £13.50, Rooms 2 twin, 2 double, 1 family (all en-suite), No smoking, Minimum age 10, Open March - November, Map Ref: H

Dalton House, Dalton nr Ponteland, Newcastle-upon-Tyne, Northumberland NE18 0AA　　　　**A696**

Dalton is a small peaceful village near Hadrian's Wall and Northumberland National Park. Ideal for exploring the beautiful county of Northumberland and convenient for businessmen who prefer to stay out of town. A warm welcome and a friendly family atmosphere are assured. Bedrooms have tea/coffee making facilities, and a guests sitting room is available to relax in. An evening meal can be provided by arrangement.

Mrs A Trevelyan
Tel: 01661 886225

B&B from £17, Dinner from £10, Rooms 1 single, 2 twin (with private bathroom), No smoking, Minimum age 12, Open April - October, Map Ref: I

North Cottage, Birling, Warkworth, Northumbria NE65 0XS　　　　**Nearest Road A1068**

Dating back to the 17th century, North Cottage has a cosy home from home atmosphere. Substantial full breakfasts are served in the dining room. Afternoon tea served free on arrival or when required. The bedrooms, which are all on the ground floor, are comfortable and well furnished with tea/coffee making facilities, electric blanket, clock radio, colour TV and the beds have either duvet or blankets. The double and twin rooms are en-suite and the single room has a wash hand basin.

John & Edith Howliston
Tel: 01665 711263

B&B from £17 (weekly rate from £112), Rooms 2 double, 1 twin, 1 single (most en-suite), No smoking, Open all year except Christmas, Map Ref: J

HIGH FORCE, TEESDALE.

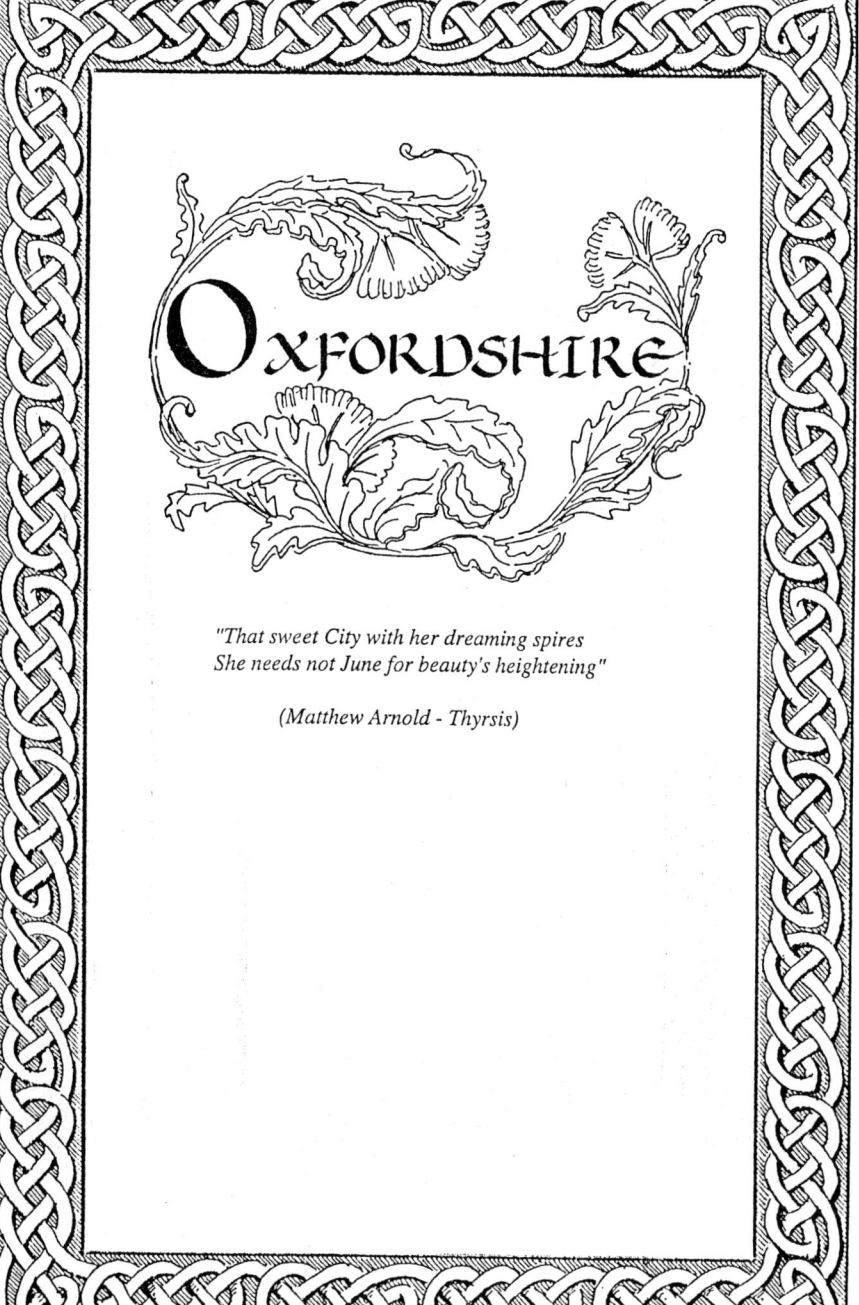

OXFORDSHIRE

"That sweet City with her dreaming spires
She needs not June for beauty's heightening"

(Matthew Arnold - Thyrsis)

OXFORDSHIRE

THE UFFINGTON WHITE HORSE

Mention Oxfordshire and the city of Oxford immediately springs to mind. A city like no other, Oxford is a seat of learning and a centre for the arts. The city, in only one square mile, has more than 600 buildings of architectural and historical interest. The medieval origins of Oxford University have produced a blend of architectural styles. It consists of 42 different colleges and halls sited in various parts of the city.

Sir Christopher Wren was Professor of Astronomy at Oxford when he designed one of the university's best known buildings, the Sheldonian Theatre, a classical amphitheatre where undergraduates ceremonially receive their degrees. The students have created their own vibrant culture from restaurants, pubs, markets and artistic events. As well as a wide variety of entertainment for the visitor from concerts to art exhibitions and museums, there are plenty of walks through the University's immaculate gardens - and there is always the famous pastime, punting!

To the South West of Oxford is the famous Vale of the White Horse. From Uffington, in the heart of the vale, there are good views of the horse cut into the chalk of White Horse Hill. There is still dispute over when the 374 feet long figure was cut into the hillside. One theory is that it was cut in Saxon times to commemorate a 9th century victory by King Alfred over the Danes. But other theories say its semi-abstract style means it could date back to as early as 350 BC and be the art of the Iron Age Celts North Oxfordshire's Cotswold country is very much the English heartland with its sleepy villages of olden ironstone or grey limestone. In the middle ages the Cotswolds wool was a major source of revenue and the wool merchants built numerous manor houses and splendid churches.

What remains of the great royal hunting forest of Wychwood overlooks the valley of the River Evenlode, giving its name to villages like Shipton-under-Wychwood. Here Tudor monarchs, including Henry VIII, hunted. Now there is a nature reserve in the 1,500 acres which survive. Burford, on the River Windrush, is a mixture of Tudor houses and Georgian facades. A feature of the High Street is the Tolsey, an upper storey supported on pillars which was where the market was held and tolls collected.

THE ROLLRIGHT STONES.

Chipping Norton, at 700 ft, is the highest town in the county. Mentioned in the Domesday Book as Norton, the "chipping" or "cheapening" meaning market was added to the name in the 13th century. Banbury is famous for its cakes, made from flaky or puff pastry filled with dried spiced fruit. The making of the cakes was first recorded in the 16th century, but they were probably made much earlier.

BANBURY CROSS.

Much of the Eastern side of Oxfordshire is off the tourist map, with its vast cornfields and wide open tracts of land. Ot Moor, a bleak expanse covering 6 square miles is surrounded by a string of attractive villages.

There are also attractive villages in the south of the area along the River Thame and the River Cherwell in the North. By the Cherwell near Bicester is Rousham House, one of the finest Jacobean mansions in the country.

OXFORDSHIRE

THE ELIZABETHAN MANOR HOUSE, MAPLEDURHAM

OXFORDSHIRE

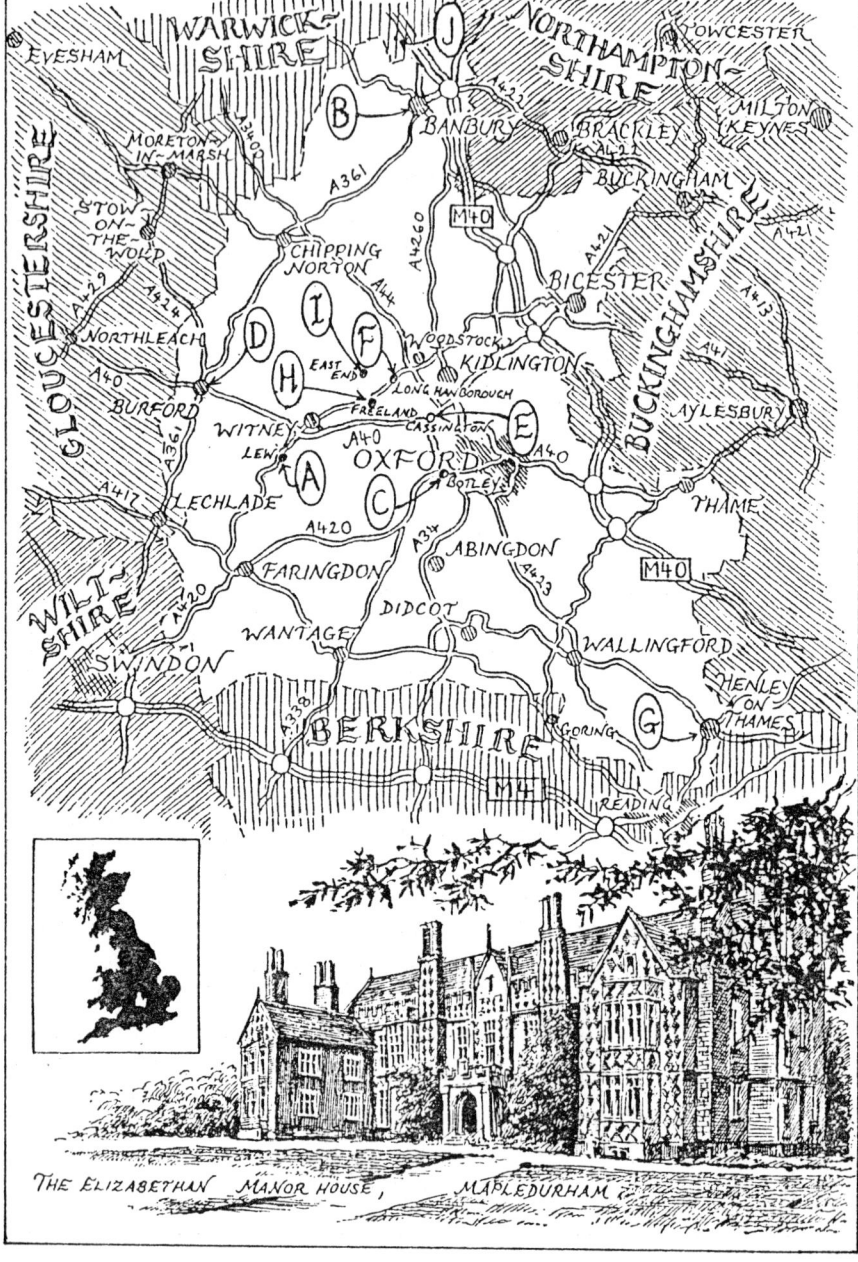

THE ELIZABETHAN MANOR HOUSE, MAPLEDURHAM

Farmhouse Hotel, University Farm, Lew, Bampton, Oxon OX18 2AU   Nearest Road A4095, A40

A charming 17th century Cotswold stone farmhouse in ½ acre of gardens including paved terraces. Pretty, colour co-ordinated, bedrooms, all en-suite, individually furnished with many extra touches. All have TV, telephone, radio, hairdryer, and hospitality tray. A honeymoon suite is available and the ground floor bedroom is equipped for disabled visitors. 2 comfortable sitting rooms with inglenook fireplaces and oak beams. A bar adjoins the dining room and an attractive conservatory leads off with views across open countryside. Traditional English food is served.

Mrs M J Rouse
Tel: 01993 850297
Fax: 01993 850965

B&B from £25, Dinner from £14.50, Rooms 2 twin, 3 double, 1 family (all en-suite), Open all year except Christmas and New Year, Map Ref: A

Home Farmhouse, Charlton, Banbury, Oxfordshire OX17 3DR   Nearest Road A43, B4100, M40

Home Farmhouse, a 400 year old listed Cotswold stone house with an attractive courtyard and garden, is a fascinating example of its kind with inglenooks, exposed beams, winder staircases; and a welcoming atmosphere. Rosemary Grove-White, an interior designer, has furnished the house in harmony with its age but with the emphasis on comfort. The bedrooms have en-suite/private bathrooms, tea/coffee makers, and TV. An excellent base from which to visit Oxford, Stratford, the Cotswolds and many houses/gardens including Blenheim, Warwick Castle, Hidcote, etc.

Mrs R J Grove-White
Tel: 01295 811683
Fax: 01295 811683

B&B from £22, Dinner from £16 (by arrangement), Rooms 1 twin, 2 double (all en-suite) Minimum age 10, Pets by arrangement, Open all year, Map Ref: B

Cotman House, Shenington, Banbury, Oxfordshire OX15 6NH   Nearest Road A422, M40

A classic 1726 stone built former Rectory standing in large terraced and walled gardens in a showpiece village amid pretty countryside. Modern plumbing, antique furniture, log fires, modern beds, combine to provide great comfort and elegance. All rooms have tea/coffee making facilitiesand TV. A full size billiards table is popular with guests. Situated 7 miles from M40 junction 11 (Banbury), 1 mile west of A422 (Banbury/Stratford Road). Convenient for Oxford, Blenheim, Cotswolds, Warwick, NEC and Silverstone.

Mrs M Hainsworth
Tel: 01295 670642
Fax: 01295 678170

B&B from £22.50, Dinner £17.50(by arrangement), Rooms 1 twin, 2 double (2 private bathroooms, 1 en-suite), Restricted smoking, Minimum age 8, Open all year, Map Ref: B

Sugarswell Farm, Shenington, Banbury, Oxfordshire OX15 6HW   Nearest Road A422

On the edge of the Cotswolds, Sugarswell overlooks fields and woodland. The interior incorporates modern conveniences with gracious style. All bedrooms have en-suite bathrooms, tea/coffee making facilities, and views of rolling countryside. A wonderful spot to relax and unwind with all the comforts of home together with the appointments expected of a large country house. Your hostess, Rosemary Nunneley, is a Cordon Bleu cook whose love of cooking is very apparent and a combination of English and French dishes are served. After dinner take a walk in the lovely garden.

Mrs Rosemary Nunneley
Tel: 01295 680512
Fax: 01295 680512

B&B from £25, Dinner from £16, Rooms 2 twin, 1 double (all en-suite, No smoking, No children, No pets, Open all year, Map Ref: B

Pond Cottage, The Green, Warmington, Banbury, Oxon OX17 1BU   Nearest Road B4100, M40

This much photographed stone built cottage in the south Warwickshire village of Warmington is within easy reach of Warwick Castle, Stratford, Upton House, Blenheim Palace, Heritage Mtr Ctr, Cotswolds and many outstanding gardens incl Hidcote Manor Garden. The pretty, en-suite, dbl room overlooks the village green and duck pond. The small single room (bathroom next door), overlooks the garden. Both have t/c making fac's. Beautifully furnished, Gr II listed house with guests sitting room. Dinner if requested at 7 pm. French spoken. A warm welcome assured.

Mrs V G Viljoen
Tel: 01295 690682

B&B from £17, Dinner from £11.80, 1 single, 1 en-suite double, No children, Open April - October (inclusive), Map Ref: J

Tilbury Lodge, 5 Tilbury Lane, Eynsham Road, Botley, Oxford OX2 9NB   M40, A34, B4044

Tilbury Lodge Private Hotel, is situated in a quiet country lane just 2 miles west of the city centre, 1 mile from the railway and 2 miles from Farmoor Reservoir with trout fishing and sailing. All rooms are en-suite with telephone, hairdryer, TV, radio and tea/coffee making facilities,. The hotel benefits from central heating, double glazing and ground floor bedrooms. There is a guest lounge, jacuzzi, 4 poster and ample parking. An ideal base for touring the Cotswolds or visiting Blenheim and Stratford-upon-Avon. AA 'Selected', RAC High Acclaimed

Eileen & Eddie Trafford
Tel: 01865 862138
Fax: 01865 863700

B&B from £25, Rooms 2 family, 5 twin/double, 2 single, Open all year, Map Ref: C

Providence Cottage, 26 Lower High Street, Burford, Oxon OX18 4RR   Nearest Road A424, A40

A delightful Cotswold stone cottage in the centre of Burford situated at the bottom of the High Street towards the bridge. Quiet bedrooms with own bathrooms. Furnished to a high standard with antiques, designer fabrics, fresh flowers and comfortable beds. Tea/coffee making facilities in bedrooms. There is a guests' lounge with colour TV. Within easy walking distance of excellent restaurants, pubs, etc. Good base for touring Cotswolds, Oxford, Stratford-upon-Avon, Cheltenham and may other places of interest. Heathrow airport 75 minutes.

Michael & Patricia Theodorou
Tel: 01993 823310

B&B from £20, Rooms 1 twin, 2 double, (en-suite), No smoking, Minimum age 14, Open all year except Christmas and New Year, Map Ref: D

Burleigh Farm, Bladon Road, Cassington, Oxfordshire OX8 1EA   Nearest Road A40, A4095

A listed stone farmhouse in a quiet position. This is a working pedigree Friesian dairy farm on the Blenheim Estate. The comfortable bedrooms, mostly have private/en-suite facilities, some have TV, and all offer tea and coffee making facilities. There is a pleasant lounge which guests have the use of. Situated conveniently for Blenheim Palace, Oxford and the Cotswolds.

Mrs Jane Cook
Tel: 01865 881352

B&B from £17.50, Rooms 1 single, 1 double, 1 family (most en-suite), No smoking, Pets welcome, Open all year, Map Ref: E

Wynford House, 79 Main Road, Long Hanborough, Oxon., OX8 8JX Nearest Road A4095, A44

Wynford Guest House is situated in the village of Long Hanborough only 1 mile from Bladon, final resting place of Sir Winston Churchill and 3 miles from famous Woodstock and Blenheim Palace. There is a warm welcome, excellent food and comfortable accommodation. All bedrooms, one of which is en-suite, have colour TV and tea/coffee making facilities. Conveniently situated for the Cotswolds. The City of Oxford is 12 miles away. Evening meal is available by arrangement and there are several local pubs and restaurants within walking distance.

Mrs C Ellis
Tel: 01993 881402
Fax: 01993 883448

B&B from £18, Dinner £9 by arrangement, Rooms 1 family, 1 twin, 1 double (1 en-suite), Restricted smoking, Pets by arrangement, Open all year, Map Ref: F

Old Farmhouse, Station Hill, Long Hanborough, Oxfordshire OX8 8JZ Nearest Road A4095, A44

A warm and friendly welcome is assured at the 17th century Old Farmhouse which is full of period charm and character, tastefully furnished with inglenook fireplace, beams and flagstone floors. Ideally situated near Oxford, Woodstock, Blenheim Palace and the Cotswolds. Lovely walks nearby. Delicious home cooking and light meals by arrangement. Excellent pubs and restaurants in picturesque local villages. French, German, Italian & Spanish spoken. ETB 2 Crowns and Highly Commended.

Mrs Vanessa Maundrell
Tel: 01993 882097

B&B from £18, Rooms 2 double (1 en-suite), No smoking, Minimum age 12, Open all year except Christmas, Map Ref: F

Little Parmoor, Parmoor Lane, Frieth, Henley-on-Thames, Oxon RG9 6NL Nearest Road M40, M4

Only 40 minutes from Heathrow and within easy reach of Windsor, Oxford, London and the Cotswolds. Little Parmoor is situated just outside the village of Frieth in the beautiful Chiltern countryside between Henley and Marlow. A pretty early Georgian country house set in an acre of garden surrounded by farmland. Comfortable rooms with colour TV and tea making facilities (one room is en-suite). Elegant panelled drawing room for guests to use. Dinner by arrangement.

Wynyard & Julia Wallace
Tel: 01494 881447
Fax: 01494 883012

B&B from £18, Dinner from £13, Rooms, 1 single, 1 en-suite double, No smoking, Open all year, Map Ref: G

Little Parmoor Farm, Frieth, Nr Henley-on-Thames, Oxon RG9 6NL Nearest Road A4155, M4, M40

Little Parmoor Farm has a relaxed, friendly atmosphere and is ideally situated for touring, fishing, golf, walking and riding. It is a 220 acre stock and grain farm in an area of outstanding natural beauty. The house itself is a 16th century brick and flint farmhouse with oak beams standing in a large garden in a rural location. Full central heating and log fires in winter. Children welcome, high chairs and cots available. Well situated for London and Heathrow. ETB listed highly commended.

Frances & Roger Emmett
Tel: 01494 881600
Fax: 01494 881600

B&B from £19, Rooms 1 double (en-suite), 2 twin, Restricted smoking, Open all year, Map Ref: G

Shepherds, Shepherds Green, Rotherfield Greys, Henley-on-Thames, Oxon RG9 4QL   **M4, M40**

Shepherds is a delightful part 18th century house which stands in its own gardens on the quiet village green. All bedrooms have either en-suite or private facilities, clock radios and tea/coffee making facilities, some have TV. Guests have their own splendid drawing room furnished with antiques and have a cosy open fire. Conveniently situated for touring Windsor, Oxford and the Chilterns. Good access to Heathrow.

Mrs Susan Fulford-Dobson
Tel: 01491 628413

B&B from £19, Dinner from £14, Rooms 2 double, 1 twin, 1 single, Minimum age 12, Restricted smoking, Open all year except Christmas and New Year. Map Ref: G

Wrestler's Mead, 35 Wroslyn Road, Freeland, Witney Oxford, OX8 8HJ   **Nearest Road A4095**

Wrestler's Mead is a chalet bungalow with a spacious garden for guests to use if required. The name of the bungalow refers to the wrestling bouts held on our ground in the 1700's and not to the antics of your hosts Babs and David, who assure you of a warm welcome. Accommodation consists of a double and single room at ground floor level and a family room on the first floor. Tea/coffee making facilities, and colour TV are provided in the double and family rooms. The family room also has en-suite shower, washbasin and toilet.

Babs & David Taphouse
Tel: 01993 882003

B&B from £16, Rooms 1 single, 1 double, 1 family, Pets by arrangement, Open all year, Map Ref: H

Gorselands Farmhouse Auberge, Boddington Lane, Long Hanborough, Nr Woodstock, OX8 6PU   **A4095**

Old Cotswold stone farmhouse with oak beams, flagstone floors and log fires in winter, situated in one acre of grounds and surrounded by idyllic countryside. Full sized billiards table and lawn tennis court for guests' use. En-suite facilities. French style evening meals by arrangement. Table licence. Ideal location for visiting Blenheim Palace, Woodstock, Oxford, Cotswold villages, North Leigh Roman Villa, etc. Lovely walks by the River Windrush. Tourist Board 2 crowns, RAC listed. Credit cards accepted.

Mrs B Newcombe-Jones
Tel: 01993 881895
Fax: 01993 882799

B&B from £14, Dinner from £10.95, Rooms 1 twin, 3 double, 1 family, (all en-suite), Restricted smoking, Pets by arrangement, Open all year, Map Ref: I

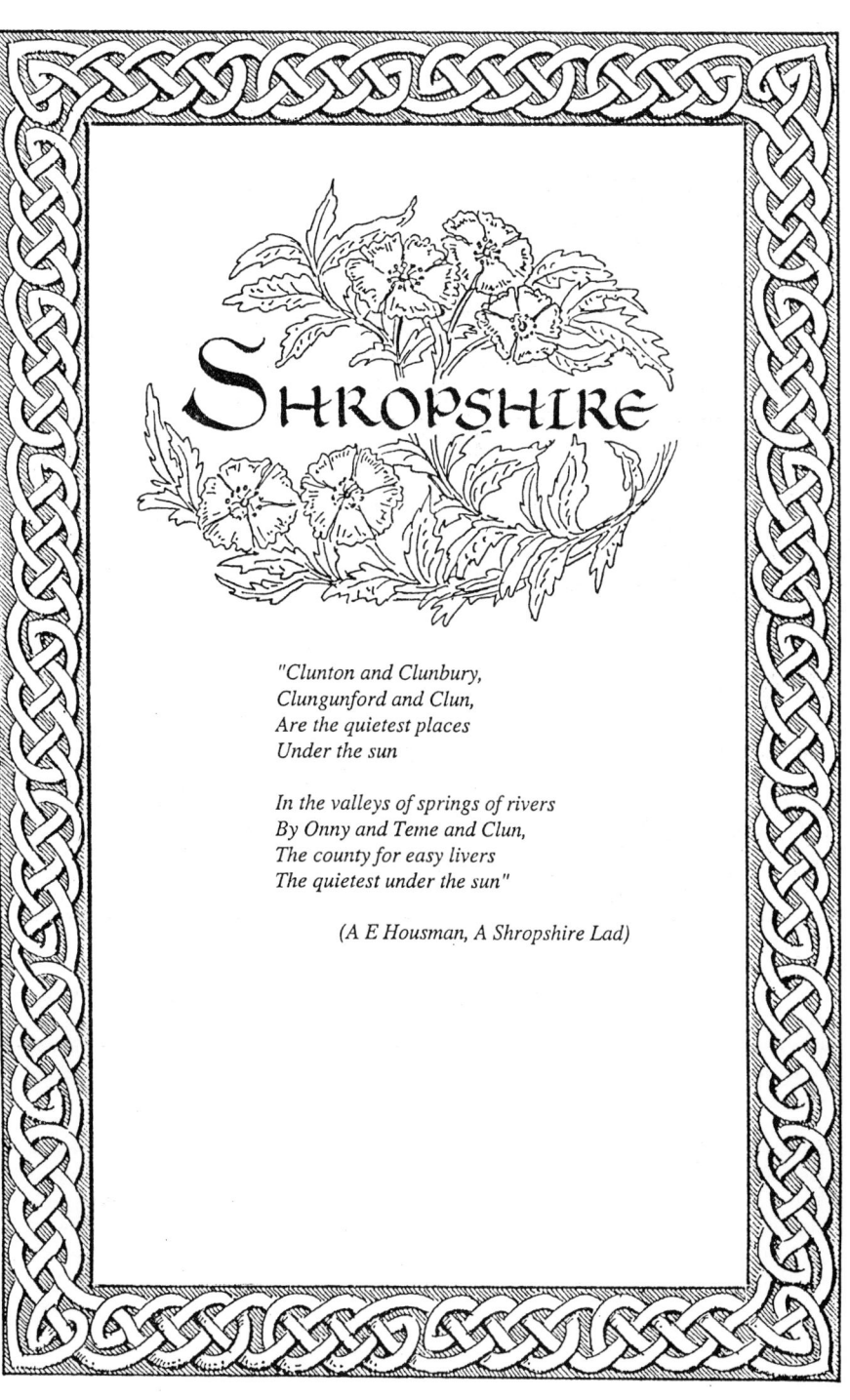

SHROPSHIRE

"Clunton and Clunbury,
Clungunford and Clun,
Are the quietest places
Under the sun

In the valleys of springs of rivers
By Onny and Teme and Clun,
The county for easy livers
The quietest under the sun"

(A E Housman, A Shropshire Lad)

SHROPSHIRE

THE WREKIN

Upland and lowland Britain meet in Shropshire; wild, high moorland encounters soft, lush lowland farms. Shropshire's contrasts give it its distinctive quality - its Roman city and 20th century new town; ruined castles and elegant country houses; the birthplace of industry and rich farmland. Shropshire is also Cadfael Country - the dark, close setting of the Medieval marches that inspired the Brother Cadfael Chronicles. Local author Ellis Peters created her best selling medieval who-dunits around the Benedictine monk at Shrewsbury Abbey.

The county's farm land is dissected by England's longest river, the Severn as it flows from the Welsh border hills to the Bristol Channel. To the North of the river the rich, arable land is broken by patches of hills, the most notable of which is the Wrekin, rising to 1,334 ft South West of Wellington and giving splendid views of the surrounding countryside Agricultural land in the south east of the county is dominated by the limestone ridge of Wenlock Edge, described by the poet A E Housman in "A Shropshire Lad". The River Corve winds through beautiful Corve Dale between Wenlock Edge and the twin hills of Titterstone Clee and Brown Clee. The valley has a wealth of attractive 15th and 16th century manor farms.

Shropshire has many small, but interesting towns, most of which have half-timbered houses. One of the most beautiful Tudor towns in England is Shropshire's county town, Shrewsbury. Lying on a peninsula of the Severn, which is spanned by twin bridges, the town's narrow streets and half timbered houses give it a unique character. The town is ornamented by its pink sandstone castle, originally Norman and renovated by Thomas Telford, the engineer and architect, whom the new town of Telford was named after. He was Surveyor Of Public Works for Shropshire and the aqueduct he designed to carry the Shropshire Union Canal at Longdon upon Tern is the oldest cast iron aqueduct in the world, dating from 1794.

EARLY 16TH CENTURY ARCHITECTURE, LUDLOW

The curiously named Ruyton XI Towns to the North West of Shrewsbury received its name in 1301 when 11 small hamlets united. As a result its village street stretches a mile, making it one of the longest in the country. Market Drayton was the birthplace in 1725 of Robert Clive - Clive of India.

The market town of Shifnal, with its fine half-timbered and Georgian houses, was described by Charles Dickens in The Old Curiosity Shop. Wem is famous for its strong ales. It was the infamous Judge Jeffreys who became Baron of Wem in 1685. Bridgnorth is built on a red sandstone ridge. The Low Town is connected to the High Town by a two-car funicular railway and flights of steep steps. The railway has a gradient of 4 in 7 and travels 201 ft between stations.

To the North of the town the River Severn flows through the Ironbridge Gorge, one of the major centres in Britain's Industrial Revolution. The 200 ft bridge which spans the gorge was built in 1779 marking the first use of iron in industrial architecture. It was designed by Abraham Darby, whose grandfather 70 years earlier was the first man to smelt iron with coke. The town of Ludlow has its own history, if not tumultuous with its Welsh border raids, and its own mellow beauty. Its ruined castle stands high above the River Teme.

South of the River Severn the landscape is studded by country houses in rich parkland. Interesting towns include Craven Arms and Bishop's Castle, both in sheep farming country, and Church Stretton. Shropshire is ideal walking country, from the lake lands in the North at Ellesmere, to the rolling hills in the South and the rugged Welsh border country. There are many trails and walks in the county. At Knighton the long distance trail, Offa's Dyke Path enters Shropshire from Wales. The 177 mile long path runs the entire length of the border between England and Wales. A 10 mile ridge called the Long Mynd to the west of Church Stretton also provides excellent walking country on its 4,530 acres of heath and moorland owned by the National Trust. A track of unknown age, The Port Way runs the entire length of the ridge.

STOKESAY CASTLE

SHROPSHIRE

Map of Shropshire showing: KIDSGROVE, CREWE, NANTWICH, STOKE-ON-TRENT, WREXHAM, CHESHIRE, NEWCASTLE-UNDER-LYME, RUABON, LLANGOLLEN, WHITCHURCH, STONE, STAFFORDSHIRE, MARKET DRAYTON, LLANGOLLEN CANAL, ELLESMERE, OSWESTRY, HODNET, R. PERRY, STAFFORD, LLYNCLYS, SHROPSHIRE UNION CANAL, ROMAN ROAD, TRENT & MERSEY CANAL, R. SEVERN, R. RODEN, NEWPORT, WALES, SHREWSBURY, The Wrekin, TELFORD, CANNOCK, WELSHPOOL, IRONBRIDGE, WOLVERHAMPTON, LONG MOUNTAIN, MONTGOMERY, MUCH WENLOCK, CHURCH STRETTON, ROMAN ROAD, R. SEVERN, LONG MYNDE, DUDLEY, NEWTOWN, WENLOCK EDGE, BRIDGNORTH, WEST BROMWICH, OFFA'S DYKE, CRAVEN ARMS, WYNN DALE, CORVE DALE, R. CORVE, R. SEVERN, CLUN, STOKESAY, WYRE FOREST, KIDDERMINSTER, KNIGHTON, LUDLOW, TENBURY WELLS, R. TEME, HEREFORD & WORCESTER, BROMSGROVE, LEOMINSTER

THE MEDIEVAL GUILDHALL, MUCH WENLOCK.

SHROPSHIRE

THE MEDIEVAL GUILDHALL, MUCH WENLOCK

Middleton Lodge, Middleton Priors, Bridgnorth, Shropshire WV16 6UR　　**Nearest Road A458/B4368**

Middleton Lodge historically the Shropshire hunting and shooting lodge of the Howard family. The original building dates back to the 17th century and is set in 20 acres of beautiful rural Shropshire countryside overlooking Brown Clee Hill. The comfortable rooms all have tea/coffee making facilities, and TV. There is a lounge for use by guests and pleasant garden. Close to Birmingham but in a quiet and peaceful, country setting.

Mary Rowlands
Tel: 0174 634 228

B&B from £20, Rooms 1 twin, 2 double all with ensuite/private facilities, No smoking, Minimum age 12, Open all year except Christmas, Map Ref: A

New House Farm, Clun, Shropshire SY7 8NJ　　**Nearest Road A488, A489**

Peaceful 18th century farmhouse set high in Clun Hills near Welsh border - a hill farm which includes an Iron Age Hill Fort called 'Caer-din-Ring'. Walks from the doorstep include 'Offa's Dyke', 'Shropshire Way' and 'Kerry Ridgeway'. Accommodation is spacious with scenic views. Tea/coffee facilities, TV and furnished to a high standard. Selection of books to browse in a country garden. Home cooked dinners and packed lunches available. "New House Farm provides a family welcome and a standard of comfort which a grand hotel would find hard to match. "B'ham Evening Post".

Luke & Miriam Ellison
Tel: 01588 638314

B&B from £15, Dinner from £8.50, Rooms 1 double, 1 family, 1 twin (all with private/en-suite facilities), Restricted smoking, Open all year except Christmas and new year, Map Ref: B

Upper Buckton, Lleintwardine, Craven Arms, Shropshire SY7 0JU　　**Nearest Road A49, A4113**

Upper Buckton is a 400 acre farm overlooking the River Teme. There is a large garden which slopes down to a mill stream. The spacious house is maintained to a high standard and all meals, except lunch are available. The farmhouse cooking is of a high standard, using locally grown produce whenever possible. Children can help with the animals, enjoy garden games, table tennis and snooker. There are many places to visit and things to do, including golf, swimming and pony trekking.

Mrs Yvonne Lloyd
Tel: 01547 540634

B&B from £20, Dinner from £14, Rooms 1 double, 2 twin, No smoking, Open all year, Map Ref: C

Strefford Hall, Strefford, Craven Arms, Shropshire SY7 8DE　　**Nearest Road A49, A489**

Strefford Hall is an imposing stone built Victorian farmhouse surrounded by 360 acres of working farmland in the picturesque hamlet of Strefford, nestling at the foot of Wenlock Edge. The bedrooms have tea/coffee making facilities, razor points and TV, all have en-suite or private facilities. Strefford Hall is the ideal centre for walking amongst the Shropshire hills. The Long Mynd and the Stretton Hills lie just to the north.

Mrs Caroline Morgan
Tel: 01588 672383

B&B from £18, Rooms 1 double, 1 twin, No smoking, No pets Open all year except Christmas and New Year, Map Ref: C

Upper House Farm, Hopton Castle, Shropshire SY7 0QF   Nearest Road A49

Upper House Farm, a stock rearing farm, is situated in the beautiful Clun Valley near the Welsh border country. It is set among wooded hills and has uninterrupted views of the peaceful valley. It forms the ideal base for exploring the unspoilt Welsh border country which is rich in ancient monuments with Upper House Farm being privileged to have its own Norman Keep being one of the finest examples in England. There is a relaxing carefree atmosphere which is run to a high standard to ensure a happy stay.

B&B from £18.50, Dinner from £10.50, Rooms 1 twin, 1 double,

Sue Williams
Tel: 015474 319

1 family (all have en-suite/private facilities), and tea/coffee makers, Open February to November, Map Ref: D

The Severn Trow, Church Road, Jackfield, Ironbridge, Shropshire TF8 7ND   Nearest Rd M54, A442

For centuries, travellers to the area have enjoyed the hospitality and comfort of The Severn Trow, a former ale house, lodgings and brothel, catering for boatmen of the river. Today, more discerning visitors are able to enjoy luxurious four-poster beds. Some rooms have TV, all have tea/coffee making facilities. Superb English breakfast served, vegetarian or special diets prepared on request. There is accommodation for guests of limited mobility. Lounge with TV. Residential drinks licence. Ample car parking space.

B&B from £18, Rooms 1 twin, 2 double, 1 family all with en-suite

Jim and Pauline Hannigan
Tel: 01952 883551

facilities, No smoking, Well behaved children by arrangement, Open January to October, Map Ref: E

The Brakes, Downton Near Ludlow, Shropshire SY8 2LF   Nearest Road A4113, A49

In the heart of beautiful rolling countryside only 5 miles from the historic town of Ludlow, The Brakes offers comfortable accommodation with excellent cuisine. A period farmhouse tastefully modernised with central heating throughout, standing in 3 acres of grounds with a beautiful garden. Bedrooms are en-suite with TV and there is a charming lounge with log fire. Excellent walking country including Offa's Dyke and the Long Mynd; also golf, riding, and fishing are available. Steeped in history with many places of interest nearby. ETB 2 Crowns Highly Commended.

Tim & Tricia Turner
Tel: 01584 77485
Fax: 01584 77485

B&B from £20, Dinner from £16, Rooms 2 twin, 1 double, (all en-suite), Restricted smoking, Minimum age 13, Open all year, Map Ref: F

---

28 Lower Broad Street, Ludlow, Shropshire SY8 1PQ   Nearest Road A49

This is a listed town house of great charm and character with a secluded walled garden, situated close to the river in a lovely Georgian town. Patricia Elms Ross is proud of the reputation she has achieved for good food and wines. Warm hospitality and quiet relaxed atmosphere. All rooms en-suite with TV and tea/coffee making facilities, and many 'thoughtful extras'. Woodland and riverside walks. Castles and lots of antique and book shops. Collection from station if required. AA QQQQ selected.

Patricia Elms Ross
Tel: 01584 876996
Fax: 01584 876996

B&B from £22.50, Dinner from £14, Rooms 2 twin, 2 double (all en-suite) Restricted smoking, Pets welcome, Open all year, Map Ref: F

The White House, Hanwood, Shrewsbury, Shropshire SY5 8LP

Nearest Road A488

The White House is a 16th century half timbered, building with 2 acres of garden in the Shropshire village of Hanwood, 3½ miles from Shrewsbury. An ideal centre for touring with easy access to north and mid Wales as well as the historic Marches area. There are ruined abbeys and churches to explore, and the ancient town of Shrewsbury. The south Shropshire hills are ideal for walking and within a few miles of The Long Mynd. Also within easy reach is Ironbridge Gorge and museum.

Mike and Gill Mitchell
Tel: 01743 860414

B&B from £20, Dinner from £12.50, Rooms 1 single, 1 twin, 4 double (2 doube are en-suite), All have tea/coffee making facilities, Restricted smoking, Minimum age 12, Open all year. Map Ref: G

Tankerville Lodge, Stiperstones, Minsterley, Shrewsbury SY5 0NB

Nearest Road A488

1100 feet up in the Shropshire hills and yet only 25 minutes from Shrewsbury, Tankerville Lodge nestles close to the Stiperstones nature reserve in a land of lore, legend and sheer natural beauty. The views from the hilltop, just a few minutes walk away, are breathtaking - a vast panorama stretching from the Brecon Beacons to Snowdonia and across Shropshire to the Peak District. Tankerville Lodge offers the ideal combination - a quiet rural haven and an ideal base for touring Ironbridge, Ludlow, Lake Vyrnwy and Cadfael country, too.

Sylvia and Roy Anderson
Tel: 01743 791401

B&B from £15.75, Dinner from £8.75, Rooms 3 twin, 1 double all have tea/coffee making facilities, Restricted smoking, Minimum age 5, Pets by arrangement, Open all year, Map Ref: H

Grove Farm, Preston Brockhurst, Shrewsbury, Shropshire SY4 5QA

Nearest Road A49

Grove Farm is a village farm of 223 acres, situated 5 miles north of Shrewsbury. The house is centrally heated throughout and all bedrooms have beverage trays and washbasins, the double room has an en-suite shower. Ideally situated for visiting Chester, Shrewsbury, Wales, the potteries and Ironbridge World Heritage site. Brochure available. HETB 1 crown commended, AA 3 Q's FHB.

Mrs Janet Jones
Tel: 01939 220223

B&B from £16.50, Rooms 1 double/family, 1 single, 1 twin, No smoking, Open all year, Map Ref: I

Foxleigh House, Foxleigh Drive, Wem, Near Shrewsbury, Shropshire SY4 5BP

A49, B5476

Foxleigh House a home of character in the heart of Wem. Relax in the spacious rooms, delightfully furnished in the style of a more leisured age; but enjoy the modern comforts of central heating and private bathrooms. Foxleigh offers bed and breakfast in 2 large twin bedded rooms each equipped with colour TV and tea/coffee making facilities. Wem is a small market town of character and charm and is an ideal touring centre for Shropshire, Cheshire and across into Wales. Wem is the home of the sweet pea but to see display gardens it is easy to travel to Hodnet and Powis.

Mrs Barbara Barnes
Tel: 01939 233528

B&B from £17, Dinner £10 by arrangement, Rooms 2 twin each with private bathroom, Pets by arrangement, Open all year except Christmas, Map Ref: J

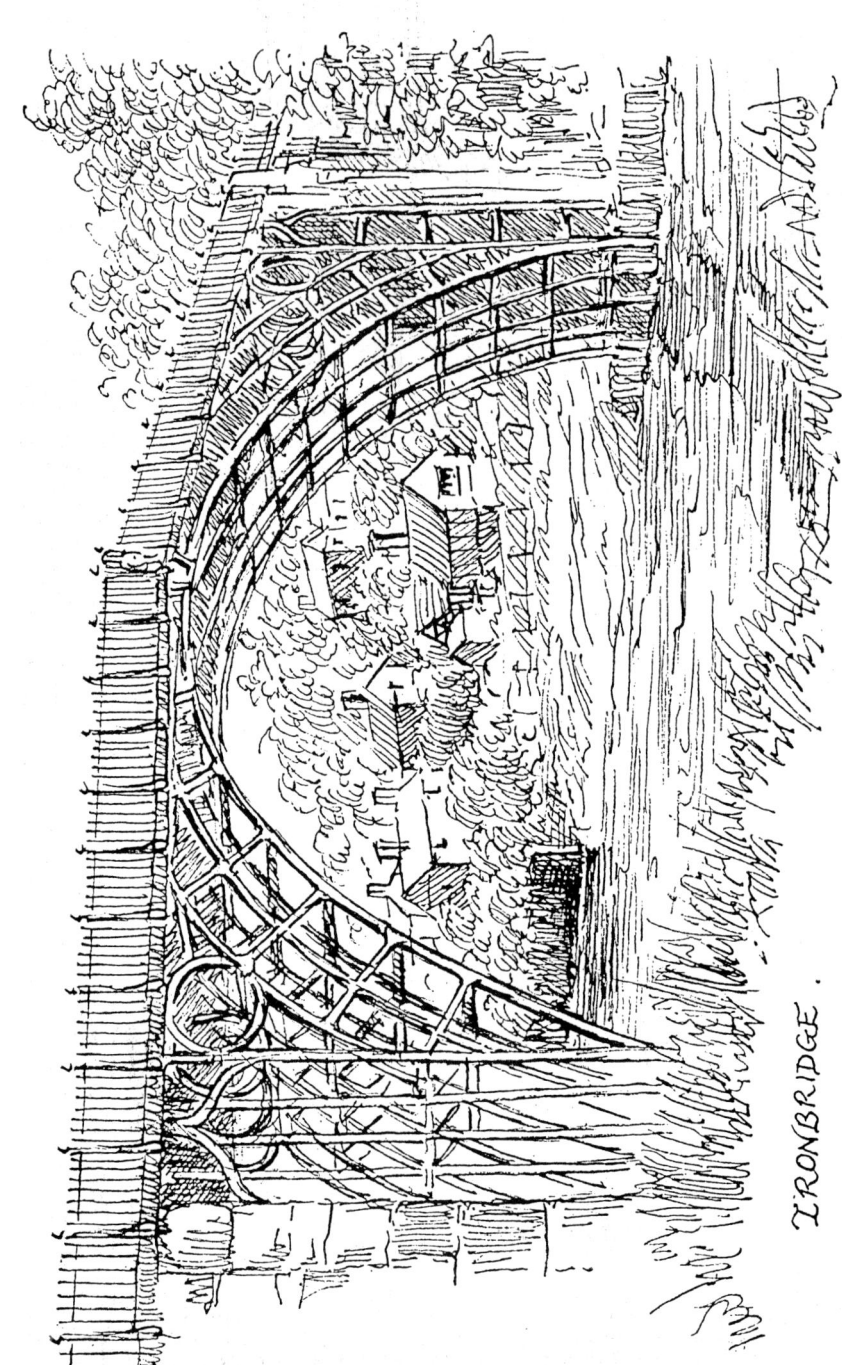

IRONBRIDGE.

SOMERSET

"Went to the hill-top. Sat a considerable time overlooking the country towards the sea . . . The Welsh hills capped by a huge range of tumultuous white clouds. The sea, spotted with white, of a bluish grey in general, streaked with darker lines. The near shores clear; scattered farmhouses half-concealed by mossy orchards"

(From Dorothy Wordsworth's Alfoxden Journal)

SOMERSET

CULBONE CHURCH.

Somerset is famed the world over for its cheddar cheese and cider. It is also well known for its varied scenery from the unspoilt countryside and country towns bordering with Dorset and Wiltshire to the wild expanse of Exmoor where it meets Devon in the West.

The Exmoor National Park covers 265 square miles from Raleigh's Cross, in Somerset to Combe Martin, in Devon and includes 3 types of landscape - coastal, pastoral moorland and heathland. The wild heather covered uplands bring to mind RD Blackmore's romantic tale of Lorna Doone, her love for Jan Ridd and her shooting at Oare Church. It is home too for the red deer and the native Exmoor ponies. Exmoor has many attractive villages including Dunster, perhaps the area's most beautiful with a wide main street of old houses and the 17th century Yarn Market. Brendon has thatched and whitewashed cottages with a medieval packhorse bridge across the East Lyn River.

Inland there are many remote lanes, leading to such windswept places as Chains Barrows, or Dunkery Beacon, the highest hill at 1,705 ft above the Bristol Channel.

The National Park coastline meets the sea at the Bristol Channel and provides some outstanding walks along dramatic cliff-top routes. Attractive towns and villages include Lynton, a Victorian creation perched on a cliff. Lynmouth's picturesque small harbour is lined by thatched houses.

CHEAP STREET, FROME.

Culbone is inaccessible by car and is best approached by a 2 mile footpath from Porlock Weir. It has the smallest church in England in regular use. In contrast, Minehead, Somerset's most Westerly town, is one of its most popular seaside resorts.

From the centuries-old harbour of Watchet, which Coleridge chose as the port of his embarkation for his Ancient Mariner, inland to Taunton, stretch the Quantock Hills. Home of the red deer, these rolling hills extending only 12 miles by 6 are to many the most beautiful part of Somerset. The hills' gentle slopes are fringed by small villages but there are no towns and villages among the inner hills. Nether Stowey was the home of Samuel Taylor Coleridge for two years. Nearby in the village of Holford is Alfoxton House which the poet William Wordsworth and his sister Dorothy rented in 1797

Somerset's county town and commercial centre, Taunton has much of interest for the tourist from its Norman castle, the grandest of the town's public buildings, to its churches. Nearby Wellington has some fine Georgian houses and it is noted for its ancient wool industry.

On the North side of the Quantocks is Bridgwater, an industrial centre and formerly a port on the River Parrett which along with the River Brue drains this area of mid Somerset.

The area is mostly low lying and a land of willows and quiet streams. Through the centre run the Polden hills, never rising above 300 ft. This an area noted for its dairy farms supplying the milk for cheddar cheese. Glastonbury is famous for its abbey which is in ruins. Arthurian legend links Glastonbury with Avalon, the place to which Arthur was taken after his death. The low lying marshy region of Sedgemoor stretches from the Mendips to Taunton and Ilminster and its willows are used for the local industry of basket making.

The Mendip Hills cover a broad band of Somerset from Weston -super-Mare to Frome 25 miles to the South East. Appearing higher than they really are because they rise from a plain, at their highest point the Mendips are 1,067 ft at Black Down. Composed of limestone covering old red sandstone, the area has a number of famous caves and swallow holes.

Cheddar is at the foot of the famous Cheddar Gorge and there are more than 400 holes or caverns in the area. Cheddar cheese originated here more than 300 years ago. To the South West is Wookey, two miles away from the famous group of caves known as Wookey Hole. The River Axe flows through the caves before widening into a lake.

The town of Shepton Mallet was an important wool market in the middle ages. Wells is famous for its cathedral, which has one of the finest West fronts in Britain, originally embellished with nearly 400 statues of angels, saints and prophets.

Yeovil is the only sizeable industrial town in south Somerset, an area of remote villages and small country towns. Cadbury Castle sits on top of a steep hill. According to legend it is from here that King Arthur set out to find his sword Excalibur.

Chard is the highest town in Somerset at nearly 400 ft above sea level and the nearby Windwhistle Hill (733f t) and Snowdon Hill (709 ft) provide superb views.

Attractive stone houses are plentiful in the small town of Wincanton and the village of Hinton St George.

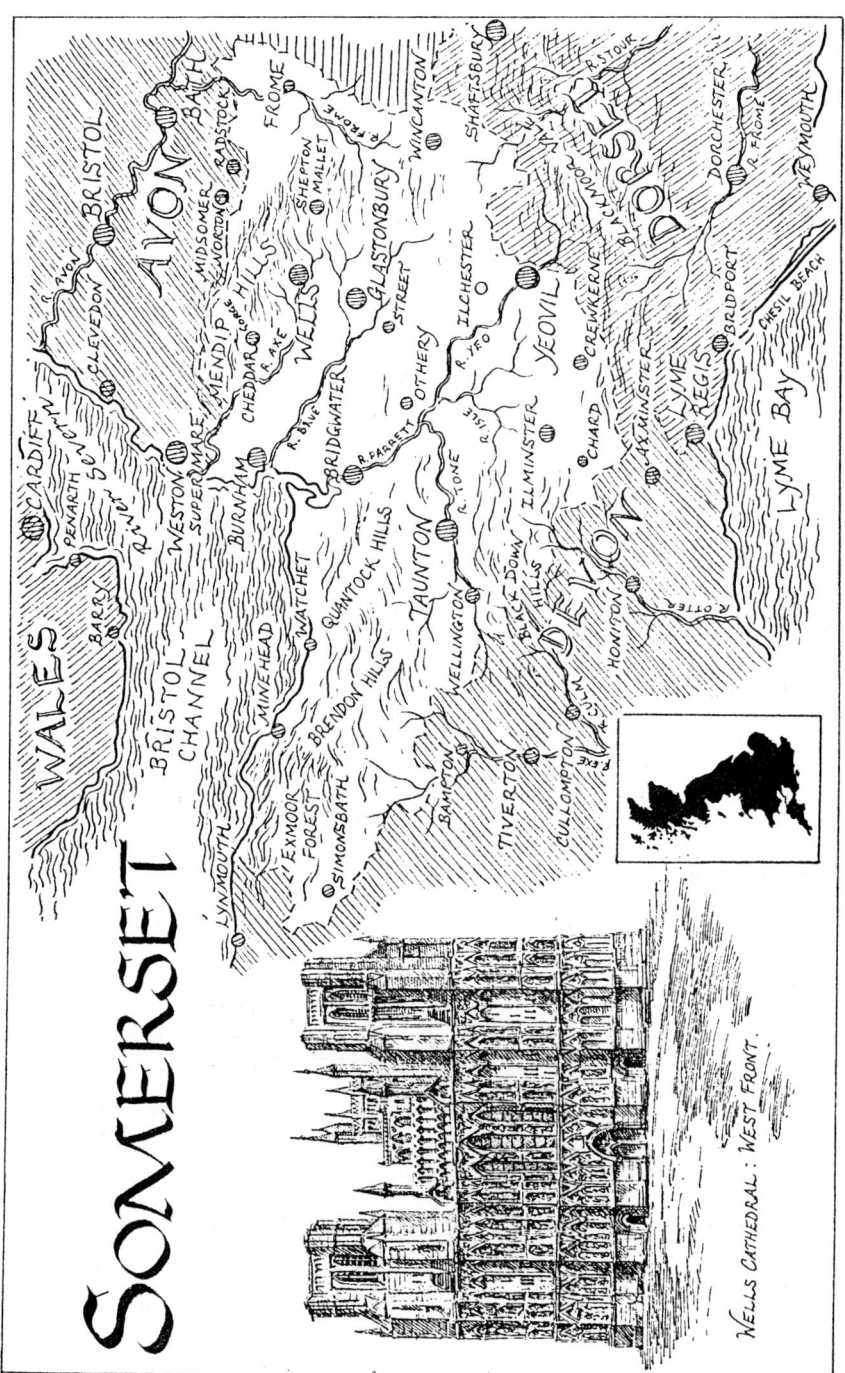

SOMERSET

WALES

BRISTOL
CARDIFF
PENARTH
CLEVEDON
R. SEVERN
R. AVON
BARRY
BRISTOL CHANNEL

AVON
BATH
MIDSOMER NORTON
RADSTOCK
WESTON SUPERMARE
MENDIP HILLS
CHEDDAR
R. AXE
R. BRUE
BURNHAM
WATCHET
MINEHEAD
LYNMOUTH
EXMOOR FOREST
SIMONSBATH
BRENDON HILLS
QUANTOCK HILLS
BRIDGWATER
WELLINGTON
BAMPTON
TIVERTON
R. EXE
CULLOMPTON
R. CULM
HONITON
BLACK DOWN HILLS
ILMINSTER
R. TONE
R. ISLE
R. PARRETT
OTHERY
STREET
GLASTONBURY
WELLS
SHEPTON MALLET
FROME
R. FROME
WINCANTON
SHAFTSBURY
ILCHESTER
R. YEO
YEOVIL
CREWKERNE
CHARD
AXMINSTER
CHARD
DEVON
R. OTTER
BLACKMOOR
DORSET
R. STOUR
DORCHESTER
R. FROME
WEYMOUTH
CHESIL BEACH
BRIDPORT
LYME REGIS
LYME BAY

WELLS CATHEDRAL: WEST FRONT.

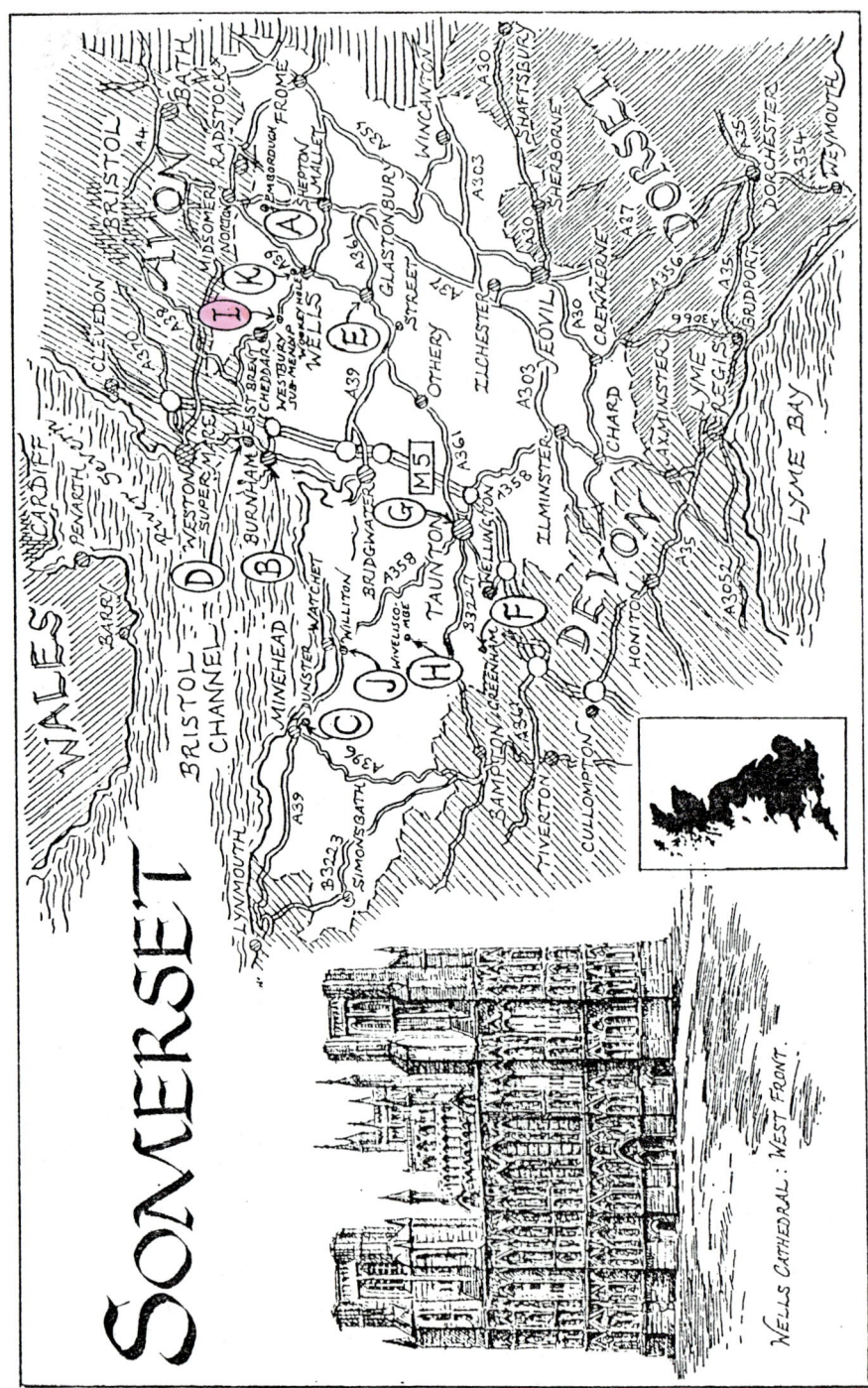

SOMERSET

WALES

CARDIFF
PENARTH, J.
B4265

BRISTOL CHANNEL

LYNMOUTH

WESTON-SUPER-MARE
D

BURNHAM-ON-SEA
B

MINEHEAD
DUNSTER WATCHET

WILLITON

A39

A396

C

SIMONSBATH
B3223

BAMPTON

TIVERTON

CULLOMPTON

DEVON

WALES
CARDIFF

CLEVEDON
A370

BRISTOL
M4 M32
A4 BATH
A4

AVON

A37

A39

MIDSOMER NORTON
RADSTOCK

A362
FROME

KILMERSDON

MARLBOROUGH
SHEPTON MALLET

A361

A I K
E
WELLS
WOOKEY HOLE
WESTBURY-SUB-MENDIP
CHEDDAR
BREAN

A38

GLASTONBURY
STREET

OTHERY

A39

A361

M5

BRIDGWATER
A358

G
WELLINGTON
F

TAUNTON

GREENHAM
H
WIVELISCOMBE

J

A38

A361

A303

ILCHESTER

A303

ILMINSTER
A358

CHARD

A30
CREWKERNE

YEOVIL
A37

SHAFTESBURY
A30

WINCANTON

A357

A303

A30

SHERBORNE
A30

DORSET

AXMINSTER

A35
HONITON

LYME REGIS
A3052

LYME BAY

BRIDPORT
A35

A3066

DORCHESTER
A354

WEYMOUTH
A354

WELLS CATHEDRAL: WEST FRONT.

Redhill Farm, Emborough, Near Bath, Somerset BA3 4SH   **Nearest Road A37**

Redhill Farm is a grade II listed farmhouse which is a small holding with a variety of animals and poultry to delight the children. Situated high on the Mendips, the perfect centre for sight-seeing. Golf, fishing and riding, are all available nearby. Leaflets are provided for local attractions. Cheddar Gorge, Wookey Hole Caves, Bath and Wells are all within easy reach. Reasonably priced pub food is available nearby and also many excellent restaurants.

Mrs Jane Rowe
Tel: 01761 241294

B&B from £14.50, Rooms 1 twin, 1 family, 1 single,
Restricted smoking, Open all year except Christmas & New Year,
Map Ref: A

The Warren Guest House, 29 Berrow Road, Burnham-on-Sea, TA8 2EZ   **Nearest Road M5, A38**

The Warren Guest House is an imposing Victorian house offering spacious accommodation 100 yards from the beach and easy walking distance from the town centre, swimming pool and golf course. All rooms have tea/coffee making facilities and radio alarms, some have en-suite facilities. Guests have use of the comfortably furnished lounge and are free to browse in the garden. A full English breakfast is served. There is a residential license. An ideal position for touring the West country. Burnham-on-Sea is a small seaside resort with many attractions.

Margaret & Peter Wheeler
Tel: 01278 786726

B&B from £13.50, Rooms 1 single, 1 twin, 2 double, 2 family,
(many en-suite) all have tea/coffee making facilities,
Restricted smoking, Pets by arrangement, Open all year, Map Ref: B

Dollons House, 10 Church Street, Dunster, Somerset TA24 6SH   **Nearest Road A396**

A Grade II listed building, Dollons House, is an attractive house believed to be much older than its early 19th century facade. The house is situated in the heart of mediaeval Dunster, with its cobbled pavements and is probably the prettiest village in the Exmoor National Park. Ideally situated for exploring the beautiful coastline. The en-suite bedrooms are individually decorated, and have tea/coffee making facilities and TV. There is a sitting room for guests which leads onto a large verandah overlooking the pleasant garden.

Major & Mrs G H Bradshaw
Tel: 01643 821880

B&B from £22.50, Rooms 1 twin, 2 double all en-suite, No smoking,
Minimum age 16, Open all year except Christmas, Map Ref: C

The Old Manor, Lower Marsh, Dunster, Somerset TA24 6PJ   **Nearest Road A39**

The Old Manor is a 15th century Grade II listed house standing in 8 acres with lovely gardens. There is a chapel over the front porch with a very fine wagon roof. Situated about 1 mile from Dunster village in a quiet, secluded spot close to Dunster Beach. It is an ideal centre from which to visit Exmoor, the famous Doone Valley, the Quantocks, and Brendon Hills.Convenient too for walking, golf, fishing and riding. Bedrooms are comfortable and there is a TV lounge where guests may relax and enjoy a cream tea. 3 self catering apartments are also available.

Mr & Mrs J Hill
Tel: 01643 821216

B&B from £18.50, Licenced, Restricted smoking, Minimum age 10,
Rooms 2 single, 4 twin, 5 double, 2 family, Open March - end October,
Map Ref: C

Conygar House, 2A The Ball, Dunster, Somerset TA24 6SD　　　　**Nearest Road A39, A358**

Conygar House is situated off the main street of Dunster. The village of Dunster has many attractions including the castle, church, working mill and yarn market and the beach which is just 1½ miles away. There is a good selection of restaurants, pubs and bars serving a wide range of meals. All bedrooms are well furnished and decorated to a high standard and have tea/coffee making facilities. Some rooms have views across the village towards the castle and moors. There is a pleasant guests' lounge which has colour television.

Mrs B Bale
Tel: 01643 821872

B&B from £15, Rooms 2 double, 1 twin, No smoking, Open March - October, Map Ref: C

Knoll Lodge, Church Road, East Brent, Somerset TA9 4HZ　　　　**Nearest Road A370, A38, M5**

Knoll Lodge is a 19th century listed Somerset house set in an acre of old orchard and is situated at the foot of Brent Knoll in the quiet Sedgemoor village of East Brent. It is 3 miles from the coast and lies on the edge of the Somerset Levels between the Mendip and Quantock Hills. It is an ideal centre for visiting Axbridge, Cheddar, Wookey Hole, Wells and Bath. All rooms are en-suite and have tea/coffee making facilities, colour TV, hairdryer, etc.

Jaqui & Tony Collins
Tel: 01278 760294

B&B from £19.50, Dinner from £9.50, Rooms 2 double, 1 twin (all en-suite), No smoking, Open all year except Christmas, Map Ref: D

No Three Magdalene Street, Glastonbury, Somerset BA6 9EW　　　　**Nearest Road A361**

Number Three - an attractive 18th century Georgian house adjoining the abbey in the historic and mystical town of Glastonbury. Its beautiful garden is floodlit at night. Internationally renowned for its high standard of cuisine No 3 is recommended by all major guides; Egon Ronay, Michelin, Good Food Guide, AA and is ETB 4 crown commended. Six luxury en-suite bedrooms designed to a high standard and rich in oil paintings and antiques. To add to the relaxation of guests, aromatherapy and massage are available by qualified therapists in beautiful and tranquil surroundings.

John & Ann Tynan
Tel: 01458 832129

B&B from £32.50, Dinner from £28, Rooms 2 twin, 3 double, 1 family all en-suite, all have tea/coffee making facilities, Open from February to November, Map Ref: E

Greenham Hall, Greenham, Somerset, TA21 0JJ　　　　**Nearest Road A38**

Greenham Hall is a large, friendly home set in a beautiful garden which is a plant lovers' paradise. There is a very large collection of perennials and plenty of room for children. For explorers and the energetic the surrounding countryside offers many varied and interesting choices including a trout fishing river, 2 nearby golf courses, horse riding, coastal trips, many historic houses, musuems, and an excellent local sports centre. There are local pubs and restaurants which offer good food.

Caro & Peter Ayre
Tel: 01823 672603

B&B from £17.50, Rooms 1 twin, 1 double en-suite, 1 family, Additional rooms available in annex, Pets are allowed by arrangement, Open all year, Map Ref: F

Strawbridges Farm Guest House, Churchstanton, Taunton, TA3 7DP   Nearest Road A303, A30, M5

ETB 2 crowns highly commended. A relaxed, peaceful atmosphere and a high standard of accommodation in a delightful area of the Blackdown Hills, an area of outstanding natural beauty. Now a non-working farm, we offer 5 tastefully decorated bedrooms each with tea/coffee making facilities, colour TV, etc. Guests have their own separate lounge and dining room. An ideal touring base only 10 minutes from Taunton and M5 and midway between north and south coasts.

Anne & Bill Slipper
Tel: 01823 601591

**B&B from £16, Rooms 2 double, 2 twin, 1 single,
Minimum age 5, Open all year except Christmas and New Year
Map Ref: G**

Watercombe House, Huish Champflower, Near Wiveliscombe, Taunton, Somerset TA4 2EE   B3227

A warm welcome awaits you at this charming country house with river frontage in a quiet secluded beauty spot in a fold of the Brendon Hills close to Exmoor. Relax from the pressures of everyday life at this modernised 18th century old school house which retains its 'olde worlde' charm. Suggestions and maps for this glorious walking, horse riding, angling, cream tea country can be provided. Easy access to north and south coasts. Recommended for good food.

Mrs Moira Garner-Richards
Tel: 01984 623725

**B&B from £18.50, Dinner from £12.50, Rooms 1 double en-suite,
1 twin, 1 single, all with modern amenities, No smoking, No pets,
Min age 10, Open March to November and Christmas, Map Ref: H**

Box Tree House, Westbury-Sub-Mendip, Wells, Somerset BA5 1HA   Nearest Road A371

A warm welcome is assured at this delightful converted 17th century farm house, located in the heart of the village next to a local inn where excellent food is served. Accommodation is in 3 comfortable rooms with en-suite and private facilities. There is a charming TV lounge. Generous breakfast with local preserves, croissants and home made muffins. Also work shops for stained glass and picture framing with many unique items for sale.

Mrs Carolyn White
Tel: 01749 870777

**B&B from £16, Rooms 2 double, 1 twin (all en-suite),
Restricted smoking, Open all year, Map Ref: I**

Stoneleigh House, Westbury-sub-Mendip, Near Wells, Somerset, BA5 1HF   Nearest Road A371

A delightful 18th century farmhouse with lovely garden situated on the southern slopes of the Mendip Hills between Wells and Cheddar. Attractively furnished bedrooms with beverage making facilities. All with private or en-suite bathroom. Television lounge with wonderful views. Continental or a delicious English breakfast is served. Vegetarians catered for. Tourist information available for guests. Good pub nearby. Ideal position for walking or touring holidays.

Mrs Wendy Thompson
Tel: 01749 870668

**B&B from £17, Rooms 2 double, 1 twin (all private/en-suite facilities),
Minimum age 10, No smoking, Open all year except Christmas,
Map Ref: I**

Curdon Mill, Lower Vellow, Williton, Somerset TA4 4LS　　　　Nearest Road A358

Curdon Mill, a licensed restaurant and hotel, nestles in a beautiful, tranquil setting at the foot of the Quantock Hills and is ideal for the country lover wishing to explore this picturesque part of Somerset. It has been carefully preserved and retains many features including its waterwheel and mill stream water garden. The pretty bedrooms all have en-suite facilities, TV, and tea/coffee trays. A large sitting room is adorned with chintzy chairs, fresh flowers and local information. Adjoining this is the period dining room where a traditional or continental breakfast is served.

Richard & Daphne Criddle
Tel: 01984 656522
Fax: 01984 656197

B&B from £25, Dinner from £16.50, Rooms 3 twin, 3 double all en-suite and have tea/coffee making facilities, Restricted smoking, Pets by arrangement, Open all year, Map Ref: J

Glencot House, Glencot Lane, Wookey Hole, Somerset BA5 1BH　　　　Nearest Road A37

Set in 18 acres of garden and parkland with river frontage, Glencot House is a grade II listed Victorian mansion which has been restored to its former glory. It is elegantly furnished and offers peace and tranquility and yet is only a short distance from Wells and Wookey Hole Caves. An ideal base for touring. All bedrooms are en-suite and have tea/coffee making facilities, TV, etc. Guests may dine at Glencot and enjoy a drink in the panelled drawing room or library in front of a log fire, or make use of the many facilities, including indoor pool, snooker, table tennis, sauna, etc.

Mrs M J Attia
Tel: 01749 677160
Fax: 01749 670210

B&B from £30, Dinner from £16.50, Rooms 7 double, 2 twin, 2 single (all en-suite), Open all year except Christmas, Map Ref: K

SUFFOLK

"The beauty of the surrounding scenery, its gentle declivities, its luxuriant meadow flats sprinkled with flocks and herds, its well-cultivated uplands, its woods and rivers, with numerous scattered villages and churches, farms and picturesque cottages, all impart to this particular spot an amenity and elegance hardly anywhere else to be found."

(John Constable)

SUFFOLK

THE WOOL HALL, LAVENHAM

Constable's description of Suffolk 200 years ago is just as fitting today. It is a county of peaceful countryside, ancient market towns and villages and unspoilt coast and estuaries. Britain's Easternmost county stretches from the heaths of Newmarket in the West to the North Sea in the East, in the South to the Forest of Breckland and to the North, Britain's newest National Park, The Broads. There is plenty to do and see in Suffolk with over 200 places to visit from stately homes and castles to abbeys, windmills, vineyards and nature reserves. Suffolk's subtle beauty has inspired some of the finest creative artists. John Constable grew up in the county and immortalised the Stour valley in paintings. Thomas Gainsborough, painter of kings and courtiers in the 18th century, grew up in Sudbury. The composer Benjamin Britten lived on the Suffolk coast and set up the Aldeburgh Festival 46 years ago.

There is plenty of opportunity for sport and recreation. An extensive network of footpaths gives plenty of choice for the walker. Several longer routes cover between 12 and 50 miles. With around 3,000 miles of country lanes it is marvellous countryside for the cyclist.

The Suffolk coast's estuaries and creeks provide great sailing. The River Waveney in the North of Suffolk is part of the great network of Broadland waterways.

Lowestoft is Britain's most Easterly point and has clean, sandy beaches. The South Beach has a Blue Flag as well as receiving the award from the English Tourist Board for the best beach in the county. Lowestoft is a fishing port with a long sea faring tradition. Nearby Southwold also boasts a Blue Flag for its beach. Broadland comes right into the town at Oulton Broad and it makes a good centre for visiting the Broads. Felixstowe grew up as a Victorian resort but is now better known as an international port. Boat trips on the estuary can be enjoyed - or even a day trip to Belgium by ferry.

FLATFORD MILL.

Ipswich is the county town of Suffolk and its origins go back to Saxon times when it was among the principal towns of England. The 16th century Christchurch Mansion is set in one of the town's many parks and has a fine collection of paintings, including the best display of Gainsborough and Constable outside London. The Ancient House, now a bookshop, is a fine example of pargetting, an external plasterwork decoration peculiar to the area.

Inland, the towns of Sudbury and Hadleigh, like so many in the area, grew up around wool and the cloth industry. Gainsborough's birthplace is in Sudbury and Hadleigh is noted for its magnificent complex of medieval buildings. Lavenham is a beautifully kept example of a Suffolk wool town with superb ancient buildings. The manufacture of cloth and preparation of wool and yarn were the main source of the town's wealth for 500 years. The 16th century Guildhall is one of the finest Tudor half-timbered buildings in the country. Dedham on the River Stour is Constable Country for it was this countryside which inspired the artist. The tower of Dedham's 16th century church is in many of Constable's paintings and a footpath leads along the river to Flatford Mill and Willy Lott's cottage, the scene of his famous Hay Wain. South of the village is Castle House, the home of the painter Sir Alfred Munnings.

Ever since the 17th century when Charles II went to Newmarket to ride, the town has been associated with horses. One of the world centres of racing, horses are bred, trained and raced here.

Bury St Edmunds has an important place in English history. It was the capital of the Saxon Kingdom of England and here in 1215 the Barons of England swore to make King John sign the Magna Carta. The plan of streets in the town centre has not changed for 900 years.

THE ANCIENT HOUSE, IPSWICH.

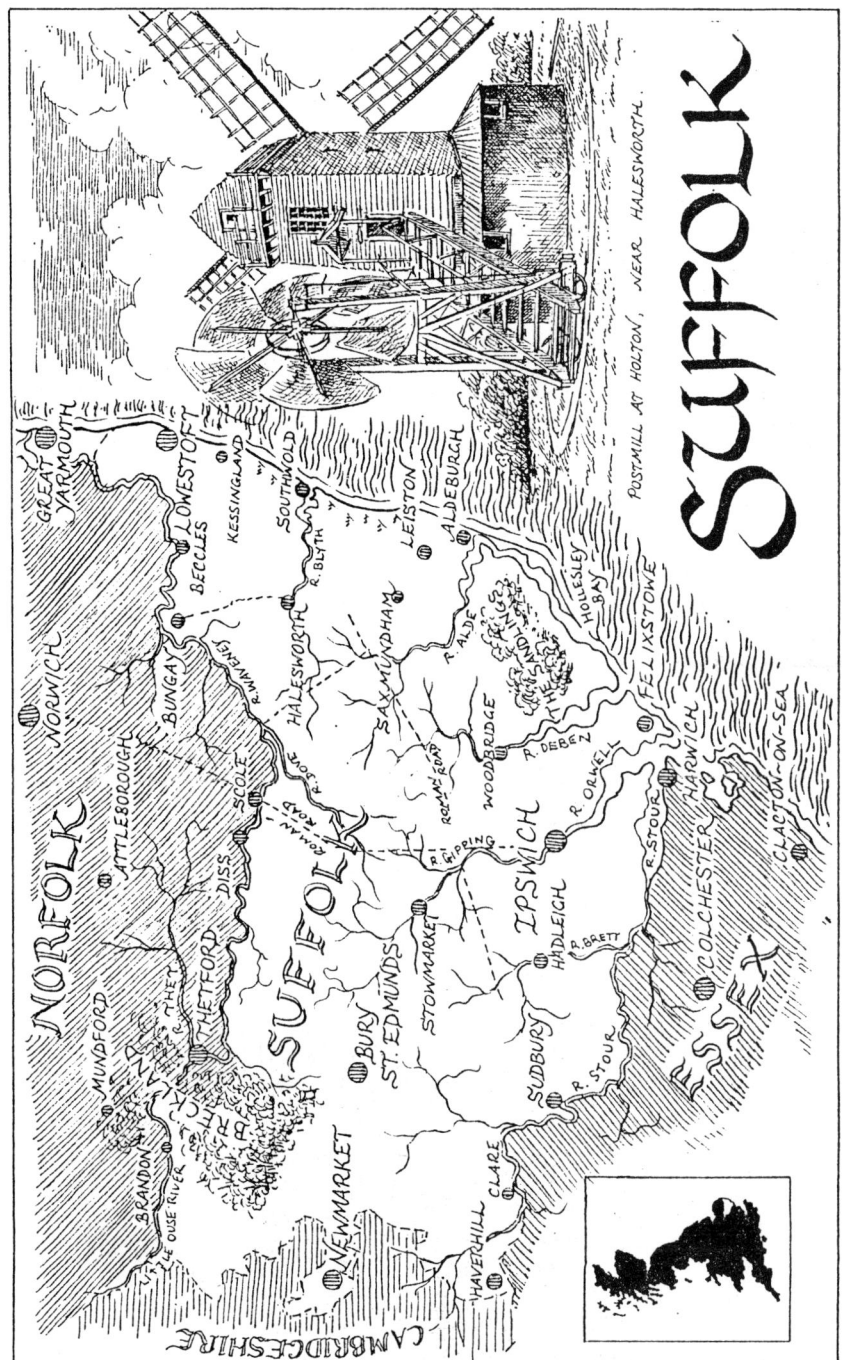

SUFFOLK

POSTMILL AT HOLTON, NEAR HALESWORTH.

NORFOLK

SUFFOLK

ESSEX

CAMBRIDGESHIRE

GREAT YARMOUTH
LOWESTOFT
BECCLES
KESSINGLAND
SOUTHWOLD
R. BLYTH
HALESWORTH
R. WAVENEY
BUNGAY
NORWICH
ATTLEBOROUGH
DISS
SCOLE
THETFORD
R. THET
MUNDFORD
BRANDON
LE OUSE RIVER
BRECK
NEWMARKET
HAVERHILL
CLARE
SUDBURY
R. STOUR
R. STOUR
R. BRETT
HADLEIGH
BURY ST. EDMUNDS
STOWMARKET
R. GIPPING
ROMAN ROAD
IPSWICH
R. ORWELL
R. DEBEN
WOODBRIDGE
ROMAN ROAD
R. ORE
SAXMUNDHAM
R. ALDE
LEISTON
ALDEBURGH
THE SANDLINGS
HOLLESLEY BAY
FELIXSTOWE
HARWICH
R. STOUR
COLCHESTER
CLACTON-ON-SEA

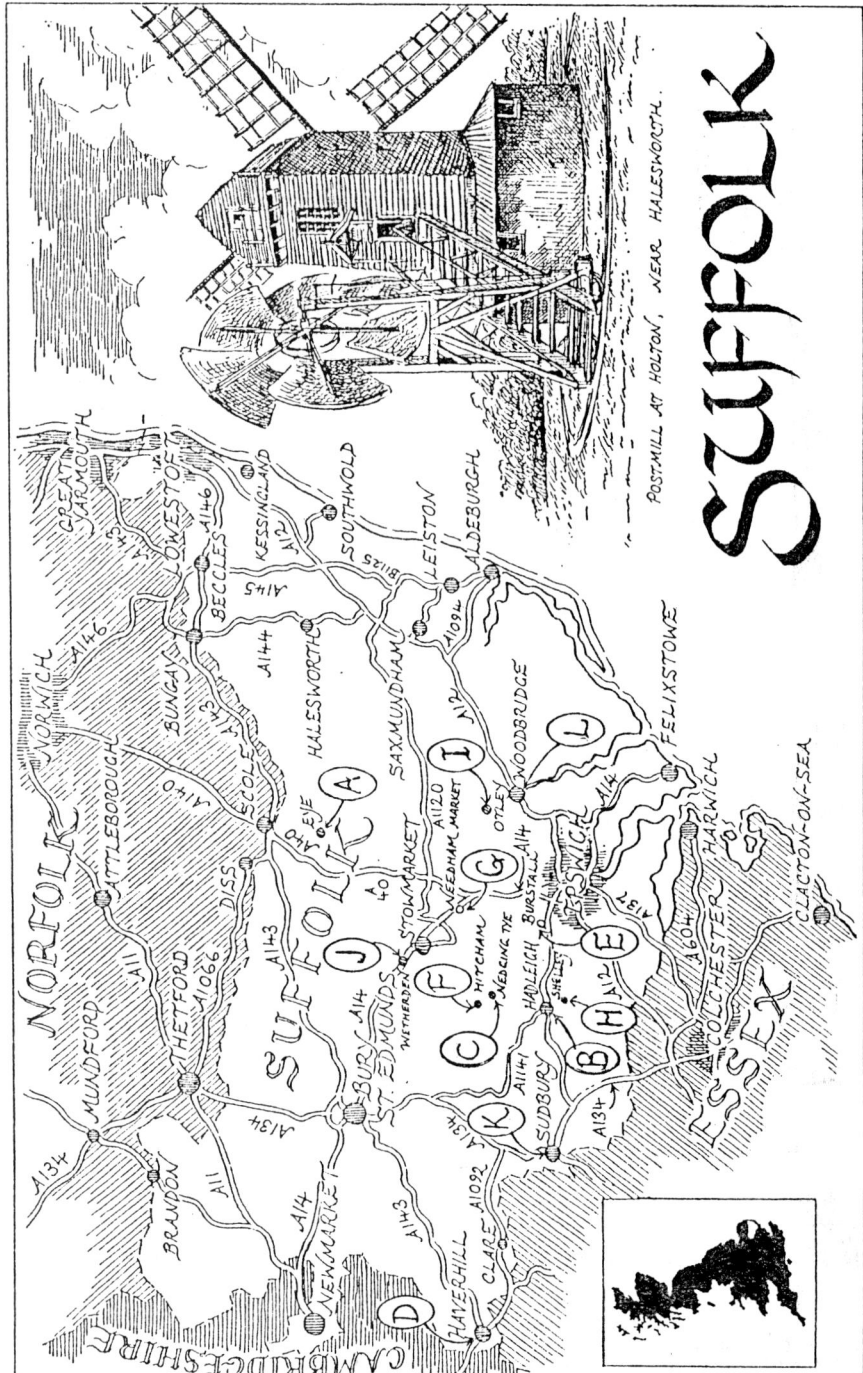

SUFFOLK

POSTMILL AT HOLTON, NEAR HALESWORTH.

Priory House, Priory Road, Fressingfield, Eye, Suffolk IP21 5PH   Nearest Road B1116

A warm welcome awaits visitors to this lovely 16th century farmhouse, peacefully set in an acre of secluded lawns and gardens. The comfortable bedrooms are provided with tea/coffee making facilities, and 2 rooms have private bathroom. Centrally heated. The house has a wealth of exposed beams, and is furnished with antique furniture. There is a guests' lounge and a pleasant dining room. Fressingfield is ideally situatuated for a peaceful relaxing holiday and also as a touring base. Excellent food available in the village only an 8 minutes walk. Colour brochure on request.

Rosemary & Stephen Willis
Tel: 01379 586254

B&B from £21, Rooms 2 twin, 1 double (2 bedrooms have private bathroom), Restricted smoking, Pets by arrangement, Open all year except Christmas, Map Ref: A

Edgehill Hotel, 2 High Street, Hadleigh, Suffolk IP7 5AP   Nearest Road B1071, A12

A beautifully restored Georgian house in a small market town. Conveniently situated in the centre of "Constable/Lovejoy" country and within easy reach of numerous pretty villages including Lavenham, Long Melford, Flatford, Dedham and Kersey and the coastal towns of Aldeburgh and Southwold. Bedrooms are elegantly furnished with en-suite facilities, tea/coffee and TV. Stunning 4-poster room. Attractive walled garden to relax in or play croquet. Traditional home cooking and personal service a speciality in this friendly family home. More rooms available in 'The Lodge House'.

Mrs Angela Rolfe
Tel: 01473 822458

B&B from £22.50, Dinner from £13.50, Rooms 2 single, 1 twin, 4 double, 2 family (all en-suite), Restricted smoking, Pets welcome, Open all year, Map Ref: B

The Old Rectory, Nedging, nr Hadleigh, Suffolk IP7 7HQ   Nearest Road B1115

Nedging is a small hamlet 6 miles east of Lavenham and 4 miles north of Hadleigh in some of Suffolk's most beautiful countryside. The Old Rectory is an elegant Georgian house in 2 acres of lovely gardens. The house has been thoroughly renovated to a high standard and each bedroom has an en-suite bathroom. Excellent 4 course dinner available if required. Ideal for a tranquil stay in peaceful surroundings. Many historic buildings and numerous golf courses nearby. Directions from Bildeston 0.4 miles south, take the small lane on the left and The Old Rectory is the first house before the church.

Tess & Rupert Chetwynd
Tel: 01449 740745
Fax: 01449 740745

B&B from £27.50, Dinner £20, Rooms 3 double, No smoking, No pets, Open all year, Map Ref: C

The Old Vicarage, Great Thurlow, Haverhill, Suffolk CB9 7LE   Nearest Road A604

Comfortable Georgian house quietly situated in lovely countryside with wonderful views. On the edge of Constable country. Well positioned for those interested in racing at Newmarket or for general exploration of East Anglia. Two of the bedrooms have en-suite or private bathrooms and all are well furnished with antique furniture. Drawing room and dining room also furnished with antiques and welcoming log fires. There is a fine garden which guests are welcome to stroll through.

Mrs Jane Sheppard
Tel: 01440 783209

B&B from £20, Dinner from £14.50, Rooms 2 twin, 1 single Minimum age 7, Restricted Smoking, Open all year, Map Ref: D

Mulberry Hall, Burstall, Ipswich, Suffolk IP8 3DP **Nearest Road A1071**

A lovely old farmhouse with log fires and good home cooking. The property, was once owned by Cardinal Wolsey during the 16th century. Henry VIII's coat of arms is over the large Inglenook fireplace in the attractive sitting room. Nicely situated in a small village 5 miles west of Ipswich and within easy access of the A12, A14, and A1071. The comfortable bedrooms are prettily furnished. Guests may also like to relax in the garden or play tennis.

Mrs Penny Debenham
Tel: 01473 652348

B&B from £17, Dinner £14, Rooms 1 single, 1 twin, 1 double, Restricted smoking, Open all year except Christmas, Map Ref: E

Mill House, Water Run, Hitcham, Ipswich, Suffolk IP7 7LN **B1115 (Stowmarket to Hadleigh)**

Mill House is a country house of the late Regency period. Set in 4 acres of beautiful grounds with peacocks, ducks, paddocks, stables tennis court and many nearby walks of natural beauty. Twin and double rooms include TV, central heating, vanity units and tea making facilities. Evening meals can be provided by arrangement. Self catering cottages are also available. Hitcham is ideally situated in the heart of Suffolk, surrounded by some of the most beautiful villages in the country and within easy reach of many market towns, and 'Constable' countryside.

Mrs Judith White
Tel: 01449 740315

B&B from £12.50, Dinner by arrangement from £6, Rooms 1 twin, 2 double (1 en-suite), Pets welcome, Open all year, Map Ref: F

Pipps Ford, Needham Market, Nr Ipswich, Suffolk IP6 8LJ **Nearest Road A45, A140**

Fine and beautiful long, low, black and white timbered house parts of which date from 1540. A house with sloping floors, beams, inglenooks, with log fires, and historic associations. The cottagey sitting rooms are filled with antique furniture and china collections and have a wonderful atmosphere. Bedrooms are attractive with en-suite bathrooms and have tea/coffee making facilities, radio/clock alarms, and hair dryers. More bedrooms in the Stables.

Mrs Raewyn Hackett-Jones
Tel: 01449 760208
Fax: 01449 760561

B&B from £17.50, Dinner from £12.50, Rooms 4 double, 3 twin, Restricted smoking, Pets by arrangement, Open all year except Christmas & New Year, Map Ref: G

Sparrows, Shelley, Hadleigh, Near Ipswich, Suffolk, IP7 5RQ **Nearest Road A12**

Sparrows is a 15th century former farmhouse set in 2 acres of garden in unspoilt countryside. Grass tennis court, table tennis and bicycles for use by guests. Beach hut available in the summer by arrangement. Within easy reach of the Suffolk coast, Constable country and many other pretty Suffolk villages. Two golf courses within 3 miles and many first class pubs and restaurants in the immediate vicinity. Dinner provided by Inglenook fireplace in dining hall at 24 hours notice. Kingsize bed, private bathroom/shower, colour TV, tea making facilities, central heating.

Mrs Rachel Thomas
Tel: 01206 337381

B&B from £17, Dinner from £12, Rooms 1 single, 1 double, 1 family, Open all year, Map Ref: H

Otley House, Otley, Nr Ipswich, Suffolk IP6 9NR   **Nearest Road A12, A140, A45**

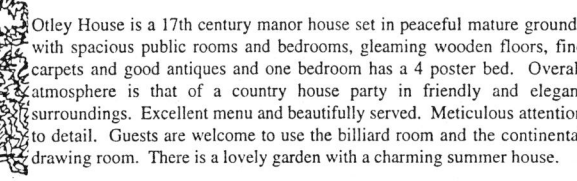

Otley House is a 17th century manor house set in peaceful mature grounds with spacious public rooms and bedrooms, gleaming wooden floors, fine carpets and good antiques and one bedroom has a 4 poster bed. Overall atmosphere is that of a country house party in friendly and elegant surroundings. Excellent menu and beautifully served. Meticulous attention to detail. Guests are welcome to use the billiard room and the continental drawing room. There is a lovely garden with a charming summer house.

Thomas & Colette Hoepli
Tel: 01473 890253
Fax: 01473 890009

B&B from £24, Dinner from £16.50, Rooms 3 double, 1 twin,
(all en-suite), Minimum age 12, Restricted smoking,
Open March - November, Map Ref: I

Bowerfield House, Helmingham Road, Otley, Suffolk IP6 9NP   **Nearest Road B1079**

Bowerfield House is a large, very handsome 17th century listed stable and barn conversion set in peaceful mature grounds with ponds, terraces and full size croquet lawn. The bedrooms all with bathrooms are beautifully furnished with antiques, TV, radio and tea/coffee making facilities. There is a billiard room and drawing room with log fires and grand piano for guests to use. Lise, who is Danish, is the winner of several East Anglian B&B awards. Full English or Scandinavian breakfast.

Lise & Michael Hilton
Tel: 01473 890742
Fax: 01473 890059

B&B from £23, Dinner from £18 (by request), Rooms 3 double rooms
with bathroom (1 four poster), No smoking, Minimum age 12,
Open mid March - end October, Map Ref: I

Wetherden Old Rectory, Wetherden, Nr Stowmarket, Suffolk IP14 3LS   **Nearest Road A5**

An 18th century house in extensive grounds overlooking the village of Wetherden. The house is delightful and is beautifully maintained with a welcoming atmosphere. The Old Rectory has a fine entrance hall and large drawing and dining rooms. Bedrooms are comfortable and have TV and bathroom. There is a croquet lawn in the garden.

Mrs J Bowden
Tel: 01359 240144

B&B from £18.75, Rooms 2 double, 1 twin, Restricted smoking,
Minimum age 15, Open mid March - end November, Map Ref: J

St Mary Hall, Belchamp Walter, Sudbury, Suffolk CO10 7BB   **A604, A134, B1058**

A very fine example of a medieval Suffolk manor house with 5 acres of lovely gardens in quiet countryside. Guests may use heated pool and tennis court and there is also a croquet lawn. A place of total tranquility. Attractive dining room and book-lined library with TV for guests use. Most attractive bedrooms one of which is huge and has a spacious en-suite bathroom. Beautiful furniture throughout.

Catherine & David Morse
Tel: 01787 237202

B&B from £24, Dinner from £16, Restricted smoking,
Pets by arrangement, Open all year except Christmas & New Year,
Map Ref: K

Grange Farm, Dennington, Woodbridge, Suffolk IP13 8BT   **Nearest Road A1120**

This is a charming house with a delightful hostess in a superb spot. The house dates from the 15th century but there has been a farmhouse on the site since the 13th century and the remains of an old moat now form a lake and ponds. There is a lovely garden with tennis court. The beamed guests' dining room and sitting room are very comfortable and beautifully furnished. Situated on the Stowmarket - Yoxford Road.

Mrs E Hickson
Tel: 01986 798388
Mobile: 03741 82835

B&B from £18, Dinner from £10, Rooms 1 double, 3 twin, 1 single
No smoking, Open all year except Christmas, Map Ref: L

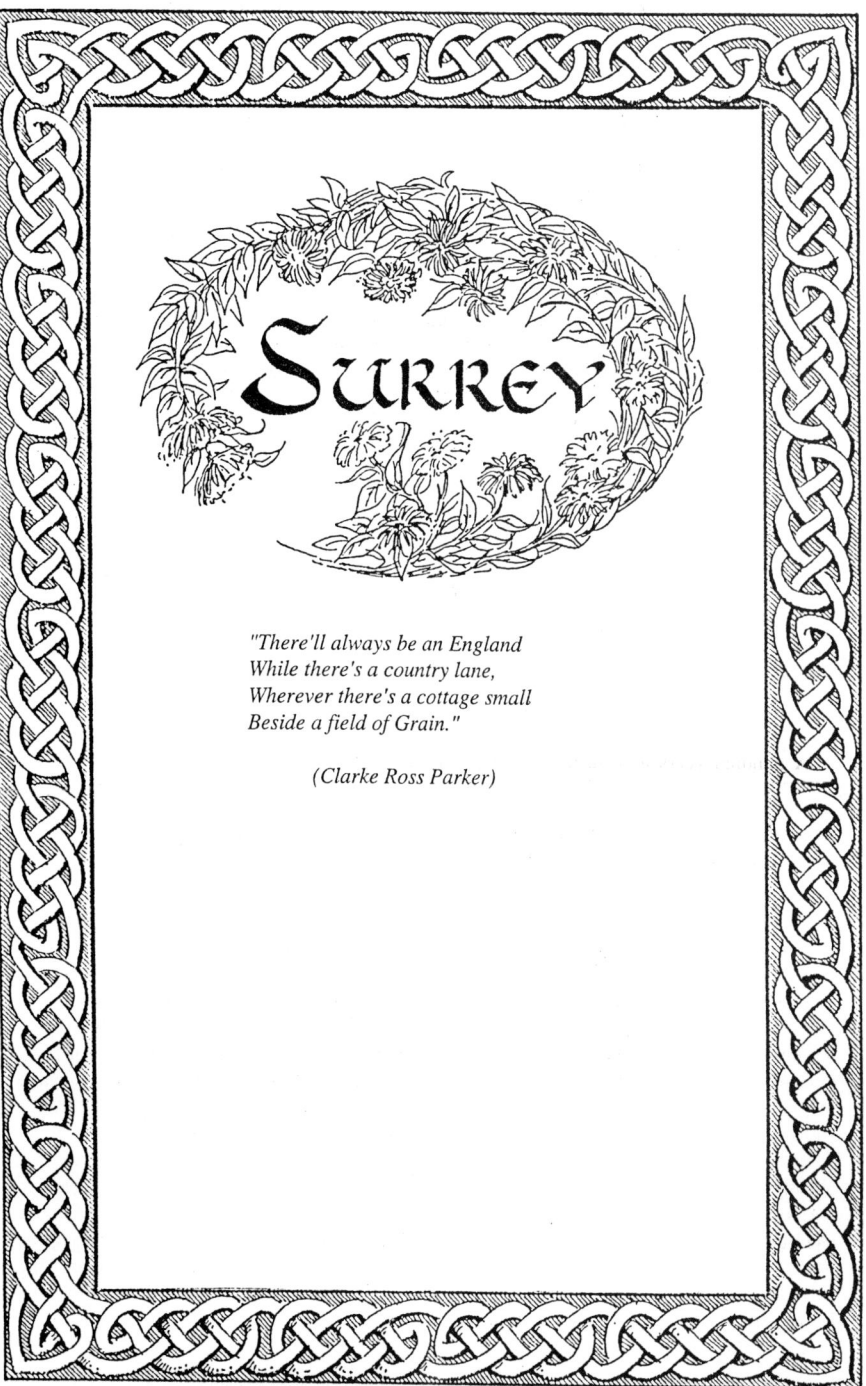

Surrey

"There'll always be an England
While there's a country lane,
Wherever there's a cottage small
Beside a field of Grain."

(Clarke Ross Parker)

SURREY

FARNHAM CASTLE.

A hundred years ago Surrey's pine and heather country was as wild as parts of Scotland. Today the county is known as the commuter and stockbroker belt, but there are still thousands of acres of commons and heaths open to the walker and picnicker giving spectacular views.

In the north of Surrey, towns like Bagshot, Esher, Camberley and Woking have become urbanised and yet are surrounded by woodlands, commons and heaths. There are also still many attractive villages like Friday Street, Abinger, Holmbury St Mary and Peaslake. Bagshot Heath was once renowned for highwaymen and it extends South to Bisley Common, famous for modern day marksmen. Three miles South West is the Royal Military Academy, Sandhurst, built in 1807. Runnymede is where King John sealed the first draft of the Magna Carta in 1215. The broad meadow alongside the River Thames belongs to the National Trust. Virginia Water is the large artificial lake at the South Eastern corner of Windsor Great Park, laid out in George III's time by landscape gardeners Paul and Thomas Sandby. The 1½ mile long lake is alive with wildfowl and coarse fish. Guildford is believed to take its name from a "ford of golden flowers" the point where the Harrow Way, an ancient track along the North Downs, crossed the River Wey. The old county town is full of well preserved houses. Nearby Godalming is an old wool town. Its narrow streets, half timbered houses and inns date back to Tudor and Stuart days. Farnham is Surrey's most Westerly town and one of the least spoilt. Here the Pilgrims' Way enters the county from Winchester. Still traceable in part along the part of the downs known as the Hog's Back, the route was used by Bronze Age traders long before medieval pilgrims. South of Farnham, at Frensham the Great Pond is one of the largest lakes in Southern England. Views from nearby hills the Devil's Jumps are among the best in Surrey.

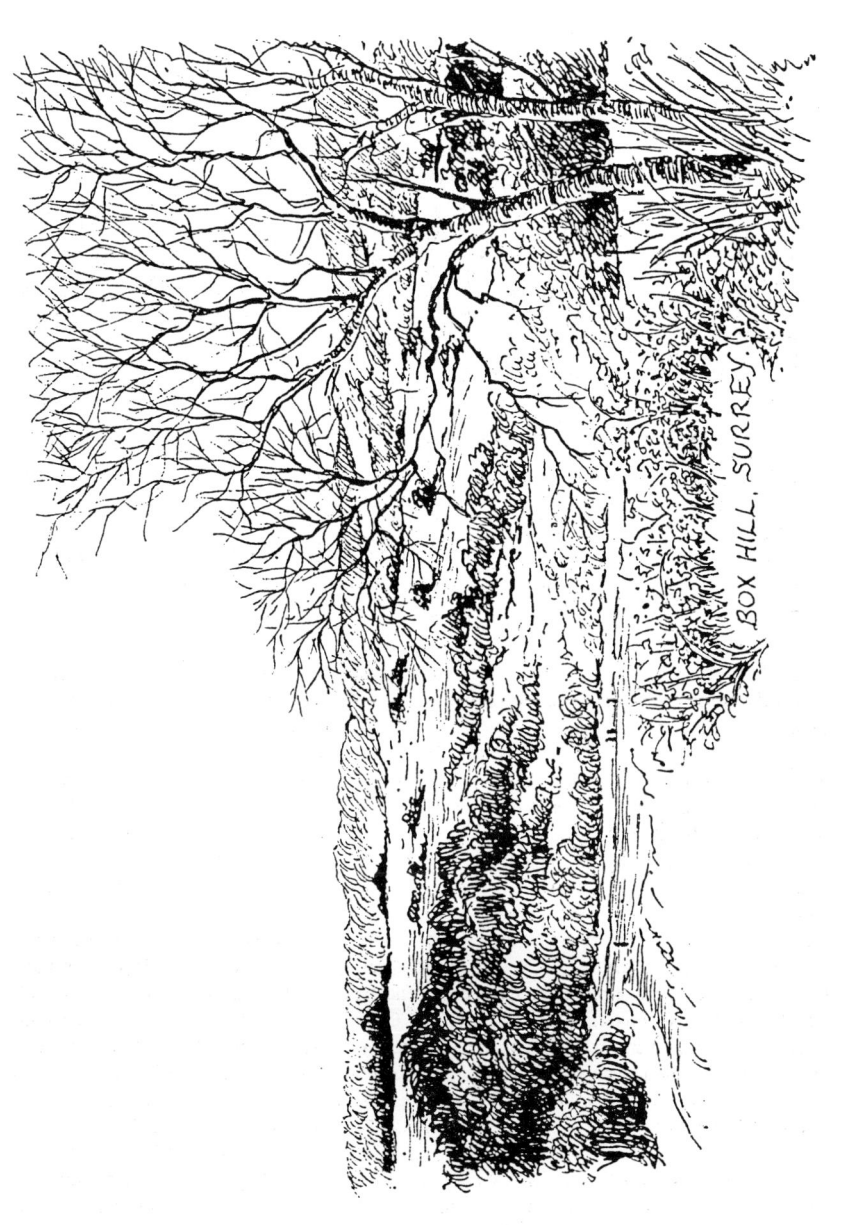

BOX HILL, SURREY.

Within 20 miles of the heart of London is excellent riding country - and the race course which hosts the world's most famous flat race, the Derby. The Derby has been run since 1780 on the downs South East of Epsom and horses can be seen at exercise early in the morning.

Dorking, where the river Mole has cut a gap through the North Downs, makes an ideal touring centre. The town's High Street follows the route of the Roman Stane Street. Charles Dickens stayed at the 400 year old White Horse Inn and the former Kings Head is said to be the Marquis of Granby in The Pickwick Papers. Just to the North of Dorking is Box Hill, a popular picnic spot as long ago as the reign of Charles II and one of the most popular viewpoints in Southern England. It derives its name from the ancient box trees on its slopes. More than 800 acres of wood and chalk downland belong the to National Trust here. Leith Hill is another spectacular viewpoint. The summit is 965 ft high and there is a 64 ft tower on top belonging to the National Trust, giving a panorama of woods and farmland. To the West of Epsom, Esher is surrounded by good open spaces. Sandown Park Racecourse is just North of the town.

BOX HILL FROM RANMORE COMMON, THE SOUTH DOWNS

SURREY

LEITH HILL TOWER, NEAR DORKING.

BERKSHIRE

WINDSOR

WOKINGHAM

SURREY HILL

CAMBERLEY

FARNBOROUGH

ALDERSHOT

HOGS BACK

FARNHAM

HAMP-SHIRE

HASLEMERE

MIDHURST

PETWORTH

SUSSEX

ARUN

BILLINGHURST

ST. LEONARDS FOREST RD

HORSHAM

CRANLEIGH

GODALMING

GUILDFORD

DORKING

WOKING

R. WEY

R. MOLE

R. THAMES

STAINES

RICHMOND

LONDON

EPSOM

LEATHERHEAD

BOX HILL

NORTH DOWNS

LEITH HILL

VALE OF HOLMESDALE

PILGRIM'S WAY

STANE STREET (ROMAN ROAD)

CROYDON

BIGGIN HILL

OXTED

REIGATE

HORLEY

CRAWLEY

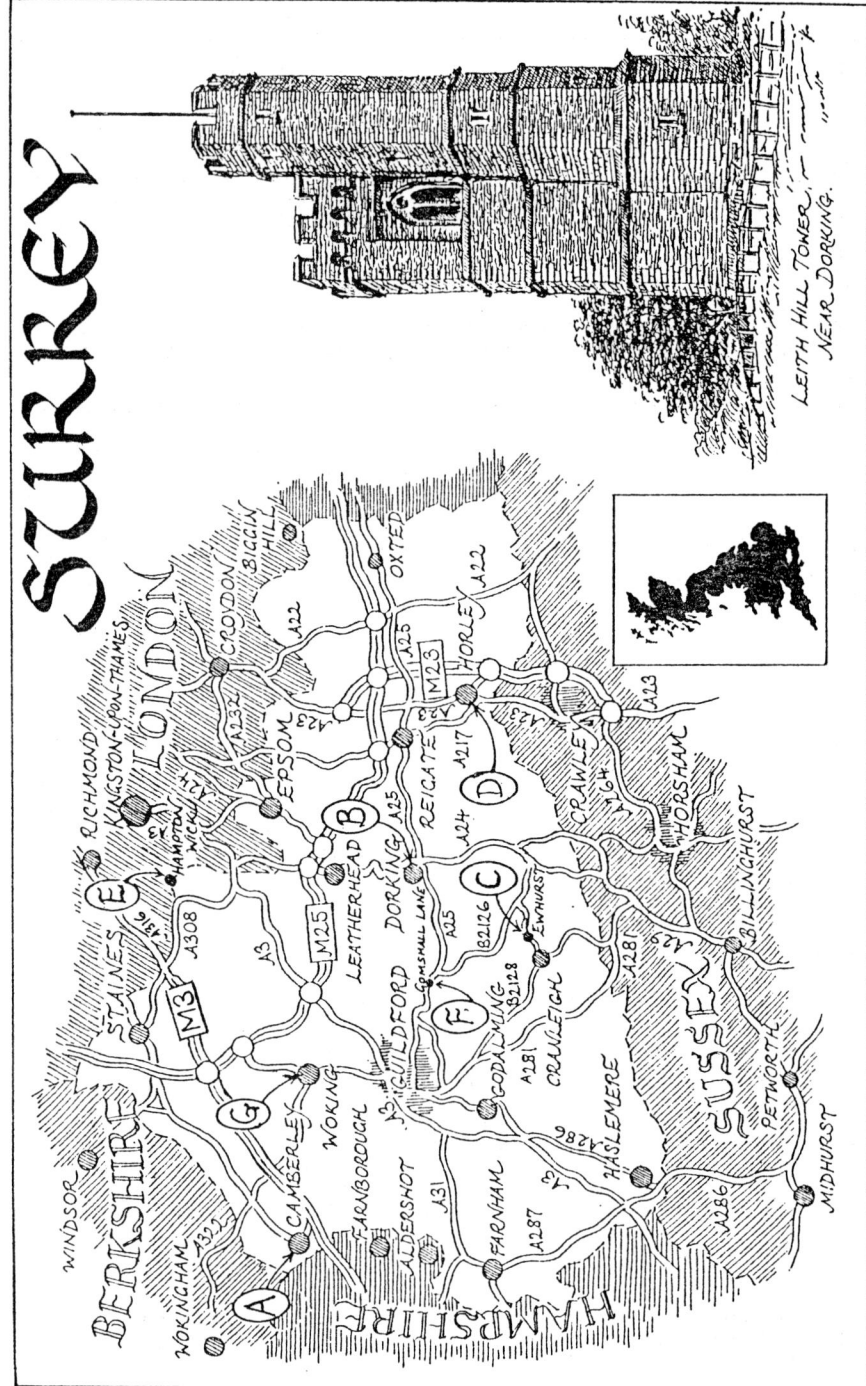

SURREY

LEITH HILL TOWER,
NEAR DORKING.

BERKSHIRE

LONDON

SUSSEX

HAMPSHIRE

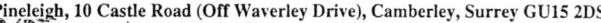

Pineleigh, 10 Castle Road (Off Waverley Drive), Camberley, Surrey GU15 2DS   Nrst Rd A325, M3

Pineleigh is a spacious Edwardian home set in half an acre of mature gardens and with ample parking. The comfortable bedrooms all have en-suite facilities, TV and hospitality trays. Conveniently situated for Ascot, Windsor, Heathrow, and Wenworth Golf Course which are a short drive away.

Ann & Tommy McCarthy
Tel: 01276 64787
Fax: 01276 64787

B&B from £20, Dinner from £20, Rooms 1 single, 1 twin, 1 double (all en-suite), No smoking, Minimum age 12, Open all year, Map Ref: A

Bulmer Farm, Holmbury St Mary, Dorking, Surrey RH5 6LG   Nearest Road A25, B2126

Bulmer Farm is a working farm set in the delightful village of Holmbury St Mary in the heart of picturesque Surrey. A 17th century house with oak beams and in inglenook fireplace. In addition to the B&B accommodation there are 2 self catering units one of which has been designed for disabled guests. All accommodation is centrally heated, have tea/coffee making facilities, and TV is provided. There is also a laundry room with washing machine and tumble dryer. The village benefits from a local shop, pubs, Victorian cottages and famous church.

Mrs Gill Hill
Tel: 01306 730210

B&B from £18, Rooms 5 twin, 3 double (many en-suite), Restricted smoking, Minimum age 12, Open all year, Map Ref: B

North Breache Manor, Ewhurst, Surrey GU6 7SN   Nearest Road A24, A39

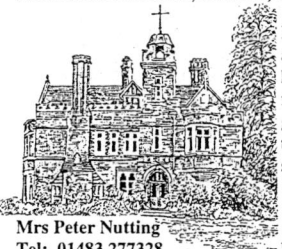

North Breache Manor surrounded by its estate has a warm and relaxed atmosphere with magnificent views over its park. The interior of the house has been totally modernised to a very high standard and each attractively furnished bedroom has its own en-suite bathroom. There are extensive gardens with about 2 acres of lawns, many shrubs and some fine specimen trees. There is a practice golf course, tennis court and heated outdoor swimming pool.

Mrs Peter Nutting
Tel: 01483 277328
Fax: 01483 276055

B&B from £40, Rooms 3 double, Restricted smoking, No pets, Open all year, Map Ref: C

The Lawn Guest House, 30 Massetts Road, Horley, Surrey RH6 7DE   Nearest Road A23

The Lawn Guest House is an attractive Victorian house set in pretty gardens just 1½ miles from Gatwick airport and 2 minutes walk from Horley town centre where there are pubs, restaurants, shops and a main line railway station to London and the south coast. The comfortable bedrooms have tea/coffee making facilities, and TV, many are en-suite. A full English breakfast is served and/or a healthy alternative of fruit, yoghurt, muesli, etc. For the comfort of all guests this is a totally non smoking home.

Mrs Janet Stocks
Tel: 01293 775751
Fax: 01293 821803

B&B from £17.50, Rooms 4 twin, 3 double, 1 family (many en-suite), No smoking, Minimum age 10, Pets welcome, Open all year, Map Ref: D

Chase Lodge Hotel, 10 Park Road, Hampton Wick, Kingston upon Thames KT1 4AS   **A308**

Originally built in 1870, Chase Lodge offers you superior accommodation and all bedrooms are equipped with tea/coffee making facilities, TV and refrigerator. Hampton Wick is adjacent to Bushy Park with Park Road itself protected by a conservation order and is acknowledged as an area of outstanding architectural/historical interest. Nearby attractions include Wimbledon, Oxford & Cambridge Boat Race, and Twickenham. Ideal touring centre for Kew Gardens, Hampton Court Palace, Richmond Theatre and Royal Windsor.

Denise & Nigel Stafford-Haworth
Tel: 0181 9431862
Fax: 0181 9439363

B&B from £22, Dinner from £12, Rooms 1 4-poster, 3 double, 1 single, 3 twin, 1 family, Restricted smoking, Pets welcome, Open all year, Map Ref: E

Cherry Trees, Comshall Lane, Shere, Surrey GU5 9HE   **Nearest Road A25**

Cherry Trees, a quiet comfortable home set in a beautiful garden is situated in the picturesque village of Shere at the foot of the North Downs, convient for local transport and shop. Good restaurant - 16th century pub serving very good food. The attractive bedrooms all have pretty outlook - TV and tea/coffee making facilities. One room is at ground floor level. Good parking. Guildford town centre is just 5 miles away

George & Olwen Warren
Tel: 01483 202288

B&B from £18.50, Rooms 1 single, 2 twin, 1 double (2 with en-suite facilities), No smoking, Open all year except Christmas. Map Ref: F

Knaphill Manor, Carthouse Lane, Woking, Surrey GU21 4XT   **Nearest Road M25 Junction 11s**

A warm welcome is assured in this large family home which dates back to the 1780's. The substantial gardens include an all-weather tennis court and a croquet lawn for visitors' use. Guest rooms are all attractively furnished and have lovely views over the garden. Each has bathroom with shower, central heating, TV/radio, and tea/coffee making facilities. Dinner is served by prior arrangement. Situated on the outskirts of Chobham, a charming Saxon village with fine restaurants and pubs. Short drive to many golf clubs and places of interest. Heathrow & Gatwick airports 30/40 mins drive.

Teresa & Kevin Leeper
Tel: 01276 857962

B&B from £30, Dinner from £20 by prior arrangement, Rooms 2 twin, 1 double (all en-suite), Minimum age 8 Open all year except Christmas and Easter, Map Ref: G

Sussex

"You came, and look'd and loved the view
Long-known and loved by me,
Green Sussex fading into blue
With one gray glimpse of sea"

(Alfred Lord Tennyson - Prologue to General Hamley)

SUSSEX

HERSTMONCEUX CASTLE.

The Sussex coast is backed by the South Downs, the land of skylarks and sheep. Valleys cut through the chalk where Stone Age man grazed his sheep 5,000 years ago - the Arun, Adur, Cuckmere and Ouse. The South Downs face the steep escarpment of the North Downs across the Weald, once covered by deep forests and now peppered with attractive villages, mansions, farms, orchards and hop gardens.

The West Sussex Downs are rich in history. Heavily wooded to within a few miles of Chichester, there are many ancient churches hidden there. The area is crossed by numerous ancient trackways. The South Downs Way runs along the Downs North of Chichester and 80 miles east across four river valleys to Beachy Head.

When the Romans arrived in AD 43 Chichester was already an important settlement for the Regni tribe. Chichester harbour has 27 square miles of navigable water, with yachting centres on numerous inlets. North of the city, Goodwood House has its own racecourse high on the downs above it famous for the Glorious Goodwood meeting starting on the last Tuesday in July and among the main events in the racing calendar. Just West of Chichester, Fishbourne is one of Britain's major roman relics, an important palace occupied during the 2nd and 3rd centuries AD during the peak of the Roman occupation.

The Normans built Arundel Castle to defend the River Arun against raiders. The valley was one of six administrative divisions in Norman times. Today the valley is a place of natural beauty, complemented by the bright, friendly seaside resorts such as Bognor Regis. Bognor is a family holiday centre with 5 miles of sand. The medieval fishing village developed as a seaside watering place from 1790, acquiring the Regis after King George V convalesced at nearby Aldwick in 1928.

THE MARKET CROSS, CHICHESTER.

Littlehampton is also a popular family resort - 900 years ago it was used by travellers to and from Normandy. Black Down is the highest point in Sussex at 919 ft above sea level, part of a plateau of nearly 500 acres to the North of Petworth. The medieval town has many narrow winding streets.

Many village and farm names end with fold, meaning a clearing in a forest, referring to the Wealden forest which once covered most of the area. One of the loveliest is Chiddingfold. Cowdray Park, with the imposing ruins of Cowdray House, built in 1530 and burnt down in 1793, is famous for its summer polo.

Some of the last remaining tracts of the Wealden forest stretches along North Sussex. From East Grinstead, minor roads run South through Ashdown Forest, the largest remaining area of heath and woods covering 20 square miles.

MoSAIC : FISHBOURNE ROMAN PALACE.

The seaside town of Worthing is an ideal touring base for the middle part of the South Downs which is ideal walking and riding country. Well signposted footpaths follow ancient tracks across the chalk downs which are peppered with ancient earthworks such as Chanctonbury Ring and Cisbury Ring. Brighton began as a tiny fishing village with a farming settlement on high ground beyond but the fishing village was almost swallowed by the sea. the village of Brightelmstone changed its character in the mid 18th century when Dr Richard Russell proclaimed the value of sea and sea bathing. Hove has many good parks and classical architecture. Lewes, which dates back to Norman times, is an excellent town from which to explore East Sussex. The White Hart was praised by William Cobbett, the 19th century traveller in his Rural Rides. The River Ouse runs through the town and nearby the Downs rise of more than 700 ft. The 813 ft Ditchling Beacon is one of the highest points on the South Downs, 2½ miles South of the village of Ditchling. The South Downs comes to a dramatic end on the coast between Beachy Head and Cuckmere Haven where 7 chalk cliffs rise to over 500 ft above the sea.

SUSSEX

BAYLEAF HOUSE, A RECONSTRUCTED 15TH CENTURY DWELLING, NEAR CHICHESTER.

SUSSEX

BAYLEAF HOUSE, A RECONSTRUCTED 15ᵗʰ CENTURY DWELLING, NEAR CHICHESTER.

Platnix Farm Oast, Harts Green, Sedlescombe, Battle, Sussex TN33 0RT   Nearest Road A21

Polished brick floor to entrance of delightful old oast house originally built in the 18th century. Lovely cottage garden. Wonderful views. All rooms have tea/coffee making facilities, and TV. Nearby there is plenty of walking around farm footpaths and coarse fishing is available on the farm. Within easy reach of Bodiam and Sissinghurst Castle. You can be sure of a warm and friendly welcome.

Mrs Benedetta Howard   B&B from £20, Rooms 1 round twin, 2 double (en-suite),
Tel: 01424 870214   Restricted smoking, Open all year, Map Ref: A

Timbers Edge, Spronketts Lane, Warninglid, Bolney, Sussex RH17 5TE   Nearest Road A272, A23

Beautiful Sussex country house set in over two acres of formal gardens with swimming pool surrounded by woodlands. Located within easy reach of Gatwick (20 minutes), Hickstead (10 minutes), Ardingly (25 minutes), Nymans and Leonardslee Gardens (10 minutes), Brighton (30 minutes). Rooms have TV and beverage making facilities.

Sally & Geoffrey Earlam   B&B from £20, Rooms 2 twin, 2 single, No smoking,
Tel: 01444 461456   Open all year, Map Ref: B

Ashlands Cottage, Burwash, Sussex TN19 7HS   Nearest Road A265

Pretty period cottage in quiet Wealden farmland within designated area of outstanding natural beauty. Glorious views, gardens and picnic spots. Kipling's 'Batemans' only 5 minutes walk across the fields and many more places of interest nearby. Ideal for walking, touring, etc. The bedrooms are comfortable and welcoming and there is a sitting room where guests may relax.

Mrs Nesta Harmer   B&B from £17, Rooms 2 twin, Restricted smoking,
Tel: 01435 882207   Minimum age 12, Open all year, Map Ref: C

White Barn, Crede Lane, Bosham, Chichester, Sussex PO18 8NX   Nearest Road A259, A27

White Barn is not a barn but a very modern house indeed (single storey), designed in recent years by architect Frank Guy and stands in the seclusion of a former orchard. The impressive dining room features a roof of exposed boards, a vast glass wall opening onto a red tiled terrace, and a brick edged flowerbed half indoors. The sitting room is built around the circular brick hearth. All en-suite bedrooms have tea/coffee making facilities. Great care is taken in the preparation and presentation of food always combining the freshest ingredients and flair to create the irresistible.

Sue & Tony Trotman   B&B from £28, Dinner from £18.50, Rooms 2 twin, 1 double
Tel: 01243 573113   (all en-suite), Restricted smoking, Minimum age 10,
Open all year, Map Ref: D

Chichester Lodge, Oakwood, Chichester, Sussex PO18 9AL — Nearest Road A27, B2178

Chichester Lodge is a charming 1840 Gothic Lodge with wonderful interior design and antique furnishings. Lots of flag stone floors, polished wood, beautiful Gothic windows, every attention to detail. Wood burning stove in hall way. There are two acres of very pretty garden with hedges and honeysuckle and hidden corners. The en-suite bedrooms are comfortable with nice decorations and furnishings and all rooms have TV. There is also a garden room with wood burning stove for winter evening. Nearby activities include fishing, golf, theatre and Goodwood.

Jeanette Dridge
Tel: 01243 786560

B&B from £20 pp, Rooms 3 double, 1 single, (all en-suite), No smoking, Minimum age 14, Open all year, Map Ref: D

Longcroft House, Beacon Road, Ditchling, Sussex BN6 8UZ — Nearest Road A23, A27, B2112

Longcroft House is situated near the foot of Ditchling Beacon in 2 acres of garden and paddock, between the vineyard and the centre of the village in easy walking distance of all amenities and easy access to reach the main roads with Gatwick. Longcroft is a beautiful house built in traditional style and offers a relaxing and comfortable stay in one of three rooms all with private or ensuite facilities & TV. Guests may chose a 4-poster bed. Beautifully decorated throughout and there is a lounge where guests may relax. Ditchling with its ancient buildings and charm has much to offer visitors.

Robert & Helen Scull
Tel: 01273 842740

B&B from £19.50, Dinner from £16, Supper £8.50, Rooms 1 twin, 2 double, (all en-suite), No smoking, Children by arrangement, Open all year, Map Ref: E

Quinces, Upper Dicker, Nr Hailsham, Sussex BN27 3RH — Nearest Road A22

Quinces is a part 16th century home with modern extensions in a pretty rural setting between Lewes, Uckfield and Eastbourne. It is near Michelham Priory close to Glyndebourne and East Sussex National Golf Club and within easy reach of Brighton and Newhaven. Accommodation is in an attractive self contained wing offering double bedroom, drawing room with log fire and TV, bathroom and kitchenette. There is also a separate single bedroom with bathroom. Hard tennis court and large heated swimming pool in lovely gardens available for use in season.

Mr & Mrs Michael Wardroper
Tel: 01323 846714
Fax: 01323 442618

B&B from £20, Dinner from £10, other meals by arrangement, Rooms 1 single, 1 twin or kingsize, Open all year, Map Ref: F

Stairs Farm House, High Street, Hartfield, Sussex TN7 4AB — Nearest Road B2110, A22

Stairs Farm house dates from the 17th century and has been carefully modernised whilst retaining various period features. Each bedroom has countryside views, TV, radio and tea/coffee making facilities. A full English breakfast is served. A tea room, restaurant and farm shop on the premises, provide home and locally produced organic and additive free food. There are 3 pubs locally serving both excellent bar snacks and restaurant meals. Local places of interest include 'Pooh Bridge', Hever Castle, Ashdown Forest and Sheffield Park. Gatwick/M25 30 minutes.

Mrs G Pring
Tel: 01892 770793

B&B from £20, Dinner from £10, Rooms 1 twin, 1 double, 1 family, No smoking, Open all year, Map Ref: G

The Tithe Barn, Woodmancote, Henfield, Sussex BN5 9ST

Nearest Road A281, A23

"Come as strangers and leave as friends", this is the motto at The Tithe Barn. This is a barn converted about 80 years ago which offers good value for money. There are 2 acres of garden and ample car parking is available. Cosy log fires in winter and sunny conservatory for summer breakfasts. All rooms have wash basin, tea/coffee making facilities, TV and a telephone can be made available for guests. Convenient for coast, Gatwick, National Trust properties. Concessionary golf 1 mile.

Mary & Michael Chick
Tel: 01273 492267
Fax: 01403 864061

B&B from £16, Rooms 2 double, 1 twin, 1 single,
No smoking, Open all year, Map Ref: H

Frylands, Wineham, Henfield, Sussex SN5 9BP

Nearest Road A272, A23

Frylands is a half timbered farmhouse dating from the 16th century which has been carefully restored. It is set in 250 acres of farm and woodlands with good coarse fishing in ponds and a stretch of the River Adur. There is a large garden with outdoor swimming pool (heated in summer) and available to guests. All bedrooms have central heating, wash basins and facilities for making hot drinks. There is a separate guests' bathroom. Transport to and from Gatwick airport can be provided at a reasonable price.

Mrs Sylvia Fowler
Tel: 01403 710214
Fax: 01403 711449

B&B from £16, Rooms 1 twin, 1 double (en-suite), 1 family,
Open all year, Map Ref: H

Cleavers Lyng Country Hotel, Church Road, Herstmonceux, Hailsham, Sussex BN27 1QJ

A271

Photogenic Cleavers Lyng is a small family run hotel adjacent to Herstmonceux Castle dating from 1577 with oak beams and inglenook fireplace. Panoramic views. Good home cooking in traditional English style and full English breakfast and lunches served daily. Fully licensed with small bar, fine wines and draught beers. TV lounge. All bedrooms are fully en-suite, centrally heated and have tea/coffee making facilities. Special attraction - badger watch!

Sally & Douglas Simpson
Tel: 01323 833131
Fax: 01323 833617

B&B from £19.75, Dinner from £12.50, Rooms 3 double, 3 twin,
2 single, Open all year, Map Ref: I

Huggetts Furnace Farm, Stonehurst Lane, Five Ashes, Nr Mayfield, E. Sussex TN20 6LL

A272, A267

Huggetts Furnace Farm is a beautiful medieval home set in the middle of tranquil countryside approached by a long farm drive. The beams and Inglenook fireplaces (with log fires when chilly) give it a timeless atmosphere. All bedrooms have en-suite/private facilities,and tea/coffee trays. There are 130 acres of grounds with a swimming pool in the summer. Dinner is available and creatively cooked from the best home grown and local produce. Lovely walks. Many National Trust properties nearby.

John & Gillian Mulcare
Tel: 01825 831220

B&B from £20, Dinner from £12.50, Rooms 2 double, 1 family,
1 twin, Minimum age 10, No smoking upstairs, Open all year,
Map Ref: J

Fairseat House, Newick, East Sussex, BN8 4PJ

Nearest Road A272

Fairseat House is an elegant Edwardian house on the edge of the picturesque village of Newick. Set in 4 acres of gardens and paddocks it enjoys rural aspects yet is easily accessible to main routes and Gatwick. Covered heated swimming pool. Open fires, chesterfields, ancestral portraits and antique books are just part of the charm Fairseat has to offer. A candlelit dinner with wine, or a relaxing light supper are available. Enjoy the luxury of a romantic night in the Edwardian room with its 4 poster bed and champagne breakfast.

Carol & Roy Pontifex
Tel: 01825 722263

B&B from £21, Dinner from £17.50, Rooms 3 double, 1 twin, Restricted smoking, Open January - December, Map Ref: K

Little Orchard House, West Street, Rye, Sussex TN31 7ES

Nearest Road A259, A268

Little Orchard House is centrally situated in peaceful surroundings. Rebuilt in 1745, the house has been lovingly renovated over the years and retains it original fascinating character. All bedrooms are en-suite one with a 4 poster. There are personal antiques, paintings, books and bears throughout the house. There is a peaceful bookroom and a sitting room with an open fire. The generous breakfast provides as much as can be eaten at a time to suit you. Large walled garden available for guests' use.

Sara Brinkhurst
Tel: 01797 223831

B&B from £28, Rooms 2 double, 1 twin, Minimum age 12, Open all year, Map Ref: L

Newbarn, Wards Lane, Wadhurst, Sussex TN5 6HP

Nearest Road A21

18th century timber framed farmhouse in 14 acres bordering Bewl Water. The house is furnished to match the peace and beauty of the surroundings. Tunbridge Wells, (The Pantiles), Sissinghurst, Scotney Castle, Bodiam, Pashley and many more places of interest, are within a short drive. London 55 minutes by train, Gatwick 60 minutes and Heathrow 90 minutes by car. Trout fishing, riding, golf, tennis, all nearby. Breakfast is served with fresh produce and home made preserves. Dinner is available at several good places in the locality.

Christopher & Pauline Willis
Tel: 01892 782042

B&B from £20, Rooms 1 single, 1 twin, 1 double, Restricted smoking, Pets by arrangement, Open all year. Map Ref: M

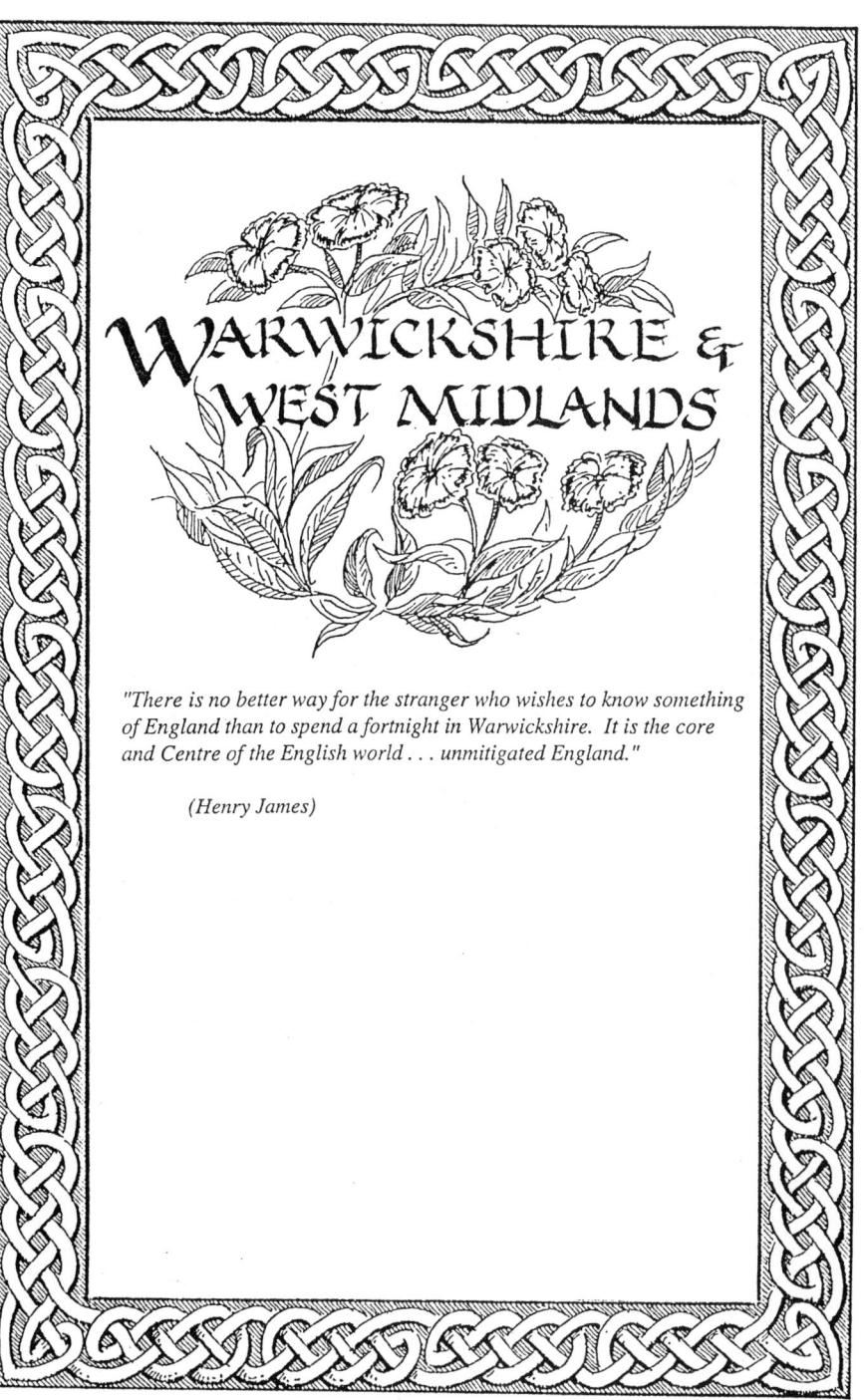

WARWICKSHIRE & WEST MIDLANDS

"There is no better way for the stranger who wishes to know something of England than to spend a fortnight in Warwickshire. It is the core and Centre of the English world . . . unmitigated England."

(Henry James)

WARWICKSHIRE & WEST MIDLANDS

SHAKESPEARES SCHOOL, STRATFORD UPON AVON.

The visitor to Warwickshire and the West Midlands can take a step back in the country's literary and industrial heritage. Yet the area's main cities, Coventry and Birmingham are excellent modern centres. No visit to Warwickshire can be complete without taking in Stratford-upon-Avon where the world's most famous dramatist, William Shakespeare was born and which is now one of the world's famous tourist centres. His mother Mary Arden was the daughter of a prosperous local farmer and his father was a glover and wool dealer who rose to become the town bailiff or mayor. Visitors can see the house in Henley Street where Shakespeare was born. Running from the Bancroft Basin in the heart of Stratford is the 200-year-old Stratford-upon-Avon Canal, the gateway to 2,000 miles of Britain's navigable waterways The city of Coventry bears little evidence of its industrial heritage - after the Second World War it was largely reduced to heaps of rubble. Now, modern shops, restaurants and cinemas are set amid flower gardens and the only evidence of the war is the shell of the former cathedral, levelled along with most of the centre by one air raid. In 1622, 22 years later, a new cathedral was consecrated, with the blackened ruins forming an approach to the new.

The county town of Warwick, in contrast with Coventry, is a blend of Georgian and Tudor architecture . Warwick Castle, overlooking the River Avon is the most visited stately home in Britain and the finest medieval castle in England. The castle's 60 acres of grounds were landscaped by Capability Brown and until 1978 it was continuously inhabited by successive Earls of Warwick. Another famous castle, Kenilworth, is now in ruins on a gentle grassy slope, a short distance from the modern town centre. It is the setting for much of the action in Sir Walter Scott's "Kenilworth".

SHAKESPEARE'S BIRTHPLACE, STRATFORD UPON AVON.

Queen Victoria granted the prefix Royal to Leamington Spa in 1838. The mineral waters first recorded in 1586 can still be taken at the Royal Pump room in the town centre Rugby is noted for its important railway junction - called Mugby Junction by Charles Dickens in a special edition of the magazine "All Year Round" - and its public school, founded in 1567. The village of Stoneleigh is probably best known as the home of the National Agricultural Centre and the Royal Agricultural Show. Birmingham and its suburbs dominate the West Midlands. In Shakespeare's day it was a market town in the heart of the English countryside - but even then it was an important industrial centre. Birmingham was noted for its smiths who used coal from the North Warwickshire mines. Birmingham became one of the world's greatest industrial cities. In recent years, massive rebuilding has transformed the city. In Shakespeare's day the Forest of Arden covered 200 square miles to the North and West of the Avon and the names of some villages still serve as a reminder of the forest, such as Henley - in-Arden and Tamworth in Arden. Henley-in-Arden, a small market town is a fine walking centre. Edgbaston is one of Birmingham's prettiest suburbs which includes Warwickshire county cricket ground, the university and botanical gardens.

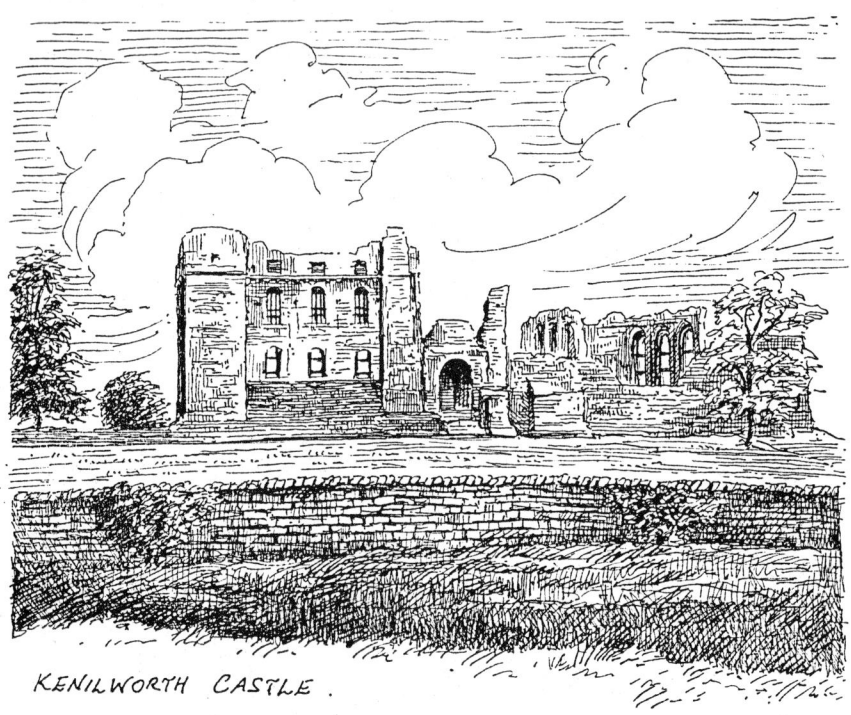

KENILWORTH CASTLE.

WARWICKSHIRE & WEST MIDLANDS

ANNE HATHAWAY'S COTTAGE AT SHOTTERY, STRATFORD UPON AVON.

CANNOCK
LICHFIELD
TAMWORTH
WOLVERHAMPTON
WALSALL
DUDLEY
SUTTON COLDFIELD
BIRMINGHAM
R. TAME
ASHBY CANAL
WATLING STREET (ROMAN ROAD) HINCKLEY
COVENTRY CANAL
NUNEATON
FOREST OF ARDEN
HUSBANDS BOSWORTH
LUTTERWORTH
R. AVON
COVENTRY
RUGBY
GRAND UNION CANAL
ROYAL LEAMINGTON SPA
WARWICK
DAVENTRY
R. LEENE
OXFORD CANAL
BANBURY
BRACKLEY
OXFORDSHIRE
SHROPSHIRE UNION CANAL
CLENT HILLS
BROMSGROVE
REDDITCH
ALCESTER
(ROMAN ROAD)
RYKNILD STREET
STRATFORD CANAL
R. AVON
STRATFORD UPON AVON
FOSSE WAY (ROMAN ROAD)
R. STOUR
EVESHAM
MORETON-IN-MARSH
CHIPPING NORTON
STOW-ON-THE WOLD
WORCESTERSHIRE

WARWICKSHIRE & WEST MIDLANDS

ANNE HATHAWAY'S COTTAGE AT SHOTTERY, STRATFORD UPON AVON.

Sandbarn Farm, Hampton Lucy, Warwickshire CV35 8AU   **Nearest Road A439, M40**

The farmhouse has been restored and is beautifully decorated throughout. There is a TV lounge for guests use. The bedrooms are all en-suite, and have tea/coffee making facilities. Hairdryers, hot water bottles and ironing board are available. A full English breakfast is served in the pleasant dining room. Vegetarian and special diets can be catered for, please ask in advance. Only a few minutes from Warwick Castle. Just 5 minutes to the centre of Stratford where there are many restaurants. There is also a local pub where good meals are available.

Mrs H P Waterworth   **B&B from £25, Rooms 3 double all en-suite, Restricted Smoking,**
Tel: 01789 842280   **Minimum age 5, Open all year except Christmas, Map Ref: A**

Snowford Hall Farm, Hunningham, Warwickshire CV33 9ES   **Nearest Road A423 Fosseway**

Snowford Hall is set in a 250 acre mixed working farm. The 18th century house stands on elevated ground overlooking the peaceful surrounding countryside. Rooms are centrally heated, have tea/coffee making facilities, and most have full en-suite facilities. A comfortable lounge with colour TV awaits the visitor. A full English breakfast is served. There are excellent pubs and restaurants nearby. Warwick, Stoneleigh Park, Exhibition Centre, Sky Blue Centre, Stratford-upon-Avon and the Motor Museum are all nearby.

Mrs R Hancock   **B&B from £17, Rooms 1 double, 2 twin, (most en-suite),**
Tel: 01926 632297   **Restricted smoking, Open all year except Christmas & New Year,**
     Map Ref: B

Crandon House, Avon Dassett, Leamington Spa, Warks CV33 0AA   **Nearest Road B4100, A423, M40**

Crandon House is set in 20 acres with beautiful views over unspoilt countryside. The attractive bedrooms all have private or en-suite facilities. Guests dining room and 2 comfortable sitting rooms 1 with colour TV and woodburning stove. Excellent breakfast menu offers traditional farmhouse or a selection of other dishes. Dinner maybe available by prior arrangement at 7 pm and there are also excellent pubs and restaurants nearby. Crandon House is situated in a peaceful part of Warwickshire within easy reach of Stratford upon Avon, Warwick, and Heritage Motor Centre.

David Lea & Deborah Lea   **B&B from £17,50, Dinner from £1250, Rooms 1 double, 2 twin,**
Tel: 01295 770652   **(en-suite), Minimum age 8, Restricted smoking,**
     Open all year except Christmas, Map Ref: C

---

8 Clarendon Crescent, Leamington Spa, Warwickshire, CV32 5NR   **Nearest Road A452, M40**

The discerning traveller will be delighted by the peace and quiet offered by this beautiful listed Regency house in a crescent with its own private dell. Elegantly furnished with many antiques and individually designed en-suite bedrooms with tea/coffee making facilities. A short walk from town centre. Warwick, Stratford, the Royal Agricultural Centre and the National Exhibition Centre are all within an easy drive.

Christine & David Lawson   **B&B from £28, Rooms, 2 double, 1 twin (all en-suite),**
Tel: 01926 429840   **Restricted smoking, Open all year, Map Ref: C**

Stonehouse Farm, Leicester Lane, Cubbington Heath, Leamington Spa, Warks CV32 6QZ　　　**A445**

A delightful, Grade II Queen Anne farmhouse set within Warwickshire's unspoilt countryside, enjoying extensive views from all of its large and comfortable rooms. Only 2 miles from the Regency town of Royal Leamington Spa, 6 miles from Warwick, and within easy walking distance of the Royal Showground at Stoneleigh. Bedrooms are comfortable and all have tea/coffee making facilities and there is a guests' lounge with television. The traditional dining room overlooks mature gardens and an orchard.

Mrs Kate Liggins
Tel: 01926 336370
Fax: 01926 336370

B&B from £17.50, Dinner from £12, Rooms 3 twin (1 en-suite), Restricted smoking, Minimum age 4, Open all year except Christmas & New Year, Map Ref: C

Lower Farm Barn, Great Wolford, Shipston on Stour, Warks CV36 5NQ　　　**Nearest Road A44, A3400**

This lovely 100 year old converted barn stands in the small, peaceful Warwickshire village of Great Wolford. The property retains much of its original form including exposed beams and ancient stonework. Now modernised and very comfortable. The beautifully furnished bedrooms have tea/coffee making facilities. A warm and welcoming sitting room with TV is for guests' use. Great Wolford has a lovely old pub, only 5 minutes walk from Lower Farm Barn, where traditional home made food is served. Convenient for Warwick and Stratford upon Avon.

Mrs R Mawle
Tel: 01608 674435

B&B from £14, Rooms 1 double 1 en-suite family, Restricted smoking, Pets by arrangement, Open all year, Map Ref: D

Wolford Fields, Shipston on Stour, Warwickshire CV36 5LT　　　**Nearest Road A44. A3400**

A large Cotswold farmhouse and gardens built by Lovel Campendown in 1857 and farmed by the Mawle family since 1901. The 3 comfortable bedrooms share 2, warmly decorated, bathrooms which are fitted with power showers. Guests may relax in the pleasant TV lounge where tea, coffee and chocolate making facilites are available. Guests may also stroll in the large garden. Space available for car parking. Conveniently situated for Stratford-upon-Avon and the Cotswolds.

Richard Mawle
Tel: 01608 661301

B&B from £14, Rooms 2 double, 1 twin, Restricted smoking, Open all year, Map Ref: D

Hardwick House, 1 Avenue Road, Stratford-upon-Avon, Warks CV37 6UY　　　**Nearest Road 439**

A delightful Victorian building dating from 1887, set within a tree-lined Avenue which has been skilfully converted to guest house accommodation of the highest calibre. Quiet home comforts, pleasant surroundings and only a short walk from all the major attractions of this historic town including the theatre and many of the shakespeare properties.. Many of the bedrooms are en-suite and all have tea/coffee making facilities, and TV. Warwick castle, Birmingham airport are a short drive away.

Simon & Drenagh Wootton
Tel: 01789 204307
Fax: 01789 296760

B&B from £19, Rooms 2 single, 2 twin, 8 double, 4 family (many en-suite), Restricted smoking, Open all year except Christmas, Map Ref: E

Ravenhurst, 1 Broad Walk, Stratford-upon-Avon, Warks CV37 6HS   Junction of B439 and A4390

Victorian town house ideally situated in a quiet part of town, centrally located for places of interest. Five minutes walk to theatre and town centre and ten minutes walk to railway station. Very popular with theatre goers. Short drive to Cotswolds and Warwick Castle. Pleasant bedrooms are all en-suite with tea/coffee making facilities, and colour TV. Four poster bed available. Enjoy a 'Ravenhurst' substantial traditional English breakfast. The Workman family, born and bred Stratfordians, offer a warm welcome and plenty of local knowledge. All major credit cards accepted.

The Workman Family
Tel: 01789 295515

**B&B from £18, Rooms 1 twin, 4 double (all en-suite),
No smoking, Open all year, Map Ref: E**

Parkfield, 3 Broad Walk, Stratford-upon-Avon CV37 6HS   Nearest Road A439

Boasting the Heart of England Tourist Board 2 crown award, Parkfield is a charming Victorian house, built around 1875. its owners, Jo & Roger Pettitt, have been giving guests a warm welcome to Stratford for almost 20 years. There are 7 comfortable bedrooms 5 of which are en-suite. Parkfield is convenient for the town centre and the RSC theatre. Nearby there are beautiful Cotswolds towns and villages including Broadway, Chipping Camden, Burford, Bourton-on-the-Water, etc. Brochure with pleasure on request.

Jo & Roger Pettitt
Tel: 01789 293313

**B&B from £16, Rooms 1 double, 4 family, 1 twin, 1 single,
(Many en-suite), No smoking, Open all year, Map Ref: E**

Thornton Manor, Ettington, Stratford-upon-Avon, Warwickshire CV37 7PN   Nearest Road A429

16th century stone manor house overlooking peaceful fields and woodland including historical sites, on a working farm. Garden, tennis court, fishing and an ideal centre for touring. The bedrooms have either a private bathroom or shower room en-suite. There is a kitchen which guests may use and a log fire in the hall to relax by with a television and a piano for musically minded guests. Conveniently situated for Stratford-upon-Avon, Banbury, Cotswolds and Warwick.

Mrs G Hutsby
Tel: 01789 740210

**B&B from £17, Rooms 1 twin, 2 double (en-suite or private facilities),
Restricted smoking, Minimum age 5,
Open all year except Christmas & New Year, Map Ref: F**

Penshurst Guest House, 34 Evesham Place, Stratford upon Avon CV37 6HT   Nearest Road A439

Karen and Yannick offer you a warm welcome to their prettily refurbished Victorian townhouse, 5 minutes walk from the town centre. Colour TV, tea and coffee, hot bedtime drink, hairdryer, iron, babysitting, and many other little extras are all available free of charge. In order to accommodate your individual plans for each day, a delicious English or continental breakfast is served at any time between 7.00 - 10.30. Home cooked evening meals by arrangement. Facilities for disabled. Brochure available.

Mrs Karen Cauvin
Tel: 01789 205259
Fax: 01789 295322

**B&B from £13.50, Dinner from £6, Rooms 2 single, 2 twin, 2 double,
2 family (some en-suite), No smoking, Open all year, Map Ref: E**

Kawartha House, 39 Grove Road, Stratford-upon-Avon, Warks CV37 6PB   **Nearest Road A439**

Overlooking the 'old town park' and located just a few minutes walk from the town centre are just two of the things that make Kawartha House well worth a visit. This lovely Victortian house, is decorated and furnished to a very high standard. Rooms are en-suite, have tea/coffee making facilities, and TV. Theatre tickets can be arranged. Special winter season mid-week breaks include dinner, bed and breakfast.

Mrs Mavis Evans
Tel: 01789 204469
Fax: 01789 262076

B&B from £12, Rooms 3 family, 2 double, 2 single,
Open all year, Map Ref: E

Winton House, The Green, Upper Quinton, Nr Stratford-upon-Avon CV37 8SX   **Nearest Road B4632**

Winton House is a historic Victorian farmhouse built in 1856. Situated in an area of outstanding natural beauty, the house overlooks Meon Hill and is steeped in witchcraft and folklore. En-suite bedrooms are decorated in traditional fashion with antique beds, old lace and handmade quilts. There is a private guest lounge with log fires. Candlelit breakfasts are a hearty choice of local specialities served with homemade jams, bread and fruit from our orchard. There is a Winton house special that changes daily. An ideal location for touring, walking and cycling. Cycles available.

Mrs G Lyon
Tel: 01789 720500
Mobile: 0831 485483

B&B from £20, Rooms 1 double, 1 twin, 1 family
(all with private bathroom), Restricted smoking,
Open all year except Christmas, Map Ref: E

Pear Tree Cottage, Church Road, Wilmcote, Stratford-upon-Avon CV37 9UX   **Nearest Road A3400**

Set in nearly an acre to shady garden this Elizabethan house is furnished throughout with country style antiques. All rooms, some of which are in the later extension, have en-suite facilities and also tea trays and TV. The village of Wilmcote is an ideal centre of long or short stays in Shakespeare country and The Cotswolds. Stratford-upon-Avon is 3½ miles away, whilst Warwick, Coventry, Oxford, Worcester and the NEC are in easy reach.

Mrs Margaret Mander
Tel: 01789 205889
Fax: 01789 262862

B&B from £21, Rooms 2 twin, 4 double, 1 family (all en-suite),
Restricted smoking, Minimum age 2, Open all year except Christmas,
Map Ref: G

Woodside, Langley Road, Claverdon, Warwick CV35 8PJ   **Nearest Road A4189**

Set in 22 acres of conservation woodland and garden. All bedrooms are spacious, furnished cottage style with antiques and period furniture, and have tea/coffee making facilities, TV and radio. Lovely outlook over woodland and garden. Full central heating, large log fire with TV and video in comfortable lounge makes for a relaxed evening after a busy day and after a home cooked dinner served to order. Or visit one of the interesting eating places locally. Doreen and her Burmese mountain dog will give you a warm welcome.

Mrs Doreen Bromilow
Tel: 01926 842446

B&B from £16, Dinner from £12.50, Rooms 1 single, 1 en-suite twin,
1 double, 1 family, Restricted smoking, Pets by arrangement,
Open all year except Christmas. Map Ref: H

Forth House, 44 High Street, Warwick CV34 4AX   **Nearest Road A429, M40**

Our rambling Georgian family home in the town centre provides two guest suites hidden away at the back. Family sized on the ground floor and a smaller first floor suite overlook the garden. Both have private bathroom and sitting room with TV, telephone, radio, fridge, hot and cold drinks. Full English breakfast at times to suit guests. Evening meals by prior arrangement. Ideal location for touring the heart of England or for those on business at the NEC or NAC.

Mrs Elizabeth Draisey
Tel: 01926 401512

B&B from £20, Dinner from £10, Rooms 1 double, 1 family (both en-suite), No smoking, Pets by arrangement, Open all year, Map Ref: H

Willowbrook Farmhouse, Lighthorne Road, Kineton, Nr Warwick, CV35 0JL   B4100, M40 (J12)

Willowbrook Farmhouse is a very comfortable house, furnished with antiques and interesting collections, surrounded by garden and paddocks in lovely rolling countryside, handy for Warwick, Stratford, the Cotswolds, NEC, NAC and the Gaydon Heritage Motor Centre. Bedrooms have beautiful views, tea/coffee making facilities, colour TV and full central heating. Guests have their own large sitting room and attractive dining room. Free range hens provide the eggs for breakfast. Friendly attentive service assured. 3 miles from Junction 12 M40.

Mrs Carolyn Howard
Tel: 01926 640475
Fax: 01926 641747

B&B from £15.50, Rooms 1 twin, 2 double (1 en-suite), No smoking, Pets welcome, Open all year except Christmas, Map Ref: I

Nolands Farm & Country Restaurant, Oxhill, Warwick   **Nearest Road A422**

The farm is just off the main A422 situated in a tranquil valley. It is a working arable farm and offers the country lover a happy relaxing stay. The bedrooms, all en-suite, most are annexed converted stables built in 1840 and now tastefully restored. There are luxury 4 poster bedrooms with bathroom. The licensed restaurant offers farmhouse cuisine made with the finest fresh ingredients and a carefully selected wine list. There is a well stocked lake with fly and coarse fishing, clay pigeon shooting, cycles for hire and horse riding nearby.

Sue & Robin Hutsby
Tel: 01926 640309
Fax: 01926 641662

B&B from £15, A La Carte £16, Restaurant non smoking, Rooms 6 double, 1 family, 2 twin (all en-suite), Minimum age 7, Open all year except Christmas and new year, Map Ref: J

The Old Rectory, Vicarage Lane, Sherbourne, Warwick CV35 8AB   **Nearest Road A46, M40 (J 15)**

A licenced Georgian country house rich in beams, flagstones and inglenooks, perfectly situated between those two tourist honeypots of Warwick and Stratford-upon-Avon. 14 elegantly appointed en-suite rooms, antique brass beds; a romantic French bed and Victorian style bathrooms. The coachhouse is ideal for families, ground floor rooms available for the elderly. Hearty English breakfasts and choices on supper menu. Walled garden and safe parking in a courtyard, pretty with flower baskets. Children and dogs welcome. Recommended by all major guides.

Martin & Sheila Greenwood
Tel: 01926 624562
Fax: 01926 624562

B&B from £19.50, Light Supper from £4.95, Rooms: 4 single, 5 double, 5 twin (all en-suite), Pets by arrangement, Open all year except Christmas, Map Ref: H

Pond Cottage, The Green, Warmington, Banbury, OX17 1BU   **Nearest Road B4100, M40**

This much photographed stone built cottage in the south Warwickshire village of Warmington is within easy reach of Warwick castle, Stratford, Upton House, Blenheim Palace, and the Cotswolds; and many gardens including Hidcote Manor Garden. The pretty en-suite, double room overlooks the village green and duck pond. The small cheerful, single room (bathroom next door), overlooks the garden. Both have tea/coffee making facilities. Beautifully furnished house with guests' sitting room. Dinner if requested at 7 pm. French spoken. A warm welcome assured.

Mrs Vi Viljoen
Tel: 01295 690682

B&B from £17, Dinner from £11.80, 1 single, 1 en-suite double, No children, Open April - October, Map Ref: M

Yew Tree Farm, Wootton Wawen, Solihull, West Mids B95 6BY   **Nrst Rd A3400, M42, M40**

Attractive Georgian farmhouse situated on A3400 in the village of Wootton Wawen, 1 mile south of Henley-in-Arden, 6 miles north of Stratford-upon-Avon. Within easy reach of Warwick Castle, Royal Showground, National Exhibition Centre and the Cotswolds. 700 acre dairy/arable farm with lake and woodland walks. Two large double, en-suite, bedrooms with tea/coffee making facilities. All rooms centrally heated. Comfortable visitors' lounge with colour TV. A hearty English breakfast served. Excellent pubs and restaurants nearby.

Mrs Janet Haimes
Tel: 01564 792701

B&B from £17.50, Rooms 1 double, 1 twin/family, No smoking, Open all year except Christmas and New Year, Map Ref: K

St Elisabeth's Cottage, Woodman Lane, Clent, Stourbridge, West Mids, DY9 9PX   **Nrst Rd A491**

Beautiful country cottage in tranquil setting with 6 acres of landscaped garden plus outdoor heated swimming pool. Lovely country walks. Accommodation includes TV in both rooms plus coffee and tea making facilities. Residents' lounge available. Plenty of pubs and restaurants nearby. Easy access to M5, M6, M42 and M40. 25 minutes from NEC and Birmingham Airport. Destinations within easy reach: Symphony Hall and Convention Centre in Birmingham, Black Country Museum, Dudley, Stourbridge Crystal factories, Severn Valley Railway.

Mrs Sheila Blankstone
Tel: 01562 883883

B&B from £20, Rooms 1 twin, 1 double (both en-suite), No smoking, No children, Pets welcome, Open all year, Map Ref: L

WILTSHIRE

"The turfe is of short sweet grasse, good for the sheep and delightful to the eye, for its smoothness like a bowling green, and pleasant to the traveller."

(John Aubrey (1626-97) English Antiquary & Biographer)

WILTSHIRE

MARLBOROUGH · HIGH STREET.

In less than an hour from London the visitor can be in the heart of rural England - Wiltshire. The county stretches from the lush countryside in the North of the county where the Cotswolds spill over from Gloucestershire to the wide open spaces of Salisbury Plain to the South. There are also many famous prehistoric monuments and sites, the most noted of which are Stonehenge, and Avebury's circle of standing stones.

From East to West of the county is the fully navigable Kennet & Avon Canal. From Bradford-on-Avon it makes its way through an impressive flight of 29 locks at Caen Hill, to just south of Savernake Forest at the Eastern edge of the county.

Bradford-on-Avon is a town unlike any other in Wiltshire with almost every route on steep incline. The bridge across the river has two original medieval arches and a domed structure on one side, which was once a chapel where pilgrims from Malmesbury to Glastonbury stopped to pray. Castle Combe is one of the most photographed villages in the country - the descent to the village is dramatic. Once a wealthy weaving centre, mellowed cottages circle the stone canopied market cross. Lacock is one of the most beautiful villages in England, dating from before the 19th century. William Henry Fox Talbot carried out many pioneering photographic experiments at his home, Lacock Abbey. At the North and South extremities of Wiltshire are two important towns - Swindon and Salisbury. Swindon is an excellent modern shopping centre and home to the Great Western Railway Museum. Salisbury, or New Sarum, was built at the meeting point of four rivers and is one of the most beautiful cathedral cities in Britain. Founded in 1220 when Bishop Richard Poore abandoned the Norman cathedral built at Old Sarum and built another, called New Sarum. The cathedral is the only English medieval cathedral in a single style.

CASTLE COMBE, WILTSHIRE

Old Sarum is the site of the original Roman fortress, Sorviodunum, is earthworks covering 56 acres and was probably first used as an Iron Age camp. The inn at Alderbury, The Green Dragon, was featured in Charles Dickens' Martin Chuzzlewit. Other interesting and attractive villages include Chilmark, with a wealth of 17th century houses, Britford, which has views to Salisbury Cathedral, Dinton and Great Wishford. Steeple Langford in the Wylye Valley has thatched brick cottages contrasting with the even older chequered flint houses. Wylye is another village with typical chequered stonework. Stonehenge, West of Amesbury, and completed around 1250 BC, retains a powerful atmosphere. The world famous Bronze Age site on Salisbury Plain probably dates back to 2150 BC. Surviving today is an outer ring of standing stores 14 ft high with lintels across the top of them and an inner horseshoe of five pairs of uprights with lintels.

THE BRIDGE AT
BRADFORD-ON-AVON.

Notable towns of the area include Amesbury, set in a bend of the River Avon which is crossed by a five arched Palladian style bridge; Devizes a pleasant old market town with fine Georgian houses; and Trowbridge, once a major settlement for Flemish weavers who brought with them great prosperity. Swindon owes the foundation of its prosperity to the old Great Western Railway works. Marlborough is a town noted for having one of the widest main streets in the country, with its splendid Georgian buildings and colonnaded shops. Nearby Avebury Circle is regarded by many experts as the most important early Bronze Age monument in Europe. It was set up around 1800 BC, 200 years earlier than the main phase in the building of Stonehenge, and is made up of 100 standing stones

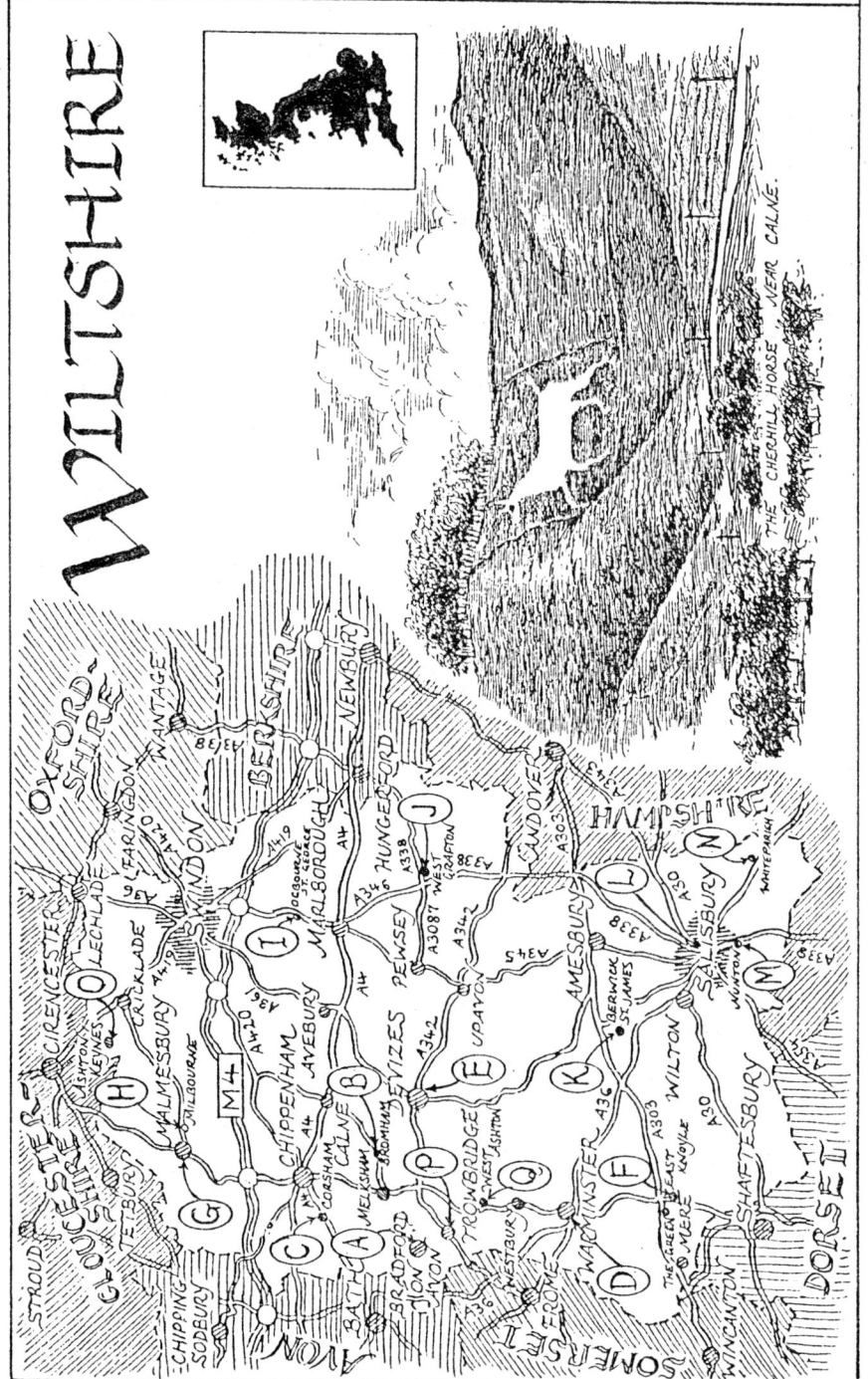

WILTSHIRE

THE CHERHILL HORSE, NEAR CALNE.

Burghope Manor, Winsley, Bradford-on-Avon, Wiltshire BA15 2LA   Nearest Road A36

Burghope Manor is a 13th century Manor House which is absolutely steeped in history. The Manor has associations with Henry VIII's prelate Archbishop Cranmer and there is a large fireplace engraved with Elizabethan writing. Despite this, however, Burghope is first and foremost a living family home with all modern day comforts including en-suite bathrooms. Situated on the edge of the village of Winsley, Burghope, is just 5 miles from Bath and the village pub and restaurant are within easy walking distance.

Elizabeth & John Denning
Tel: 01225 723557
Fax: 01225 723113

B&B from £30 per person, Rooms 2 double, 1 twin, Minimum age 10, Open all year except Christmas, Map Ref: A

The Cottage, Westbrook, Bromham, Chippenham, Wiltshire SN15 2JZ   Nearest Road A342

The Cottage formerly a farmhouse is reputed to have been a coaching inn built between 1450 and 1505. There is over an acre of garden and paddock. Westbrook is a small hamlet situated in beautiful countryside and was once the home of Thomas Moore, the Irish poet. The area is steeped in history and is ideal walking country. The accommodation is in a recently converted barn, originally the ostlery. The en-suite bedrooms are comfortable and all have have tea/coffee making facilities. Breakfast is served in the beamed dining room. Packed lunches available on request.

Richard & Gloria Steed
Tel: 01380 850255

B&B from £20, Rooms 2 twin, 2 double (all en-suite), Open all year, Map Ref: B

Boyds Farm, Gastard, Nr Corsham, Wiltshire SN13 9PT   Nearest Road A4

A relaxing stay is assured on this arable farm whicn is idyulically situated in the peace and tranquility of the unspoilt Wiltshire countryside. As featrued by the Daily Express, this delightful 16th century farmhouse accommodates individuals, couples and families. The house is centrally heated and guests have their own lounge with woodburning stove. Bedrooms have washbasins and tea/coffee making facilities. Good pub food is available locally. Ideal for Stonehenge, Bath Lacock, Castle Combe and the M4.

Mrs Doroth Robinson
Tel: 01249 713146

B&B from £16, Rooms 2 double, 1 family, Restricted smoking, Open all year. Map Ref: C

Sturford Mead Farm, Corsley, Warminster, Wiltshire BA12 7QU   Nearest Road A362

Sturford Mead Farm is on the A362 between Frome and Warminster, nestling under the historic monument of Cley Hill (National Trust) and opposite Longleat with its safari park, lake and grounds. Stourhead, Cheddar Gorge, Wooky Hole and the prettiest English village of Castle Combe are close by. The cathedral cities of Wells and Salisbury are within easy distance as is Bath. A real steam train still runs at the East Somerset Railway. The comfortable bedrooms, all with private facilities, have tea/coffee makers, and TV.

Ms Lynn Corp
Tel: 01373 832213

B&B from £17, Rooms 2 twin, 1 double (all en-suite or private facilities) Restricted smoking, Open all year, Map Ref: D

Springfield House, Crockerton, Near Warminster, Wiltshire BA12 8AU   **Nearest Road A36, A350**

Situated in the beautiful Wylye Valley, on the edge of the famous Longleat Estate, Springfield House is a charming village home dating from the 17th century. Rachel & Colin welcome you to their home with its beams, open fires, fresh flowers, and private or en-suite bedrooms which overlook the gardens and grass tennis court. Marvellous base for touring, walking, or just relaxing. Bath, Salisbury, Wells, Glastonbury, Stonehenge, Stourhead Gardens easily reached.

Rachel & Colin Singer
Tel: 01985 213696

B&B from £17, Dinner from £14, Rooms 2 double, 1 twin
(all with private/en-suite facilities), No smoking, Open all year,
Map Ref: D

Eastcott Manor, Easterton, Devizes, Wiltshire SN10 4PL   **Nearest Road A3098**

Eastcott Manor, a Grade II Elizabethan Manor House, stands in its own grounds of approximately 20 acres. Rooms are of good size and bedrooms well equipped with up to date facilities including tea/coffee makers. Good food is a feature of a stay at Eastcott. A four course dinner to Cordon Bleu standards may be booked in advance, wine is included. Light suppers are also available by arrangement. Eastcott is an ideal location for a country holiday with much to see locally and many sporting activities including the International Horse Trials at Badminton close by.

Malcolm & Janet Firth
Tel: 01380 813313

B&B from £20, Dinner from £12, Rooms 2 single, 2 twin
Pets by arrangement, Open all year except Christmas, Map Ref: E

Milton Farm, East Knoyle, Wiltshire SP3 6BG   **Nearest Road A303**

A very nice warm welcome at picturesque Milton Farm with a friendly personal service. Rooms are full of character; low beams, log fires, uneven floors, nice old furniture, antiques and silver, lots of space, and plenty of books. In the stable gallery, next to the farmhouse, hand painted Portugese ceramics are for sale. There is an outdoor heated swimming pool which guests may use. The comfortable bedroms with private/en-suite facilities, have tea/coffee making trays and TV. Dinner can be provided by prior arrangement

Mrs Janice Hyde
Tel: 01747 830247

B&B from £19, Dinner by arrangement, Rooms 1 twin, 1 double,
(ensuite/private facilities), Open February to November, Map Ref: F

Stonehill Farm, Charlton, Malmesbury, Wiltshire SN16 9DY   **Nearest Road B4040**

Stonehill Farm is a 15th century Cotswold stone farmhouse situated on a working dairy farm in the lush and rolling countryside on the Wiltshire/Gloucestershire border. One of the bedrooms has its own shower room en-suite and all rooms have tea/coffee making facilities. Children and dogs are welcome and full English breakfast is served in the guests sitting/dining room. Ideal for 1 night or several days. Oxford, Bath, Stratford-upon-Avon, Stonehenge and the delightful Cotswold Hills and villages are all within easy reach by car.

Mrs Edwards
Tel: 01666 823310

B&B from £14, Rooms 2 double, 1 twin
Open all year, Map Ref: G

Southfields Cottage, Milbourne, Malmesbury, Wiltshire SN16 9JB   Nearest Road A4

A friendly welcome to this charming, comfortable, 17th century stone cottage, situated on the Wiltshire Cycle Way. In the tradition of re-cycling the main beams are ship's timbers salvaged from wrecks in the Severn estuary. The Breakfast Room has deep pink walls and a large fire place filled with dried flowers from the garden. Attractive bedrooms with TV, radio, hairdrier, tea, coffee & herbal tea and many thoughtful extras. Malmesbury perched on a hill in a loop of the river Avon, with its famous 17th c Abbey and Norman carved stone entrance, is a delight to explore

Mrs Christine Meller
Tel: 01666 823168

B&B from £18, Rooms 1 double, 1 twin both en-suite,
No smoking, Minimum age 12, Pets by arrangement,
Open all year, Map Ref: H

Laurel Cottage, Southend, Ogbourne St George, Marlborough, Wiltshire SN8 1SG   Nearest Road A346

This picturesque 16th century thatched cottage, lovingly restored, lies in a fold of the Downs 2 miles north of Marlborough. The pretty bedrooms are individually styled, some with en-suite facilities and every effort has been made to provide comfortable and well appointed furnishings. The rebuilding of an old coach house in the grounds now provides private accommodation for 2 in 'The Ridgeway Suite'. Breakfast is taken in the low beamed dining room around the family table and there is a full and varied breakfast menu. ETB highly commended, AA 5Q selected.

Mrs Adrienne Francis
Tel: 01672 841288

B&B from £16.50, Rooms 2 twin, 1 double, 1 family, (some en-suite),
No smoking, No pets, Open March - October, Map Ref: I

Mayfield, West Grafton, Marlborough, Wiltshire SN8 3BY   Nearest Road A338

A delightful thatched farmhouse surrounded by well kept gardens. The property has been carefully extended to provide 3 comfortably sized bedrooms and 2 bathrooms. There is a choice of lounge and guests share a single table in the breakfast room. Mayfield is decorated with taste and style and is furnished with antiques. Guests are welcome to use the tennis court and heated swimming pool. ETC highly commended, AA 5Q premier selected.

Mrs Angela Orssich
Tel: 01672 810339
Fax: 01672 811158

B&B from £19, Dinner from £10, Rooms 2 double, 1 twin,
Open all year except Christmas & new year, Map Ref: J

The Mill House, Berwick St James, Nr Salisbury, Wiltshire SP3 4TS   Nearest Road A303, A36

Diana welcomes you to the beautiful Mill House set in acres of nature reserve abounding in wild flowers and infinite peace. An island paradise with the River Till running through the working mill and beautiful garden. Diana's old fashioned roses long to see you as do the lovely walks; Stonehenge, Antiquities Houses and noted 'Carriers' at Stockton. Built by the miller in 1785 the bedrooms, all with tea/coffee making facilities, and TV, command magnificent views. Fishing or swimming in the mill pool and close to golf courses and riding. Attention to healthy and organic food.

Diana Gifford Mead
Tel: 01722 790331

B&B from £20, Rooms 11 single, 11 twin, 11 double
(2 double rooms are en-suite), Minimum age 5, Open all year,
Map Ref: K

Pigeon House Cottage, The Green, Britford, Salisbury, Wiltshire, SP5 4DU   Nearest Road A338

A picturesque 17th century cottage lying 1 mile from Salisbury. Exposed beams and sympathetic restoration create a warm and friendly atmosphere in this charming and peaceful location. Views of Salisbury Cathedral across water meadows extend from one side of the property with a stream and open fields on the other. Two twin bedded rooms with adjoining bathrooms are available each with tea/coffee making facilities. A hearty English breakfast is served in the cosy farmhouse style kitchen. Centrally heated. Many good pubs and restaurants nearby.

Mrs Gaye Bonallack
Tel: 01722 329950

B&B from £17, Rooms 2 twin, No smoking, No Pets,
Open all year except Christmas, Map Ref: L

Stratford Lodge, 4 Park Lane, Castle Road, Salisbury SP1 3NP, Wiltshire   Nearest Road A36

Stratford Lodge is a small friendly hotel tucked down a quiet lane overlooking a large park, a few minutes from the centre of Salisbury. A secluded, pretty, lawned garden has tables and chairs which are an enticement in the summer. The bedrooms are furnished with antiques, the beds covered with beautiful lace bedspreads. The breakfast room is the conservatory and the gracious dining room is open to non-residents. The dinner menu is exciting and worth studying over a glass of complimentary sherry. There is a heated swimming pool for guests to use.

Mrs P J Bayly
Tel: 017223 25177

B&B from £23, Dinner from £16, Rooms 2 single, 2 twin, 3 double,
2 family (all en-suite/private facilities), No smoking, Minimum age 8,
Open all year except Christmas, Map Ref: L

Moors Farm, East Knoyle, Salisbury, Wiltshire SP3 6BU   Nearest Road A303, A350

Moors farm is a working dairy farm peacefully situated one mile from the picturesque village of East Knoyle. The surrounding area is designated to be of outstanding natural beauty and there are many historic houses, monuments and gardens to visit in the area. The farmhouse dates from mid 17th century and the first floor accommodation forms part of an extension added after the Napoleonic wars. The accommodation consists of 2 large bright comfortable rooms comprising bedroom with twin beds, bathroom and adjoining sitting room. Easily adaptable to cater for a family.

Mrs June Reading
Tel: 01747 830385

B&B from £20, Rooms 1 twin/family with bathroom and sitting room,
Minimum age 8, Open all year except Christmas, Map Ref: F

---

1 Riverside Close, Laverstock, Salisbury, Wiltshire SP1 1QW   Nearest Road A30

Charming, well appointed home, in a quiet area 1½ miles from Salisbury Cathedral. Tastefully furnished suites enjoying their own en-suite bath or shower room, TV and drink making facilities. Salisbury is the centre of an area steeped in antiquity, rich in natural beauty, with many places of outstanding historical interest. Your hosts take endless care to ensure the well being of their guests and are happy to plan itineraries for them.

Mrs Mary Tucker
Tel: 01722 320287
Fax: 01722 320287

B&B from £19.50, Dinner from £12 (with 48 hours notice),
Rooms 1 double, 1 family, No smoking, Open all year, Map Ref: L

Newcourt Lodge, Nunton Drove, Nunton, Salisbury, Wiltshire SP5 4HZ   Nearest Road A338

Newcourt Lodge lies in the peaceful village of Nunton which is just 3 miles from Salisbury. The house stands in large mature gardens and affords panoramic views of the Wiltshire countryside. Bedrooms are nicely furnished and include TV, central heating, hot & cold water, and tea/coffee making facilities. There are ample country pubs nearby which serve evening meals. Newcourt Lodge is well situated for visiting Stonehenge, the New Forest, Salisbury and the West Country.

Mrs Jill Johnson
Tel: 01722 335877

B&B from £16, Rooms 2 twin, 1 single, Minimum age 8, No smoking, No pets, Open all year except Christmas, Map Ref: M

Farthings, 9 Swaynes Close, Salisbury, Wiltshire SP1 3AE   Nearest Road A36

Central but veryquiet, Farthings is the charming home of Mrs Gill Rodwell. Parking is no problem in this peaceful Close. The comfortable, nicely furnished, bedrooms all have tea/coffee making facilities, and there is a good choice of breakfast. The breakfast room, with its interesting collection of old family photo's, opens onto a delightful garden. This is an ideal base for visiting this old Cathedral/market town and the surrounding area.

Mrs Gill Rodwell
Tel: 01722 330749

B&B from £16, Rooms 2 single 1 twin, 1 double, (twin and double rooms are en-suite), No smoking, Minimum age 4, Open all year except Christmas, Map Ref: L

Brickworth Farmhouse, Whiteparish, Salisbury, Wiltshire SP5 2QE   Nearest Road A36

A perfectly situated 18th century listed farmhouse, renovated and furnished to maintain its period charm. The comfortable bedrooms offer tea/coffee making facilities, and TV. Salisbury, Stonehenge, Romsey, the New Forest, Winchester and Bath are all within easy reach and Sue Barry is a registered tourist guide and will assist you to plan ideal excursions. There are excellent local pubs which provide good meals at realistic prices.

Mrs Sue Barry
Tel: 01794 884663
Fax: 01794 884581

B&B from £15, Rooms 1 single, 2 double, 1 family, (double rooms are en-suite), Open all year except Christmas, Map Ref: N

---

1 Cove House, Ashton Keynes, Swindon, Wiltshire SN6 6NS   Nearest Road A419

No 1 Cove House is a 17th century manor house situated at the centre of a pretty lower Cotswold village with the infant River Thames running beside the High Road. The house is surrounded by ¾ acre of beautiful walled garden. The garden room is always open for guests to enjoy. Mr & Mrs Threlfall take a keen interest in interior design, this is evident throughout the house which includes a recently renovated ballroom. A sitting room is located in the converted attic for sole use of guests, with colour TV, stereo, local information and maps.

Mr & Mrs R C Threlfall
Tel: 01285 861226

B&B from £22, Rooms 2 double, 1 twin, No smoking, Open March to October, Map Ref: O

Spiers Piece Farm, Trowbridge, Wiltshire BA14 6HG   **Nearest Road A361**

Try our 'home away from home' farmhouse bed and breakfast in the heart of the Wiltshire countryside. Spacious Georgian farmhouse, large garden, great views, peace and tranquility. Adjacent to an historical, picturesque village. Many tourist attractions including Bath and Stone Henge within easy reach. All rooms have tea/coffee making facilities. Guests own luxury bathroom, sitting room/colour TV and dining room. Great breakfasts to last you all day.

Mrs Jill Awdry
Tel: 01380 870266

B&B from £15, Rooms 2 double, 1 twin,
Open February - November, Map Ref: P

Welam House, West Ashton, Wiltshire BA14 6AZ   **Nearest Road A350**

Welam House, built of Bath stone in 1840 and a former vicarage, is a fine example of mid Victorian Gothic architecture. The house retains many of its original period features with elegant stained glass windows in the hall. The house is centrally heated, has an attractive dining room with separate sitting room for guests to relax in. The drawing room which has Jocobean style ceiling panels overlooks the bowling green. Very comfortable accommodation offers extensive views of garden and open countryside. Tea/coffee making facilities available in all rooms.

Mr & Mrs Cronan
Tel: 01225 755908

B&B from £16, Rooms 1 twin, 1 double, 1 family
(all with private/en-suite facilities), Restricted smoking,
Open March - Dec, Map Ref: Q

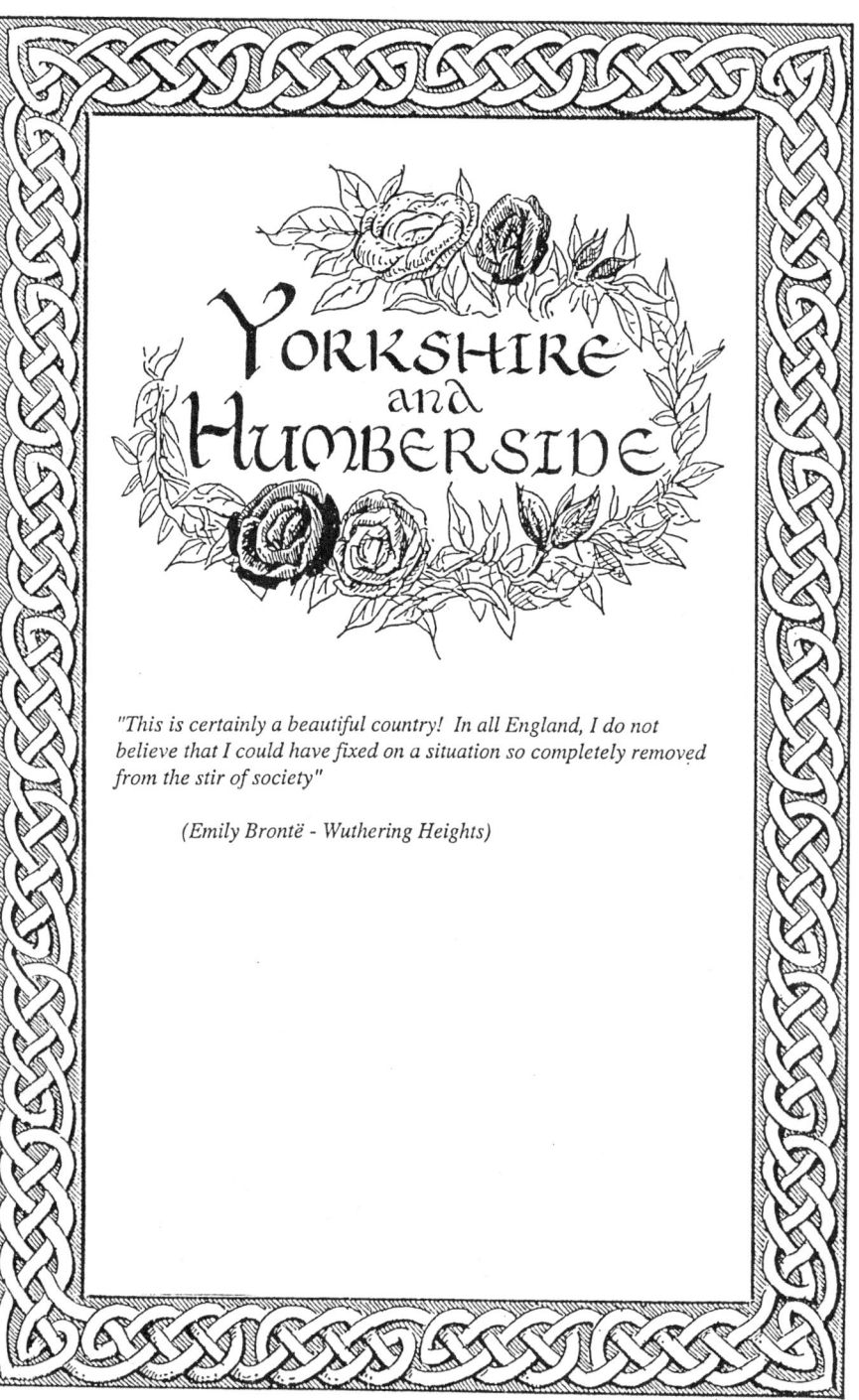

Yorkshire and Humberside

"This is certainly a beautiful country! In all England, I do not believe that I could have fixed on a situation so completely removed from the stir of society"

(Emily Brontë - Wuthering Heights)

YORKSHIRE

RIEVAULX ABBEY.

Yorkshire is a county of unspoilt beauty and a wealth of heritage. The county has some spectacular scenery from the Dales to the predominantly cliff lined coast. The region's historical capital, York, dates back to the Romans nearly 2,000 years ago and one of the city's quaint streets, the Shambles, is the best preserved medieval thoroughfare in Europe. Perhaps Yorkshire's most breathtaking scenery is the natural limestone landscape of upper Airedale, around Malham. The village of Malham itself is set in an amphitheatre of hills, with the giant overhang of Malham Cove a mile to the North.

Grassington is Upper Wharfedale's principal village where a medieval bridge spans the River Wharfe. To the North of the village, lead mining on Grassington Moor brought a boom in the late 18th and 19th centuries. While the Dales look purely pastoral today, moors like Grassington and gill-sides bear the scars of lead mining which declined in the 1880s because of foreign imports. Kettlewell must be one of upper Wharfedale's most attractive villages, dominated by great Whernside at 2,310 ft while 3 miles to the South is Kilnsey Crag which attracts serious rock climbers. In the Yorkshire Dales National Park upland moors sweep to a score of summits of more than 2,000 ft.

The view from the top of Richmond's 11th century castle keep is one of England's finest. More unspoilt countryside can be found in the firsts, hills and vales of the North Yorkshire Moors, where heather covered moorland stretches from the Vale of York to the sea. The North Yorkshire Moors Railway is among the most scenic in Britain, and is one of many steam railways in the area. Helmsley is the main town beneath the rim of the moors and a fine centre for walking. Two miles North is Rievaulx Abbey, founded in 1131, the first Cistercian house in the North of England and one of the country's most magnificent monastic ruins.

THE SHAMBLES, YORK.

One of Yorkshire's most famous sons was Captain James Cook, who was employed as a grocer's apprentice in the attractive fishing village of Staithes. As a young man he lived in Whitby and he sailed the Whitby-built Endeavour for Tahiti via Cape Horn in 1768. The fishing port is dominated by its abbey, high above the town. Its first abbey was founded in AD 657 by St Hilda. Robin Hood's Bay is another seaside village well worth a visit.

The Romans chose the site of York for their fortress of Eburacum. Later the Danes founded a colony here and the clock can be turned back to the Viking city in the Yorvik Viking Centre. The Normans also built their fortifications at York . Four medieval gates lead in through the ancient city walls, built on Roman foundations and girding the old city for 3 miles.

The spa town of Harrogate is an attractive town with its banks of flowers and well planned open spaces. It is also well known as a conference centre. At nearby Knaresborough, Georgian houses line the narrow streets and steep steps and alleys lead down to the River Nidd. Opposite the ruined castle is the Dropping Well, where water dropping on to an overhang forms a limestone deposit, petrifying a curious assortment of objects.

Among the many Yorkshire market towns to visit are Bedale, with its wide cobbled verges, and Boroughbridge, where 3 stone monoliths dating from 2000 to 1500 BC stand at up to 30 feet high, and are known as the Devils Arrows.

YORK MINSTER

YORKSHIRE & HUMBERSIDE

THE 13th CENTURY RUINS of WHITBY ABBEY

YORKSHIRE & HUMBERSIDE

The 13th CENTURY RUINS of WHITBY ABBEY

Elmfield Country House, Arrathorne, Bedale, North Yorkshire, DL8 1NE   Nearest Road A684, A1

Nestled in the heart of 'Herriot Country', this award winning country house provides the ideal location for both holiday and business visitors. Situated in its own grounds with uninterrupted views; relaxing and enjoyable base from which to explore the Dales and Moors. Bedrooms are all en-suite, have tea/coffee making facilities, and TV. Two ground floor bedrooms ideal for disabled guests. Superb home cooked evening meals and full English breakfast with home-made preserves. There is a games room, solarium, lounge bar, and garden where guests may relax.

Jim & Edith Lillie
Tel: 01677 450558   **B&B from £19.50, Dinner from £11.50, Rooms 3 twin, 4 double,**
Fax: 01677 450557   **2 family (all en-suite), Open all year, Map Ref: A**

Low Green House, Thoralby, Bishopdale, Yorkshire DL8 3SZ   Nearest Road A684

There is a warm welcome and a truly personal service at Low Green House in beautiful Bishopdale. The en-suite, pleasant, bedrooms all have central heating, colour TV, and hot drinks making equipment. Breakfast and set dinner menu's are varied and interesting home cooking making use of local produce and fresh vegetables. Guests can relax in front of a log fire in the lounge where there is a good selection of books, guides and maps of the area. This is an ideal base for touring; Thoralby being almost the centre of the Yorkshire Dales.

Marilyn & Tony Philpott   **B&B from £18.50, Dinner £11, Rooms 1 twin, 3 double**
Tel: 01969 663623   **(all en-suite), No smoking, Pets by arrangement,**
                                 Open all year except Christmas, Map Ref: B

Brafferton Hall, Brafferton, York YO6 2NZ   Nearest Road A1, A19

Brafferton Hall, home of John and Sue White, is in a quiet corner of the historic village of Brafferton/Helperby. A warm welcome and the opportunity to relax in a comfortable environment is assured. Ideal for an overnight stopover or for exploring many Yorkshire attractions. Guest rooms have private or en-suite bathroom, TV and tea/coffee makers. Dinner, by arrangement, is taken 'en-famille' in the candlelit dining room. Fresh fruit and vegetables, homemade bread, free-range eggs and local cheeses are all to be appreciated at this perfect retreat from the stresses of a busy world.

John & Sue White   **B&B from £27.50, Dinner from £17, Rooms 3 double, 1 single,**
Tel: 01423 360352   **(all with en-suite/private bathroom), No smoking,**
Fax: 01423 360352   **Open January - December, Map Ref: C**

The Old Vicarage, Crakehall, Near Bedale, Yorkshire DL8 1HE   Nearest Road A684 (off A1)

The Old Vicarage is a delightful Georgian house built in 1842 and extended in 1897 presenting a fine example of a stone Yorkshire dwelling. The spacious bedrooms some with en-suite facilities shaver points, colour TV, tea/coffee making facilities, radio alarm, central heating and hairdryer. There is a private lounge, with log fire, for guests' use. The owners enjoy having guests to stay in their home and there is a friendly relaxed atmosphere. Crakehall is in the heart of Herriot country and enjoys access to York, Ripon, The Dales and Harrogate

Mrs J C Young   **B&B from £20, Rooms 3 double, 2 twin, No smoking,**
Tel: 01677 422967   **Open all year except Christmas, Map Ref: A**

Halfway House, Crayke, York, YO6 4TJ

Nearest Road A19

Built during the latter part of the 19th century, Halfway House, stands on rising ground on the edge of the pretty village of Crayke, with superb views over to the Dales in the west. The house and Georgian outbuildings have been sympathetically restored maintaining many original features. Rooms are decorated and furnished to a high standard with many antiques as well as TV, radio/alarm, tea/coffee making facilities, and many other welcoming touches. 1992 & 1993 winner of the Yorkshire & Humberside Best B & B Award and winner in the All England Award of Excellence 1993

Mrs Belle Hepworth
Tel: 01347 822614
Fax: 01347 922942

B&B from £30, Dinner £18, Rooms 2 double (one 4-poster), 1 twin, (all en-suite), Restricted smoking, Minimum age 12, Open January - December, Map Ref: C

Holme House, Piercebridge, Darlington, DL2 3SY

Nearest Road B6275

Holme House is a spacious 18th century farmhouse on a working farm. We offer a warm welcome to our guests and invite you to share our family home. The house is comfortably furnished and peaceful with views of open countryside from all rooms. You can relax in the sitting room in front of a blazing log fire. The bedrooms have a private bathroom and facilities for making tea and coffee. Piercebridge is a picturesque village on the River Tees famous for its Roman remains. A convenient area from which to visit the attractive market towns of Richmond, Barnard Castle and nearby Dales.

Mrs Anne Graham
Tel: 01325 374280

B&B from £15, Rooms 2 twin, Restricted smoking, Pets welcome by arrangement, Open January - February, Map Ref: D

Alderside, Thirsk Road, Easingwold, York YO6 3HJ

Nearest Road A19

Alderside is a comfortable Edwardian former school house set in large private gardens. Easy access to York and the North Yorkshire Moors via the A19. Full English breakfast using local produce and home made preserves. The 2 double rooms have TV, clock/radio, hairdryer, beverage tray and their own bathroom. Although dinner is not available here, there are good nearby pubs and restaurants which serve excellent food. There is an additional room available for any accompanying friend or relative.

Daphne Tanner-Smith
Tel: 01347 822132

B&B from £16.50, Rooms 2 double with private bathroom, No pets, No children, No smoking, Open March - November, Map Ref: E

Manor House Farm, Ingleby Greenhow, Great Ayton, North Yorkshire TS9 6RB

Nearest Road A172

Delightful farmhouse (part 1760) built of Yorkshire stone, set in 164 acres of park and woodlands at the foot of the Cleveland hills in the North York Moors National Park. Environment is tranquil and secluded. Ideal for nature lovers, relaxing, touring and walking. Accommodation is attractive with exposed beams and interior stonework. Atmosphere is warm and welcoming. Guests have separate entrance, lounge and dining room.. Bedrooms are pleasing and bright with private facilities and tea/coffee equipment. Evening dinners served, special diets if required, excellent wines, brochure.

Dr & Mrs M Bloom
Tel: 01642 722384

Dinner, Bed & Breakfast From £35, Rooms 2 twin, 1 double (all have en-suite/private facilities), No smoking, Minimum age 12, Open all year except Christmas, Map Ref: F

Laskill Farm, Hawnby, York YO6 5NB   **Nearest Road B1257**

Charming, warm country farmhouse on 600 acre farm in the north Yorkshire National Park in the heart of James Herriot and Heartbeat country. All rooms are lovingly cared for and well equipped. Lovely garden with own lake, peace and tranquillity. Lots of places of historical interest and stately houses nearby. York only 45 minutes away. Generous cuisine of high standard using fresh produce whenever possible. Natural spring water.

Mrs S Smith
Tel: 01439 798268

B&B from £17.50, Dinner from £10.75, Rooms 4 double, 1 single, 3 en-suite twin, Open all year, Map Ref: C

Alexa House, 26 Ripon Road, Harrogate, North Yorkshire HG1 2JJ   **Nearest Road A61**

Built for Baron de Ferrier this fine old Victorian house retains all its former charm and splendour and now offers 13 en-suite bedrooms all individually decorated with central heating, colour TV, tea/coffee making facilities, direct dial telephone, hair dryer and radio clock alarm. The former stable block has been converted to provide outstanding ground floor accommodation suitable for elderly/disabled guests. Bargain breaks and traditional home cooked dinner available. Large car park, residential licence and comfortable lounge.

John & Roberta Black
Tel: 01423 501988
Fax: 01423 504086

B&B from £24, Dinner from £10, Rooms 5 double, 1 family, 4 twin, 3 single (all en-suite), Open January - December, Map Ref: G

Ruskin Hotel & Restaurant, 1 Swan Road, Harrogate, Yorkshire HG1 2SS   **Nearest Road A61**

The Ruskin is something rather special. This small select highly acclaimed Victorian hotel is set in lovely grounds in Harrogate's old conservation area. Pretty antique furnished bedrooms, including 4-poster, offering every comfort and facility. Delightful bar/restaurant with Victorian balcony serving award winning English/French food. Relaxing guest lounge with open fire. Only 3 minutes walk into town centre, exhibition halls and magnificent gardens. Ideal base for excursions to the Dales. Large private car park. A very warm welcome awaits you at this charming hotel.

John & Maria Simmons
Tel: 01423 502045
Fax: 01423 506131

B&B from £28, Dinner from £14.95, Rooms 3 double, 2 family, 2 single (all en-suite), Restricted smoking, Open January -December, Map Ref: G

High Winsley Cottage, Burnt-Yates, Nr Harrogate, Yorkshire HG3 3EP   **Nearest Road A61**

A traditional Yorkshire Dales stone cottage situated well off the road in peaceful countryside with lovely views all around and ideally placed for both town and country. A warm welcome, good food, and comfortable accommodation are assured. All bedrooms are en-suite, and have tea/coffee making facilities. There are 2 guests' sitting rooms with television, books, magazines, local guides and maps. Great care is taken to provide first class fare and includes home bred beef, fresh fruit and vegetables from the garden, free range eggs and home baked bread.

Clive & Gill King
Tel: 01423 770662

B&B from £18.50, Dinner from £12.50, Rooms 3 twin, 2 double (all en-suite), Residential licence, Restricted smoking, Minimum age 11, Open March - December, Map Ref: H

Springfield, Cragg Road, Cragg Vale, Hebden Bridge, West Yorkshire HX7 5SR   Nearest Road B6138

Springfield extends a warm welcome to guests. It is well situated in an acre of garden within a wooded valley in the south Pennines and there are excellent views of moorland and woods. All rooms are comfortably furnished and offer TV and tea/coffee making facilities. One of the rooms has en-suite facilities. Mrs Nelson is the winner of the West Yorkshire Hospitality Award for 'Best Bed & Breakfast Establishment' and 'Best Yorkshire Breakfast'. Close to Calderdale Way and Alternative Pennine Way.

Mrs N W Nelson
Tel: 01422 882029

**B&B from £15, Rooms 1 double, 1 twin, 2 single, No smoking,
Open January - December, Map Ref: I**

Crib Farm, Long Causeway, Luddenden Foot, Yorkshire HX2 6JJ   Nearest Road A58

Crib Farm was built in the 1600's as a coaching inn and was used by many travellers who crossed the south Pennines from Lancashire to Yorkshire. In the 1800's it became a dairy farm and it still offers a warm welcome to the many travellers who venture to this unspoilt region of west Yorkshire. Set on the hills above Luddenden Foot near the town of Hebden Bridge the farm provides an excellent location for both holidaymakers and businessmen alike. All bedrooms are comfortable and have tea/coffee making facilities. Guests have use of a pleasant lounge with TV.

Mrs Pauline Hitchen
Tel: 01422 883285

**B&B from £15, Dinner from £8 (by request),
Rooms 1 single, 1 twin, 2 double, Restricted smoking,
Open all year except Christmas & New Year, Map Ref: J**

Porch House, High Street, Northallerton, Yorkshire DL7 8EG   Nearest Road A684

Porch House was built in 1584 and took its name from the porch that still frames the main entrance. Throughout its history Porch house has offered comfort and shelter to many travellers including royalty - James (VI of Scotland/I of England) and Charles I. Jackie and David extend a royal welcome to guests. All rooms are en-suite, have tea/coffee making facilities and TV. Traditional English Breakfast/Vegetarian. There is a residents lounge; original fireplaces and beams; walled garden; private parking; central position (opposite church)

Jackie Smith &
David Summers
Tel: 01609 779831

**B&B from £20, Dinner from £12 by arrangement, Rooms 1 single,
1 twin, 2 double, 1 family (all en-suite), No smoking, No pets,
Open all year, Map Ref: K**

The Old Farmhouse Country Hotel, Raskelf, York YO6 3LF   Nearest Road A19

The Old Farmhouse is an award winning friendly hotel ideal for York Moors and Dales. The comfortable bedrooms all have en-suite bathroom with bath or shower, tea/coffee making facilities, direct dial phones and colour TV. There are 2 lounges and a large dining room featuring local hand made oak chairs. There is full central heating and open fires in chilly weather. There is an extensive breakfast menu with homemade bread, marmalade and jams. A 4-course evening meal with choice, and a restaurant and residential licence.

Bill & Jenny Frost
Tel: 01347 821971
Fax: 01347 822392

**B&B from £25, Dinner from £16, Rooms 2 twin, 6 double, 2 family,
(all en-suite), Restricted smoking, Pets by arrangement,
Open February - December, Map Ref: L**

Walburn Hall, Downholme, Richmond, North Yorkshire DL11 6AF   **Nearest Road A6108**

Walburn Hall is one of the few remaining fortified farmhouses in England. Dating from the 14-16 centuries it has an enclosed cobbled courtyard and terraced gardens. Accommodation for guests includes, 2 double/twin and 1 double/family both with en-suite bathrooms. Rooms also benefit from tea/coffee making facilities, and there is a guests' lounge and dining room with beamed ceilings and stone fireplaces with log fires. Your stay at Walburn Hall offers you the opportunity to visit places of historic interest - Richmond, Bolton & Middleham castles, and numerous abbeys.

Diana Greenwood
Tel: 01748 822152
Fax: 01748 822152

B&B from £19, Rooms 2 double/twin, 1 double/family (all en-suite), No pets, No smoking, Open March - November inclusive, Map Ref: M

Busby House, Stokesley, Yorkshire TS9 5LB   **Nearest Road A172**

This is a lovely old farmhouse sympathetically altered to include what was once the adjacent cottage with dairy and outbuildings. The principal rooms look south over the large garden and fields to the hills beyond. To the rear is a cobbled courtyard. The atmosphere is peaceful and relaxed and exudes warmth and friendliness. Busby House is very well located for exploring the moors, dales and coast and within easy reach of York, Durham and many places of historic interest. The house is only 25 minutes from the A1 and so makes a good stop between the south and Edinburgh.

Mrs Anne Gloag
Tel: 01642 710425

B&B from £27, Dinner from £16.50, Rooms 2 twin, No smoking, Open all years except Christmas & New Year, Map Ref: N

Thornborough House Farm, South Kilvington, Thirsk, North Yorkshire YO7 2NP   **Nearest Road A19**

Thornborough House Farm is a 200 year old farmhouse which provides first class accommodation and a warm welcome. Guests can enjoy their own sitting and dining room which has an open fire and colour TV, Two of the bedrooms are en-suite and the third has a private bathroom. All rooms are warm and comfortable and have tea/coffee making facilities, and colour TV. Families are very welcome and a cot and high chair are available. The houses lies 1½ miles north of Thirsk, the town made famous by James Herriot. 2 Crown commended.

Mrs Tess Williamson
Tel: 01845 522103
Fax: 01845 522103

B&B from £13, Dinner from £8, Rooms 1 double, 1 twin/single, 1 family, Open all year, Map Ref: O

Brandymires, Muker Road, Hawes, Wensleydale, Yorkshire, DL8 3PR   **Nearest Road A684**

Brandymires is a 3 storey house built in local stone circa 1850. The house has magnificent views from all windows, full central heating and an open fire in the lounge. The 4 comfortable bedrooms have washbasin with hot and cold water and shaver point. The special bedrooms have mahogany and oak 4 poster beds. Great care is taken in the preparation and cooking of all meals and fresh produce is used whenever possible. Bread is home-made as are the conserves. Brandymires has a drinks licence. No TV.

Gail Ainley and
Ann Macdonald
Tel: 01969 667482

B&B from £16.50, Dinner £10 (not Thursday), Rooms 3 double, 1 twin, Minimum age 8, Pets by arrangement, No smoking, Open February - October, Map Ref: P

Barbican Hotel, 20 Barbican Road, York YO1 5AA **Nearest Road A19**

The Barbican Hotel is a Victorian residence of charm and character built in 1888. Lovingly restored it retains many of its original features. All bedrooms are en-suite and have TV and tea/coffee making facilities. One room is at ground floor level. There is a comfortable guests' lounge and the dining room retains a classic 19th century cooking range where a full English breakfast is served. Central York is only a 5 minute walk away and the Barbican Leisure Centre a 100 yards. A private car park is situated at the rear of the hotel.

Elsie & Len Osterman
Tel: 01904 627617
Fax: 01904 627617

B&B from £20, Rooms 1 twin, 5 double, 1 family (all en-suite),
No smoking, Open all year, Map Ref: C

Grange Lodge, 52 Bootham Crescent, Bootham, York YO3 7AH **Nearest Road A19**

The Grange Lodge offers a warm and friendly welcome. Accommodation is in a choice of 7 comfortable and attractively furnished bedrooms, many with en-suite facilities and all have TV and tea/coffee making facilities. Conveniently located for all of York's attractions and only 10 minutes away from York Minster. An ideal place for touring this most beautiful region.

Jenny Robinson
Tel: 01904 621137

B&B from £13, Dinner from £8, Rooms 3 double, 2 family, 1 twin,
1 single (many en-suite), No pets, Open all year, Map Ref: C

Hobbits Hotel, 9 St Peter's Grove, Clifton, York, YO3 6AQ **Nearest Road A19**

Hobbits is a comfortable, Edwardian house, situated in a quiet cul-de-sac only 10 minutes walk from the city centre. Bed and breakfast in a home-from-home style, in beautifully decorated bedrooms, all with private facilities. Each room has central heating, colour TV, mini bars, and tea/coffee making facilities. There is a licence for alcohol and a comfortable guests' lounge. The city centre offers a wide variety of attractions including York Minster and museums. Within a short drive it is possible to get to the coast, moors, dales and wolds. Parking available.

Mrs Rosemary Miller
Tel: 01904 624538/642926

B&B from £27, Rooms 2 single, 2 twin, 3 double/family (all en-suite),
Restricted smoking, Pets by arrangement, Open all year except
Christmas, Map Ref: C

The Hazelwood, 24-25 Portland Street, Gillygate, York, YO3 7EH **Nearest Road Gillygate**

The Hazelwood is a non-smoking Victorian town house with private car park situated in an extremely quiet, yet central, location only 400 yards from York Minster. We pride ourselves on our high quality and generous breakfasts. All our comfortable bedrooms (some with 4-poster beds) have colour TV, radio alarm, hair dryer and tea/coffee making facilities. Relax in our quiet garden or residents' lounge with its range of guides and maps. We are only too pleased to assist in planning your stay in York. Special winter rates between November and Easter.

Ian & Carolyn McNabb
Tel: 01904 626548
Fax: 01904 628032

B&B from £16, Rooms 2 single, 5 twin, 8 double, 1 family,
(mainly en-suite), No smoking, Open all year, Map Ref: C

Dairy Guest House, 3 Scarcroft Road, York YO2 1ND   **Nearest Road A64, A19**

The Dairy Guesthouse is a tastefully renovated Victorian town house, offering thoughtfully planned and individually styled rooms. Situated only 200 yards south of the medieval city walls, it is within easy walking distance of the city centre and attractions such as the 'Jorvik Viking Museum', 'York Castle Museum' and 'National Railway Museum'. The house is tastefully decorated and furnished throughout. It has full central heating and a lovely enclosed courtyard. The bedrooms, 3 of which are en-suite, have colour TV, hot drinks facilities, and hairdryer.

Keith Jackman
Tel: 01904 639367

B&B from £15, Rooms 2 twin, 2 double, 2 family (some en-suite), No smoking, Open February - December, Map Ref: C

---

4 South Parade, York. YO2 2BA   **Nearest Road A1036**

Number 4 South Parade is one of twenty Grade II listed houses, forming an elegant Georgian terrace built in 1824. All bedrooms are en-suite and have teletext remote control TV with a video channel and direct dial telephone. The main bathroom, which is available to guests, has a jacuzzi. Traditional English breakfast is served with some special dishes being available if ordered the previous evening or, if preferred, a lighter continental breakfast South Parade is a private cobbled street situated just outside the city walls by Micklegate Bar.

Robin & Anne McClure
Tel: 01904 628229
Fax: 01904 628229

B&B from £34 pp for a double/twin room; single from £58, Rooms 3 double/twin, No smoking No children, Open all year, Map Ref: C

Holmwood House Hotel, 114 Holgate Road, York YO2 4BB   **Nearest Road A59**

Holmwood House Hotel was built as two private houses in the 19th century, backing on to one of the prettiest squares in York. The 2 listed buildings have been lovingly restored to retain the ambience of a private home and provide peaceful elegant rooms where the pressures of the day can be eased away. Bedrooms have their own bath/shower room, TV, hairdryer, telephone, tea/coffee making facilities, etc. There is a car park to the rear of the hotel where guests may prefer to leave their car as the city walls are only 5 minutes walk away.

Mr & Mrs C Gramellini
Tel: 01904 626183
Fax: 01904 670899

B&B from £27.50, Rooms 3 twin, 9 double (all en-suite), Restricted smoking, Minimum age 8, Open all year, Map Ref: C

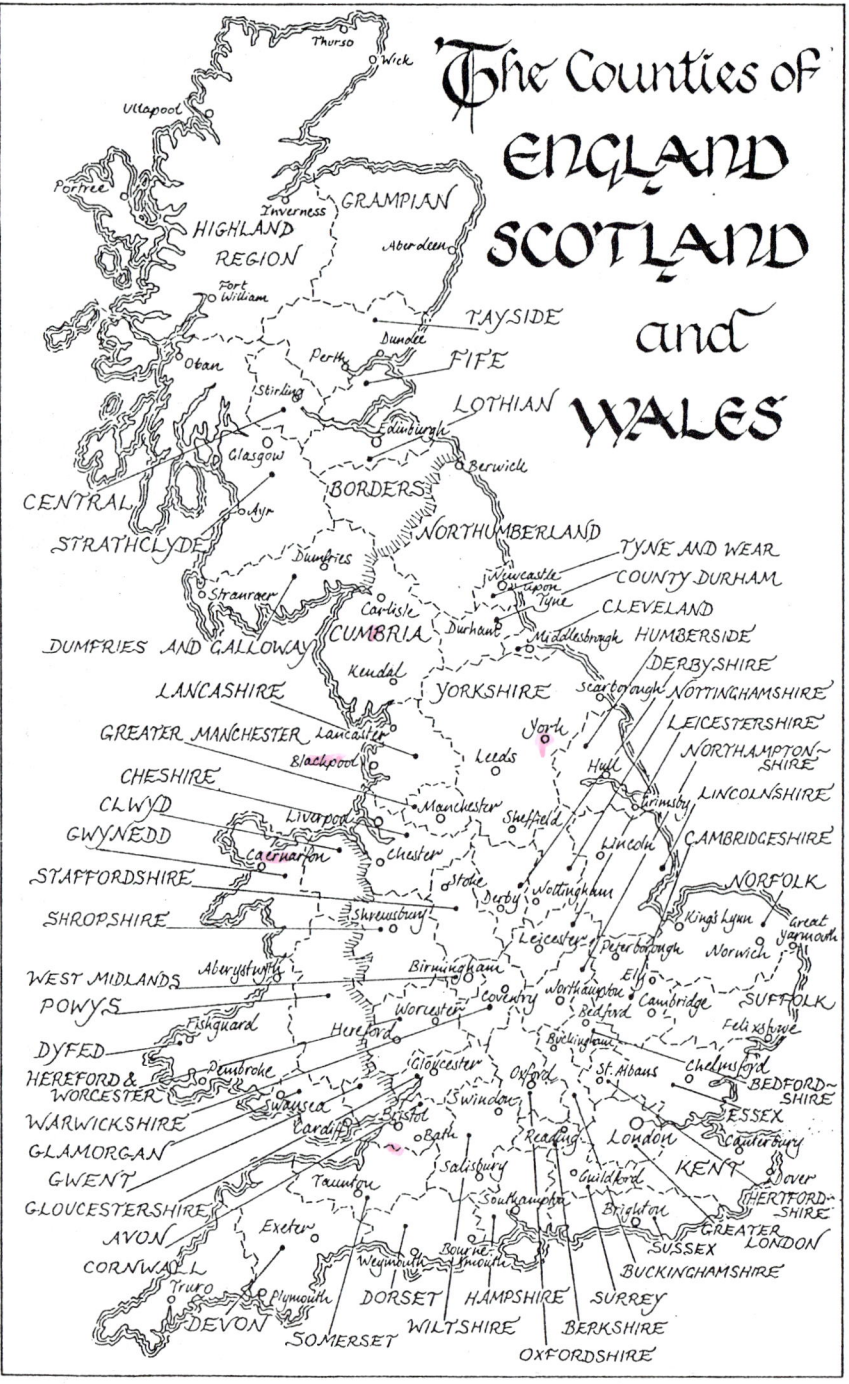

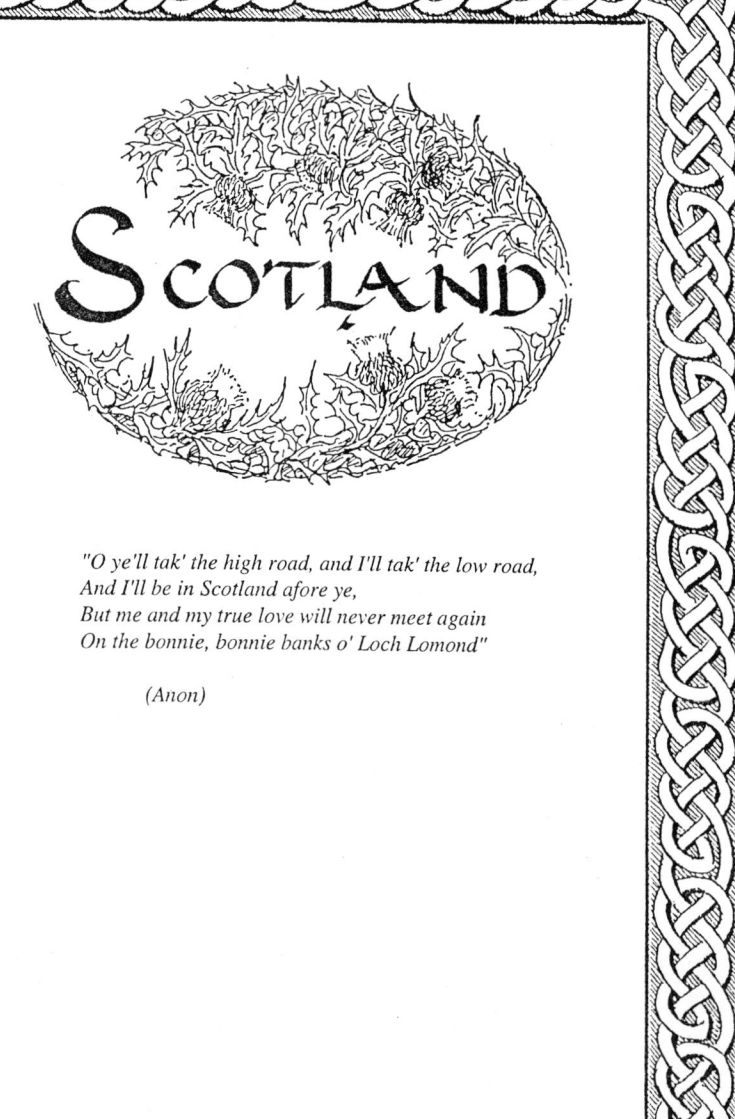

SCOTLAND

"O ye'll tak' the high road, and I'll tak' the low road,
And I'll be in Scotland afore ye,
But me and my true love will never meet again
On the bonnie, bonnie banks o' Loch Lomond"

(Anon)

SCOTLAND

Scotland is unique to any other part of the British Isles. Its major cities are well under 10 hours' coach travel from London. Scotland's history and its people have brought visitors from all over the globe, many in search of their heritage. It has breathtaking scenery and wide open spaces - thanks to a population of just over 5,000,000 living in an area just over a third of the total area of Britain. Scotland's uniqueness is also found in its food and drink and distinctive cloths. The country's food is famous for its quality with wild salmon and native brown trout coming from its rivers and lochs while fresh sea fish are favourites on many menus. As well as quality beef and lamb, Scotland's countryside holds a good stock of game from venison, grouse and pheasants. Perhaps the best known Scottish dish is haggis, always served at Burns Suppers, recalling Scotland's bard, Robert Burns. Scotch whisky is a leading Scottish export, recognised worldwide as a quality drink, both blended and malt whisky. Scotland's tweeds, tartans and woollens are manufactured in the Hillfoots towns, east of Stirling, the Borders as well as the Outer Hebrides, especially Harris which gives its name to the distinctive tweed.

LOCH SUNART

"My heart's in the Highlands, my heart is not here;
My heart's in the Highlands, a-chasing the deer;
A-chasing the wild deer, and following the roe -
My heart's in the Highlands wherever I go."

(Robert Burns)

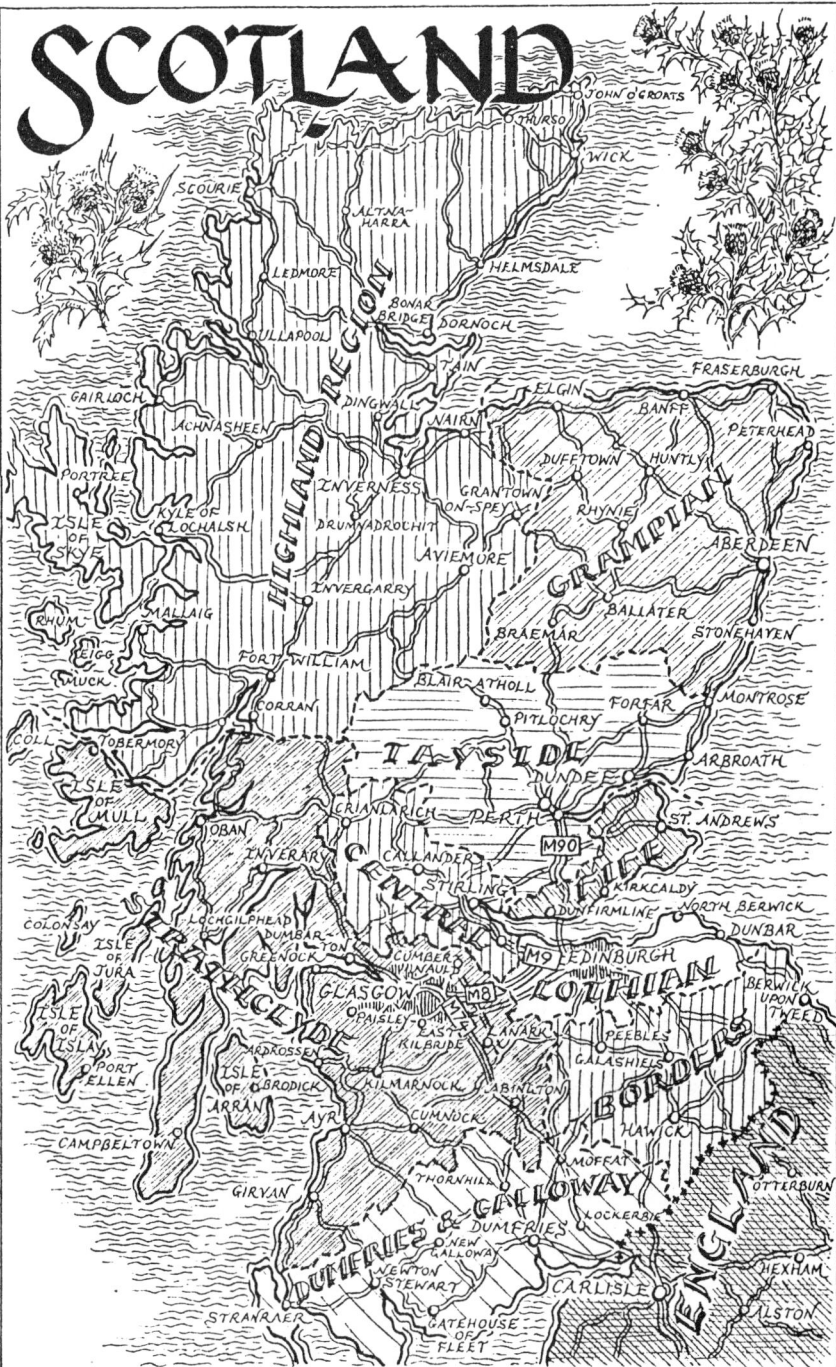

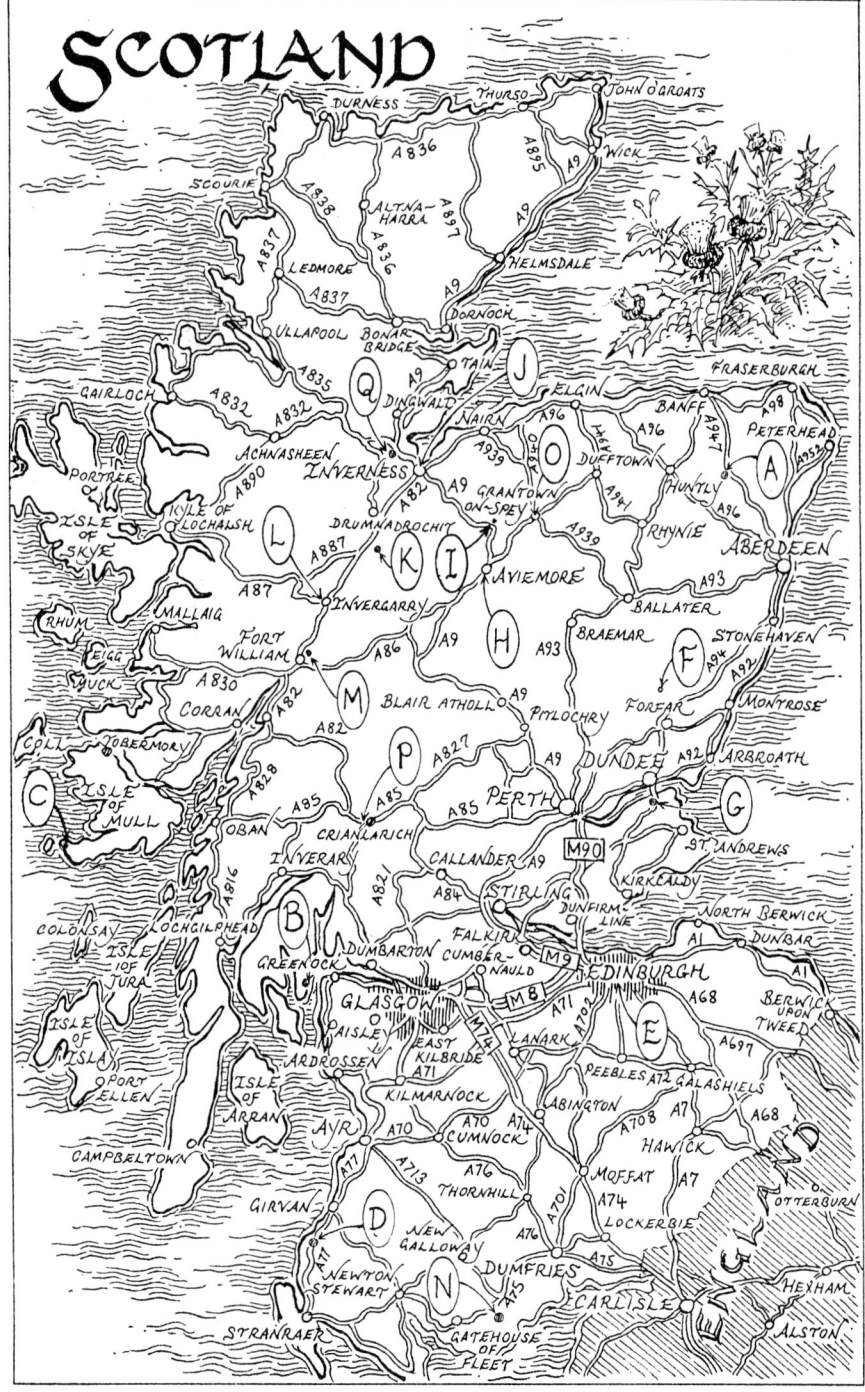

ABERDEENSHIRE

Queen Victoria & Prince Albert helped popularise Scotland for the visitor 150 years ago. They chose Deeside which along with the valley of the River Don, has around 150 castles, the best known of these being Balmoral, home of today's Queen. Bought by Queen Victoria and Prince Albert in 1853, it was rebuilt as a castle mansion in Scottish baronial style. Six miles South West is Braemar, famous for its Royal Highland Gathering held in September which is usually attended by the Queen.

Meikle Camaloun Farm, Fyvie, Aberdeenshire AB53 8JL   **Nearest Road A947**

Meikle Camaloun is a large farmhouse in a quiet rural location (which is on the "Whisky Trail")! It is off the main road and overlooks Fyvie Castle. Rooms are tastefully decorated and have tea/coffee making facilities. There is a private bathroom and an en-suite. The house boasts a friendly atmosphere. Close by activities include fishing and golf. Forty minutes away is Aberdeen for shopping.

Mrs Marjory Wyness   **B&B from £15, Rooms 1 double, 1 twin**
Tel: 01651 891319   **No smoking, Open March - October, Map Ref: A**

ARGYLLSHIRE

Dramatic Argyllshire is cut up into peninsulas and islands, crowned with bleak, savage mountains in the North. Ruins of castles overlook stretches of water and along the sea coast are holiday villages and towns. The Gulf Stream's influence makes the climate warmer than in the Highlands. The area's lochs and streams make it a paradise for anglers and boating enthusiasts. Northern Argyll ranges from the highland peaks of Glencoe, notorious for the massacre of 1692, to the jagged coastline and great sea lochs, the haunts of gannets, divers and wading birds. Oban is the key port for the Western Isles and a centre for the Gaelic culture. Memories of the past are still kept alive in an area which has associations with Mary Queen of Scots, Robert the Bruce and Flora MacDonald.

Abbot's Brae Hotel, West Bay, Dunoon, Argyllshire PA23 7QJ   **Nearest Road A815**

Friendly, family run Victorian house hotel in secluded 2 acre woodland glen with breathtaking views of the sea and hills. Spacious and tastefully furnished bedrooms all en-suite with colour TV, radio, direct dial telephone, tea/coffee making facilities, and full central heating. Unwind with a drink by the fire in the well appointed lounge and dine in the cosy dining room with delicious à la carte menu and select wine list. Residential licence. The perfect base to explore Argyll and the Western Highlands. Only one hour from Glasgow airport.

Carole & Duncan Nairn
Tel: 01369 705021   **B&B from £20, Dinner from £13.50, Rooms 4 double, 3 family**
Fax: 01369 705021   **(all en-suite), Open March - October, Map Ref: B**

Red Bay Cottage, Deargphort, Fionnphort, Isle-of-Mull, Argyll PA66 6BP   **Nearest Road A849**

Red Bay Cottage is a modern house built on the shoreline of the south west coast of Mull. John and Eleanor have built up a very good reputation for the quality of food in their adjoining restaurant and guests can eat in the pleasant dining room, overlooking Iona Sound and the white sands of Iona. An ideal base for touring Mull, Iona and the Treshnish Isles. Eleanor is a qualified practising silversmith so why not enjoy a winter break. Send for details of residential silversmithing courses.

John & Eleanor Wagstaff   B&B from £15.50, Dinner from £7.50, Rooms 2 twin, 1 double,
Tel: 01681 700396   Pets by arrangement, Open all year, Map Ref: C

AYRSHIRE

Ayrshire is famous for its association with Scotland's national poet, Robert Burns (1759-96), the son of a farmer who had moved to the county from Kincardineshire. Burns was born in Alloway, just South of the traditional seaside resort of Ayr and his birthplace, now Burns Cottage & Museum is close by the picturesque old Brig o'Doon, made famous in Burns' poem Tam o' Shanter. It is also the starting point of the Burns heritage trail which traces the life of the poet South to Dumfries, where he died. Ayrshire is a landscape of vivid green pasture with an attractive coastline providing some fine coastal links golf courses including the famous Turnberry. Although the county's history is bound up with some industrial development, there is an excellent range of country parks and fine birdwatching areas.

Cosses Country House, Ballantrae, Ayrshire KA26 0LR   **Nearest Road A77**

Deluxe accommodation within the beautiful home of Susan and Robin Crosthwaite with en-suite facilities, hospitality trays, TV and a log fire to welcome you on a chilly evening. Hidden in a secluded valley of woodland and garden, we are within easy reach of Ayrshire, Dumfries and Galloway's beautiful countryside, 18-hole golf courses, castles (including Culzean) and gardens, walking (lovely walks from the house), cycling and fishing. The kitchen and herb gardens supplement local produce for delicious "Taste of Scotland" meals. 30 mins from Irish ferry terminals.

Susan & Robin Crosthwaite   B&B from £30, Dinner from £18, Rooms 1 double, 2 family, (all en-
Tel: 01465 831363   suite), Pets by arrangement, Open all year except Christmas and
Fax: 01465 831598   New year, Map Ref: D

EDINBURGH

Scotland's capital city, Edinburgh, is every inch a world capital, offering the perfect blend of year round entertainment and culture. The city's history begins with the Old Town dominated by its magnificent castle and Royal Mile. The New Town was built from the late 18th century onwards and today its neoclassical grandeur survives. Throughout the year the city stages numerous festivals, the most famous being the Edinburgh International Festival in August, now the largest festival of the arts in the world.

Sonas Guest House. 3 East Mayfield, Edinburgh, EH9 1SD   **Nearest Road A7**

Sonas Guest House is a lovely stone terraced building dating from 1876. Its well proportioned bright rooms have been carefully refurbished to provide comfortable, centrally heated bedrooms, each with full en-suite bathroom, colour TV, tea/coffee making facilities, hair dryer, etc. Situated just over one mile south of the city centre on a quiet road between the A7 and A701. Ideally located for the university, the commonwealth swimming pool and general sight seeing. Private parking available. A delicious Scottish breakfast is served each morning.

Mr & Mrs D R Robins
Tel: 0131 667 2781   **B&B from £18, Rooms 3 double, 3 twin, 1 family (all en-suite)**
Fax: 0131 667 0454   **Open all year except Christmas, Map Ref: E**

Ellesmere House, 11 Glengyle Terrace, Edinburgh EH3 9LN   **Nearest Road A702**

Attractive and comfortable house centrally located in a residential area and facing south over a park. The castle, Royal Mile (Edinburgh old historic town), and Princes Street (one of Britain's best shopping venues) are all within very easy reach. Rooms are spacious, individually decorated and well equipped with TV, heating and tea/coffee making facilities. Most rooms are en-suite and a 4-poster bed is available. There are many varied restaurants and pubs locally. Scottish Tourist Board Award 2 crowns Highly Recommended, AA 4 Q Selected.

Celia & Tommy Leishman
Tel: 0131 2294823   **B&B from £17, Rooms 1 single, 2 twin, 2 double, 1 family (most en-**
Fax: 0131 2295285   **suite), Minimum age 10, Open all year, Map Ref: E**

Meadows Guest House, 17 Glengyle Terrace, Edinburgh EH3 9LN   **Nearest Road A702**

An attractive and comfortable double flat centrally located in a residential area within easy walking distance of Edinburgh's attractions including The Castle, The Royal Mile, and Princes Street. Rooms are spacious, tastefully decorated and well equipped. Each has TV, tea/coffee making facilities, and most have en-suite shower and toilet. There are many varied restaurants nearby. Because there is so much to see and do in an around Edinburgh advance bookings of less than 3 consecutive nights are not accepted.

Mr & Mrs J Stuart
Tel: 0131 229 9559   **B&B from £22, Rooms 1 single, 1 twin, 1 double, 3 family,**
Fax: 0131 229 2226   **Open all year except Christmas, Map Ref: E**

FIFESHIRE

Fife, an area between the 2 wide river estuaries, the Forth and the Tay, was often referred to as a kingdom when its people were fiercely independent. Today it is easy to reach from the South by the Forth Bridges. Its landscape is one of scattered woods, grain fields and a beautiful coastline. On the way to St Andrews the visitor taking the coastal route reaches the East Neuk, neuk being Scottish for corner. Dutch influence on the local architecture recall the area's European links and has created picturesque waterfronts at Pittenweem and Crail. St Andrews is the former ecclesiastical capital of Scotland and also boasts the oldest university in the country as well as being the home of golf.

The Old School House, Fern, Angus Glens, By Forfar, Angus, DD8 3QW   Nearest Road A90

A tiny village in the heart of the Angus Glens yet only 3 miles off the new A90 Dundee - Aberdeen road. The Old Schoolhouse has great character, and the house dates from the 17th century. The guests' dining and sitting rooms are the old Victorian school itself which has been carefully restored and now forms part of the main house. Original wood panelling and open fires are special features. The bedrooms are en-suite and furnished to a high order. A complete retreat in a beautiful and little known area.

David & Sarah Sayers   **B&B from £17.50, Dinner from £7.50, Rooms 1 twin, 2 double (all en**
Tel: 01356 650289   **suite), No smoking, Open July to September inclusive, Map Ref: F**

Forgan House, By Newport-on-Tay, Fife DD6 8RB   Nearest Road A92

Forgan House is a listed Georgian country house standing in 5 acres of garden, orchard and grounds between Dundee and St Andrews. The bedrooms, with their own private facilities, are individually furnished and decorated with views over unspoilt countryside. We offer a warm, friendly and personal service within an informal and relaxed atmosphere. This historical area with its small fishing communities is renowned for its golf courses and there are miles of clean, sandy beaches. STB Highly Commended Three Crowns.

Mrs Patricia Scott
Tel: 01382 542760   **B&B from £22.50, Dinner from £15, Rooms 2 twin, 2 double (all with**
Fax: 01382 542760   **private facilities), Restricted smoking, Open all year, Map Ref: G**

INVERNESS-SHIRE

The historic town of Inverness is at the head of the Great Glen. This coast to coast valley was formed in ancient geological times and as well as holding the Inverness to Fort William Road, it has the string of lochs, which includes Loch Ness, joined to form the Caledonian Canal. Two exhibitions in Drumnadrochit explore the theme of the Loch Ness Monster. Fort William is the Southern gateway to the Great Glen, dominated by Britain's highest mountain, Ben Nevis (4,406 ft). Fort William, a popular tourist centre, is often described as being on the Route to the Isles.

Alvie Manse, By Aviemore, Inverness-shire PH22 1QB   **Nearest Road A9**

A charming secluded former old manse set on a private peninsula by Loch Alvie. A warm welcoming family home attractively furnished with log and peat fires. Drying facilities available. An ideal base for touring and exploring the surrounding countryside.

Helen & Jim Gillies   B&B from £15, Dinner from £12, Rooms 1 double, 1 twin, 1 single,
Tel: 01479 810248   No pets, No smoking, Open all year, Map Ref: H

Feith Mhor Country House, Station Road, Carr-bridge, Inverness-shire PH23 3AP   **B9153**

The peaceful secluded setting of Feith Mhor, 1½ miles from the village, enables you to relax and enjoy the beauty of the Highlands. This lovely late 19th century house, set in 1½ acres of attractive garden, offers a warm welcome and traditional comfort. The pleasantly furnished bedrooms are all en-suite with colour TV, radio and tea/coffee making facilites,. We offer good home cooking and like to use local and garden produce whenever possible. This is a wonderful area for birdwatchers, tourists, walkers, fishing and golf. STB 3 crowns commended, AA 3Q's.

Penny & Peter Rawson   B&B from £20, Dinner £11, Rooms 3 twin, 3 double (all en-suite),
Tel: 01479 841621   Restricted smoking, Minimum age 10, Pets by arrangement,
                                                    Open all year, Map Ref: I

Easter Dalziel Farmhouse, Dalcross, Inverness IV1 2JL   **Nearest Road A96/B9039**

A warm welcome is assured at this Victorian farmhouse which is set amidst 210 acres of prime farmland of breeding beef cattle and grain. The 3 charming bedrooms have tea/coffee making facilities and share 2 bathrooms. There is a large dining room, lounge with colour TV, and on colder evenings a welcoming roaring log fire to sit around. Breakfast is served at the large oak dining table and guests are offered a choice which includes full Scottish breakfast of porridge, kipper and poached eggs. Many attractions and activities are within easy reach.

Mrs Margaret Pottie   B&B from £15, Dinner from £10 (by arrangement and some evenings
Tel: 01667 462213   only), Rooms 1 Twin/Double, 2 double, Pets by arrangement,
Fax: 01667 462213   Open March - November, Map Ref: J

Craigard House, Invergarry, Inverness-shire PH35 4HG

Nearest Road A82

Set in the breathtaking splendour of the highlands, Craigard, a large country house on the western outskirts of the village of Invergarry is the perfect base for a relaxing and varied holiday. Each of the well furnished bedrooms has a washbasin and tea/coffee making facilites. Guests can enjoy a quiet drink in the relaxed atmosphere of the residents' lounge and on cooler evenings pull up to a roaring log fire. A separate TV lounge provides added comfort. The magnificent scenery surrounding Craigard makes it an ideal point for touring.

Mr R L Withers
Tel: 0180 9501 258

B&B from £16, Dinner from £12, Rooms 2 double, 1 single, (all en-suite), Minimum age 8, Open all year, Map Ref: K

Foyers Bay House, Lower Foyers, Loch Ness, Inverness-shire IV1 2YB

Nearest Road A82, A9

In its own magnificent grounds of wooded pine slopes abundant rhododendrons and apple orchard with fabulous view of Loch Ness, nestles the splendid Victorian villa of Foyers Bay House. The grounds are set amid beautiful forest, nature trails and adjoin the famous Falls of Foyers. The villa is tastefully and luxuriously refurbished. Provided in every room are telephone, TV and en-suite bath or shower room, tea/coffee making facilities, fresh fruit and bath/shower gel, compliments of your hosts Otto & Carol Panciroli, ensuring a first class and comfortable stay.

Mr & Mrs O E Panciroli
Tel: 0456 486624
Fax: 0456 486337

B&B from £17, Dinner from £6.25, Rooms 1 double, 2 twin, Open all year, Map Ref: L

Invergloy House, Spean Bridge, Inverness-shire PH34 4DY

Nearest Road A82

Invergloy House welcomes non-smokers. This is a converted coach house and stables set in 50 acres of attractive wooded grounds. Guests have their own large sitting room with magnificent views over Loch Lochy and mountains. All rooms are tastefully and traditionally furnished. Two public bathrooms with shower. The house lies 5½ miles north of Spean Bridge on the main road to Inverness overlooking Loch Lochy where free fishing is available from a private shingle beach, reached by footpath. Rowing boats for hire. Hard tennis court. SAE for details.

Mrs M H Cairns
Tel: 01397 712681

B&B from £16, Dinner from £9, Rooms 3 twin, Minimum age 8, No smoking, Open all year, Map Ref: M

Riverside, Invergloy, Spean Bridge, Inverness-shire PH34 4DY

Nearest Road A82

The bungalow is set in extensive woodland gardens beside the small River Gloy, where it flows into Loch Lochy. It is conveniently situated off the A82 midway between Fort William and Fort Augustus. The furnishings are traditional and comfortable, and the guests' lounge has a lovely outlook and an open log fire for chilly evenings. There are six excellent restaurants within a 5 mile radius.

Mr & Mrs D E Bennet
Tel: 01397 712684

B&B from £17, Rooms 1 double with private bathroom, 1 family with en-suite shower, Open all year, Map Ref: M

KIRKCUDBRIGHTSHIRE

Kirkcudbrightshire's South facing coastline is a sun trap, backed by farmland and woods, with moors and hills beyond. Picturesque Kirkcudbright is popular with artists and nearby Newton Stewart is the gateway to the Galloway Forest Park, with its lochs, woodland and craggy hill slopes. Wanlockhead is Scotland's highest village - higher than any community in the Highlands. Whithorn, whose early Christian heritage is portrayed in a visitor centre, was a place of pilgrimage for generations of Scottish Monarchs. The Queen's Way - today's A712 to New Galloway - follows the footsteps of the most famous of them, Mary Queen of Scots.

Rose Cottage Guest House, Gelston, Castle, Douglas, Kirkcudbrightshire DG7 1SH   **A75**

Rose Cottage is an excellent centre for touring Galloway. The roads, which are quiet and good, make motoring a pleasure. The scenery includes hills, lochs, forest, moorland and sea. Golf, fishing, boating and walking are available, or simply relax in comfort, sit in the garden by the steam and waterfall and admire the surrounding countryside. There is ample parking. STB commended 2 crowns; AA Recommended QQQ; DGTB good services award.

Kerr & Sheila Steele   **B&B from £15, Dinner £8.50, Rooms 2 double (1 en-suite),**
Tel: 01556 502513   **3 twin, Open January - November, Map Ref: N**

MORAYSHIRE

Tomintoul, to the North of the wild heathery Grampian hills, is part of the unique Malt Whisky trail in the valley of the River Spey in Morayshire. The signposted route takes in 8 famous distilleries and around 70 miles of beautiful countryside and small towns. Sometimes called the Scottish Riviera, the Moray Coast has many sandy beaches and a mild, dry climate. Its coast is peppered with important fishing centres and is dissected by rocky, red sandstone headlands. The main town of Elgin is famous for its ruined 13th century cathedral, one of the finest ecclesiastical buildings in Scotland.

Ardconnel House, Woodlands Terrace, Grantown-on-Spey, Moray PH26 3JU   **Nearest Road A95**

Ardconnel House is situated at the southern fringe of Grantown-on-Spey opposite Lochan and Pine Forest and within a short walk to the famous River Spey. All bedrooms have en-suite private facilities and are extremely comfortable being equipped with colour television, welcome tray and hairdryer. Excellent home cooking using fresh local produce is complemented by a well selected modestly priced wine list. Quality food and accommodation at realistic prices. Ample private parking. AA 5Q premier selected, STB 3 crown deluxe, Taste of Scotland selected.

Barbara & Jim Casey
Tel: 01479 872104
Fax: 01479 872104

B&B from £21, Dinner from £13.50, Rooms 1 single, 3 twin, 6 double,
2 family (all en-suite), No smoking, Minimum age 10,
Open February - November + New Year, Map Ref: O

Culdearn House, Woodlands Terrace, Grantown-on-Spey, Morayshire PH26 3JU   **Nrst Road A95**

Culdearn House has been sympathetically modernised and upgraded by the Scottish proprietors, Isobel and Alasdair Little. Each of the guest rooms have en-suite facilities, colour TV, welcome tray, hairdryer, etc and are furnished to a high standard. The spacious lounge and dining room are furnished and decorated in a most pleasing way and boast log fires when needed. The whole house is double glazed and heated. "Taste of Scotland" membership recognises the good food served here and all rates include dinner. 3 & 7 day breaks available. AA Guest House of the Year.

Alasdair & Isobel Little
Tel: 01479 872106
Fax: 01479 873641

Dinner Bed & Breakfast £48, Rooms 5 double, 3 twin, 1 single,
Open March - October, Map Ref: O

Kinross House, Woodside Avenue, Grantown-on-Spey, Morayshire PH26 3JR   **Nearest Road A95**

Kinross House sits on a quiet and pretty avenue in Grantown-on-Spey, a charming country town in the heart of the Scottish Highlands. Lovely en-suite bedrooms are warm and restful, all with TV and welcome trays; one is on the ground floor. Delicious meals are served by David dressed in his MacIntosh kilt. We are 'Taste of Scotland' members and have 3 crowns highly commended from the Scottish Tourist Board. Enjoy highland hospitality and comfort at its very best with your Scottish hosts. Send for our brochure.

David & Katherine Elder
Tel: 01479 872042
Fax: 01479 873504

B&B from £21, Dinner from £11.50, Rooms 2 single, 2 twin,
1 double, 1 family, No smoking, Minimum age 7,
Open early April - end October, Map Ref: O

PERTHSHIRE

The city of Perth was once Scotland's capital. The "Fair City" was made a Royal Burgh in 1210 and fortified by Edward I of England in 1298. Perth served as capital of Scotland for a century until 1437 when James I of Scotland was murdered there and his widow and her son, James II moved the court to Edinburgh. Nearby Scone was the coronation place of Scottish kings, the last to be crowned there was Charles II in 1651.

In his novel published in 1828, The Fair Maid of Perth, Sir Walter Scot wrote: *"Amid all the provinces of Scotland, if an intelligent stranger were asked to describe the most varied and most beautiful, it is probable he would name the county of Perth..."* Scott's comments are true of the county today, with its mountains and moors, lush farmland, lochs and glens.

Allt-Chaorain Country House, Crianlarich, Perthshire FK20 8RU   **Nearest Road A82**

Allt Chaorain House is a small residential house affording guests amenities, comfort and atmosphere of your own home. The lounge has a log fire, a trust bar, and an adjoining sunroom which offers one of the most picturesque views of the Highlands with Ben More dominating the landscape. Situated in an elevated position between Crianlarich and Tyundrum on the A82, the perfect touring centre for Oban, Fort William, Pitlochry, Crieff & Perth. Comfortable bedrooms all with private facilities, TV, telephone, tea/coffee making facilities, and central heating throughout, etc.

Roger McDonald
Tel: 01838 300283
Fax: 01838 300238

B&B from £30, Dinner from £15, Rooms 4 twin, 4 double (all en-suite), Minimum age 9, Restricted smoking, Pets by arrangement, Open early March - end October, Map Ref: P

ROSS-SHIRE

Scotland North from the Black Isle to Caithness is wild and remote - and has remained largely unspoilt. The Black Isle is a green and wooded peninsula and Strathpeffer, to the West, still has the air of a Victorian spa resort. Dornoch, now even more easily reached by the new Dornoch Firth road bridge, is an attractive old burgh. The road which hugs the Eastern seaboard offers many opportunities to stop and explore this dramatic coastline. It eventually reaches Wick and on to John o'Groats and the impressive seascapes nearby, although the most Northerly mainland point is Dunnet Head, a little to the West. Thurso is Scotland's most Northerly mainland town and makes a good base for visits into the Caithness countryside.

The Dower House, Highfield, Muir-of-Ord, Ross-shire　　　　　　　　　　**Nearest Road A9**

Highfield house, which was the baronial home of the MacKenzie-Gillanders, no longer exists but the Dower House was converted to the cottage orné style around 1800 and has retained all its charm to this day. Nestling in 3 acres of mature grounds the house is traditionally furnished and offers an informal and relaxing atmosphere, whether for the individual guest or private house party. The bedrooms all have private bathrooms which are also traditional with cast iron baths and period brass fittings.

Mr & Mrs R G Aitchison　　　　　　**B&B from £35, Dinner from £25, Rooms 2 double, 3 twin,**
Tel: 01463 870090　　　　　　　　**No smoking, Open all year, Map Ref: Q**

EILEAN DONAN CASTLE.

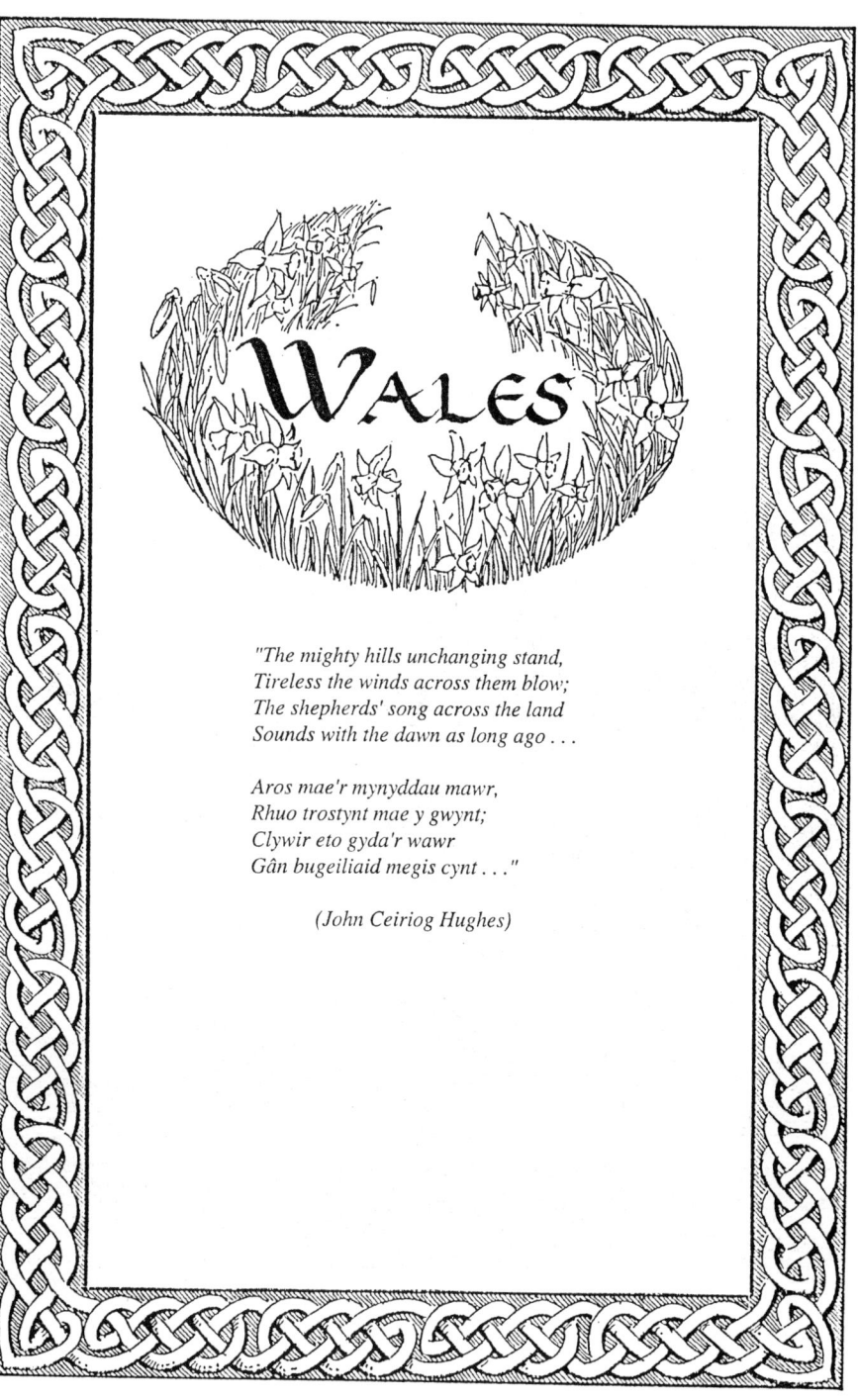

WALES

"The mighty hills unchanging stand,
Tireless the winds across them blow;
The shepherds' song across the land
Sounds with the dawn as long ago . . .

Aros mae'r mynyddau mawr,
Rhuo trostynt mae y gwynt;
Clywir eto gyda'r wawr
Gân bugeiliaid megis cynt . . ."

(John Ceiriog Hughes)

WALES

Wales, from its rugged coast to spectacular mountains, is steeped in history and legend. The country's backbone is the Cambrian Mountains, their highest point being the 3,560 feet Snowdon, in North Wales, which is only 10 miles from the sea. The popularity of North Wales stems from Snowdonia, which takes its name from Snowdon, and its sea and great beaches. From the Snowdonia National Park to the East the landscape rises again to the Clywdian Range, an area of outstanding natural beauty. The peaceful Isle of Anglesey and the Llyn Peninsula are also areas of outstanding natural beauty.

Mid Wales is a place to get away from it all along old drovers' roads, beside silent lakes and in cool forests. Surprisingly most of the Snowdonia National Park is in Mid Wales and to the East are the more rounded hills of the border country. Cardigan Bay runs along the entire length of Mid Wales with its huge beaches, picturesque harbours and mountain backed coastline.

South Wales has plenty to offer the visitor. There are 2 National Parks and 2 Areas of Outstanding Natural Beauty, as well as cities and valleys, many of which portray the region's industrial heritage, along with forests and places to visit.

HARLECH CASTLE

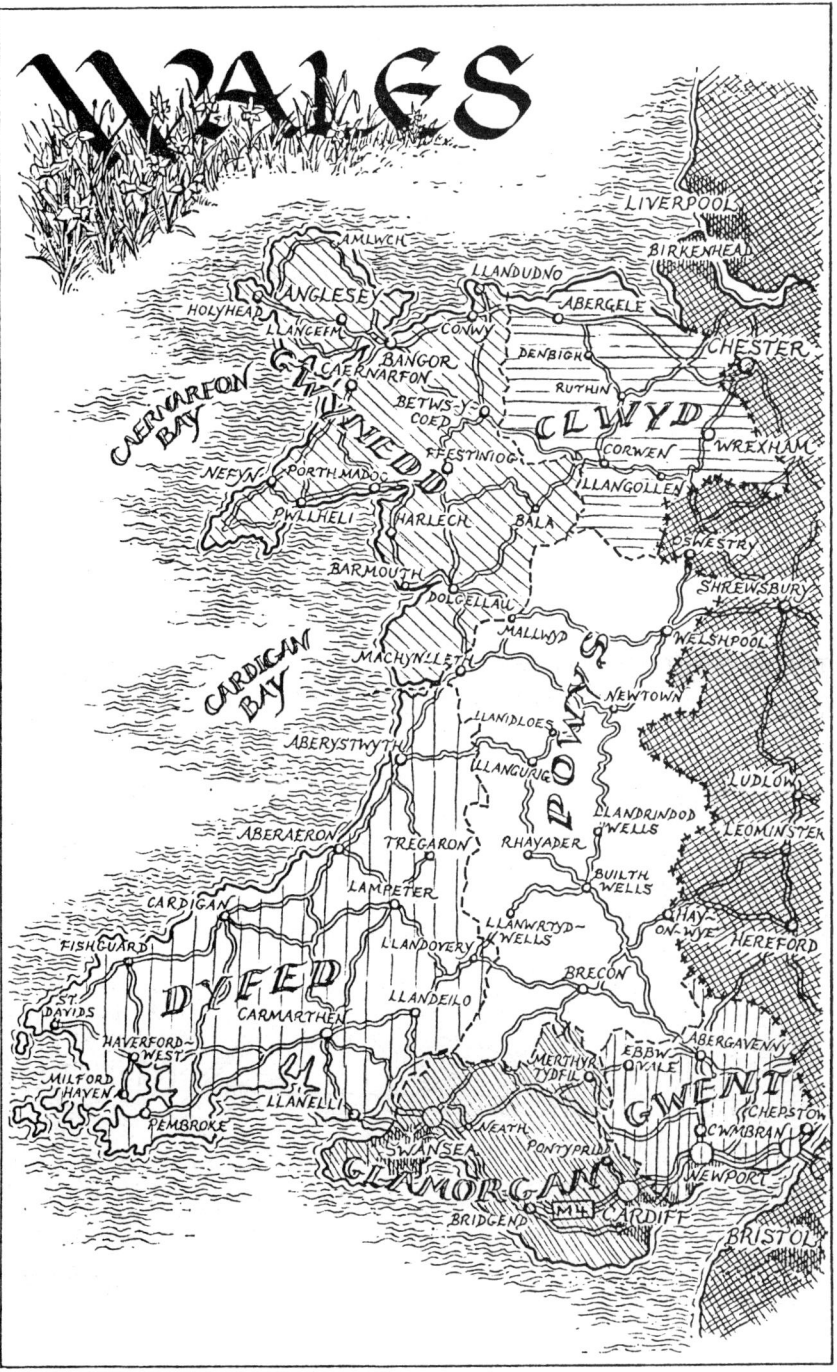

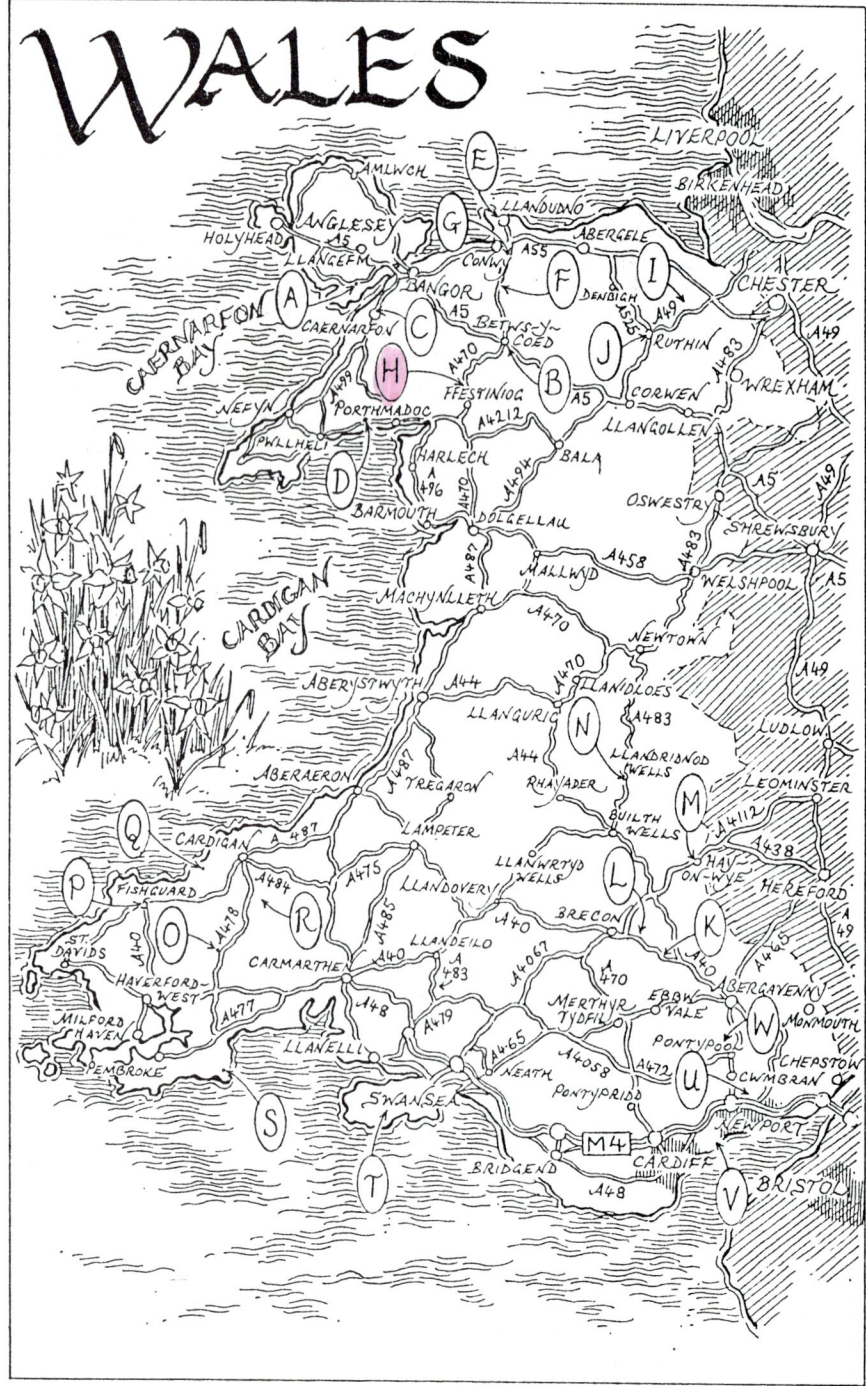

CLWYD

A few miles over the border into Wales is Llangollen with its unmistakably Welsh countryside. Mountains and rocky escarpments surround the town which stands gracefully on the banks of the River Dee. Clwyd's coast is the place for those seeking a seaside holiday with plenty of resorts and miles of sandy beaches. Inland, Wrexham in recent years, has successfully exploited its rich industrial heritage, becoming a business and tourist centre for the Welsh borders. The town has plentiful recreational facilities as well as a large number of historical places of interest. On the outskirts Erddig Hall which has gained the unique reputation as "the most evocative upstairs downstairs house in Britain" because the Yorke family, owners of the house since 1733, never felt the urge to move with the times.

The Old Mill Private Hotel, Melin-y-Wern, Denbigh Road, Nannerch, Mold, Clwyd CH7 5RH   A541

Forming part of a complex of rural mill buildings and situated in the Melin-y-Wern conservation area The Old Mill private hotel has been created by the careful conversion of the original Wern Mill stable buildings. The hotel gardens feature paths and quiet sitting areas which overlook the lawn, borders and various tree lined waterways. The en-suite bedrooms are furnished to excellent standards and fully equipped with telephone, TV, beverage tray, hair drier and trouser press. Extensive table d'hote evening menu and wine list.WTB 3 Crown Highly Acclaimed, AA 2 Star, RAC Highly Acclaimed.

Susan & Neil Evans
Tel: 01352 741542
Fax: 01352 740254

B&B £27.50, Dinner from £12.25, Price reduction for 2 night break, Rooms 1 twin, 3 double, 2 family (all en-suite), No smoking, Pets allowed by arrangement, Open all year, Map Ref: I

Rhianfa, Ffordd Llanrhydd, Ruthin, Clwyd LL15 1PP   **Nearest Road A525**

A detached Victorian house in a quiet area of the historic market town with extensive attractive gardens and patio. Convenient walking distance for the centre, the Ruthin Castle Medieval Banquet, and local walks, eg Offa's Dyke. Parking available. The double and twin rooms are fully en-suite and have tea/coffee making facilities. Guests' lounge/library with TV. Drying room and cycle garage.

Mrs Margaret Ranson
Tel: 01824 702971

B&B from £16, Dinner from £7, Rooms 2 double, 1 twin, (all en-suite) No smoking, Open all year, Map Ref: J

Eyarth Station, Llanfair DC, Ruthin, Clwyd LL15 2EE   **Nearest Road A525**

This beautifully converted railway station dates from the glorious days of steam. It is situated in the beautiful Vale of Clwyd 1 miles from the medieval town of Ruthin where banquets are held in the castle. Ideal touring centre for Chester, Snowdonia and the many historic castles of north Wales. All rooms have en-suite facilities and tea/coffee. An outdoor heated swimming pool and sun terrace is available. Eyarth Station is found off A525 Wrexham/Ruthin Road. Ample car parking. 3 crowns, highly recommended.

Jen & Bert Spencer
Tel: 01824 703643
Fax: 01824 707464

B&B from £19, Dinner from £11, Rooms 2 double, 1 family, 3 twin (all en-suite), Open all year, Map Ref: J

DYFED

The sea is never far away in South Wales. The Pembrokeshire National Park, in Dyfed, is one of Europe's finest stretches of coastal natural beauty and it is Britain's only shore-based national park, running for about 180 miles. The park can be divided into 4 sections: in the South there are sandy beaches; in the upper reaches of the Haven is the unexplored Daugleddau; the huge horseshoe shaped St Bride's Bay in the far West is fringed with cliffs; and the rugged part are the rock bound North facing shores between St David's and Cardigan.

Inland, Carmarthen is rich in legend and history, its chief claim being the birthplace of the wizard Merlin, whose father was said to be king of the region in the Dark Ages. Carmarthen has Roman associations as the site of Moridunum, their most Westerly fortress in Britain.

Yethen Isaf, Mynachlogddu, Clynderwen, Pembrokeshire, Dyfed SA66 7SN   **Nearest Road A478**

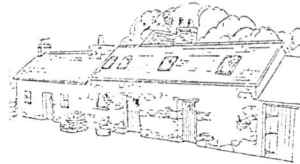

Built in 1747 when land settlement was granted if a home with a stone hearth could be built in 24 hours, Yethen Isaf was originally a Ty Nos which roughly translated means an overnight house. The farmhouse retains much of its 18th century character yet has all the comforts of the 20th century. A working farm with a herd of pedigree Welsh black cattle and a flock of Beulah Speckleface sheep. Self catering also available on our other farm which is only 9 miles from the coast.

Brian & Ann Barney
Tel: 01437 532256   **B&B from £16-£19, Dinner from £9.50, Rooms 1 double, 2 twin**
Fax: 01437 532256   **(1 en-suite), Open all year, Map Ref: O**

Manor House, Fishguard, Dyfed SA65 9HG   **Nearest Road A40, A487**

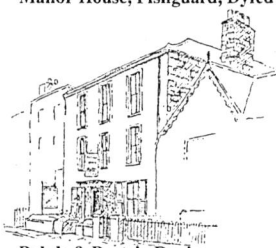

Manor House Hotel is a Georgian Town House overlooking the picturesque Lower Fishguard Harbour. It is ideal as a touring centre or as an overnight stop for travellers to Ireland. The comfortable bedrooms all have tea/coffee making facilities, and some have TV. There is a delightful residents' lounge and an award winning licenced restaurant. At the rear of the hotel is a sheltered, walled garden with superb views of Lower Town Harbour and Dinas Head. On warmer days breakfast or pre-dinner drinks may be taken on the terrace overlooking the sea.

Ralph & Beatrix Davies   **B&B from £16.50, Dinner from £12, Rooms 2 single, 1 twin, 2 double,**
Tel: 01348 873260   **1 family, (many en-suite) Pets by arrangement,**
                              Open all year except Christmas, Map Ref: P

The Old Vicarage, Moylegrove, Dyfed, SA43 3BN   **Nearest Road A487, B4582**

The Old Vicarage is a spacious Edwardian house situated in an acre of paddock and gardens. It stands in an elevated position with superb views over the small coastal village of Moylegrove and out to sea. All bedrooms are fitted with vanity units hand wash basin and most have en-suite bathroom. Comfortably furnished and decorated in traditional Edwardian style and all have tea/coffee making facilities. There is a spacious dining room, and a large and comfortable lounge with TV. Washing and drying room is available. Situated in the Pembrokeshire coastal national park.

Anthony & Peggy Govey   **B&B from £20, Dinner from £12.50, Rooms 1 single, 4 double (many**
Tel: 01239 86231   **en-suite), Restricted smoking, Children welcome by arrangement,**
                              Open February to November, Map Ref: Q

Awel-y-Grug, Boncath, Pembroke, Dyfed SA37 0JP   **Nearest Road B4332**

Conveniently situated for touring, beaches, walking, golf, fishing and riding. Two of the bedrooms are en-suite and have colour TV and all have tea/coffee making facilities. There is a residential licence and a varied menu which includes a choice of vegetarian. A television lounge and indoor games room are available for residents and there is a pleasant garden. There is also a utility room with washing machine, drying and ironing equipment. There are also 2 self contained and fully equipped flats converted from an old barn for self catering.

B&B from £16, Dinner from £9.75, Rooms 1 twin, 1 double,
Ensuite + 2 twin, Restricted smoking, Pets by arrangement,

Tel: 01239 841260   Open late March to end October, Map Ref: R

Wychwood House, Penally, Near Tenby, Dyfed, SA70 7PE   **Nearest Road A4139**

Large country house offering sea views from all its elegant and spacious bedrooms, some with large sun balcony and all with tea/coffee making facilities, and TV. Dine by candlelight and relax and enjoy Lee's interesting and freshly cooked 4-course menu of the day. Open fires in lounge and dining room. 2 miles south of Tenby, Penally lies ¼ mile off the A4139. Near by is an excellent beach, which you can walk along to the ancient walled town of Tenby. Boat trips are also available to visit the monastic Island of Caldey.

Lee & Mherly Ravenscroft   B&B from £17.50, Dinner from £12.50, Rooms 3 double
Tel: 01834 844387   (1 with private bathroom), 1 family, Restricted smoking,
          Pets by arrangement, Open all year, Map Ref: S

GLAMORGAN

The fresh cockles on sale at Swansea market come from the sands off Penclawydd on the Gower Peninsula's Northern shores. The peninsula was the very first piece of Britain to be declared an Area of Outstanding Natural Beauty in 1956. Gower's villages are small, so holiday accommodation is limited, although there are plenty of places in nearby Mumbles and Swansea. The peninsula's low lying Northern coastline is completely different from the South with its limestone cliffs and sandy bays.

Swansea was described by its famous son Dylan Thomas as an 'ugly, lovely town'. It now boasts one of Europe's most stunning and successful waterfront developments. And its sandy beaches at Swansea Bay are a few minutes away from a modern shopping centre.

Fairfield Cottage, Knelston, Gower, Glamorgan SA3 1AR   **Nearest Road A4118**

Fairfield Cottage is a charming 18th century Gower cottage set in ½ acre of pleasant gardens in the hamlet of Knelston on the Gower peninsula. The cottage is situated close to all bays with their sandy beaches and coastal walks. There is a comfortable lounge with an inglenook fireplace. The cottage has attractive double bedrooms and home cooking is to a very high standard with locally produced vegetables when in season. There is ample parking within the grounds. Swansea is 12 miles away with its leisure centre and excellent shopping facilities.

Mrs Caryl Ashton
Tel: 01792 391013

B&B from £17, Dinner from £10, Rooms 1 single, 1 twin, 2 double,
No smoking, Minimum age 5, Open all year except Christmas,
Map Ref: T

Stoney-Forge, Knelston, Reynoldston, Swansea, Glamorgan SA3 1AR   **Nearest Road A4118**

Stoney-Forge Guest House is a modern house which is situated 100 yards off the main road and is tastefully decorated throughout. All bedrooms have h&c, tea/coffee making facilities, colour TV, and one bedroom is en-suite. Comfortable lounge and separate dining tables. It is the ideal spot for seeing the beautiful Gower Peninsula and only 4 miles from Rhossili Bay and 3 miles from Porteynon Beach. Evening meal is available with good home cooking using fresh local produce when in season. Highly commended by the Wales Tourist Board.

Ms Margaret Davies
Tel: 01792 390920

B&B from £16, Dinner from £8.50, Rooms 1 twin, 1 double, 1 family
Restricted smoking, Open March - November, Map Ref: T

GWENT

Gwent is a county of river valleys, from the lush famous fishing grounds of the Usk and the Wye to the former industrial and coalmining communities of the West. Monmouth in the East, stands on the Rivers Monnow and Wye and is a history lover's paradise. Henry V was born at Monmouth Castle in 1387, was in the famous battle of Agincourt in 1415 and there is a statue of him in the town's handsome Agincourt Square. The town's second famous son was Charles Stewart Rolls, co-founder of Rolls Royce.

Newport is the county's principal town. St Woolo's Cathedral has witnessed religious worship since the 6th century. The town's modern heart is centred around John Frost Square, named after the leader of Newport's 1839 Chartist Uprising.

Great House, Isca Road, Old Village, Caerleon, Gwent NP6 1QG　　　**Nearest Road M4, B4596**

A delightful period riverside house packed with character and comfortably furnished. Its large well maintained garden backs onto the River Usk. This is a Grade II locally listed building with full central heating. The M4 is about 1½ miles away. Approach along B4596 turn right before tbe bridge then immediately left into Old Village, Great House is on the left further up near Bell Inn and continue parallel to river. Great House is on the left. Excellent golf courses, Roman amphitheatre and museums within walking distance. Historic village.

Mrs Dinah L Price　　　**B&B from £18, Dinner from £6 by arrangement, Rooms 2 twin,**
Tel: 01633 420216/312　　　**1 single, Minimum age 10, Open all year, Map Ref: U**

The West Usk Lighthouse, St Brides, Wentloog, Nr Newport, Gwent NP1 9SF　　　**B4239, M4 (J28)**

Grade II listed, The West Usk is a real lighthouse built in 1821 to a unique design. Rooms are wedge-shaped within a circular structure. The entrance hall is slate-bedded and leads to a central stone spiral staircase and the internal collecting well! The views are panoramic from the roof patio. All the bedrooms are en-suite and have been individually furnished to include a king size waterbed and 4-poster bed. Guests can try the flotation tank for deep and immediate relaxation. Most amenities are close by and there are many interesting places to visit in the area. Distinctly different.

Frank & Danielle Sheahan　　　**B&B from £22, Dinner from £10 (by arrangement only),**
Tel: 01633 810126/815860　　　**Rooms 3 double (with en-suite facilities), No smoking, Pets by**
Fax: 01633 815582　　　**arrangement, Open all year, Map Ref: V**

Ty'r Ywen Farm, Lasgarn Lane, Mamhilad, via Trevethin, Pontypool NP4 8TT　　　**Nearest Road A472**

A 16th century Welsh longhouse on a mountainside, with breathtaking views down the Usk Valley and across the Bristol Channel. Retaining many original features every modern comfort has been embodied including 1 room with its own jacuzzi. From Pontypool town centre follow the sign for Blaenavon, at the roundabout turn right over river (sign Trevethin), take 2nd right at Yew Tree Inn, carry on for ¼ mile to top of hill, turn right into Lasgarn Lane (sign Pontypool Golf Club), carry on for 1 mile to end of lane, through gate, turn right up a concrete ramp. Proceed with care.

Mrs Susan Armitage　　　**B&B from £19, Light supper £2.50, Rooms 3 double (4 poster beds),**
Tel: 01495 785200　　　**1 twin, (all rooms en-suite), Minimum age 14, No smoking,**
Fax: 01495 785200　　　**Open all year, Map Ref: W**

GWYNEDD

Gwynedd's beauty ranges from the flat fertile farmlands of Anglesey to the spectacular mountains of Snowdonia. The Gwynedd coastline is famous for its castles. Caernarfon, overlooking the Menai Strait is the ceremonial capital of Wales. In the castle, which dominates the town, was born Edward I who became the first English Prince of Wales in 1284. In 1969 Prince Charles was invested there as Prince of Wales. and the town walls were completed in 4 years. Llanberis attracts serious climbers, walkers and visitors to its lakeside setting at the foot of Snowdon. The Llanberris Pass claws its way up from the town to Pen-y-Pass, a popular starting point for 2 paths to the summit of Snowdon. Llandudno is Gwynedd's best known seaside resort yet it is relatively unspoilt. Its unique charm comes from the way its original character has been preserved.

Plas Trefarthen, Brynsiencyn, Anglesey, Gwynedd LL61 6SZ　　　　　**Nearest Road A487**

A beautifully Georgian large farmhouse on 200 acre working farm which affords panoramic views of Caernarfon Castle, Snowdonia and Menai Straits. Most of the spacious rooms have private bathrooms and are fully centrally heated. A full size billiard table and table tennis are available. There is also a nearby sea zoo. Self catering holidays are also available. Brynsiencyn is on the A4080 from Llanfair PG.

Marian Roberts　　　　**B&B from £17.50, Dinner from £10, Rooms 1 double, 7 family**
Tel: 01248 430379　　　**(6 en-suite), Open all year, Map Ref: A**

Royal Oak Farm Cottage, Betws-y-Coed, Gwynedd LL24 0AH　　　　**Nearest Road A5**

An attractive conversion of an old mellow stone farm cottge and buildings set in a sunny courtyard on the banks of the beautiful River Llugwy. The house is close to the village centre yet quiet and secluded. The en-suite bedrooms are tastefully furnished and decorated and all have tea/coffee making facilities. Shops, motor museum and golf are all available locally.

Mrs Kathleen Houghton　　　**B&B from £14, Rooms 1 twin with private facilities, 2 double en-suite,**
Tel: 01690 710760　　　　　**Restricted smoking, Open all year except Christmas, Map Ref: B**

Fron Heulog Country House, Betws-y-Coed, Gwynedd LL24 0BL　　　　**Nearest Road A5**

"The Country House in The Village", Fron Heulog offers the welcome for which Wales is famous. This is a stone built house of Victorian charm with an excellent standard of comfort and modern amenities. The atmosphere is friendly and the home cooking delicious. For Fron Heulog, turn off the busy A5 road over picturesque Pont-y-Pair Bridge (B5106), immediately turn left between village shop and river bank. Fron Heulog is up ahead 150 metres from bridge in quiet peaceful wooded riverside scenery.

Jean & Peter Whittingham　　　**B&B from £14, Dinner £15 by arrangement,**
Tel: 01690 710736　　　　　　**Rooms 2 double, 2 twin, 1 single (all en-suite),**
　　　　　　　　　　　　　　　　Minimum age 15, No smoking, Open all year, Map Ref: B

Ty'n-y-Celyn House, Llanrwst Road, Betws-y-Coed, Snowdonia Nat Park, N Wales Ll24 0HD   A470

Ty'n-y-Celyn House is a large Victorian house that nestles in a quiet, elevated position overlooking the picturesque village. It is superbly and tastefully refurnished for comfort and relaxation. Rooms have colour TV, hairdryer, trouser press/ironing board, radio/cassette/alarm clock, electric blankets on beds and beverages making facility. There are beautiful views of the Llugwy Valley, surrounding mountains and the Conwy and Llugwy rivers. Robust breakfast and warm welcome. Highly rated by AA, RAC, Tourist Board and others.

Ann & Clive Muskus
Tel: 01690 710202
Fax: 01690 710800

B&B from £20, Rooms: 8 Single, 6 double, 2 family, 8 rooms en-suite), No smoking, Open all year, Map Ref: B

The White House, Llanfaglan, Caernarfon, Gwynedd LL54 5RA   Nearest Road A487

A comfortably appointed modern country house enjoying splendid views of the Menai Straits and Snowdonia. A haven for bird watchers and sea anglers. A swimming pool is available for guests. Caernarfon Golf Club is only 2 miles away. Access to The White House is via the A487 Caernarfon/Porthmadog, on leaving Caernarfon, cross the bridge, turn right for Saron/Llanfaglan. Set mileometer to zero and proceed for 1.6 miles and turn right. The White House is on the left in half a mile, last house before the sea.

Beverley & Richard Bayles
Tel: 01286 673003

B&B from £16.50, Rooms 2 double, 3 twin, Pets by arrangement, Open all year, Map Ref: C

Trefaes Guest House, Y Maes, Criccieth, Gwynedd LL52 0AE   Nearest Road A497

A fine Edwardian building with a commanding view over an historic town, castle and the sea. All rooms are comfortably appointed and have en-suite or private bathroom, TV, tea/coffee making facilities, and heating. There is a lounge for guests and private parking in the drive. Trefaes can easily be found at the top of the village green on the right, by turning off the A497 and onto the B4411 for about 300 yards.

Mrs Pat Clayton
Tel: 01766 523204
Fax: 01766 523013

B&B from £20, Dinner from £13.50 (vegetarian meals available), Special break rates, Rooms 2 double, 1 twin, (all en-suite) Minimum age 10, Pets by arrangement, Open all year, Map Ref: D

White Lodge Hotel, Central Promenade, Llandudno, Gwynedd LL30 1AT   Nearest Road A470, B5115

White Lodge Hotel is in an excellent position on the promenade and has retained the character of the Victorian period. A well kept hotel with a friendly and relaxing atmosphere. The en-suite bedrooms are all spacious and individually decorated, with tea/coffee making facilities, and colour TV. Breakfast and dinner are served in the pleasant dining room. Guests may relax in the lounge, enjoy a drink in the licensed bar and have use of the nearby swimming pool. There is a private carpark. Well situated for Llandudno's many attractions.

Eileen & Peter Rigby
Tel: 01492 877713

B&B from £19.50, Dinner from £6.50, Rooms 4 twin, 6 double, 2 family (all en-suite, Minimum age 5, Pets by arrangement, Open March - November, Map Ref: E

Firs Cottage, Maenan, Nr Llanrwst, Gwynedd LL26 0YR

Nearest Road A470

17th century Firs Cottage offers comfortable accommodation central to all north Wales attractions. Situated in a convenient and pleasant location with clear views to hills. Tea and coffee will be made on request and home made bread and jams will be served on the breakfast table. A beautiful garden with patio as well as 2 TV lounges are available for guests' use. Close by places of interest to visit include Conway castle, Llandudno, Betws-y-Coed and Bodnant Garden.

B&B from £14 per person per night, Rooms 2 twin, 1 double,

Mary & Jack Marrow
Tel: 01492 660244

Restricted smoking, Well behaved pets by arrangement,
Open all year except Christmas, Map Ref: F

The Old Rectory, Llansanffraid Glan Conwy, Gwynedd LL28 5LF

Nearest Road A470

The Old Rectory has a fine and exclusive tradition earning the AA Red Star status and the RAC Blue Ribband for outstanding service, food, ocmfort and hospitality. It boasts the highest rated restaurant on the North Wales coast. Extra murally it offers outstanding views of the Conwy estuary, castle and Snowdonia. It is set in 2½ acres of mature garden. The Old Rectory is located on the A470 approximately 2 miles south of its junction with the A55. 2 miles Llandudno junction station. 1½ hours Manchester Airport. Car hire arranged to meet trains.

B&B from £34, 2 days break from £129, Dinner from £27.50,

Michael & Wendy Vaughan
Tel: 01492 580611

Rooms 4 double, 2 twin, Main house non-smoking, Pets by
arrangement, Open February - mid December, Map Ref: G

Cae Du Guest House, Manod, Gwynedd LL41 4BB

Nearest Road A470

Cae Du is a comfortable part 16th century farmhouse up in the mountains looking down the Vale of Ffestiniog in the centre of the Snowdonia National Park. Keith & Liz give you a warm welcome to their home where you will find Liz cooking with as much local produce as possible with vegetarians and those on special diets also being well cared for. Off the main A470, 500 yards up a gated road, one arrives at Cae Dus' spectacular views from where you are within easy reach of most of Snowdonias' many attractions including mines, castles, gardens, beaches, and much more.

Liz & Keith Lethbridge
Tel: 01766 830847

B&B from £16.50, Dinner from £10, Rooms 3 twin, 4 double
(most en-suite), No smoking, Open all year, Map Ref: H

POWYS

The sparsely populated Central Powys relies on hill farming, tourism and forestry for its livelihood. Its market towns became prosperous in Victorian times as Spa towns.

To the North West is the Elan Valley where a chain of 4 reservoirs pipe water to Birmingham 73 miles away. The poet Shelley (1792-1822) lived with his first wife in a house now submerged beneath the water of Caban-coch. When the reservoirs were constructed between 1892 and 1903, 18 farmhouses, a school and a church were destroyed.

In the South, Brecon stands at the heart of the Brecon Beacons National Park, just a short distance from the highest peaks in South Wales.

The Old Rectory, Llansantffraed, Brecon, Powys LD3 7YF　　　　**Nearest Road A40**

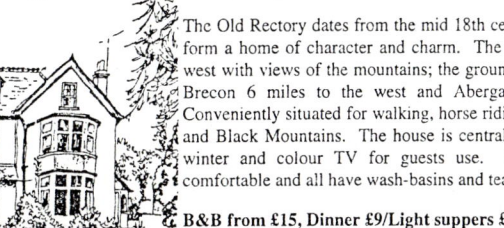

The Old Rectory dates from the mid 18th century. It has been extended to form a home of character and charm. The back of the house faces south west with views of the mountains; the grounds run down to the River Usk. Brecon 6 miles to the west and Abergavenny 14 miles to the east. Conveniently situated for walking, horse riding or motoring in the Beacons and Black Mountains. The house is centrally heated with log fires in the winter and colour TV for guests use. Bedrooms (one en-suite) are comfortable and all have wash-basins and tea/coffee making facilities.

B&B from £15, Dinner £9/Light suppers £5 by arrangement, (Wine can be brought in),Rooms 2 double (1 en-suite), 1 twin, Restricted smoking, Open all year, Map Ref: K

Mrs Margaret Howard
Tel: 01874 676240

Dolycoed, Talyllyn, Nr Brecon, Powys LD3 7SY　　　　**Nearest Road A40**

An attractive Edwardian house in mature gardens offering home comforts in a beautiful part of Wales at the foot of the Brecon Beacons, 5 miles from Brecon. Directions to Dolycoed are: from Brecon A40/A470 take the A40 for Abergavenny, left onto the B4558, turn right at the post office and next right, the house is on the right before the next 'T' junction.

Brian & Mary Cole
Tel: 01874 858666

B&B from £15, Rooms 2 twin, disabled guests welcome, Open all year, Map Ref: L

York House, Cusop, Hay-on-Wye HR3 5QX　　　　**Nearest Road A438**

York House is a warm comfortable late Victorian residence, situated at the edge of Hay-on-Wye with a beautiful large, southerly garden which does much to enhance the Country House atmosphere. Lovingly refurbished and retaining many of its original features to create a haven of comfort and convenience. All rooms are individually decorated and have TV, and hospitality trays. The lounge is peaceful and equipped with playing cards, and scrabble, and is an ideal place to relax over after dinner coffee. Breakfast is a choice of full English or lighter choice of fruit, yoghurt, etc.

B&B from £17.50, Dinner from £12, Rooms 1 twin, 2 double, 2 family (many en-suite), No smoking, Minimum age 8, Pets allowed by arrangement, Open all year, Map Ref: M

Peter & Olwen Roberts
Tel: 01497 820705

Guidfa House, Crossgates, Llandrindod Wells, Powys LD1 6RF   **Nearest Road A44, A483**

This stylish Georgian guest house offers superior en-suite accommodation which is delightfully complemented by a spacious sitting room with its chandelier and open log fireplace. Meals are prepared by Cordon Bleu trained Anne and accompanied by an amazing, value for money, wine list. Guidfa House makes an ideal base for exploring mid Wales.

Anne & Tony Millan
Tel: 01597 851241
Fax: 01597 851875

B&B from £21, Dinner from £9.50, Rooms 2 double, 3 twin, 2 single (all en-suite), All bedrooms non smoking, Minimum age 10, Open all year, Map Ref: N

NOTES

NOTES

BOOKING FORM - (FOR LONDON ADDRESSES ONLY)
Please send the completed form to:
London Home-to-Home, 19 Mount Park Crescent, London W5 2RN

Guests' Names	
Mr/Mrs/Miss/Ms	Mr/Mrs/Miss/Ms
Mr/Mrs/Miss/Ms	Mr/Mrs/Miss/Ms

Please state ages of any children listed in the party

Permanent Address

Home Phone No	Work Phone No	Fax No

Please Reserve	Single	Twin	Double	Family
Private Bathroom Require				

For the nights of:	Dates	Total Number of Nights

Date you will beging your overseas trip	Arrival Date	Time

Arriving at Heathrow/Gatwick/Station
Flight no (if applicable)
Will you be going direct to your accommodation
Will you have a car in London

PAYMENT OF DEPOSIT:

By cheque. Cheques made payable to "London Home-to-Home". I enclose my cheque for £

By Credit Card - Visa, MasterCard, Eurocard

My credit card number is ☐☐☐☐☐☐☐☐☐☐☐☐☐☐☐☐ Amount £

Cardholder's Name	Signature
Date	Expiry Date

PERSONAL INFORMATION (OPTIONAL)

Occupations
Age Group
Smokers

Please list 3 of the homes that appeal to you. Where possible we will book one of these for you	First Choice	Second Choice	Third Choice

If none of these is available we will select a comparable alternative for you

It would be helpful if you could tell us a little about yourselves such as your interests and your reasons for visiting London

How did you learn about London Home-to-Home

It is important to note that London Home-to-Home acts only as a booking agent between paying guests and hosts. The Information provided is based upon the circumstances normally in existence in the homes; London Home-to-Home does not itself actually provide the accommodation nor does it own or control in any way those who do provide the accommodation. Further your contract for the accommodation is with the hosts. London Home-to-Home does not accept any responsibility for any matters which arise as a result of events beyond its control. London Home-to-Home reserves the right to transfer the accommodation should it consider this necessary, or offer a full refund of monies paid and will notify guests of any change as soon as possible.

Signed	Date